THE GOOD Cook

THE GOOD Cook

70 ESSENTIAL TECHNIQUES
250 STEP-BY-STEP PHOTOGRAPHS
350 EASY RECIPES

ANNE WILLAN
Founder of La Varenne Cooking School

Photographs by ALISON HARRIS

STEWART, TABORI & CHANG
NEW YORK

Published in 2004 by

Stewart, Tabori & Chang

15 West 18th Street

New York, NY 10011

Canadian Distribution:

Canadian Manda Group

One Atlantic Avenue, Suite 105

Toronto, Ontario M6K 3E7

Canada

Library of Congress Cataloging-in-Publication Data

Willan, Anne.
    The good cook : 70 essential techniques : 250 step-by-step photographs : 350 easy
    recipes / Anne Willan ; photographs by Alison Harris.
        p. cm.
    Includes bibliographical references and index.
    ISBN 1-58479-328-7
    1. Cookery. I. Title.

TX714.W522 2004
641.5—dc22
                                                    2004048235

Design by Galen Smith and Hotfoot Studio

Food styling by Marie Leteure-Roux

Index by Elizabeth Parson

Printed in China

10 9 8 7 6 5 4 3 2 1

Stewart, Tabori & Chang is a subsidiary of

LA MARTINIÈRE
GROUPE

contents

Anne and daughter Emma at the market.

ACKNOWLEDGMENTS

Anne Willan would like to thank:

Chef Randall Price, kitchen director, for his recipe-testing expertise and sheer inventiveness
with new ideas and ingredients, all in the midst of pressure;

Kate Rowe, for her tireless dedication to *The Good Cook* and for her skill
with every aspect of research and editing;

Brittany Williams, a key player at the closing stages of the book and also during the photo shoot,
where she and Monica Hulshizer worked so patiently as the "hands";

Anu Duggal, Cathy Huyghe, and Andrew King, roving team members;

All my thanks, too, to photographer Alison Harris, who delivered magic with her camera in concert
with David Downie. The appeal of the book owes much to both of them, as it does to the expertise
and guiding hands of Leslie Stoker, Sarah Scheffel, and Galen Smith at Stewart, Tabori & Chang.

INTRODUCTION

For the lucky ones, good cooking begins at home, and I've been lucky. When I was a child, there was almost always someone in the kitchen. We were a half mile from the nearest farmhouse and I learned early to rely on the garden—my mother grew onions among the roses and her raspberries were a triumph. Thursday was baking day, the best day of the week, with the chance to roll dough and lick cake batter from the spoon. When our children, Emma and Simon, grew up, they too were often in the kitchen, whisking the vinaigrette and whirling the crumbs for pastry dough in the processor. Poking, tasting, and asking questions was all part of an adventure and, bite by bite, two good cooks were born.

My early experiences in the family's kitchen paved the way for my culinary career, which began with three years of professional training in London and Paris. Then came food journalism in the U.S. and my initiation into writing cookbooks. Side by side with writing is the passion I have for teaching that led me to launch Ecole de Cuisine La Varenne in Paris in 1975. That's still my favorite pursuit, whether directing La Varenne's summer programs at Château du Feÿ in Burgundy or our winter program at The Greenbrier in West Virginia.

All along, I've been aware that a surprising number of my students and, I suspect, many readers of my books have not had the good fortune of learning how to cook at home as I did. Yes, they have the right instincts and a love of food, but if they are at a loss when it comes to chopping an onion or whisking up a hollandaise sauce, cooking becomes a frustration, not a pleasure. To execute any recipe successfully, and ultimately create good recipes of your own, you must know your basic cooking techniques.

Here's where *The Good Cook* comes in. The techniques you'll find in this book—there are more than 70 of them—cover everyday basics such as chopping herbs, whisking egg whites, and making gravy, as well as essential skills like how to shuck oysters, roast a beef tenderloin, and carve the Thanksgiving turkey. Step-by-step, you'll learn how to whip up the perfect soufflé, roast and peel a red pepper, and grill the ideal juicy steak. You'll triumph when a crêpe flips perfectly, and groan when the hollandaise curdles to oil (don't worry, we'll fix it). Everywhere you'll find tips on the best methods and how to mend mistakes. In fact, there is so much to say that I've concentrated on the savory side of cooking, leaving desserts for another time.

Recipes remain the heart of this book, and I have chosen more than 350 of my favorites to share with you. All of the modern classics are included and most of the recipes have a personal twist. My tempura batter for vegetable fritters includes sparkling water for crispness, and in tapenade I use green olives instead of black for a fresher effect. Many recipes have just a few ingredients, and run to only a half dozen lines of text; follow my techniques and you'll easily master them all. Often recipes include a seasoning, a sauce, or a quick accompaniment that makes the dish memorable. Consider a green herb gremolata with grilled fish, for instance, or a ginger scallion glaze for duck magret.

I know free time is in short supply, but if you give a little of it to learning some culinary techniques, you'll discover that the more you know, the more fun cooking becomes. After that, all you need to become a good cook is curiosity and a sense of adventure. Bon appétit!

Anne Willan
www.annewillan.com

Key Ingredients

Butter

The best butter for cooking is unsalted as you can then control the amount of salt in a dish more easily. Unsalted (also known as sweet) butter also contains slightly more butterfat and less whey (i.e. water and milk solids) and is less likely to burn when used for frying. All the recipes here assume you use unsalted butter. This does not mean you need to buy expensive artisan or imported butter for cooking—gourmet butters are intended for the table.

Crème Fraîche

Crème fraîche has an inimitable, nutty taste and unctuous consistency that is just thick enough to fall from the spoon. Heavy cream does not add the same *je ne sais quoi* to soups, wine sauces, and stews. You can buy crème fraîche in gourmet markets, and also make it easily at home.

For 3 cups crème fraîche, stir together 2 cups heavy cream with 1 cup active culture buttermilk and a squeeze of lemon juice. The richer your heavy cream is, the better will be your crème fraîche. Warm the cream mixture, stirring gently, to body temperature—dip in your little finger to test. Half cover the cream (it needs air) and set it aside in a warm place. After 8 to 12 hours, it should be lightly thickened but if still thin, leave it a few more hours. Store crème fraîche covered in the refrigerator; it keeps up to 2 weeks.

Eggs

Eggs should be as fresh as possible. The size normally called for in recipes is "large," which weigh 2 ounces each. Store eggs in the refrigerator, but let them come to room temperature if making recipes such as mayonnaise or cake batters. Chilling reduces the risk of salmonella contamination, but the bacteria are only destroyed by cooking to a temperature of at least 155°F. Lightly cooked eggs, for example, when soft-boiled, scrambled, or in sauces such as hollandaise, may not reach this temperature and should not be served to small children or anyone with a compromised immune system.

Flour

As a pragmatist, I tend to go for whatever is readily available. In the case of flour, that means unbleached all-purpose flour, the kind you find on every supermarket shelf. It will vary slightly from region to region in the U.S., but for the pasta and pastries we are making in this book, all-purpose is fine. When any other type of flour is called for (whole wheat, for instance) this is specified.

Herbs

When I call for herbs in this book, I mean fresh herbs. I love their perfume and color. You can assume that the average large bunch of fresh leafy herbs such as basil and tarragon weighs 2 ounces, a medium bunch weighs 1 1/2 ounces, and a small bunch is 1 ounce. Parsley is often needed in more generous amounts, and comes in bunches of up to 3 ounces. You'll need a bit less of pungent herbs such as thyme and rosemary, even when they are fresh (most herbs are stronger when dried). Bay leaf is an exception as, oddly, when fresh it has disagreeable overtones of camphor. It should be used dried and ideally still fragrant.

The bundle of aromatic herbs called a bouquet garni is used for flavoring slowly cooked dishes, such as stocks, sauces, and stews. It always includes sprigs of thyme and parsley with a bay leaf, tied together with string. Sometimes a piece of green leek or celery stalk may be added. A bouquet garni can be made entirely with dried herbs but is better with fresh; it is always removed before serving.

Nutmeg

I single out nutmeg among spices because its flavor and fragrance, freshly grated, is greatly superior to packaged nutmeg powder. Whole nutmeg keeps its flavor for years so I always have several on hand, ready to grate as needed. It is used in sweet as well as savory dishes, and is particularly good with vegetables such as spinach and pumpkin. You'll also find nutmeg in some meat dishes, and it is an important seasoning in white sauce.

Oils

You'll find many different kinds of oil for cooking. **Olive oil** is one of the most versatile, good for sautéing or pan-frying, tasty in dressings, and available in a wide range of flavors from many different countries. Best of all is extra-virgin olive oil, cold pressed from the ripe fruit. Color varies from yellow gold to deep green and is no indication of quality, though the flavor varies. Not surprisingly extra-virgin oil costs more (sometimes much more) than regular olive oil extracted with the help of heat and solvents. You'll appreciate extra-virgin oil in dressings and for drizzling on grilled fish or vegetables, but if you heat it, you might as well use something more modest. It's fun to compare different bottles and pin down which one you prefer for dressings and which one will do for cooking.

I'm a great advocate of **nut oils**, particularly walnut and hazelnut. They too can be expensive but just a spoonful or two of cold-pressed nut oil adds amazing fragrance to salads and grilled foods. You should look for an artisan product as commercial nut oil has often been thinned with anonymous oils—it's worth reading labels carefully. Buy nut oil in small quantities as it turns rancid after a month or two unless kept in a tinted bottle in a cool place. In the refrigerator, oils cloud but they become clear again if you warm them.

Standard **vegetable oils** from seeds such as corn, sunflower, safflower and canola (a.k.a. rapeseed or colza) are often odorless and virtually tasteless, although sesame and some peanut oils are exceptions. As you might expect, bland oils don't contribute much flavor to a dish, but they are useful for mixing with stronger types, for example olive oil, when frying or making dressings. Most oils can be used for pan-frying, though nut oils tend to break down and lose flavor even at low temperatures. For deep-frying, fresh oil with a high smoke point is important—peanut, safflower, and canola oils are good choices. You'll find more about using oils in dressings under How to Make Vinaigrette (page 72).

Salt

I like to use fine salt for seasoning almost everything except boiling water and hot soups and sauces, when I can be sure coarser crystals will dissolve completely. You'll find **sea salt** in

both fine and coarse crystals, sometimes in flakes. Some sea salts, such as Maldon salt or the pink salt from Hawaii, are produced on an artisan basis at a corresponding mark-up. **Kosher salt** is less expensive but equally pure and comes coarse or fine. To ensure it pours freely in humid conditions, fine **table salt** includes an anti-caking agent. Some cooks think this gives a slightly bitter taste though less than 1 percent is added. All measures in this book assume you use fine salt, of whatever type.

Seasoning

When I say "season to taste," I mean to adjust seasoning with fine salt and freshly ground black pepper (or white pepper for sauces such as hollandaise where black pepper would be unsightly). When other seasonings may be needed, they are specified. You should taste a dish often, at the start of cooking, halfway through if you like, and above all at the end, before it goes to table. (Remember that some ingredients such as ham, cheese, olives, and anchovy are already salty.) To some extent, adding salt to food is a matter of personal taste, but without a minimum of salt almost all foods are bland. In the West we are accustomed to seasoning with pepper as well as salt.

Vinegar

For most purposes, my choice would be **red wine vinegar** as its flavor is well-rounded. You'll easily find a reliable brand that has good acidity without being harsh. For light-color foods, notably fish, you'll want to use a **white wine vinegar**—many are flavored with tarragon, but that's fine. **Cider vinegar** adds a pleasantly fruity touch. **Malt vinegar**, made from beer rather than wine, has a distinctive taste. The only vinegar I shy away from in cooking is distilled **white vinegar**. Harsh and with high acidity, it is intended only for pickling—and cleaning the coffee maker! For specific uses of vinegar, see How to Marinate (page 51), and How to Make Vinaigrette (page 72).

Wines and Spirits

I like to think of wine as a primary ingredient, as endlessly adaptable as onion or vinegar. Just a few spoonfuls of **red or white wine** will add depth to marinades, sauces, and soups, not to mention pan gravy. Did you know a little bit of wine cuts elasticity in pasta dough, and provides acidity as well as flavor to many marinades?

I'm a great believer in using whatever wine happens to be open in the kitchen. My only hesitation is with high-tannin reds, as their roughness on the tongue mellows only with long simmering. There's certainly no need to buy a fine vintage for cooking as nuances of flavor will be lost as soon as the wine is heated. If you wonder about alcohol content, 90 percent or more evaporates even before a dish reaches the boiling point, and the rest will be gone after an hour.

Fortified wines such as port, sherry, and vermouth are also useful in the kitchen. Since they are concentrated, you need less of them. When substituting dry white vermouth for white wine, for example, I usually use half the quantity of vermouth. Fortified wines have a clear flavor profile and maintain it when heated, a useful attribute in dishes like Spanish Mussels with Sherry. Cooking with **spirits** is another matter. To keep their character (and some alcohol), Cognac, rum, and other distilled liquors are fine in dishes that are not heated or they may be added to hot dishes at the last minute. Both fortified wines and spirits are used for flambéing (see How to Flambé, page 131).

CHAPTER ONE essential flavors

First things first. As cooks, where would we be without the essential flavors of herbs, together with the onion family, including garlic, shallot, and onions themselves? Add the heat of chiles or ginger and a dish already starts to take shape. To make the most of each of these flavorings, there are simple but specific techniques. Garlic, for example, should be peeled and chopped differently from ginger. Herbs divide into two categories and can be disappointing if not treated right. Basil, tarragon, dill, and other tender, fragrant varieties are mainly used fresh, while tougher aromatics like bay leaf and thyme only yield their flavors after long simmering in soups and stews.

Chile peppers were never a favorite of mine until I traveled in Mexico and found varieties that are not fiery hot. Once launched, with Emma's help I've gone exploring so that now I feel initiated. Several times I've suffered chile burns on my hands, so take care when chopping! Last of all in this chapter I've added tomatoes—not precisely a flavoring but they're such a basic element in cooking I feel they qualify as essential.

To peel, slice, dice, and chop all of these ingredients, you need a good knife, so you might want to take a look at Knife Skills on page 20 and review what you have. The ability to chop onions to large or small dice or to reduce a bushy pile of herbs to a fine shower of green without bruising the leaves is one of the tests of a professional chef. Don't worry. You can work at a quarter the speed and achieve just the same result.

Finally, for me no kitchen is complete without a stockpot on the simmer, so I've included recipes for beef, veal, chicken, fish, and vegetable stock here, right up front. With just one of these five basics on the stove or in the freezer, you can tackle almost any soup, sauce, or stew.

HOW TO CHOP FRESH HERBS

There's nothing like a sprinkling, or better still a shower, of fresh herbs for brightening a dish, adding vivid taste and color. I'm talking about tender, aromatic herbs like chives, chervil, tarragon, parsley, cilantro, and mint. Together, the first three make a classic mix called *fines herbes*. In her back garden in Los Angeles, Emma grows all of these, and in Burgundy where I live for much of the year, we have sage, oregano, dill, bay leaves, and a dozen more. Just a few freshly picked leaves bring unmatched fragrance to the kitchen and the food. All are good chopped, provided they are fresh and have soft leaves (much depends on their maturity and how they have been grown).

The taste of any herb is liveliest when it is added raw to salads or scattered on cooked dishes as a decoration. Parsley blends with most foods, and fresh cilantro (also called Chinese parsley) would be my first choice for Latin American or Asian dishes. I think of chopped spearmint in Lebanese tabbouleh, and peppermint or Vietnamese mint with crispy spring rolls. Watch out, however, for pungent herbs like rosemary and thyme—their flavors are often improved when mellowed by cooking.

When you are choosing herbs, look for crisp, colorful leaves and firm stems. Tired, wilted leaves are difficult to chop without crushing them so they deteriorate still further. To prepare the herbs, rinse them under the tap (or soak them briefly in water if they are very gritty) and dry them on paper towels. Pull the leaves from the tough stems. When the leaves are small, as with tarragon or the spikes on rosemary, strip them from the stem by running your finger and thumb from tip to base—you'll find they fall off easily.

Most cooks chop herbs with a large knife as you see below, but the Italians have a neat two-handled knife called a mezzaluna, or half-moon. Its curved blade makes chopping large quantities easy. To chop a mound of herbs, both our teenage children took to using two large knives, one in each hand. Not only do you have double the chopping power, but with two big blades it is easy to stop the herbs straying to the edge of the board. I like to keep fresh herbs on the stem in a pot of water on the counter, where they are decorative and last for several days.

1 Pile the leaves (here parsley) on a chopping board. Cut the herbs into small pieces, holding the tip of the blade against the board and rocking the handle up and down.

2 Continue until the herbs are evenly chopped, coarsely or finely as you wish. They should be fine enough to fall in an even shower, but take care not to go too far. Some of these herbs, notably tarragon and chervil, bruise easily if overchopped, losing their fragrance.

herbal hints

* Basil needs careful handling as it bruises easily, so I prefer to shred it in a chiffonade (page 24).
* Bay leaf is so strong it is never chopped to use fresh, though occasionally it is crumbled as a background seasoning when dried.
* Some cooks suggest chopping herbs in the food processor but I've never found that method satisfactory. At best the leaves will be coarsely chopped in uneven chunks, at worst when you don't stop in time, the herbs will turn to a dirty green mush. However, if herbs are chopped in the processor with other ingredients, they do just fine.
* Chopped fresh herbs are best used at once, but leftovers, of parsley for instance, can be refrigerated for a few hours in a small pot covered with a damp paper towel.

White Asparagus with Green Sauce

This Italian bread-thickened green sauce *(salsa verde)* is designed for grilled or fried fish, pasta, and lamb, but I love it with vegetables, too. The asparagus may be served hot or at room temperature.

Serves 4

> **2 pounds white or green asparagus**
> **salt and pepper to taste**
>
> **FOR THE GREEN SAUCE**
> **2 slices white bread, crusts discarded**
> **1/2 cup red wine vinegar**
> **large bunch of flat-leaf parsley**
> **3 tablespoons capers, rinsed and drained**
> **4 garlic cloves, crushed and peeled**
> **4 anchovy fillets**
> **2/3 cup olive oil**

To peel the asparagus: With a vegetable peeler or small knife, scrape the length of each stalk, starting below the tip and cutting almost to the stem end. Break off the woody end of the stem, together with the peel. Divide the spears into 4 portions. Bunch each portion together, tips downward on the work surface, and tie the bundles with string. Trim the stalks to the same length with a knife.

Bring a large pan of salted water to a boil. Add the asparagus, cover, and bring it back to a boil. Simmer uncovered until the stems are tender when poked with a knife, 8 to 15 minutes depending on size and age of the asparagus. Drain it in a colander, rinse with cold water to set the color of the tips, and leave to cool until tepid.

Meanwhile, make the sauce: Soak the bread in a small bowl with the vinegar for 10 minutes. Pull the leaves from the parsley stems and coarsely chop them. Put the capers, crushed garlic cloves, and anchovy fillets in a food processor. Squeeze the bread dry, tear it into pieces, add to the processor, and work it to a purée. With the motor running, gradually add the olive oil with a little salt and pepper. Pour the sauce into a bowl, stir in the chopped parsley, and taste for seasoning.

To finish: Set a bunch of asparagus on each of 4 serving plates and discard the strings. Coat the center of each bunch with 1 to 2 tablespoons sauce, leaving the tips and ends exposed so you can see what you are eating. Serve the remaining sauce separately.

GETTING AHEAD: Green sauce can be made up to 4 hours ahead and kept covered at room temperature. Cook the asparagus just before serving to serve hot, or up to 2 hours ahead if serving at room temperature.

Warm Herb Potato Salad

I make this all summer long, varying the herbs according to what is flourishing in the garden. You may want to use pretty red-skinned potatoes, as they do not need to be peeled for serving. A firm, waxy variety is best.

Serves 4

> 1½ **pounds small new potatoes**
> ⅓ **cup white wine**
> ⅓ **cup olive oil**
> ¼ **cup chopped fresh chives**
> ¼ **cup chopped fresh parsley**
> ¼ **cup chopped fresh mint**
> **salt and pepper to taste**

Put the potatoes, unpeeled, in a saucepan of cold salted water and bring them to a boil. Simmer them until tender when pierced with the point of a knife, 15 to 20 minutes. Drain them thoroughly.

While still warm, halve or thickly slice the potatoes into a bowl. Pour the wine over them and toss until it is absorbed. Pour in the olive oil, toss again, and finally toss with the herbs. Try to do this tossing with a flick of the bowl, as stirring with a spoon tends to break up the potatoes. Taste the salad, season, and serve while still warm.

GETTING AHEAD: The salad can be tossed with the wine and olive oil up to 8 hours ahead and kept at room temperature. Add the herbs and mix gently just before serving.

Herb and Shallot Butter

Delicious with broiled steak and vegetables. For fish, leave out the garlic and add a tablespoon of lemon juice.

Enough for 4 servings

Chop 2 shallots and 1 clove garlic. Add a handful (about ¼ cup packed) of mixed herb sprigs such as parsley, tarragon, chervil, oregano, and thyme (cilantro is good, too, but on its own). Chop the herbs together with the shallots and garlic until quite fine. Cream 4 tablespoons butter and stir in the herb mixture with a generous amount of freshly ground black pepper and a little salt. Taste and adjust the seasoning—the flavor should be lively. Roll the butter into a cylinder in wax paper or plastic wrap, and chill until firm. It can be kept 1 to 2 days. For serving, slice it in rounds to put on hot food at the last minute.

Warm Herb Potato Salad

how to make a persillade

A persillade is so useful! This combination of parsley leaves and garlic, with or without shallot, is added to sautéed meats and vegetables near the end of cooking, or just before serving. The point is to keep the persillade's fresh fragrance, while at the same time adding color and the bite of raw greens. For me, a persillade is almost a necessity with wild or cultivated mushrooms, potatoes sautéed in olive oil or butter, sautéed bell peppers, and pan-fried fish. A persillade is best fresh, but can be kept up to an hour or so.

Persillade

Enough for 4 to 6 servings

Coarsely chop a medium-sized handful of parsley sprigs (about 3/4 ounce). Peel and chop a large shallot or crush and peel 2 garlic cloves. Add the shallot or garlic to the parsley and continue chopping until the persillade is evenly cut.

Green Herb Gremolata

Gremolata is an Italian flavoring mix, usually composed of chopped fresh garlic, citrus zest, and parsley. It is traditionally sprinkled on Italian osso buco and other dishes when they go to table. I'm crazy for this green herb version, delicious on top of sautéed fish or grilled vegetables. Herb gremolata can be kept up to an hour.

Enough for 4 servings

Chop the leaves from a medium bunch of flat-leaf parsley. Mix them in a bowl with the white and green part of 1 scallion, very thinly sliced on the diagonal, the grated zest of 1 lemon or lime, and 1 tablespoon capers, rinsed, drained, and coarsely chopped. Season with a little salt and plenty of freshly ground black pepper.

Tabbouleh

Traditionally tabbouleh is one of many little dishes of *mezze*, the appetizers that open all Middle Eastern meals, but I also enjoy it with kebabs and grilled lamb chops. Couscous is a good substitute for the bulghur.

Serves 6

> **1¼ cups bulghur wheat**
> **1 pound tomatoes, peeled, seeded, and chopped**
> **3 scallions, including green parts, thinly sliced**
> **1 cup chopped fresh parsley**
> **1 cup chopped fresh mint**
> **1 teaspoon ground coriander**
> **½ teaspoon ground cumin**
> **grated zest of 1 lemon**
> **salt and pepper to taste**
> **½ cup olive oil**
> **½ cup lemon juice, more to taste**

Put the bulghur in a large bowl and cover it generously with cold water. Leave to soak for 1/2 to 1 hour.

Drain the bulghur in a strainer, squeezing with your fists to extract as much water as possible. Return it to the bowl and stir in the tomatoes, scallions, parsley, mint, coriander, cumin, lemon zest, salt, and pepper. When mixed, stir in the olive oil and lemon juice. Taste, adjust seasoning with more lemon if you like, and serve the salad at room temperature.

Herb Vinaigrette

Classic with green salad, pasta salad, or potato salad, and good with almost anything. For a lighter dressing, substitute half vegetable oil for the olive oil.

Makes about 3/4 cup vinaigrette, enough for 1 to 1 1/2 pounds salad greens

Whisk 2 tablespoons balsamic vinegar with 1/2 teaspoon Dijon mustard, salt, and pepper until mixed. Gradually whisk in 3/4 cup olive oil so the dressing emulsifies and thickens slightly. Whisk in 3 to 4 tablespoons chopped fresh herbs of your choice, taste, and adjust the seasoning. Use within 30 minutes or the herbs will discolor.

Knife Skills

For success in the kitchen, you need a good knife, so review your collection before you start. A sturdy chef's knife is a priority, in large or medium size to suit your hand. Cooks feel lost without their favorites: for some it may be a short, stubby boning knife, for others the curved blade of the little knife called a parrot's beak. I'm addicted to the thin, flexible blade that the French refer to as a fish knife, perfect for carving meats and cutting very thin slices from poultry breasts. Here and throughout the book, you'll be introduced to a variety of knives and see how to hold them comfortably. With a sturdy knife or two, plus the know-how to tackle these few essential flavoring ingredients, we're ready to go. Let me say up front that I'm not an advocate of the food processor for dicing and chopping—for small amounts, it takes as much time as a knife and results are mixed. I am far more partisan to a mandolin slicer for thin, even slices and julienne strips (see How to Use a Mandoline, page 22).

how to choose and handle a knife

Good knives are the most important tool in the kitchen. They are expensive but will last for years. Don't be tempted to buy cheap knives: they lose their edges quickly and make cooking much more difficult. I follow the advice of Randall Price, a chef and good friend, who is also a knife connoisseur. He points out that a knife should feel sturdy, comfortable, and balanced, so try it in your hand before you buy it. The blade should be full tang, which means it is composed of a single piece of steel that continues to the end of the handle. Less expensive stamped blades often end just inside the handle and lack strength. The handle itself must be nonslip (be wary of synthetic materials).

Knife blades may be made with stainless-steel, carbon steel, or a blend of the two. Shiny knives with a high stainless-steel content are easy to clean and keep their edge longer. The drawback is that once stainless knives have lost their edge, they are much

harder to sharpen at home. Most serious cooks prefer high-carbon knives, which are easier to keep sharp, though the blade tarnishes and loses its shine. Three knives make up a basic set: a medium chef's knife with a 7- to 8-inch blade; a lighter knife with a narrower 6- to 7-inch blade for carving and more delicate slicing; and a 3-inch vegetable or utility knife for paring and small-scale chopping and slicing. The bigger your hands and the more adept you are with your knives, the larger you will want them to be.

When using a knife for slicing and chopping, grip the handle firmly with all four fingers—letting your first finger stray along the top of the blade weakens your hold. Looking at the pictures throughout this book, you'll see that one hand grips the knife handle and the other is masked by the blade. It is this second hand that guides the knife, so that your curved knuckles are brushed with each stroke of the blade. The movement feels odd at first but it is key to all slicing and chopping.

how to sharpen a knife

Knives are wonderfully sharp when they are new, but they won't stay that way. Keeping knives sharp involves regular sharpening and occasional honing. Various tools exist for sharpening knives—some electric, some hand-operated—but nothing in my view replaces a traditional sharpening steel and a flat Carborundum stone. The steel is for sharpening the blade each time you use it. Less often—after perhaps a couple hundred uses—your knife will need to be honed, that is ground against an abrasive stone. Serrated knives cannot be resharpened.

1 To sharpen a blade: Hold the knife against the steel at an angle of about 20 degrees and draw one side and then the other rapidly along it, taking care to run the full length of the blade. With practice, you will get quite fast at this.

2 To hone a blade: Wipe the Carborundum stone lightly with mineral oil (sold with the stone). Hold the knife at a very slight angle to the stone. Rub the blade against it on one side and then the other until the blade feels very sharp to your touch.

how to use a mandoline

A mandoline slicer has a flat plastic, metal, or wooden frame with adjustable cutting blades for slicing and shredding vegetables. The inexpensive, plastic-based mandolines that are widely available do an excellent job, so there's no need to invest in a heavy-duty professional model. The simplest type has a single fixed blade that will only slice, but most mandolines have interchangeable blades that allow you to slice in several thicknesses and cut strips varying from fine julienne to thin French fry size (*frites*). Some models come with a guard to hold the vegetable and protect your hand, or you can use a heavy cloth or glove. With practice, you probably won't need to bother, and just use your hand.

1 For slices: Work the vegetable (here peeled potato) up and down across a plain blade, adjusting it for thin or thick slices. If you like, protect your hand with a cloth.

2 For julienne: Use the julienne blade and work the vegetable (here unpeeled zucchini) up and down across the blade.

Daikon Hors d'Oeuvre

These crispy little cones make charming cocktail hors d'oeuvre or garnishes for marinated fish, smoked salmon, and cold soups. For the filling, use a soft goat cheese, and flavor it with chives and your favorite herb. For an even quicker filling, you can substitute herb- and garlic-flavored Boursin cheese.

Makes 40 to 50 cones to serve 8 to 10

> **2 medium daikon or black radishes**
> **(about ¾ pound)**
> **½ cup white wine vinegar, for soaking**
> **½ pound fresh goat cheese**
> **1 tablespoon chopped fresh chives**
> **1 tablespoon chopped fresh herb,**
> **such as basil, mint, or tarragon**
> **salt and pepper to taste**

Peel the radishes, trim the tops, and cut 40 to 50 very thin rounds on the mandoline. (They should be 2 to 3 inches in diameter.) Spread them in a shallow baking dish, pour the white wine vinegar over them, and leave to soak for 15 to 30 minutes.

For the filling: Put the cheese in a bowl and crush it to break it up if necessary. Using a fork so the cheese remains light, stir in the chives and herb, and season with salt and freshly ground black pepper.

Drain the radishes on paper towels. Make a single cut from the center of each round to the edge. Put a teaspoon of filling next to the cut and roll the radish into a cone around the cheese. Continue stuffing and rolling the cones until you've used all the radish rounds and filling. Place the cones on a platter, cover it tightly with plastic wrap, and chill well before serving.

GETTING AHEAD: The cones can be made up to 8 hours ahead and stored, covered, in the refrigerator.

Emma's Medley of Summer Squash

When cutting the julienne, remove only a couple of layers from the surface of the squash, leaving the soft interior and seeds behind.

Serves 4

> **3 small zucchini (about ¾ pound)**
> **3 small yellow squash (about ¾ pound)**
> **juice of 2 lemons**
> **juice of 2 limes**
> **1 tablespoon finely chopped fresh ginger**
> **salt and pepper to taste**
> **½ cup olive oil**
> **medium bunch of cilantro**

Trim the zucchini and squash and cut them into 2-inch lengths. Slice them in julienne on the mandoline, rotating them so all the skin and an underlayer of flesh is removed; discard the central core. For the vinaigrette, whisk the lemon and lime juice in a small bowl with the ginger, salt, and pepper. Whisk in the olive oil. Pull the leaves from the cilantro, reserving 4 sprigs for decoration. Chop the leaves and stir them into the dressing.

Toss the vegetable julienne with the dressing, taste, and adjust the seasoning. Pile the salad on 4 serving plates and top each with a cilantro sprig.

GETTING AHEAD: The salad can be served at once, or after an hour or so when it has wilted slightly. Don't be tempted to keep it in the refrigerator as it is best at room temperature.

HOW TO MAKE A CHIFFONADE

When you cut leafy vegetables and herbs into shreds with a large knife, you have a chiffonade. For greens and herbs with delicate leaves that bruise easily—basil, arugula, and baby spinach—thin slicing is kinder than chopping. Lettuce, particularly romaine and iceberg, is often cut in a coarser chiffonade to be used as a bed for other ingredients or in sandwiches and wraps. Tougher vegetables such as cabbage, kale, turnip greens, and bok choy can be sliced into a fine chiffonade to serve raw, in cole slaw, for example. More often, however, you'll do best to blanch a chiffonade of these tougher greens in boiling water for a minute to soften them slightly, or you can quickly stir-fry them with seasonings until they're wilted.

A chiffonade is so simple and quick I always wait until the last minute. To prepare the leaves, wash them to remove any grit, then drain and dry them thoroughly on paper towels. (Moisture on delicate leaves makes them all the more liable to bruise.) Cabbage needs special treatment because its ribs are so tough. Hand cutting with a large knife is the rule for almost all chiffonades, but the firm, tight heads of cabbage and iceberg lettuce can also be sliced on a mandoline (see How to Use a Mandoline, page 22).

The name chiffonade puzzled me until I remembered chiffon fabric, which forms a sunburst of pleats that look like shreds when you scrunch them in your fist. I tried it with one of Emma's party dresses, and we both laughed as that's how a chiffonade of vegetables or herbs should look—fine needle slivers in a haphazard fluffy mound. So we went downstairs and tried it in the kitchen.

Chinese Egg Ribbons

Very thin ingredients such as crêpes, tortillas, and these Chinese egg pancakes may be cut in a chiffonade, forming pretty ribbons to mix in salads, stir-fries, and sometimes soups.

Enough for 4 servings

Whisk 2 eggs with a pinch of salt until frothy. Brush a 7-inch nonstick frying pan with vegetable oil and heat until very hot. Add about a third of the beaten egg, swirling the pan so it is completely coated. Cook over medium heat until the pancake is brown, about 1 minute. Flip and brown the other side. Remove the pancake and cook two more in the same way. Stack, roll them, and cut into 3/8-inch strips.

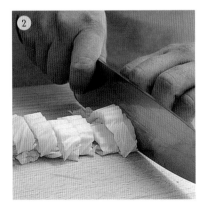

1 Separate the leaves (here a head of Napa cabbage). If the leaves have tough ribs, fold them in half lengthwise and cut out the ribs. Stack them and roll the pile tightly.

2 Slice across the roll to make fine or coarse strips, depending on the leaves you are using. Herbs should be cut about 1/8 inch wide, while a lettuce or cabbage chiffonade can be up to 1/2 inch wide.

Tomato, Mozzarella, and Basil Salad *(Insalata Caprese)*

Everyone enjoys this simple Italian summer salad, especially when made with buffalo-milk mozzarella, a softer, creamier cheese than the cow's milk version.

Serves 6 as a first course

- **1 pound fresh mozzarella in liquid**
- **1 pound plum tomatoes**
- **large bunch of basil**
- **salt and pepper to taste**
- **¹/₂ cup olive oil, more to taste**

Drain the mozzarella and thinly slice it. Core the tomatoes and cut them crosswise in thin slices. Strip the leaves from the stems of the basil, reserving a few sprigs for decoration. Cut the leaves in a ¹/8-inch chiffonade.

Arrange alternating slices of mozzarella and tomatoes on individual plates. Season with salt and pepper and drizzle with the olive oil. Just before serving, sprinkle the chiffonade of basil on top. Decorate with the reserved basil sprigs.

GETTING AHEAD: Prepare the salads up to 30 minutes ahead and leave them at room temperature. The flavors will blend and mellow.

Herb Topping for Pasta

The simplest topping for any cooked pasta, courtesy of Emma.

Serves 4 to 6

Cut in a chiffonade a generous handful of leaves of any fragrant herb such as sage or basil. Put them in a warm pasta bowl and add freshly cracked black pepper to your taste. Heat 4 to 5 tablespoons olive oil until smoking and pour over the herbs. Drain and add 1 pound very hot cooked pasta. Toss and serve at once.

how to shred cabbage

For cole slaw, cabbage soup, braised cabbage, indeed almost all its uses, cabbage must be finely or coarsely shredded. It is important to remove all the stalk and thick ribs, cutting the remaining ribs across so they cook at the same speed as the leaves. To do this, discard tough or wilted outer leaves and quarter the cabbage with a large knife. Cut the core from each wedge. Set one-quarter firmly on the chopping board and cut crosswise in fine or coarse slices, working across the ribs. At the end of chopping, discard any thick pieces of rib. The yield of shredded cabbage from a tightly packed head is surprisingly large, but like many greens, cabbage will lose half or more of its volume when it is cooked.

German Hot Bacon Slaw

A warming version of cole slaw.

Serves 3 to 4

Finely shred one-half of a white cabbage (about 3 pounds). Heat 1 tablespoon vegetable oil in a large saucepan and fry 3 ounces diced bacon and 1 chopped onion until starting to soften, about 2 minutes. Stir in 1¹/₂ tablespoons sugar and cook over medium heat until caramelized to a good brown, 1 to 2 minutes more. At once add ¹/₄ cup red wine vinegar, standing back so the vapor does not sting your eyes. Stir to dissolve the caramel, add the shredded cabbage, and toss thoroughly. Cover and cook over low heat, until the cabbage has softened but still has some crunch, 8 to 10 minutes. Add plenty of freshly ground black pepper, taste, and adjust seasoning.

HOW TO PEEL AND CHOP GARLIC

I was brought up British, with not a clove of garlic on my plate until I went to France in my early teens, so I feel disloyal when I say that every notable cuisine in the world makes generous use of garlic. Now I'm a garlic enthusiast like so many other cooks. I can't do without it in salad dressings, in sauces like French *aïoli* and Greek *skordalia*, dips such as *bagna cauda*, and on croutons and garlic bread. Garlic is not just a flavoring; it so enhances other ingredients that it is indispensable to many marinades, braises, and stews. Some say garlic soup will cure a cold and a fresh clove in a bag around your neck wards off the evil eye. To health food advocates, garlic is a multi-purpose tonic, used for everything from a head cold to rheumatism. That's fine by me, I love it.

The strength of garlic varies widely with variety and age, and so therefore does the amount you need in a recipe. Always adjust quantities to taste. The three main types—white, violet, and red-skinned—range from strong to mild. Giant elephant garlic is mildest of all and is best treated as a vegetable rather than a seasoning. The more papery the outer skin of a garlic head, the drier and more pungent are the cloves. Stronger, drier garlic tastes better when mellowed by cooking, but young garlic is mild—sweet enough to rub raw on a slice of bread moistened with olive oil, or to chop very finely and scatter in a salad. When you cut open a clove, you may find a small green shoot of leaves ready to sprout. These garlic sprouts have the strongest taste of all; you may want to discard them.

There are lots of gadgets for dealing with garlic, but nothing beats your fingers. Yes, I know they will smell after you've handled garlic, but rubbing them with a cut lemon will work wonders. Basically there are no short cuts to first separating the head of garlic into individual cloves, and then peeling them. Use a large knife for chopping garlic, as a garlic press bruises garlic and makes it taste acrid, while even a small food processor

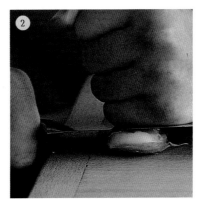

1 To separate the garlic cloves, smash the head with your hands. Alternatively, pull off a single clove with your fingers.

2 To peel a garlic clove, set your fist on the flat side of a large knife and in one motion strike the clove. This loosens the skin so you can peel it easily. (Take care that the handle of the knife does not overlap the cutting board or you will bang your knuckles.)

3 Crush the peeled clove again with the flat of the knife. Chop the flattened clove, moving the knife blade back and forth.

works only for industrial quantities. Some cooks like to crush garlic cloves to a purée with a pinch of salt, but I find this coarsens the taste.

Peeled garlic cloves can be kept 2 to 3 days in an airtight jar in the refrigerator. (Do not store them in oil as there is a very slight danger of botulism.) Once chopped, you should use garlic within a few hours as it quickly turns strong. Watch out, too, that you do not over-brown garlic—when scorched it becomes eye-wateringly bitter.

Garlic Focaccia

Garlic tossed with olive oil toasts to golden brown on top of this focaccia; coarse sea salt adds contrasting bite. If you use an electric mixer, the dough takes only 5 minutes to mix.

Makes a 12-inch focaccia to serve 6 to 8

> **1 tablespoon active dry yeast**
> **1½ cups lukewarm water**
> **3½ cups flour, more if needed**
> **1 teaspoon salt**
> **1½ tablespoons olive oil, more for brushing the bowl and baking sheet**
>
> **FOR THE TOPPING**
> **6 garlic cloves**
> **½ cup olive oil**
> **1½ teaspoons coarse sea salt**

Sprinkle the yeast over ¼ cup of the warm water in a small bowl. Leave for 5 minutes, until the yeast is dissolved and starts to bubble. Sift the flour and salt into the bowl of an electric mixer fitted with a dough hook. Make a well in the center of the flour and add the dissolved yeast with the remaining 1¼ cups water and the olive oil. With the mixer on low speed, stir the liquid into the flour to make a smooth dough. Turn the speed to medium-high and knead the dough until very smooth and elastic, 2 to 3 minutes. If the dough seems sticky, work in more flour during kneading; it should be soft and pulling away from the sides of the bowl. Alternatively, you can mix and knead the dough by hand.

Shape the dough into a ball, transfer it to an oiled bowl, and turn it over so the top is oiled. Cover with a damp cloth and leave it in a warm place until doubled in bulk, 1 to 1½ hours. Meanwhile, finely chop the garlic and stir it into the olive oil. Heat the garlic oil gently in a small saucepan until hot, cover, and set it aside to infuse while the dough rises.

When risen, work the dough lightly on a floured work surface to knock out the air, then roll it into a 10-inch round and transfer it to an oiled baking sheet. Cover with a damp cloth and leave it to rise in a warm place until it has almost doubled in bulk, ¾ to 1 hour. The dough will spread a bit on the baking sheet, so leave plenty of room for the dough to rise and expand.

Preheat the oven to 400°F. Flour your hands and, using your fingertips, vigorously dimple the surface of the dough all over, including the edges, making deep indentations. Brush generously with the garlic-infused olive oil so that the oil pools in the indentations. Sprinkle the dough with coarse sea salt and bake until browned, 25 to 30 minutes. Serve warm, as soon as possible after baking.

GETTING AHEAD: The dough may be kneaded and left to rise overnight in the refrigerator; cover the bowl tightly with plastic wrap. Let the dough come to room temperature, then shape and bake it just before serving.

Garlic Bread

Garlic bread is a rival for focaccia (page 27) any day and a quick accompaniment for soup and salad.

Makes 1 loaf

> ½ cup (1 stick) butter, plus 2 tablespoons
> 3 to 4 garlic cloves, finely chopped
> 2 tablespoons chopped fresh parsley
> 2 tablespoons chopped fresh thyme or basil
> ½ teaspoon salt
> ½ teaspoon pepper
> 1 loaf crisp Italian bread

Melt the 2 tablespoons butter in a small saucepan and sauté the garlic over medium heat until fragrant, about 1 minute. Add the remaining butter and heat until melted. Stir in the parsley, thyme, salt, and pepper. Heat the garlic-herb butter until very hot, then let cool. Cut the bread into 1¼-inch slices, cutting almost but not quite through each slice. Brush between the slices with the garlic-herb butter. Put the loaf on a sheet of foil and gather up the sides, leaving the top open.

Preheat oven to 350°F. Bake bread until very hot, brown, and crisp on top, 12 to 15 minutes.

GETTING AHEAD: The bread can be prepared 3 to 4 hours ahead and baked just before serving.

Garlic Broth

A great pick-me-up when served with grated Parmesan cheese and a baguette. For a more substantial soup, simmer a handful of vermicelli noodles or orzo (tiny, rice-shaped pasta) in the broth just before serving.

Serves 6

> 6 garlic cloves, chopped
> 1 tablespoon olive oil
> 1½ quarts water
> pared zest of 1 orange
> 2 bay leaves
> 2 sprigs thyme
> 2 sprigs rosemary
> 1 whole clove
> salt and pepper to taste

In a soup pot, sauté the garlic in the olive oil until soft, about 1 minute. Add the water, orange zest, bay leaves, thyme and rosemary sprigs, whole clove, salt, and pepper. Cover and simmer until the broth is very fragrant, 10 to 15 minutes. Traditional cooks do not strain the soup before serving, but you may wish to do so as the flavorings are not meant to be eaten. Serve at once, while still fresh and fragrant.

Roasted Whole Garlic Heads

how to roast garlic and shallots

Garlic and shallots, roasted in their skins to retain their juices and taste, make a luxurious accompaniment to roast meats, poultry, and vegetables. Cooking mellows the flavor, giving garlic in particular a deep, caramelized sweetness. The soft pulp of garlic is also good spread on bread or used to flavor vegetable dishes and sauces. When served whole at the table, roasted shallots pop out of their skins easily enough, but to extract the pulp from garlic cloves, you need to mash them with a knife or fork. Hearty eaters like me often take a direct approach, chewing on the whole roasted cloves and then discarding the skin. Be sure to save any oil leftover from roasting garlic or shallots—it is excellent for grilling and sautéing vegetables, or as a topping for focaccia.

Roasted Whole Garlic Heads

For roasting, trim the tops of heads of garlic so the heat reaches the inside of the cloves.

Preheat the oven to 375°F. Trim the heads of garlic so the tops of the cloves are exposed, allowing one head per person. Pack them in a small baking dish and pour over enough olive or vegetable oil to almost cover them. Cover tightly with a lid or aluminum foil and roast in the oven until the garlic is very tender, 1 to 1¹/₂ hours. Drain the heads and serve hot, reserving the flavored oil for another use.

Roasted Garlic Cloves

For quicker results, pull the heads of garlic apart so the individual cloves can be cooked in their skins.

Separate the garlic cloves and toss them with olive or vegetable oil, allowing one head of garlic and 1 tablespoon oil per person. Put the cloves in a single layer in a baking dish, cover, and roast them in a preheated 350°F oven until the skins are browned and the pulp is tender when poked with a knife, 35 to 45 minutes.

Roasted Shallots

Shallots may be halved or left whole for roasting.

Trim the roots and discard any loose skin from some shallots, allowing 2 to 3 shallots per person. If you like, cut them in half through the root, but do not peel them. Toss them with olive or vegetable oil and roast them as you would garlic cloves until tender when pierced with a knife. Allow 25 to 35 minutes if the shallots are halved, or 10 minutes longer if they are left whole.

Roasted Shallot

HOW TO PEEL AND CHOP SHALLOTS

Finicky things, shallots. I'm often tempted to use an onion instead, until I taste the results. No onion can match a shallot's layers of flavor—perfumed and piquant without being sharp. Raw chopped shallot is agreeably crunchy and brisk in salads or sprinkled over grilled fish or vegetables. Sliced or chopped shallots are much used to flavor vinegars, marinades, and vinaigrettes.

Like onions, the taste of shallots varies if they are lightly cooked, when they retain an aromatic bite, or more thoroughly browned, which mellows and concentrates their flavor. If you roast shallots whole (page 29), they will be bursting with flavor, losing none of their intensity. Note that chopped shallot cooks rapidly and burns all too easily, so take care not to brown it beyond a light gold. Sliced shallots hold up better during cooking, but they too need more careful attention than common onions.

You're pretty safe buying shallots unless the poor things have started to sprout green tendrils. If you've a choice, the pink- or purple-tinged varieties are superior; please do avoid the giant shallots shaped like a torpedo. Like so many oversized vegetables, they are short on taste. At home, shallots should be stored like onions, in a cool place in the dark. Emma puts them in an airy, covered basket in a corner of the counter, where they keep happily several weeks. Every now and again she browns and caramelizes them for the delicious marmalade, sharpened with a few spoonfuls of wine vinegar, that follows.

① To peel a shallot: Separate the bulbs at the root if necessary, then remove the skins from each section. Trim the top and leave a small part of the root to hold the shallot bulb in one piece.

② To chop a shallot: Set a section flat side down on a chopping board. (If it is rounded on all sides, cut a thin slice from one side to form a base.) Hold the shallot firmly in your fingers, and with a vegetable knife, slice horizontally toward the root, leaving the slices attached at the root end.

③ Slice vertically through the shallot, again leaving the root end uncut. Cut across the shallot to make small dice. For finer texture, continue chopping with a large knife.

④ To slice a shallot: Peel the shallot, trimming the root. Set the shallot, flat side down (if necessary trim off a small slice so the shallot sits flat) and cut lengthwise in thin or thick slices.

Lemon Shallot Vinaigrette

Perfect on fish or a cooked vegetable salad such as green beans, cannellini beans, and potatoes. Toss the vegetables with the dressing while they are still warm.

This recipe makes enough vinaigrette for 1 pound cooked vegetables. As an approximate guide, 1 pound green beans or 2 pounds potatoes serves 4.

Makes 1 cup vinaigrette, enough for 1 to 1½ pounds cooked vegetables to serve 4

Put 2 finely chopped shallots in a small bowl and whisk in 2 tablespoons lemon juice, 2 tablespoons white wine, salt, and pepper. Gradually whisk in ½ cup olive oil so the dressing emulsifies and thickens slightly.

Crunchy Shallot Steak

When you think steak, think tuna or swordfish as well as beef.

Grill your steaks (see page 122 for fish, page 190 for beef) and warm a metal serving dish. Chop 2 shallots for each person. When the steaks are cooked through, sprinkle half the shallots in the hot serving dish. Set the steaks on top, sprinkle with the remaining shallots, and serve. Juices from the steaks will moisten the shallots, but they will stay crunchy.

Emma's Shallot Marmalade

As a child, Emma didn't like onions so I never thought of offering her shallots. It took a neighborhood restaurant and the familiar name of marmalade to persuade her. This recipe is also good made with yellow onions. Try it with cold roast pork or chicken, or spread a thin layer on crusty bread or bruschetta.

Makes 2 cups

> 2 pounds shallots
> 4 tablespoons butter
> salt and pepper to taste
> 2 tablespoons sugar
> 3 tablespoons red wine vinegar
> ⅔ cup chicken or veal stock

Peel the shallots and thickly slice them. Melt the butter in a heavy frying pan over medium heat. Add the shallots, season with salt and pepper, and brown them, stirring frequently, 8 to 10 minutes. Sprinkle with the sugar and cook 1 to 2 minutes longer, until the shallots are caramelized—you will be able to smell the caramel. Deglaze the pan with the vinegar, stirring to dissolve the pan juices. Add the stock and bring to a boil.

Cover the pan and cook over low heat, stirring occasionally, until the shallots are brown and meltingly tender, 20 to 30 minutes. The juices should be reduced so the shallots have become a thick conserve. If necessary, cook the marmalade without the lid until all liquid has evaporated and the shallots are deep golden brown.

GETTING AHEAD: Shallot marmalade keeps well in the refrigerator in an airtight container for up to a month.

HOW TO PEEL, SLICE, AND DICE ONIONS

Here we're looking at the familiar globe onion. How could we cook without it? Think of life without French onion soup, creamed onions, stuffed onions, deep-fried onion rings, and our more recent indulgences, lusciously rich onion chutneys and confits. Many quiches and stews are unimaginable without a foundation of onions, and vegetable salads would be dull indeed.

The quick slicing and chopping of an onion is more useful than any other technique. With a sharp large knife and a firmly anchored chopping board (put a damp cloth or paper towel underneath to immobilize it), you're ready to start. I wish I had a magic remedy for the tears that onions elicit—it is the juice between the layers that causes the trouble. Hold a piece of bread in your teeth advises an old cookbook of mine, so you breathe through your mouth, not your nose. A well-aired kitchen helps, as does rinsing your hands often in cold water. And take care never, ever to touch your eyes.

choosing onions

Which onions should you choose? Good onions are heavy (therefore juicy) and firm when you pinch them, with no green sprout peeking out. To some extent, the color of an onion's skin indicates its pungency: red onions are usually sweet, white ones of medium strength, and yellow onions the most astringent. Personally I always go for yellow onions unless I need red ones to use raw in a salad. I find that white onions are bland when cooked, and lack the complexity that makes yellow onions so indispensable. Remember that an onion is milder when fresh, so layers of dry, papery skin suggest the taste will be stronger. Soil plays its part too: the famously sweet Bermudas and Vidalias taste different when grown elsewhere. So, as with apples and tomatoes, you simply have to try a variety of onions until you find the ones you like.

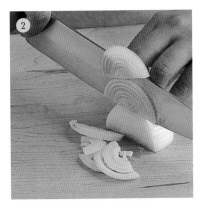

① To peel an onion: Trim the stem and root ends of the onion, leaving enough of the root to hold the onion together. If you plan to slice or dice the onion, halve it through the root—you'll find the skin can be stripped off easily.

② To slice an onion crosswise: Set the peeled onion half flat on a chopping board, and with a large knife, slice across, working from top to root and cutting slices of the thickness you want. (Hold the onion firmly, guiding the knife with your bent fingers.) Discard the root end of the onion.

③ To slice an onion lengthwise: Set the onion half on a chopping board and cut it in fine wedges through the stem and root, in thick or thin slices, starting with the knife almost flat against the board, gradually increasing the angle to vertical in the center of the onion. The slices form crescents.

You can slice onions crosswise or through the root, or you can dice them or cut them in rings. You'll find that onions have a mind of their own, falling apart easily when cut crosswise, but clinging together when cut through the root. Slices cut through the root end hold together in attractive crescents when cooked over moderate heat. Chopped onions cook more quickly; in fact, they almost disappear into the background of a slow-cooked sauce or stew.

The speed at which you cook onions makes a big difference. If you sauté or sweat them very slowly, under a cover of parchment paper or aluminum foil pressed down to keep in the juices, they gradually soften until meltingly tender, almost sugary. This is the right technique for delicate onion tarts and flans. If you sauté onions more quickly; without a cover, they color to a sunny gold and taste both tart and sweet with a hint of caramel—the right stuff for soups, stews, and braised vegetables. When cooked even further, so their sugars caramelize to a rich mahogany, onions work magic in confits, chutneys, French onion soup, and homemade hash browns. (Did your mother make those—mine did!) Ultimately, onions burn black and scorch, but you have to be really careless to let that happen.

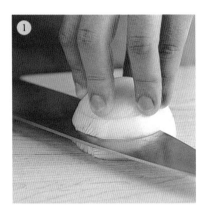

1 To dice an onion: Halve the onion through the root, peel it, and set a half flat on the chopping board. With a large knife, make a series of horizontal cuts from the stem toward the root. Cut just to the root but not through it, so the slices hold together. Thick slices will yield large dice, thinner slices are needed for chopped onion.

2 Make a series of lengthwise vertical cuts of the same thickness, slicing almost but not quite through the root.

3 Finally, cut the onion crosswise so that it falls into dice. Guide the knife with your bent fingers.

4 To chop the onion into smaller pieces: Continue chopping, moving the knife back and forth on the board and holding the point down with one hand. Continue until the onion is chopped as finely as you want.

onion rounds and rings

Onions are sliced into thick rounds for grilling or roasting in the oven. First brush them with oil and sprinkle with salt, pepper, and a little sugar. Thinner rounds may be added raw to salads, or separated into rings for deep-frying. Very thin slices fall naturally into rings and make decorative toppings when raw, or lacy garnishes when sautéed or deep-fried. For onion rings, strip the skin and leave the onion whole.

To cut onion rounds or rings: First peel a large onion, and trim the stem and root ends. Turn the onion on its side, hold it securely on the board with one hand, and cut thick or thin slices crosswise in downward strokes. Leave the slices whole or push them apart into rings.

Cotton Onions

Deep-fried cotton onions are a Southern specialty. They should be light and fluffy as a ball of cotton. They are not to be confused with deep-fried onion rings, which are cut thicker, then breaded or battered, and not nearly so delicate. For perfectly even slices, use a mandoline. Tobacco onions are a simple variation: when seasoning the flour, add a teaspoon of gumbo filé powder (a key ingredient in gumbo) and a large pinch of cayenne.

Serves 3 greedy people

> 2 large onions, thinly sliced into rings
> about 1 quart buttermilk
> deep oil for frying
> 1½ cups flour
> 1 teaspoon salt, more for sprinkling
> 1 teaspoon paprika
> ½ teaspoon freshly ground black pepper

Separate the onion rings, put them in a bowl, and pour the buttermilk over them to cover. Refrigerate for 15 to 30 minutes. Heat deep oil to 375°F. Put the flour in a large plastic bag with the salt, paprika, and black pepper. Shake to mix.

Using tongs, lift a generous handful of onion rings out of the buttermilk and add them to the flour. Toss until lightly coated. Still using tongs, transfer them from the flour to the hot oil and fry them until lightly golden and crisp, 1 to 2 minutes. Drain the rings on paper towels and fry the rest in the same way. Just before serving, sprinkle them with a little salt. Serve hot.

GETTING AHEAD: Cotton onions will stay crisp for about 15 minutes if you don't crowd them.

Confit of Onions in Red Wine

Onion confit is wonderful with steak and rich meats like pork and duck—and that's just a beginning. Use it as a topping for pizza, a filling for quiche, and as a flavoring for soups and sautéed vegetables. A fruity red wine, such as a Merlot or Gamay, is best.

Serves 4 to 6

> 5 tablespoons butter
> 2 pounds onions, sliced lengthwise
> 1 tablespoon sugar, more to taste
> salt and pepper to taste
> 1 cup fruity red wine

Melt the butter in a sauté pan and stir in the onions with the sugar, salt, and pepper. Press a piece of aluminum foil on top, cover the pan to keep in the onion juices, and cook them over low heat until reduced and soft, stirring often, 20 to 30 minutes.

Remove the lid and foil, increase the heat to medium, and continue cooking, stirring often, until the onions are caramelized and very dark brown, 15 to 20 minutes longer. Pour in the wine and simmer, stirring, until the liquid has evaporated and the onions are dark brown, concentrated, and meltingly tender, 8 to 10 minutes. Taste and adjust the seasoning, including the sugar.

GETTING AHEAD: Confit can be kept, tightly covered, in the refrigerator for 1 month or more. The flavor will mellow over time.

Double Onion Salad with Orange

I like this as a first course and best of all with roast duck or pork. You can vary the mix by adding some sliced avocado if you like.

Serves 4

> **2 large oranges (about 1 pound total)**
> **3 medium sweet red onions (about 1 pound total), cut into rings**
> **2 to 3 scallions, including some of the green parts, sliced**
>
> FOR THE CITRUS DRESSING
> **1 cup sour cream**
> **grated zest and juice of 1 lime**
> **½ teaspoon ground cumin**
> **salt and pepper to taste**

For the citrus dressing: Whisk the sour cream, lime zest and juice, cumin, salt, and pepper until smooth. The dressing should be thin enough to pour—whisk in a little water if necessary. Taste and adjust seasoning. Spoon about half the dressing onto 4 individual plates.

To slice the oranges: Using a serrated knife, cut a slice from the top and bottom. Set the orange cut side down on the work surface. Working from top to bottom and following the curve of the fruit, cut away rind, pith, and skin. Continue until all the peel has been removed, then cut the orange crosswise in 3/8-inch slices.

Arrange the orange and onion slices overlapping on top of the pool of dressing on each plate. Spoon the remaining dressing over the orange and onion slices to partially coat them. Sprinkle with sliced scallions, cover loosely, and chill for up to 30 minutes before serving.

GETTING AHEAD: Up to 6 hours ahead, slice the oranges and onions, arrange them on plates, cover tightly with plastic wrap, and chill. Make the dressing and refrigerate it. Shortly before serving, bring the dressing to room temperature and whisk it until emulsified again. Spoon it over the salad and top with the sliced scallions.

Real French Onion Soup

Don't let commercial canners fool you, real French onion soup can only be made at home. The onions—and they must be the pungent yellow ones—are browned for 30 minutes or more, so they caramelize to dark brown and give the soup its robust flavor.

Serves 4 to 6

> **¼ cup butter**
> **2 pounds onions, thinly sliced lengthwise**
> **salt and pepper to taste**
> **1 tablespoon sugar**
> **1½ quarts beef, veal, or chicken stock**
> **½ baguette, cut into ½-inch slices**
> **¾ cup (2½ ounces) grated Gruyère cheese**
> **4 to 6 deep heatproof soup bowls**

Melt the butter in a large pot and stir in the onions with salt and pepper. Sauté very gently over low heat, stirring often, until the onions are soft and starting to brown, 15 to 20 minutes. Stir in the sugar and continue cooking over medium heat, stirring until the onions are reduced, concentrated, and very dark brown, 10 to 15 minutes longer. It is this browning that gives the soup its flavor.

Add the stock and simmer the soup, 10 to 15 minutes. Meanwhile, preheat the oven to 350°F. Set the baguette slices on a baking sheet and bake in the oven until crisp and brown, 10 to 15 minutes.

To finish: Reheat the soup if necessary. Preheat the broiler and heat the soup bowls. Add 1 to 2 slices of the toasted bread to each one and pour the soup over the toast. Sprinkle with the grated cheese and broil until browned. Serve at once; onion soup must be scalding hot.

GETTING AHEAD: The flavor of onion soup actually improves if you make it a day or two ahead and refrigerate it. Finish it by reheating and adding the toast and grated cheese just before serving.

HOW TO PEEL AND CHOP FRESH GINGER

I wish I could grow fresh ginger in my garden—many food plants thrive in Burgundy's moist, temperate atmosphere—but ginger needs tropical heat to survive. Like most Western cooks, I've come to think of fresh ginger as part of my standard repertoire, though as a child I knew it only as a dried spice in ginger cookies. Just a hint of raw ginger in salad dressings and marinades adds unexpected depth to tomatoes, squash, eggplant, and other vegetables. Be careful, though, not to overdo it. As with an excess of garlic, all you will taste is the ginger.

When cooked, usually by sautéing, the flavor of fresh ginger mellows but retains a surprisingly warm bite that wakes up any fish dish or stir fry. With garlic and scallion, ginger forms part of a classic Asian seasoning trio that has become familiar worldwide. The popular sushi condiment, pickled ginger, is easy to buy. Chop and sprinkle it over broiled fish or vegetables, or serve it instead of the usual grated horseradish with shrimp cocktail or oysters on the half shell.

The best fresh ginger is firm, plump, and slightly pliable, with the cut surfaces moist to the touch. It is sold by the "hand," no explanation needed. Loosely wrapped ginger keeps well for a couple of weeks in the refrigerator, so it rivals garlic and onion as a standby seasoning. Simply break off a piece when you need it. When recipes call for chopped ginger by the tablespoon, just remember that a 1 1/2-inch piece of ginger yields about 1 tablespoon after chopping.

I long ago learned the trick of scraping the peel off ginger with a teaspoon so the flavoring elements just under the skin are unharmed. Unlike garlic and the rest of the onion family, ginger does not bruise easily. In fact, to release maximum flavor, it needs quite violent crushing to break up its fibrous texture. "Watch out, Mom!" the children would say when I used the flat of a knife or cleaver to whack slices of ginger with a satisfying thump. Perhaps they feared I might thump them as well.

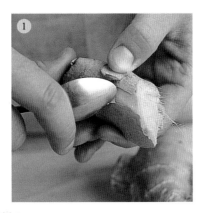

① Using a teaspoon, scrape the peel from the piece of ginger. Slice it with a large knife, cutting across the fibrous grain.

② Set the blade flat on each slice of ginger and crush it with the heel of your hand or your fist.

③ Assemble the flattened ginger slices and finely chop them.

Vietnamese Stir-Fried Fish with Ginger

This versatile stir fry suits scallops and shrimp as well as all sorts of white fish. Serve it with rice or noodles. Chinese fermented black beans add their characteristic yeasty flavor—you'll find them in Asian markets and some supermarkets.

Serves 3 to 4

>   1 pound sole or other thin fish fillets
>   1-inch piece of ginger, peeled and chopped
>   3 garlic cloves, finely chopped
>   1 tablespoon Chinese fermented black beans,
>   finely chopped
>   1 tablespoon sesame seeds
>   2 tablespoons vegetable oil
>   2 scallions, including green parts, sliced
>   1 tablespoon soy sauce, more to taste
>   1 tablespoon rice wine or sweet sherry
>   1 teaspoon dark sesame oil, more to taste

Rinse the sole fillets, pat them dry on paper towels, and cut them diagonally into strips. In a small bowl, mix the ginger, garlic, and black beans. Heat a wok over medium heat, add the sesame seeds and toast them, stirring constantly, until browned, 1 to 2 minutes. Remove and set them aside.

Heat the wok over high heat for about 30 seconds. Drizzle the vegetable oil around its sides, add the ginger mixture, and stir-fry until aromatic, about 30 seconds. Add the fish and cook over very high heat, tossing and stirring just until it is firm, about 1 minute. Stir in the scallions, soy sauce, and rice wine and toss over high heat until the fish is cooked through, about 1 minute longer. Remove from the heat and stir in the toasted sesame seeds and sesame oil. Taste, adjust the seasoning, including soy sauce and sesame oil, and serve at once.

GETTING AHEAD: I like to prepare all the ingredients for a stir fry an hour or two ahead, storing the fish in the refrigerator. Frying is done at the last minute.

Chicken Wings with a Ginger Glaze

The dark anise-tinged glaze for these wings is picked up just before serving with a shower of finely chopped fresh ginger.

Serves 4 to 6

>   24 to 30 chicken wings (about 1½ pounds)
>   2-inch piece of ginger, peeled and chopped
>   ⅓ cup soy sauce
>   ⅓ cup water
>   1 tablespoon sweet sherry or vermouth
>   2 tablespoons sherry vinegar
>   1 star anise
>   2 whole cloves garlic, peeled
>   ¼ cup brown sugar
>   1 scallion, including green parts, sliced

Set aside half the ginger. Mix the soy sauce, water, sherry, sherry vinegar, star anise, remaining ginger, and garlic in a large deep bowl. Add the chicken wings, stir to mix well, cover, and chill for at least 6 hours or overnight.

Transfer the wings and marinade to a wok and stir in the brown sugar. Bring to a boil, reduce the heat to low, cover, and simmer the wings until the meat is tender and just begins to pull away from the bones, 25 to 35 minutes depending on the size of the wings. Stir often so they are always coated with marinade and do not stick to the pan.

Remove the lid and boil, stirring often, until the sauce has thickened to a rich brown glaze. Discard the anise and garlic. Sprinkle the wings with the scallion slices and reserved ginger and serve.

GETTING AHEAD: These chicken wings are delicious cooked up to a day ahead and reheated or served at room temperature.

HOW TO CORE, SEED, AND CHOP FRESH CHILE PEPPERS

The world of peppers is composed of the hot varieties and the essentially mild bell peppers. It is hot chiles that we are looking at here. There are dozens of varieties, ranging from piquant jalapeños all the way up the heat scale to Scotch bonnets and habaneros, which are so hot they can cause nasty burns. To mention a few of the most common, jalapeño peppers are dark green, pointed, and 2 to 3 inches long. Their heat is mild to medium. Poblanos are also mild to medium in strength, and similar in color but an inch or two longer, with plump shoulders and a sunken stem. Lighter green serranos are smaller and a bit hotter, with an herbal note. Habaneros can be orange or green and look like little Chinese lanterns; watch out, they are fiery hot.

I could go on and on, but happily all chiles are treated the same on the chopping board. Many hot varieties are too powerful to be served in slices, so they are halved lengthwise and chopped only after the seeds and core have been scooped out. Chile seeds and ribs contain a good deal of heat, and cooks who live dangerously like to throw them in, though white seeds can spoil the appearance of a colorful sauce. Personally I remove the seeds and core. Milder, fleshy chiles such as serrano, poblano, and jalapeño can also be roasted and peeled like bell peppers (see How to Roast and Core Bell Peppers, page 255) before chopping. Tiny hot chiles give off acrid smoke if scorched, so most recipes call for them to be simmered or baked without browning.

Lazy cooks are quickly betrayed by chunks of chile peppers in their salsa, so give extra time to your knife work. The hotter chiles will sting your skin and eyes when you are chopping, but luckily a single chile goes a long way. If you keep your hands away from your face and wash as soon as you're done, you'll be fine. When dealing with larger quantities, you may want to wear rubber gloves.

1 Halve the chile pepper lengthwise and cut or scrape out core and seeds with a vegetable knife. Cut away the fleshy white ribs.

2 Slice each half lengthwise into very thin strips. Gather the strips together and cut them crosswise into fine dice. If necessary, chop the dice even smaller using a large knife.

Chile Cilantro Relish, page 40

Chile Cilantro Relish

This brilliant green relish, popular in southern India, should be freshly prepared so it bursts with flavor. Serve it with mild curries, or spread it on flat bread and top it with sliced cucumber.

Makes 1 cup relish to serve 4 to 6

large bunch of cilantro
3 jalapeño or serrano chiles, cored, seeded, and cut in large pieces
½ cup grated fresh or unsweetened dried coconut
2-inch piece of ginger, thinly sliced
juice of 1 lemon
1 teaspoon salt
1 teaspoon sugar
2 tablespoons vegetable oil
2 teaspoons mustard seeds

Pull leaves from stems of cilantro, wash the leaves, and pat them dry on paper towels. Put them in a food processor with the chiles, coconut, ginger, lemon juice, salt, and sugar. Purée until the relish is finely chopped, 2 to 3 minutes.

Heat the vegetable oil in a small frying pan over medium heat and fry the mustard seeds until they pop, 1 to 2 minutes. With the processor blades running, pour the seeds and oil into the relish and process just until combined.

GETTING AHEAD: Unlike many relishes, this is best when very fresh, served after a maximum of 30 minutes' chilling.

Chiles with a Soft Heart

These stuffed peppers make a lively garnish for steak and pork chops.

Serves 3 to 4

Slit 6 to 8 jalapeño or serrano chiles down one side and scoop out the cores and seeds. Cut strips the same length as the chiles from a 4-ounce piece of mild Cheddar or Monterey Jack cheese. Stuff the cheese into the chiles. Pour 2 to 3 tablespoons olive oil onto a plate, coat the chiles in the oil, and then lay them in a small baking dish. Cover with aluminum foil and bake in a preheated 350°F oven until the chiles are tender, 25 to 30 minutes.

Mauritian Hot Cakes

I enjoy these crispy hot cakes with cocktails, or as an accompaniment to chicken and meat curries or stews.

Makes 24 to 30 cakes to serve 6 to 8

½ pound red lentils
1 onion, cut in pieces
1 garlic clove, cut in pieces
3 jalapeño peppers, cored, seeded, and cut in chunks, more to taste
3 tablespoons chopped fresh cilantro
¼ teaspoon baking soda
salt and pepper to taste
¼ cup vegetable oil

Rinse the lentils and leave them to soak in cold water, 6 to 12 hours. Drain them. Work the onions, garlic, and peppers in a food processor until finely chopped. Add the lentils and pulse until they are finely chopped also. Work in the cilantro, baking soda, salt, and pepper. Taste and adjust the seasoning, adding more pepper if you like heat.

Heat half the oil in a skillet until very hot. Drop heaping tablespoonfuls of the mixture into the hot oil and flatten with the back of the spoon. Fry the cakes until golden brown, 2 to 3 minutes. Turn them and brown the other side, 1 to 2 minutes longer. Heat the remaining oil and fry the remaining mixture. Serve warm or at room temperature.

GETTING AHEAD: Hot cakes keep well at room temperature for up to a day.

HOW TO PEEL, SEED, AND CHOP TOMATOES

Peeling, seeding, and chopping a tomato is easy when you know how, and well worth the time. A quick dunk in boiling water will cook a tomato sufficiently so it can be peeled without trouble. Tomato seeds are messy, chewy, and often bitter, so for most recipes they are best removed, too. Chopping is more obvious, a matter of slicing the halved tomato, turning it, and slicing again before chopping into coarse or small dice. You'll need this technique to make tomato sauce for pizza or pasta, salsa (there are several recipes in this book), and colorful little garnishes for fish,

poultry, and vegetables. Have you ever made your own fresh tomato juice? With ultraripe tomatoes from the farmers' market, it's a revelation.

Tomatoes commonly masquerade as vegetables, but botanically they are a fruit and they behave like one in the kitchen. Ripe tomatoes cook rapidly to a purée, and for a tomato soup or sauce a pinch of sugar (truly just a pinch, this is not dessert) can work wonders. Identifying a ripe tomato recently picked from the vine is easier said than done. In general, deep color is a sign of ripeness, but some heirloom varieties never

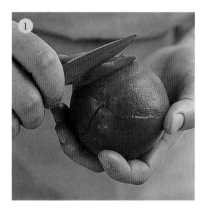

1 To peel a tomato: Bring a large pan of water to a boil. With a vegetable knife, cut a shallow cross in the flower end. If the tomato is large, cut out the core. Immerse the tomato in boiling water until the skin curls away from the cross, 8 to 15 seconds depending on ripeness. You can do several tomatoes at a time, but a large quantity must be scalded in batches. Transfer tomatoes to a bowl of cold water, then peel them.

2 Alternatively, to peel just a few tomatoes, spear each one on a two-pronged fork and toast it over an open flame until the skin chars and can be removed easily.

3 To seed a tomato: Cut the tomato crosswise and squeeze each half, scraping away the seeds with a knife. For large quantities, it is worth sieving the seeds in a strainer to extract the tomato juice.

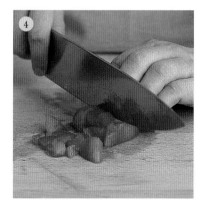

4 To chop a tomato: Set a tomato half cut side down and slice it with a large knife. Give the slices a half turn on the board and slice again. Then chop the tomato chunks as coarsely or finely as you want.

progress beyond a greenish orange. Wooly texture is almost impossible to detect without cutting the fruit open. The best bet of all is to grow your own, or failing that, to buy fresh tomatoes at a roadside stand or farmers' market. Connoisseurs have their favorite picturesque heirloom varieties, be it brandywine, mortgage lifter, Cherokee purple, or striped German, so experiment to discover your own. Back home, resist the temptation to refrigerate tomatoes as chilling stops them from ripening further.

tomato tips

* Red tomatoes are green before they ripen, but a yellow tomato is a distinct variety.
* Ultraripe, sweet, soft tomatoes are best for soups and sauces; the crisp texture of greener tomatoes is appropriate for salads. Plum tomatoes are less juicy, which makes them ideal for a concentrated sauce.
* Perish the thought of unnecessary work: when tomatoes are to be sieved for a soup or sauce there is no need to peel them.
* The skin of many plum tomatoes is thin, so here's another instance where peeling may not be necessary.
* Thyme, basil, bay leaf, orange, cheese, anchovy, and garlic are the natural partners of tomato.

Concassée of Tomato

A vivid topping of raw tomato is useful with broiled and sautéed fish, poultry, and vegetables. A concassée can be little more than chopped tomatoes seasoned with salt and pepper, or it can be brisk with herbs and a touch of lemon, as I like it.

Makes 1 cup topping to serve 4

Peel, seed, and chop $1/2$ pound tomatoes. Transfer to a colander, stir in a little salt and pepper, and let the tomatoes stand for 30 minutes to drain excess juice. Stir in 1 tablespoon chopped fresh basil, oregano, or flat-leaf parsley, a squeeze of lemon juice, and a pinch of sugar. Taste and adjust the seasoning.

Fresh Tomato Cocktails

If you've only tasted canned tomato juice, here's a whole new world. Make the cocktails at the height of the season when tomatoes are full of flavor and bursting with juice.

SUNSET SPECIAL

Serves 4

Peel and seed 2 pounds very ripe tomatoes and cut them in pieces. Put them in a food processor with $1/4$ cup Pernod or other anise liqueur, 2 tablespoons chopped fresh tarragon, and $1/2$ teaspoon salt. Purée until smooth, then chill for serving.

VIRGIN MARY

Serves 4

Follow the recipe for Sunset Special, but instead of the Pernod, tarragon, and salt, substitute 2 tablespoons Worcestershire sauce, 1 teaspoon celery salt, and a dash of Tabasco. For a classic Bloody Mary, add a shot of vodka to each glass.

Tomato Sauce for Pizza

It's tempting to use store-bought tomato sauce to top a pizza, but if you're making the dough, please follow through with a fresh tomato sauce. You'll be happy with the results!

Makes 1 quart sauce, enough for two 14-inch pizzas

> ⅓ **cup olive oil**
> **3 onions, chopped**
> **4 garlic cloves, chopped**
> **3 pounds plum tomatoes, seeded and chopped**
> **4 to 5 tablespoons tomato paste**
> **3 to 4 tablespoons chopped fresh oregano or thyme**
> **1 bay leaf**
> **salt and pepper to taste**
> **pinch of sugar**

Heat the oil in a large saucepan, stir in the onions, and sauté them over medium heat until they are soft and lightly browned, 5 to 7 minutes. Add the garlic and sauté until fragrant, about 1 minute more. Stir in the tomatoes, tomato paste, oregano, bay leaf, salt, pepper, and sugar. Cover and cook gently until the tomatoes are very soft, 10 to 15 minutes. Remove the lid and continue cooking, stirring often, until the sauce is thickened and just falls from the spoon, about 20 minutes longer. Taste and adjust the seasoning.

GETTING AHEAD: Tomato sauce keeps well, covered in the refrigerator, for up to a week. It can also be frozen, so when you find plum tomatoes that are cheap and ripe it is well worth making a double or triple batch of pizza sauce.

Tomato Sauce for Pasta

Follow the recipe for Tomato Sauce for Pizza, but simmer it uncovered for just 10 to 15 minutes, so it remains soft enough to pour. You'll have enough sauce for 2 pounds pasta to serve 8.

Salsa Mexicana

This classic condiment for tacos, enchiladas, quesadillas, burritos, and tortilla chips is standard on every Mexican table. Note that it is a dip rather than a side dish, so the ingredients should be chopped quite small.

Makes 2 cups dip to serve 4 to 6

> **small bunch of cilantro**
> **1 pound tomatoes, peeled, seeded, and chopped**
> **1 medium onion, finely chopped**
> **2 garlic cloves, finely chopped**
> **2 serrano or jalapeño chile peppers, cored, seeded, and finely chopped, more to taste**
> **juice of 1 lime**
> **salt to taste**

Pull the cilantro leaves from the stems, reserving one or two sprigs for decoration, and chop the leaves. Mix the chopped tomatoes, onion, garlic, and chiles in a bowl and stir in the cilantro and lime juice. Taste and adjust the seasoning with salt and more chile pepper as you wish.

GETTING AHEAD: If you want to keep the dip more than an hour or two, add salt just before serving so the tomatoes do not make the salsa watery.

Stock Basics

It's common knowledge in my family that I'm never happy without a pot of stock simmering on the stove. Stock is the basis of so many soups and sauces, to me it's like money in the bank. Good stock is full-flavored and rich with gelatin extracted from the bones of fish, chicken, or meat. (Vegetable stock is the exception as it uses no bones.) Stock should be simmered without a lid, never boiled, or it will become cloudy. (Once more there's an exception, as fish stock is brought to a boil, then simmered rapidly.) Stock is easy to make at home and will simmer quietly on the back of the stove while you look after other dishes.

After the ingredients have been strained out, stock is often simmered again to reduce and concentrate it. In this way, the flavor is intensified—taken to the limit, the reduced stock becomes a glaze (see How to Make a Glaze, page 88). For this reason, I do not add salt, as stock can easily become too salty when reduced. Stock can be kept for up to 3 days in the refrigerator, or longer if you boil it for 5 minutes on the stovetop every couple of days, then return it to the refrigerator. I often simmer stock until it's concentrated, freeze it in ice cube trays, and store the cubes in a plastic bag to use in small quantities.

Talking of stock cubes and cans, I find that most commercial versions are a poor substitute for the real thing. They tend to taste insipid and lack gelatins; too much salt can be a problem, too.

Brown Beef or Veal Stock

Veal stock is made with veal bones only, whereas beef stock is made with half veal bones and half beef. If your butcher saws the bones in half, you'll be able to extract all the more flavor. The vegetables I suggest here are just a start: you can add many others such as leeks, carrot tops, and tomatoes for color, and herbs for taste. Do not, however, include roots as they disintegrate. Bones and vegetables for brown stock must be well browned and the easiest way is to roast them in the oven.

Makes about 2 ¹/₂ quarts stock

> **5 pounds veal bones (or half veal, half beef)**
> **2 unpeeled onions, quartered**
> **2 carrots, quartered**
> **1 celery stalk, cut in pieces**
> **1 bouquet garni of 5 to 6 parsley stems,**
>   **3 to 4 thyme stems, and 2 bay leaves**
> **1 teaspoon peppercorns**
> **1 tablespoon tomato paste**
> **3 to 4 garlic cloves, unpeeled (optional)**
> **5 quarts water, more if needed**

Preheat the oven to 500°F. Put the bones in a roasting pan and roast until they are well browned, 30 to 40 minutes. Stir, add the onions, carrots, and celery, and continue roasting until the bones and vegetables are very brown, almost charred around the edges, 30 minutes longer.

Transfer the bones and vegetables to a stockpot and add the bouquet garni, peppercorns, tomato paste, garlic if using, and enough water to cover. Bring slowly to a boil, skimming often. Simmer very gently for 5 to 6 hours, skimming occasionally, and adding more water if needed to cover. Strain, and if the flavor is thin, boil the stock until it is reduced and concentrated. Chill and skim off any fat before using.

White Veal Stock

White veal stock is made like brown stock, but instead of being browned, the bones are blanched in boiling water before they are simmered.

Makes about 2 1/2 quarts stock

In the recipe for Brown Beef or Veal Stock, do not brown the bones. Put them in a large pot, cover them with cold water, and bring them slowly to a boil. Simmer them for 5 minutes, drain in a colander, and rinse with cold water. Put the bones in a stockpot with the remaining ingredients and continue as described.

Chicken Stock

Chicken stock is also made like brown veal stock, but the chicken bones are not browned before they're simmered.

Makes about 1 1/2 quarts stock

In a stockpot, combine 3 pounds raw chicken backs, necks, and bones with 1 quartered onion, 1 quartered carrot, 1 celery stalk cut in pieces, a bouquet garni of 5 to 6 parsley stems, 3 to 4 thyme stems, and 2 bay leaves, 1 teaspoon peppercorns, and 4 quarts water. Simmer for 2 to 3 hours, skimming often, to extract the full flavor from the bones. Add more water if necessary to keep the bones covered. At the end of cooking, strain the stock, and if necessary, boil it to concentrate the flavor.

Fish Stock

Fish stock is the only kind that is simmered rapidly for a short time. In this way, maximum flavor is extracted from the bones while still retaining a fresh taste. If the bones are not washed carefully, or if they are cooked too long, fish stock may become bitter. Heads and bones of white fish such as cod, snapper, sole, and halibut are best—the flavor of stock from rich fish such as salmon can be oily.

Makes about 1 quart stock

Cut 1 1/2 pounds fish bones and heads into pieces and wash them very thoroughly. Put them in a large saucepan with 1 sliced onion, a bouquet garni of 5 to 6 parsley stems, 3 to 4 thyme stems, and 2 bay leaves, 1 teaspoon peppercorns, 1 cup dry white wine or 4 tablespoons white wine vinegar, and enough water to just cover. Bring to a boil, skimming often, then simmer rapidly for 20 minutes, skimming occasionally. Strain the stock and boil, if necessary, to concentrate the flavor.

Vegetable Stock

This mild, fresh-tasting stock can be substituted for beef or chicken stock, if you like. If frozen, vegetable stock tends to become tasteless, but you can refrigerate it for up to 3 days.

Makes about 1 1/2 quarts stock

In a large saucepan, combine 3 sliced onions, 3 thinly sliced carrots, 3 sliced celery stalks, and 2 lightly crushed garlic cloves if you like. Add 2 quarts water, a bouquet garni of 5 to 6 parsley stems, 3 to 4 thyme stems, and 2 bay leaves, and 1 teaspoon peppercorns. Bring the stock slowly to a boil and simmer, uncovered, for about 1 hour, skimming occasionally. Remove the stock from the heat and strain.

CHAPTER TWO tips from the pros

Tips from the Pros follows naturally from the basic techniques we looked at in the last chapter. It's all about expertise, becoming familiar with methods that are easy if you know how. With a particular pan, or a certain flick of the wrist, it is all so much simpler. I remember the day I showed Emma how to stir-fry, and the day she introduced *me* to her mini food processor for grinding spices. Eureka!

Increasingly I find that machines solve many tiresome jobs in the kitchen. When puréeing soup, for instance, a food processor or blender is a vast improvement upon the slow old days of working it by hand through a sieve. Throughout this chapter, I try to help you with that perennial question—which machine is right for the job? Deep-frying is also high on my list of pro techniques—easy if you learn the rules and enormously impressive. You're everyone's friend if you can batter-fry fish or deliver a veal escalope to the table in a crisp golden coating of breadcrumbs.

Stir-frying is another sleight of hand that wows the crowd. Don't be discouraged by the chef in the Chinese restaurant who swirls and flips vegetables in his wok with such ease. With a bit of practice, you'll soon be stir-frying almost without thinking, adding all the ingredients in the right order at the right time, then tossing them over the highest possible heat so they end up fragrant and perfectly cooked. As with so much successful cooking, prepping ahead is the key.

Another basic trick of the trade is marinating to add flavor. A bland food like chicken breast or raw salmon is transformed by an appropriate mix of wine, citrus juice, herbs, and the lift of chile, garlic, and fresh ginger. Here I tell you how to create your own mixes to match the dishes of your choice. Marinating is all about understanding ingredients, nurturing foods, and developing flavors. Brining and salting have an important place in the kitchen, too.

Lastly I take a little look at the simple bread-based extras that can make a dish shine. Italian bruschetta and crostini come in here, as do French croûtes and croutons. Now we're firing up the stove and putting our hands to the dough, as they say in France. *Allez! Avanti!* Let's go!

HOW TO PUREE SOUPS AND VEGETABLES

Thank heaven for machines. Only a masochist would insist on puréeing soups and vegetables by forcing them through the flat sieve called a tamis—it's tough work, time-consuming, and messy. Three electrical assistants are now available—the immersion blender, the upright blender, and the food processor. An immersion blender, often called a wand, is a hand-held rod with a rotary blade that can be immersed in liquids and semi-solids to work them to a purée. I love it, particularly for small quantities. A traditional upright blender is outstanding for soups and fruit sauces, reducing fairly liquid foods to an impressively smooth emulsion. However, an upright blender needs liquid otherwise it has trouble breaking down firm ingredients such as cooked vegetables. Here's where the food processor takes over. I consider it the four-wheel drive of the kitchen, powerful enough to reduce liquids and solids to a smooth but still slightly textured purée.

A more general problem is that no machine strains out the seeds, fibers, or skins that you find in vegetables such as celery or asparagus, and fruits like raspberry or tomato. In such cases, a recipe will tell you to push the mixture by hand

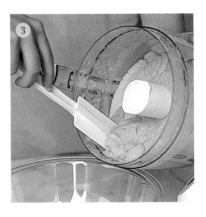

1 A hand-held immersion blender produces a slightly rough-textured soup or purée (here carrot purée). To avoid splashing, if necessary tip the pan. Do not start the motor until the blade is completely immersed in the purée. To help the purée form, start and stop the motor as you do the pulse button on a food processor.

2 A blender is best for small quantities and plenty of liquid (here pea soup). Hold the lid firmly before starting the motor as the liquid will surge.

3 The food processor does best with stiffer purées using small amounts of liquid (here you see orange lentil purée). Start with the pulse button before turning on full power and, when necessary, stop to scrape down the sides of the bowl. As an alternative, work by hand with a potato masher and you'll find you can make a quick stiff purée with a slightly uneven texture.

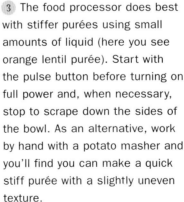

4 To purée an ingredient with seeds or fibers (here raspberry coulis), work it through a food mill, turning the handle to force the mixture through the sieve. Alternatively, first purée the ingredient in a food processor, then push it a little at a time through a bowl strainer with a wooden spoon.

through a food mill, flat sieve, or bowl strainer. All the same, using a machine for puréeing will already have saved you a lot of hard work. Potatoes follow their own rules—they contain a lot of starch so they need special treatment when you mash and purée them (page 240).

Moving beyond the technical side, machines open a whole world of green and golden vegetable soups and velvety purées made from spinach or squash. On a dinner plate, what a striking contrast an orange purée of carrot or rutabaga makes beside a creamy white spoonful of root celery or turnip. Remember, all purées need plenty of seasoning to compensate for vegetables that may be bland after thorough cooking. A dash of herb or spice can work wonders—for example chopped oregano is a natural with tomato, and cumin or nutmeg with lentils and dried kidney beans. Fruits are easy to purée, and their bright colors and intense flavors are a guaranteed success. Some, such as raspberries and strawberries, do not even need to be cooked before puréeing.

purée pointers

* To purée easily, cooked vegetables or lentils and other legumes must be very soft. Drain them thoroughly after cooking so flavors are as concentrated as possible.

* For smooth-textured soups, set aside some of the cooking liquid. Purée the solids with just a bit of liquid, then thin the purée to the consistency you want with additional cooking liquid.

* To prepare a purée an hour or two ahead, spread it out in the saucepan and moisten the top with stock, milk, cream, or water. When reheating, simply stir in the extra liquid.

* A soup or purée often thickens on standing, so adjust the consistency with more liquid just before serving.

Squash Soup with a Crunch

The crunch is provided by toasted sunflower seeds. Pumpkin can be substituted for the butternut squash.

Serves 6 to 8

> 1 butternut squash (about 3 pounds)
> 3 tablespoons butter
> 2 onions, chopped
> 2 garlic cloves, chopped
> 1-inch piece of ginger, chopped
> salt and pepper to taste
> 1 quart chicken stock, more if needed
>
> FOR THE GARNISH
> 3 tablespoons sunflower seeds
> 2 teaspoons vegetable oil
> 1 teaspoon curry powder
> ½ teaspoon nutmeg
> ½ cup crème fraîche or sour cream

Peel the squash, scoop out the seeds, and cut the flesh into 3/4-inch chunks (page 262). Melt the butter in a large pan and add the onion, garlic, and ginger. Cook, stirring, until soft, 2 to 3 minutes. Add the squash and season with salt and pepper. Pour in the stock and bring to a boil. Cover and simmer gently, stirring occasionally, until the squash is very tender, 30 to 40 minutes.

Meanwhile, make the garnish: Preheat the oven to 375°F. Toss the sunflower seeds with the oil and toast them on a baking sheet until browned, stirring occasionally, 6 to 8 minutes. Remove from the oven and toss with the curry and nutmeg. When cool, taste and adjust seasoning.

Take the squash from the heat and let cool slightly. Purée it with an immersion blender, or in batches in a blender or food processor. Reheat the soup, stirring well to mix. If it is too thick, add more stock. Taste and adjust seasoning.

To finish: Reheat the soup if necessary and ladle it into bowls. Add a spoonful of crème fraîche and sprinkle with the sunflower seeds.

GETTING AHEAD: The soup can be made up to 2 days ahead and kept in the refrigerator.

Fragrant Lentil Purée

Lentils on their own are plain stuff, but I do appreciate this lentil purée with spiced sausages, curries, and marinated roast meats—dishes that stand firm beside an extra burst of spice. If you thin the purée with veal or chicken stock, you'll have an excellent winter soup.

Serves 4 to 6

> ½ **pound lentils**
> 1 **onion, cut in pieces**
> 1 **carrot, cut in pieces**
> 1 **whole clove**
> 3 **cups water**
> 2 **tablespoons vegetable oil**
> 1 **onion, sliced**
> 1 **garlic clove, chopped**
> 1 **teaspoon ground cumin**
> 1 **teaspoon ground nutmeg**
> **salt and pepper to taste**

In a saucepan, combine the lentils, onion, carrot, and clove and stir in the water. Cover the pan and simmer until the lentils are very tender, 1 to 1½ hours. Add more water as necessary so that at the end of cooking the lentils are soupy. Do not add salt and pepper until halfway through cooking to avoid toughening the lentil skins.

When the lentils are tender, discard the clove (if you can find it!) and purée the lentils and liquid in a food processor or using an immersion blender. In a frying pan, heat the oil and sauté the sliced onion until soft. Stir in the garlic, cumin, and nutmeg and sauté gently, stirring until fragrant, 2 to 3 minutes.

To finish: Reheat the purée if necessary and stir in the spiced onion. Reheat, stirring, for 3 to 5 minutes until very hot. Taste and adjust seasoning.

GETTING AHEAD: Purée the lentils and make the onion flavoring up to a day ahead, storing them separately in the refrigerator. Just before serving, reheat the purée, adding a little water if it has stiffened on standing, stir in the onion, and heat until very hot.

Carrot Purée with Orange

Delicious with chicken, pork, ham, and game.

Makes 3 cups to serve 6 to 8

Put 2 pounds thickly sliced carrots in a pan of cold salted water, cover, and bring to a boil. Simmer until very tender, 15 to 20 minutes, then drain. Purée the carrots in a food processor with the juice and grated zest of 1 orange, or purée them with the orange juice and zest in the pan using an immersion blender. Reheat purée in the pan with 1 to 2 tablespoons butter and a large pinch of sugar. Season to taste with salt and pepper.

Raspberry Coulis

Also called Melba sauce, the tart taste and brilliant red color of raspberry coulis is indispensable with creamy mousses, charlottes, fresh and poached fruits, and ice creams. Unsweetened frozen raspberries make a good coulis if fresh fruits aren't available.

Makes 1 cup sauce to serve 4 to 6

Work 2 cups fresh or frozen raspberries through a food mill or a strainer to remove seeds. Stir in 1 to 2 tablespoons kirsch or raspberry liqueur and confectioners' sugar to taste. Chill thoroughly.

Spicy Applesauce

Serve with cold pork, duck, goose, or simply on its own for breakfast or dessert.

Makes 1½ cups applesauce

Quarter and core but do not peel 1½ pounds tart apples. Put them in a pan with ½ cup water, a stick of cinnamon, 4 whole cloves, and a generous grating of fresh nutmeg. Cover and cook gently until pulpy, stirring occasionally, 30 to 40 minutes depending on the type of apple and their ripeness. Work the pulp through a food mill or sieve, discarding the cinnamon and cloves. Return purée to the pan and cook, stirring, until thick, 1 to 2 minutes. Stir in 2 to 3 tablespoons sugar and 2 tablespoons butter. Taste and adjust the sweetness, adding ground cinnamon if you like.

HOW TO MARINATE

A marinade is designed to flavor and tenderize raw foods. As a quick way to put your personal stamp on a recipe, marinades are unrivaled. The mixture may be spicy or cooling, liquid or dry; it can consist only of aromatics or may include vegetables as well. It can be very simple: vinaigrette (page 73) makes a useful marinade, as does a pot of plain yogurt with a few dry spices—Emma's favorite. My own 10-minute quickie consists of a soaking in wine or beer. There's only one essential: a marinade must contain enough acidity (typically from wine, vinegar, or lemon juice) to penetrate foods beyond the surface.

A marinade provides ethnic identity—a plain chicken breast takes on instant character as a satay with an Indonesian mix, or as a curry with Indian spices. With a thin marinade, you can baste roast meats to form a glaze—a teriyaki mixture, for instance, broils to a glistening caramel brown on meats and fish. Thicker marinades doubling as barbecue sauces include the time-honored blend of ketchup, vinegar, and brown sugar for pork. In classic coq au vin, the wine marinade forms the basis of a dark, complex sauce that is the essence of French cuisine.

Marinating can be done at room temperature for quick results, but if you are soaking food for more than an hour it is wiser to chill it. In any case, be sure a cooked marinade is completely cold before pouring it over food. Ceramic or glass containers are best for marinating; stainless steel is okay, too, but with other metals, particularly aluminum, there's a chance that wine or other acids may react and impart a metallic tang. You can avoid a bowl altogether by putting everything in a plastic bag—by squeezing out air, a maximum of ingredients come into contact with the liquid. In case of leaks, keep the bag in a container!

A few well-known dishes, particularly of fish, start and end with a marinade (see Simple Marinades for Fish, page 125). I'm addicted to marinated raw salmon, made by thinly slicing salmon, brushing it with olive oil and lemon juice, then sprinkling with chopped capers or green peppercorns. Latin-American seviche takes a similar approach—the fish (or shellfish) is not cooked at all but simply marinated in lime or lemon juice with lively seasonings such as chile pepper, garlic, and cilantro. For presentations where the fish is not cooked, buy only very fresh fish from a trusted source.

1 When marinating, the marinade must completely cover the food (here chicken in a red wine marinade for coq au vin). Be sure a marinade is cold before adding it, particularly to meats and chicken. Cover the bowl and store it in the refrigerator. The longer you leave food in a marinade, the more pungent its flavor will become. Half an hour can be enough for thin fillets of fish, but a roast of beef or game may be left for as long as 3 days so full-bodied, intense flavor develops. Note that after soaking, leftover marinade will contain raw juices from the food and must be cooked at once or discarded.

Red Wine Marinade

This is the classic French red wine marinade for coq au vin and stews such as boeuf bourguignon. The character of the marinade depends very much on the wine—light, fruity, or full-bodied and complex, it's your choice.

Makes 3 cups marinade, enough for 1 chicken or 3 pounds stew meat

> **2 tablespoons olive oil**
> **2 onions, sliced**
> **1 carrot, sliced**
> **1 celery stalk, sliced**
> **1 bottle (750 ml) red wine**
> **½ cup red wine vinegar**
> **bouquet garni of 2 bay leaves and**
>   **a few sprigs of thyme and parsley**
> **2 garlic cloves, chopped**
> **12 whole peppercorns**
> **12 juniper berries**

In a saucepan, heat the oil and sauté the onions, carrot, and celery until soft, about 5 minutes. Add the wine, vinegar, bouquet garni, and garlic cloves. Tie the peppercorns and juniper berries in a piece of cheesecloth and pound with a rolling pin to crush them. Add the bag to the wine mixture, bring to a boil, and simmer until the vegetables are tender, 15 to 20 minutes. Let cool and then chill before using.

GETTING AHEAD: Cooked marinades like this keep well in the refrigerator up to 2 days before use.

Beer Marinade

For beef.

Makes 3 cups marinade, enough for 3 pounds stew beef or beef steak

In the recipe for Red Wine Marinade, substitute 3 cups dark beer for the red wine.

White Wine Marinade

Marinate thin fish fillets for half an hour, while chicken needs at least 2 hours.

Makes 1 cup marinade for 4 fish fillets or chicken breasts

Remove the sprigs from a bunch of thyme or rosemary and pound them with a rolling pin to release the flavor. Mix them with 1 cup dry white wine, 2 bay leaves, and a sliced onion, pour over the food, and refrigerate 1 to 2 hours.

Soy Barbecue Marinade

This Asian mix can double as a marinade and barbecue sauce for pork ribs, duck, and chicken satay.

Makes ¼ cup sauce

> **¼ cup sake**
> **¼ cup soy sauce**
> **¼ cup water**
> **¼ cup brown sugar**
> **juice of 1 lemon**
> **1-inch piece of ginger, finely chopped**
> **2 tablespoons vegetable oil**

In a saucepan, mix the sake, soy sauce, and water. Stir in the brown sugar, lemon juice, and ginger. Heat, stirring, until the sugar has dissolved and then boil to reduce by more than half, 8 to 10 minutes. Take from the heat and stir in the vegetable oil. Let cool before use—the sauce will thicken on standing.

GETTING AHEAD: This sauce can be refrigerated a week or two in a covered container, so I like to double or triple the quantity to use as needed.

Emma's Lazy Coq au Vin

There's no way I could persuade Emma to spend the 3 days needed for a classic coq au vin. Instead she's devised this version that has the flavor of the original with far less work. When time is really short, she cooks the chicken without marinating and it is still delicious.

Serves 4

> **1 chicken (4 to 5 pounds), cut into 8 pieces (page 148)**
> **1 recipe Red Wine Marinade**
> **1 tablespoon oil**
> **4 thick slices of bacon, diced**
> **2 tablespoons flour**
> **2 cups chicken stock**
> **salt and pepper to taste**

Marinate the chicken pieces in the Red Wine Marinade, refrigerating for 12 to 24 hours if you have time. Drain the pieces on paper towels, straining and reserving the marinade, with the bouquet garni and cheesecloth bag, and vegetables separately. (If you are short of time, go straight ahead without marinating.)

In a sauté pan, heat the oil and brown the chicken pieces on all sides, taking 10 to 15 minutes. Remove them, add the bacon, and fry until it starts to brown. Stir in the reserved vegetables and brown them also. Stir in the flour and cook until browned, 1 to 2 minutes. Add the reserved marinade, and bring to a boil, stirring until it thickens slightly. Simmer 2 minutes so the wine reduces thoroughly. Stir in the chicken stock and replace the chicken pieces, pushing them down into the sauce.

Cover the pan and simmer on the stove, or in a preheated 350°F oven, until the chicken pieces are very tender when pierced with a two-pronged fork, 35 to 40 minutes. Turn the pieces halfway through cooking. If the sauce gets thick, stir in more stock. At the end of cooking, the sauce should lightly coat the back of a spoon. If it is thin, remove the chicken pieces and boil it to the right consistency. Discard the bouquet garni and cheesecloth bag of spices—the vegetables are left in the sauce. Replace the chicken pieces.

Reheat them, taste, and adjust seasoning of the sauce.

GETTING AHEAD: Coq au vin reheats superbly, so make it 2 to 3 days ahead of time.

Emma's Lazy Coq au Vin

Salty Stories

Apart from seasoning, salt has two major uses in the kitchen. Dry salt sprinkled on raw food pickles it and, if left long enough, cures it sufficiently to be stored a long time—salt cod is an example. Alternatively, the salt may be dissolved in water as a brine, usually with aromatic flavorings added. Brine has a similar pickling and curing effect, as in corned beef and pastrami. Often salting or brining is combined with smoking the food as well—consider the many traditional kinds of ham. A third side effect of salt is that it extracts moisture, useful with vegetables such as cucumber and eggplant (see How to Salt Vegetables, page 259).

The type of salt used for salting and brining affects the flavor of the food. Sea or kosher salt is best as it contains none of the bitter-tasting additives in table salt. Sea and kosher salts are generally sold as large crystals, fine for brining when they are dissolved. The same coarse crystals can also be used for long-term salting over several days (as in gravlax), which gives them time to draw out moisture and dissolve evenly over the surface of the food. However, food that is salted only briefly (typically fish fillets) will be unevenly cured with coarse salt, so you should use kosher or sea salt that is finely ground.

how to dry-salt

Dry-salting is quicker than brining, an easy way to add a hint of salty pickled flavor. The worst mistake is to add too much salt, or to leave the food for too long, so be cautious and follow the recipe carefully on quantity and timing. Just a few minutes of dry-salting can be enough—count 10 minutes for small fish fillets or up to an hour for a large beef roast. Use fine kosher or sea salt.

Larger pieces of food, ranging from a side of fish to whole hams, can be preserved by immersion in coarse salt. The salt draws out the juices forming a wet crust, sometimes almost a brine. Note that if you want to brown the food after salting, its surface must first be thoroughly dried on paper towels.

1 Sprinkle the salt (here mixed with sugar and pepper for gravlax) over the food, spreading it evenly with your fingers or the back of a spoon. Cover the food, adding a weighted plate to ensure a more even cure, and chill. At the end of salting, wipe or rinse and dry the food before use.

Gravlax of Salmon

Homemade gravlax, cured with salt, sugar, and pepper and seasoned with dill, is more succulent and far cheaper than commercial versions.

Serves 6 to 8

In a small bowl, mix 3 tablespoons coarse sea or kosher salt, 2 tablespoons sugar, and 1 teaspoon crushed black pepper. Set a 12-ounce fillet of salmon skin side down in a shallow dish. Sprinkle with half of the salt mixture and cover with a large bunch of dill sprigs. Sprinkle with the remaining salt and lay an equal-sized fillet of salmon on top, head to tail with the skin up. Set a weighted plate on top of the salmon, cover, and refrigerate 2 days. Turn the salmon every 12 hours and baste with juice drawn out by the salt. After 2 days, drain and rinse the salmon, discarding seasonings and dill. Pat it dry. To serve, cut it in very thin diagonal slices. It will keep 2 days.

Briskly Brined Pork Roast

This all-purpose spicy brine suits poultry and meat, particularly pork. This recipe makes 1 quart brine, enough for a 2-pound roast.

Serves 4

In a saucepan, combine 5 cups water with $1/4$ cup each of sea salt and sugar, 3 bay leaves, 1 cinnamon stick, 1 teaspoon whole cloves, 1 teaspoon peppercorns, 5 to 6 thyme sprigs, 3 to 4 star anise, and 1 whole dried red chile pepper. Bring to a boil, simmer 5 minutes, and let cool. Pour the brine over a 2-pound loin or sirloin pork roast, cover, and refrigerate 6 to 12 hours. Preheat the oven to 350°F. Drain the pork and pat it dry with paper towels. Heat a tablespoon of oil in a small roasting pan and brown the pork on all sides—it browns easily because of the sugar cure. Cover with foil and roast 1 to $1^1/4$ hours, basting occasionally. The meat is done when a meat thermometer inserted in the center registers 160°F.

how to brine

The original purpose of a brine was to pickle foods so they could be stored for months at a time. Today brining for a shorter time is a popular way to tenderize food and add flavor together with spices and herbs. The brine is in effect a marinade with generous amounts of salt. Portions of food such as chops or fish fillets may be brined for an hour or two, with a maximum of 24 hours for a large pork roast. Brining the Thanksgiving turkey for up to a day has become quite a tradition as the dry white breast meat is much improved. Before cooking, usually by roasting or simmering in water, drain the food and discard the brine. Remember that quick brining like this does not preserve the food but simply adds moisture and taste.

1 Make the brine, let it cool, and then chill it until cold. Set the food (here a pork roast) in a deep nonmetallic bowl and pour the brine over it. The brine should cover the food completely. If necessary, weigh it down with a heavy plate so it does not float. Cover and keep in the refrigerator. At the end of brining time, drain and dry the food before cooking it. The brine is discarded.

rubbing it in

Dry marinades, often called rubs, are spice and herb mixes that flavor and cure foods before broiling or roasting. There are dozens, even hundreds, of possibilities. Curry powder, Chinese five-spice powder, Indian garam masala, herbes de Provence, and Cajun seasoning can all be used as dry marinades. Less well known are mellow Indonesian *sambals*, aromatic Ethiopian *berbere*, the Moroccan herbal mix called *ras el hanout*, and the red hot rubs used for jerk dishes in the Caribbean. Many of these rubs are available commercially so you've plenty of choice.

Making your own rub is fun and better than commercial mixes, which may be stale. The sensory impact of freshly ground herbs and spices is astonishing. For grinding, a mortar and pestle is the grandmother of all homemade rubs, but as far as I am concerned electricity has taken over. Every now and again, I use my electric coffee grinder to pulverize black peppercorns, cinnamon stick, mustard seed, fenugreek, cumin, turmeric, and chile pepper for my curry powder. The exotic tinge to the next brew of coffee takes everyone by surprise. For larger quantities of spice, I use Emma's small electric food processor. A dry spice mix lasts several months in an airtight container, gradually losing its punch.

To moisten a rub and turn it into a paste, I add garlic, fresh ginger, or vegetable oil. A paste can be spread on food more generously and it sticks better than a dry rub, but it can be kept only about a week in the refrigerator. Use a moist rub for meats, poultry, and robust fish such as tuna.

Herbal Garlic Paste

For pork, lamb, and chicken. Meat rubbed with this paste is especially good grilled to serve cold.

Makes about ¹/₂ cup, enough for 1 chicken, 1 leg of lamb, or 6 pork chops

In a small food processor, combine 20 garlic cloves, cut in pieces, 2 tablespoons fresh thyme leaves, 4 crushed dried bay leaves, 2 teaspoons freshly ground pepper, and 1 tablespoon sea or kosher salt. Add ¹/₄ cup olive oil and purée the mixture to a paste. Spread the paste on meat or chicken and chill 1 to 2 hours. Scrape off the paste before cooking.

Garam Masala

This is my favorite garam masala, the basic seasoning mixture for northern Indian meat and rice dishes. It makes an excellent rub for poultry as well as meat.

Makes about ¹/₄ cup, enough for 2 large chickens or 3 pounds stew beef or lamb

In an electric coffee grinder, combine a cinnamon stick, broken in pieces, 1 bay leaf, 1 tablespoon cumin seeds, 1 tablespoon coriander seeds, 2 teaspoons black peppercorns, 3 whole cloves, the seeds from 6 cardamom pods, and 1 teaspoon ground nutmeg. Grind to a fine powder.

Cajun Seasoning

Cajun seasoning is the main element of the famous New Orleans blackened fish, and is great for grilled vegetables, too. As with all spice mixes, there are many versions, and here's mine.

Makes about ¹/₄ cup, enough for 1¹/₂ pounds fish fillets

In a coffee grinder, mix a tablespoon of fresh thyme leaves, a teaspoon each of paprika, fennel seeds, cumin seeds, black peppercorns, mustard seeds, and sea or kosher salt, and a pinch or more of cayenne pepper to your taste. Work to a powder.

HOW TO STIR-FRY

Quick, simple, with an emphasis on fresh ingredients, stir-frying suits the way I like to cook. I can swing it light or substantial, Asian or Western, according to mood and occasion, be it a quick supper such as Stir-Fried Chile Chicken or a full-scale dinner for the family of Stir-Fried Bream with snow peas and black mushrooms plus my favorite seasoning sauce. That's another advantage of a stir fry—it provides a complete meal cooked in a single pot, a wok. If you don't already have one, I urge you to pick up a simple $20 wok of cast steel from your nearest Chinese grocery. It may come with a curved, spoon-like stirrer, or you can use a wooden spatula. Expensive, Western-style woks are not nearly so efficient and easy to use. Be sure to read the label, as before use your wok will need "proving" by heating with oil.

A stir fry moves fast once cooking begins so ingredients must be chopped and sliced ahead. Dense ones such as raw chicken breast should be cut small, with more fragile greens or sprouts in larger pieces that are still bite-sized. Vegetables are half the secret, offering contrast of texture, both tender and crisp, and colors, green, white, golden, and red. Greens, roots, stalks, sprouts, almost any vegetable will blend happily in a stir fry provided each is cut into even pieces that cook at the same speed. Fish, poultry, or meat can be almost an afterthought, cut small in strips or slices so as to cook quickly, spreading flavor throughout the rest of the mix. The meat may be raw or precooked, an opportunity to use leftover chicken, pork, or beef.

Except when ingredients are cooked in batches for better control, stir-frying follows a careful ritual. Here I quote my good friend Martin Yan, a brilliant Asian chef. "Hot, hot, hot," he advises, "Intense cooking seals flavor, seals juices, and seals nutrients while leaving foods crisp." First add the flavorings such as chopped ginger, chile, garlic, and scallion and stir-fry them until fragrant, just a few seconds—I said we'd move fast. Next come the slow-cooking foods, which may require a few minutes' steaming over lower heat, covered with a lid. Last of all

2 Add remaining ingredients as instructed in the recipe, and spread them over the full surface of the pan so they are in maximum contact with the heat. Toss and turn them constantly with a wok stirrer or wooden spatula so they cook evenly. (Here we show Stir-Fried Bream.)

1 On your most powerful burner, heat an empty wok about 30 seconds. Drizzle vegetable oil around the sides of the pan and continue heating— in a few seconds the whole pan will be coated with hot oil. As soon as it is smoking, add aromatic flavorings. Stir-fry until fragrant, about 30 seconds.

come greens and other delicate items, with the heat at full throttle again. "Stir, stir, stir," I quote Martin once more. "Don't load the wok with vegetables and meat and just stand there and stare at it. It's stir-fry, not stare-fry!"

Asian cooks are adept at marinating ingredients in piquant seasonings such as soy sauce, rice wine or vinegar, lemon or lime juice, fish sauce (*nam pla*), chopped garlic, and fresh ginger; the final seasoning is adjusted with similar condiments. Soy sauce and dark sesame oil define an Asian fry. Herbs and lemon juice are more Western. Need I add that a stir fry does not wait but should be served at once, steaming hot with a tantalizing blend of aromas.

Stir-Fried Bream

Bream is a popular fish in Chinese restaurants, but this basic fish stir fry works well with any white fish fillets. Chinese black mushrooms provide contrasting color at a low price, but any dried mushroom can be substituted.

Serves 4

- 1 ounce dried mushrooms (Chinese black or other dried variety)
- 1 pound bream fillets, free of skin and bones
- ¾ pound snow peas
- 2 scallions
- 3 tablespoons vegetable oil
- ½-inch piece of ginger, finely chopped
- 2 garlic cloves, finely chopped
- 2 whole dried red chile peppers
- ½ cup fish or chicken stock
- 2 tablespoons soy sauce, more to taste
- 1 tablespoon rice wine
- 1 tablespoon cornstarch mixed to a paste with 2 tablespoons water

Soak the dried mushrooms: Put them in a bowl and pour boiling water over them to cover generously. Leave them to soak 20 to 30 minutes, then drain and dry them on paper towels. Trim any tough stems and cut them in 2-inch pieces. Rinse the fish fillets, dry on paper towels, and cut them in 2-inch strips. Trim the ends of the snow peas

and pull the strings down the pods. Repeat at the other end, pulling the string from the other side. Trim and slice the scallions, including the green tops, and separate the green from the white.

Heat a wok over high heat until very hot. Pour oil around the sides to coat the pan, reserving 1 tablespoon. Heat over high heat for 30 seconds. Add the ginger, garlic, and chile peppers and stir-fry until very fragrant, about 30 seconds. Add the fish and white scallions and stir-fry rapidly until the fish turns white, 2 to 3 minutes. Transfer the fish mixture to a bowl and set aside. Discard the chile peppers.

Wipe the wok with paper towels and heat again until very hot. Add the remaining oil and heat for 15 seconds. Add the snow peas and mushrooms and stir-fry over high heat, 3 to 4 minutes. The snow peas should be tender but still crisp and the mushrooms should be hot. Stir in the stock, soy sauce, and rice wine, mixing thoroughly.

Return the fish mixture to the wok and stir well. Add the cornstarch paste and continue stirring over high heat until the sauce thickens, 1 to 2 minutes. Remove the wok from the heat, sprinkle the stir fry with the green scallions, taste and adjust the seasoning with soy sauce. Serve immediately.

GETTING AHEAD: Like all classic stir fries, you can prepare the ingredients ahead, 3 to 4 hours in this case. Stir-fry them at the latest possible moment.

Stir-Fried Chile Chicken

Sunday night supper would be my name for this versatile stir fry that adapts to beef, pork, and lamb as well as chicken, plus almost any green-leafed vegetable. The vegetables should be cut in small pieces so they take only 3 to 5 minutes to cook. Serve some rice noodles on the side.

Serves 4

2 boneless chicken breasts (about ¾ pound total)
4 scallions
10 to 12 leaves of green, Savoy, or Napa cabbage
1 tablespoon vegetable oil
1 red bell pepper, cored, seeded, and cut in thin strips
pinch of dried hot red pepper flakes, more to taste
3 tablespoons soy sauce, more to taste
1 tablespoon honey, more to taste
3 tablespoons chopped fresh cilantro
a few drops of dark sesame oil

Cut the chicken breasts in diagonal ¼-inch slices. Trim and slice the scallions, keeping the white and green parts separate. Shred the cabbage leaves, discarding stems and thick ribs.

Heat a wok, drizzle oil around the sides, and heat a few seconds until smoking. Add the chicken and cook, stirring constantly, about 1 minute. Add the red pepper and cook 1 minute longer. Stir in the sliced white scallions with dried hot red pepper flakes to your taste. Toss a few seconds, then add the shredded cabbage, soy sauce, and honey. Toss and stir over high heat until the cabbage wilts, 2 to 3 minutes. Stir in the green scallion tops, cilantro, and a little sesame oil. Taste, adjust seasoning, including soy sauce and honey, and serve at once.

GETTING AHEAD: For any stir fry, you should measure and prepare all the ingredients, then cook them at the last possible moment.

Mango and Chard Steak Stir Fry

Sautéed vegetables can be multinational, like this lively mix of Swiss chard and mango with Asian flavorings. Napa cabbage or red beet greens can replace the chard.

Serves 4

1½ pounds Swiss chard
1 firm mango
3 scallions
1 lime
3 tablespoons vegetable oil
1½-inch piece of ginger, chopped
3 garlic cloves, finely chopped
¾ pound flank steak, trimmed and cut in ¼-inch-thick slices
½ red bell pepper, cored, seeded, and diced
2 tablespoons cider vinegar
2 tablespoons soy sauce

Trim the chard, discarding tough outer stems, and wash it. Cut stems and leaves crosswise in ½-inch slices and set the green leaves aside. Cut the peel from the mango with a small knife. Slice on each side of the pit to remove the flesh and coarsely dice it. Trim and slice the scallions, keeping the white and green parts separate. Halve the lime and squeeze the juice from one half. Cut the other in wedges.

To cook the stir fry: Heat 2 tablespoons of the oil in a wok, add half the ginger and garlic and all the white scallions and sauté until fragrant, about 30 seconds. Add the beef and stir-fry until it is no longer pink, 1 to 2 minutes. Remove it, heat the remaining oil, add the remaining ginger and garlic, and stir-fry until fragrant, about 30 seconds. Add the sliced chard stems and stir-fry until almost tender, 3 to 5 minutes. Stir in the chard leaves and continue cooking, stirring, just until wilted, about 1 minute. Add the mango, red pepper, and beef and heat about 30 seconds. Stir in the vinegar and soy sauce and cook, stirring, 1 minute longer. Take from the heat, sprinkle with green scallions, and lime juice, and serve at once, with lime wedges on the side.

HOW TO DEEP-FRY
IN BATTER

Tempura, fish and chips, fried zucchini flowers, or shrimp scampi—can any of us ignore the temptations of crisply fried fritters of fish and vegetables? I have fond memories of munching on battered cod on the waterfront of Whitby in northern England, and a golden *fritto misto* of shellfish on the Venice lagoon. But deep-fried foods are all or nothing: they can be sublime, or they can be heavy, soggy, and depressing. So much depends on how the food is fried.

Deep-frying, so called because of the generous amount of oil or fat involved, is done at a high temperature. Ingredients need a coating of batter, sometimes of breadcrumbs (see How to Make Breadcrumbs, page 65), for protection. Frying should brown the coating at the same time as cooking food inside. If the food is already cooked, as with mashed potato croquettes coated in breadcrumbs, the filling heats and softens while the coating fries to be temptingly crisp.

Fresh oil with a high smoke point is important for deep-frying—peanut, safflower, and canola oils are good choices. The oil must be hot enough to seal the coating of batter or breadcrumbs so the food inside is not soaked with oil.

Bite-sized ingredients need a temperature of 375°F, with 365°F for larger items, measured with a fat thermometer or using a pan with a thermostat. A simple test for the temperature of hot oil is to add a few drops of batter or water: batter should brown within 1 to 2 seconds and water should sizzle at once. If the oil starts to smoke, it is too hot and will scorch the coating before the food inside is done. Turn off the heat at once and let it cool to the right temperature. When oil is too cool, the food is not sealed during frying, but soaks and turns soggy.

Deep-frying needs your full attention as hot oil in contact with moist foods can overflow the pan and cause a fire. Never fill a pan more than half full with oil, and thoroughly dry ingredients before immersing them in hot oil. It is always best to use a frying basket so food such as French fries can be lifted out quickly. If a pan does catch fire, do not attempt to move it and never use water to smother flames. Turn off the heat at once and cover the pan of oil with a lid or baking sheet. Baking soda or salt help douse flames if you don't have a fire extinguisher.

2 Fry the fritters until light golden, turning them once, 2 to 5 minutes depending on the food and size of the pieces. Lift them out with the frying basket or with a draining spoon and drain them at once on paper towels; large pieces of chicken or fish drain well when the towels are set on a rack.

1 Heat oil to the temperature indicated in the recipe. To coat with batter, dip the piece of food into the batter using tongs or chopsticks, let excess drain on the side of the bowl for a second or two, and lower the food quickly into the hot fat (here we see shrimp). Add as many pieces as can conveniently fit in the pan. If you add too many at once, the fat temperature will be lowered and your fritters will be soggy.

batters for coating

A batter coating is suited for delicate foods such as vegetables and small pieces of fish or shellfish that cook quickly. A basic batter is thickened with flour (or another starch) to give body, but it should be thin enough to pour and is sometimes bound with eggs. The lighter the batter, the better it is. Sparkling liquids such as beer or mineral water may be included, or whipped egg whites or a raising agent such as yeast or baking powder. My favorite recipe is fizzy with Champagne (actually I use sparkling white wine at half the price).

Champagne Batter
Ideal for tempura of shellfish and vegetables. See Shrimp and Vegetable Clouds (page 63) for tips on preparing the vegetables.

Makes 1 1/2 cups batter, enough for tempura for 3 people

Sift 3/4 cup flour with an equal amount of cornstarch and 1 teaspoon salt into a bowl. Slowly whisk in 1 cup Champagne or sparkling white wine. Chill the batter, 15 to 30 minutes, so the flour starches expand and thicken it slightly. After standing, it should be the consistency of thin pancake batter; if too thick, add a little more sparkling wine before coating shellfish and vegetable pieces for frying.

Mushrooms and Cauliflower in Pancake Batter
This quickie of Emma's uses packaged pancake mix.

Serves 4 to 6

Trim the stems of 6 ounces button mushrooms, halving them if they are large. Cut the florets from a medium cauliflower, discarding the stem. Florets should be about the same size as mushrooms. Prepare 2 cups packaged pancake mix according to directions—there should be about 2 cups batter. Heat about 1-inch oil to 375°F in a sauté pan or very deep frying pan. Dip mushrooms in batter and fry in 1 or 2 batches until browned and tender, 3 to 4 minutes. Drain on paper towels and keep warm in a low oven with the door open while dipping and frying the cauliflower. Serve with lemon wedges.

pans for deep-frying

A traditional bath of oil is at least 2 inches deep so that larger ingredients such as fish fillets in batter can float freely. For safety, you need a pan that is purpose-designed for deep fat and wide enough to take plenty of fritters, with sides high enough to prevent bubbling oil from spilling. Specially designed deep fat pans are available with a metal basket to make transferring food easy and safe. Electric models with thermostats are common, but avoid those with a lid as the contents will stew rather than fry to be crisp. Less oil is needed for sliced vegetables and other items cut small enough to be generously covered by a 3/4-inch layer. Here you can use a sauté pan but the average skillet or frying pan may be too shallow, depending on what is being fried.

Shrimp and Vegetable Clouds

Stuffed Fried Zucchini Flowers

Like everyone who grows zucchini, in midsummer we have a surplus of yellow trumpet-shaped flowers, perfect for stuffing. For a quicker recipe, leave out the stuffing and simply fry the flowers in batter. Concassée of Tomato (page 42) is an excellent accompaniment.

Serves 4

1 recipe Champagne Batter (page 61)
12 zucchini flowers
oil for deep-frying

FOR THE FILLING
½ cup fresh or dry goat cheese
1 tablespoon chopped fresh parsley
2 teaspoons chopped fresh thyme
½ teaspoon pepper
a little salt

Make Champagne Batter and leave to stand. Meanwhile rinse and dry the zucchini flowers, keeping stems intact for dipping. Using a fork, crush together the goat cheese with the parsley, thyme, pepper, and salt. Fill the flowers with this stuffing, twisting the petals closed.

To finish: Heat a ³/₄-inch layer of oil to 375°F in a sauté pan or deep frying pan. Dip a few flowers in batter and fry until brown, 3 to 4 minutes, turning them once. Drain on paper towels and keep warm while frying the rest in batches.

GETTING AHEAD: By all means make the Champagne Batter and stuff the flowers an hour or two ahead, keeping both in the refrigerator. Dipping and deep-frying, however, must be done at the last minute.

Shrimp and Vegetable Clouds

Feel free to try other vegetables not listed here, or for a shortcut, choose just two or three from the list. Sparkling water helps lighten the batter, and a mild vinegar, such as cider or rice wine, makes a good dipping sauce. For a delicious vegetarian entrée, leave out the shrimp.

Serves 6 as a main course

> **1 medium sweet potato, peeled and cut in 3/8-inch slices**
> **1 medium zucchini, cut in 3/8-inch diagonal slices**
> **small head of broccoli, cut in florets**
> **4 1/2 ounces snow peas or green beans, trimmed**
> **1 red bell pepper, cored, seeded, and cut in strips**
> **6 small scallions, trimmed, with green tops**
> **1 1/2 pounds large shrimp, peeled and deveined, tails left on**
> **oil for deep-frying**
>
> **FOR THE TEMPURA BATTER**
> **1 2/3 cups flour**
> **1 1/2 cups cornstarch**
> **1 teaspoon salt**
> **2 cups sparkling water, more if needed**
> **1/4 cup sesame seeds**

Mix the tempura batter: Sift the flour, cornstarch, and salt into a large bowl and set it over a bowl of ice water. Slowly whisk in the sparkling water, then stir in the sesame seeds. Leave the batter for 15 to 30 minutes so the flour starches expand and thicken it slightly. After standing, it should be the consistency of thin pancake batter. If it is too thick, stir in more sparkling water.

To finish: Heat a 3/4-inch layer of oil to 375°F in a large sauté pan or skillet. Coat and fry the vegetables and shrimp until golden, working in batches. Allow 2 to 3 minutes for shrimp; for vegetables the timing will vary from 3 to 5 minutes, depending on the type. Transfer the cooked shrimp and vegetables to a rack lined with paper towels and keep them warm in a low oven with the door open while you fry the rest.

To serve: Pile the fritters loosely on a large platter, or arrange a sampling on individual plates. Be sure not to pile them too closely together or they will steam and lose their crispness.

GETTING AHEAD: Prepare the batter, vegetables, and shrimp up to 4 hours in advance, storing them covered in the refrigerator. Fry everything at the very last moment.

insiders' tips

* During frying, food will need turning at least once with tongs or the special draining spoon called a spider; you can also use wooden chopsticks.

* You can keep fried foods warm, uncovered, for perhaps 15 minutes in a 350°F oven with the door open, but they are best served at once.

* To keep oil free of debris after frying, leave it to cool and then strain it through cheesecloth. The same oil can be reused but after half a dozen times it will be dark and taste strong, particularly when fish and shellfish have been deep-fried, and must be discarded.

* Lemon or lime, cut in halves or wedges so the juice can be squeezed, complements fried fish, shellfish, and vegetable fritters. Other traditional accompaniments include piquant sauces such as tartar, tomato ketchup, and tomato salsa.

HOW TO COAT AND FRY IN BREADCRUMBS

I like to fry in batter, Emma goes for breadcrumbs. She has a point—a coating of breadcrumbs contributes much more to a dish than the ephemeral frost of a batter. Think of Southern fried catfish, crunchy with cornmeal and browned in oil in a blackened cast-iron skillet. Picture a vegetable platter with items such as breaded sliced eggplant, crusty cauliflower, and almond-coated sweet potato. Remember fried green tomatoes. Need I say more?

Foods with a breadcrumb coating are, on the whole, easier to fry than those in batter, which need to swim in deep fat. Breaded ingredients such as fish fillets, veal escalopes, and sliced vegetables can be cooked with little fuss in a shallow layer of fat. The temperature need not be as high or as carefully controlled as when deep-frying in a batter, so more interesting fats such as olive oil and lard can be used. Part oil, part butter is called for in classic recipes such as Italian veal cutlet

1 Line up a shallow plate of flour seasoned with salt and pepper, a second shallow plate with an egg broken onto it, and a third plate of dry white breadcrumbs. Add a pinch of salt and a tablespoon of water to the egg, and whisk with the flat of a fork until mixed and frothy. Dip the piece of food (here a veal escalope) into flour and pat both sides so the flour adheres.

2 Using the fork, dip the food in egg, letting the excess drain off. With two fingers, strip off any excess egg.

3 Transfer the food to the plate of breadcrumbs and turn it in the crumbs until evenly coated. Lay it on a plate or sheet of parchment paper. Repeat with more pieces.

4 Heat the fat until very hot— food should sizzle at once when added. Lower each piece gently into the hot fat, adding as many as fit easily into the pan without overcrowding. Cook the pieces of food until golden brown, turning them once. Time will vary from 2 to 5 minutes, depending on the size of the piece. When done, a breadcrumb coating should be a generous golden brown, a bit darker than battered fritters. Lift out pieces with a fork and drain them on paper towels.

Milanese in a breadcrumb coating flavored with grated Parmesan cheese.

The breadcrumbs themselves are usually made from white bread and should be dry so the coating sticks firmly to the food—you can make them at home or buy a package. Variants include full-flavored cornmeal and Japanese panko crumbs, which are light and dry. Flavorings for the crumbs range from chopped nuts to spices such as paprika and curry powder, or dried herbs such as thyme. Grated Parmesan is my all-time favorite.

To form an even coating that sticks firmly, the food must first be dipped in flour, then in beaten whole eggs, and finally in the bread-crumbs. Coating in flour is easy, but food gets slippery once it is dipped in egg, so be sure you are well organized to move on at once to the crumbs. To make a breadcrumb coating even crisper, leave the coated food uncovered in the refrigerator for an hour or two before frying.

Roast Tomatoes Provençale

These roast tomatoes topped with garlic, breadcrumbs, and parsley add a Mediterranean touch to steak, roast chicken, and vegetable entrées. The topping makes a good stuffing for mushrooms as well.

Serves 3 to 4

Preheat the oven to 400°F and oil a baking dish. Core 3 medium tomatoes and cut them crosswise in half. Set them in the baking dish cut side up. In a small bowl, mix $1/4$ cup browned bread-crumbs, 3 to 4 tablespoons chopped fresh pars-ley, and 1 chopped garlic clove with generous amounts of salt and pepper. Stir in 3 tablespoons olive oil. Spread the crumb mixture on the toma-toes. Roast them in the oven until tender and the skins split, 20 to 25 minutes. Serve them hot or at room temperature.

how to make breadcrumbs

We all have leftover bread so why not make crumbs? They are extraordinarily useful. Fresh crumbs are used to bind stuffings and thicken sauces. Dry white bread-crumbs are needed to coat food for frying. Browned breadcrumbs may be sprinkled on gratins and baked dishes for color and crunch. If you buy packaged breadcrumbs, you'll find they are usually browned—the best have no added seasonings.

Fresh White Breadcrumbs

Crumbs will be more even if you use frozen sliced bread. Discard the crusts from fairly dry white bread and cut it in large cubes. Work the cubes in a food processor or blender, not more than 2 slices at a time. Keep the crumbs tightly covered and use within 2 days so they do not mold.

Dry White Breadcrumbs

Discard crusts from sliced white bread and dry the slices in a warm place or very low oven until crisp and dry. Timing depends on the dry-ness of the bread. Work the bread to crumbs in a food processor or blender. Dry crumbs can be stored in an airtight jar for at least a month.

Dry Browned Breadcrumbs

Make as for dry white breadcrumbs, letting the bread dry and brown in the oven. Brown bread-crumbs will keep for several months in an air-tight jar.

Todd's Veal Escalopes

Emma's husband Todd is an inventive cook. For this recipe he pounds veal escalope or chicken breast to flatten it, then coats it in Japanese panko crumbs flavored with paprika, chile pepper, or Parmesan cheese as the mood takes him. Asked for an accompaniment, he said, "How about some thinly sliced zucchini sautéed in olive oil with a bit of garlic and ground cumin?"

Serves 4

> 4 large, thinly cut veal escalopes
>   (about 1¼ pounds)
> ½ cup flour seasoned with ½ teaspoon salt
>   and ¼ teaspoon pepper
> 2 eggs, lightly beaten with 2 tablespoons cold
>   water and a pinch of salt
> ¾ cup panko or dry white breadcrumbs
> 6 tablespoons grated Parmesan cheese
> 5 tablespoons butter
> 2 tablespoons oil
> 1 lemon, cut in wedges, for serving

Put the escalopes between two sheets of wax paper or plastic wrap and pound them with a heavy pan or rolling pin to flatten them to a ¹/8-inch thickness. For more even results, rotate the escalopes in a circle while pounding them. Coat them thoroughly with the seasoned flour, dip them in the egg, and finally in the breadcrumbs mixed with Parmesan cheese.

To finish: In a large frying pan or skillet, heat half the butter and a tablespoon of the oil until foaming. Add 2 escalopes to the pan and fry them over medium heat until golden brown, about 2 minutes. Do not move them during frying or the coating will fall off. Turn the escalopes and brown the other side, about 2 minutes longer. Drain them on paper towels. Transfer the escalopes to a platter and keep warm in a low oven while frying the rest in the remaining butter and oil. Serve immediately, with lemon wedges.

GETTING AHEAD: Pound and coat the escalopes up to 6 hours ahead of time, refrigerating them uncovered and not touching each other.

Firemen's Catfish Fry

In the rural South, a catfish fry is a social event and a traditional way for volunteer firemen to raise funds. The mandatory accompaniment is tartar sauce.

Serves 4

> 4 to 6 skinned fillets of catfish
>   (about 1½ pounds)
> ¾ cup flour seasoned with 1 teaspoon salt
>   and ½ teaspoon pepper
> 2 eggs lightly beaten with 2 tablespoons cold
>   water and a pinch of salt
> 1 cup coarse white or yellow cornmeal,
>   more if needed
> ¼ cup vegetable oil, more if needed
> 2 lemons, cut in wedges, for serving

Trim, rinse, and dry the catfish fillets. Set out the seasoned flour, beaten eggs, and cornmeal on 3 plates. Coat the fillets in each and refrigerate them 1 to 2 hours (they should be uncovered and should not touch each other).

To finish: Heat the oil in a large frying pan until very hot. Fry half the fillets until golden brown and crisp, about 2 minutes each side. Drain the fillets on paper towels and keep warm in a low oven with the door open while frying the rest, in more oil if needed. Serve with lemon wedges.

GETTING AHEAD: The fish will be crisper if the fillets are coated ahead and refrigerated so the coating dries a bit. Frying must be done as late as possible, keeping the first batch of fried fish warm in a low oven with the door open while cooking the rest.

HOW TO MAKE CROUTES AND CROUTONS

Think twice before throwing away dry bread—you'll be surprised what delicious things you can do with it. For example, in no time at all you can transform leftover country bread into fried or toasted croûtes for serving with soups such as French onion, and for dipping in stews with broth or a rich sauce. The open Italian sandwiches called bruschetta and crostini, based on crusty ciabatta bread, actually toast all the more crisply with bread that is a bit stale. In under 10 minutes, you can make the consummate Italian snack of toasted bread brushed with olive oil and topped with prosciutto, oil-cured olives, and some marinated artichokes or peppers. And I always seize the chance for the perfect Sunday brunch of herbed scrambled eggs on a croûte of whole wheat bread fried in liberal amounts of butter. A toasted croûte often consists simply of a slice of bread, while a baked one can be made from a hollowed bread roll, creating a pleasantly crisp container for creamed mushrooms or possibly soup. If you like, brush melted butter or oil on baked croûtes before putting them in the oven.

Croutons are made from sliced bread diced in $1/4$- to $1/2$-inch cubes, and like croûtes, they can be toasted, baked, or fried. Rich and crunchy, they are one of our family's winter treats. When Simon comes home for Christmas, he won't let a bowl of seasonal soup go by without frying up a batch. We spice the buttery nuggets with nutmeg and allspice, or toss them with chopped herbs like parsley or thyme. Flavored croûtes or croutons are delicious in salads, too, perhaps with the lift of a clove of very finely chopped garlic.

For baked croûtes:

1 Cut a baguette or another crusty loaf in even slices. If you like, brush them on both sides with olive oil or melted butter. Toast the slices on a baking sheet in a preheated 350°F oven for 10 to 15 minutes until lightly brown, turning them once. I find it simplest to turn them with my fingers, but you may prefer to use tongs or a spatula. Note that they tend to cook unevenly near the borders of the baking sheet.

For fried croûtes and croutons:

2 Heat a $1/4$-inch layer of oil, or oil and butter, in a frying pan until a piece of bread sizzles at once when dipped. (Don't be tempted to skimp on fat or the bread will brown unevenly.) Add the rest of the bread, stirring constantly so the croutons brown evenly.

3 As soon as they are lightly browned, pour them into a strainer so the oil drains into a bowl. For croûtes, as soon as one side is brown, turn with tongs and brown the other side. Drain croûtes and croutons on paper towels. Keep a close watch on both as they color quickly.

Baked Herb Croutons

Delicious in green salads, omelets, and scrambled eggs, and with mushroom or asparagus soup.

Serves 3 to 4

Discard crusts from 4 thick slices of white or whole wheat bread and brush generously with melted butter. Cut the bread in ¹/₂-inch cubes and bake in a preheated 350°F oven until lightly browned, stirring occasionally, allowing 8 to 10 minutes. While still warm, toss the croutons with 1 teaspoon chopped fresh thyme or rosemary and 1 tablespoon chopped fresh parsley.

Fried Spiced Croutons

The classic accompaniment to winter soups of squash, chestnut, and celery root.

Serves 3 to 4

In a small bowl, mix 1 teaspoon ground allspice or curry powder and ¹/₂ teaspoon each of ground nutmeg and coriander. Cut 4 thick slices of white bread in ¹/₂-inch cubes, discarding crusts, and fry in oil and butter. Drain, and while still warm toss with the spices.

Mozzarella and Anchovy Crostini

Almost any cheese can be used for these crostini, which make an excellent supper with a green salad.

Serves 6

Preheat the oven to 350°F. Set 6 thick slices of country bread on an oiled baking sheet and sprinkle each one with 1 to 2 tablespoons dry white wine. Top with 8 ounces fresh mozzarella cheese, drained and sliced. Scatter a thinly sliced onion on the cheese and sprinkle with salt and pepper. Bake the crostini in the oven until the bread is toasted and the cheese is browned and bubbly, 20 to 25 minutes. Melt 2 tablespoons butter and stir in 7 to 8 finely chopped anchovy fillets. Heat 1 minute, spoon over the crostini, and serve at once.

Cherry Tomato Bruschetta

The high roasting temperature here brings out the sweetness of the tomatoes. Try adding other vegetables as you like, such as mushrooms or fennel, cutting them in small pieces so they roast at the same rate as the more tender ones. For bread, Italian ciabatta is traditional but any crusty bread does fine.

Serves 4 as an appetizer

> **1 pound cherry tomatoes**
> **2 onions, peeled and sliced into thin crescents**
> **8 garlic cloves, peeled and halved lengthwise**
> **¹/₃ cup olive oil, more if needed**
> **salt and pepper to taste**
> **8 slices of bread, cut ³/₄-inch thick**
> **1 tablespoon balsamic vinegar, more to taste**
> **1 tablespoon coarsely chopped fresh flat-leaf parsley**
> **2 to 3 tablespoons coarsely chopped fresh basil**

Preheat the oven to 500°F. Discard the stems from the tomatoes and toss them with the onions and garlic in a tablespoon of the olive oil. Season with salt and pepper. Spread them in a pan just big enough to hold the vegetables in a single layer. Roast them in the oven until they are very tender and browned, stirring once, 20 to 25 minutes.

If possible toast the bread slices in a wide-rack toaster. If one is not available, use the oven: When vegetables are done, remove them and lower oven temperature to 350°F. Put bread slices directly on an oven rack and toast them in the oven until golden, turning once, 10 to 15 minutes.

Brush the toasted croûtes generously with the remaining olive oil. If necessary reheat the vegetables on top of the stove. Toss the hot vegetables with the vinegar and chopped herbs. Taste and adjust the seasoning, adding more vinegar if you like. Top the slices of bread with the roasted vegetables and serve at once.

GETTING AHEAD: By all means cut the vegetables and slice the bread an hour or two ahead, but cooking must be done at the last minute.

Cherry Tomato Bruschetta

CHAPTER THREE saucery

Two essentials stand out in a good sauce: an appropriate consistency and a clear, vivid flavor, from delicate to intense. Throughout this chapter, you'll find expressions such as "lightly emulsified" or "just coats a spoon" that define the fine line between a sauce that is too thin and watery, and one that is overconcentrated and heavy. A heavy sauce can usually be thinned by adding more liquid, but a thin sauce can be harder to rescue. Remedies depend on the type of sauce.

The other characteristic of a good sauce—a clear, vivid flavor—depends on the ingredients and how they are assembled. Reduction of the pan juices to an intense glaze, which forms the basis of many sauces, is critical. Careful seasoning is also vital to balance salt, pepper, and other condiments such as grated nutmeg. Remember, the only way to judge a sauce is to taste it, and taste again when you've added it to the food it accompanies. The more you taste and adjust the seasoning, the better the sauce will be!

You'll be happy that not more than half a dozen ingredients are needed for any one of the seven basic sauces in this chapter. At its simplest, vinaigrette requires only minutes to whisk up. Recently cooks have taken to adding chopped herbs, chile pepper, tomato, saffron, and other cheerful seasonings to the basic oil and vinegar mix. Vinaigrette is invaluable not only for salads but also for marinating and basting grilled foods, particularly vegetables and fish.

Mayonnaise plays a richer role, comparable to that of hollandaise, its warm counterpart. Both of these glossy golden emulsions are merely suspensions of oil or butter in egg yolk. You'll find I have a handy ruse or two for holding their delicate consistency together. Even simpler are butter sauces, which contemporary cooks revamp in hundreds of ways by adding pan juices, wine, stock, and finely chopped seasonings such as herbs and shallot.

I was prepared to defend the importance of old-fashioned white sauce in this chapter, when I discovered to my surprise that Emma makes it all the time for favorites like macaroni and cheese. She thinks like I do that a sauce improves almost any dish, moistening the food, adding layers of flavor and sometimes color, too. Just think how much béarnaise sauce adds to a good steak, or hollandaise to grilled fish or steamed asparagus. We agree that green salad without vinaigrette dressing is fit only for rabbits, and festive turkey is as good as naked without a generous spoonful of rich pan gravy.

HOW TO MAKE
VINAIGRETTE

Vinaigrette sounds as if it is made with vinegar, and indeed it often is. Basic vinaigrette is a combination of just four ingredients: oil, vinegar, salt, and pepper. You can use olive oil, or one of the nut oils such as walnut, hazelnut, or pecan. Turn to oil made from peanuts (botanically separate from the nut family), grapeseed oil, or plain vegetable oil and the field widens. The vinegar can be red wine, white wine, or sherry; it can have balsamic sweetness or the fragrance of fruit. It can be replaced altogether by another acid such as citrus juice, particularly lemon or lime. Some of my favorite combinations are olive oil with lemon, walnut oil with sherry vinegar, and hazelnut oil with raspberry or balsamic vinegar.

For vinaigrette flavorings, first option is a traditional teaspoonful of Dijon mustard, which helps emulsify the dressing. Moving on, just small amounts of soy, Worcestershire sauce, or spices such as ground coriander or cayenne lend instant international flavor. Fresh seasonings like chopped garlic, ginger, and shallot add depth, though they can be heavy if the dressing is kept more than an hour or two. Fresh herbs wilt even faster and should be added at the last minute. Like me, Emma is addicted to fresh herbs and

has a nice little herb patch out back where she grows chives, tarragon, dill, parsley, and basil for her salads.

A good vinaigrette should be lightly thickened by vigorous whisking so it clings to salad leaves or whatever it dresses. A small quantity can be quickly whisked by hand. Best advice on making vinaigrette is "Be a prodigal with the oil, a miser with the vinegar, and whisk like the devil himself." Emma makes large amounts of dressing in a screw-top jar (plastic with a very tight lid), and emulsifies it each time she uses it by shaking hard. I mix my dressing with an upright blender or an immersion blender in a tall jar, adding all the ingredients to the container at once and then blending them.

The aim is to emulsify the vinaigrette so it coats the ingredients rather than separating and running off in a puddle. A small spoonful of heavy cream, mayonnaise, or Dijon mustard all help to stabilize the emulsion.

Classic proportions for a vinaigrette dressing are three parts of oil to one of vinegar, but the bite of lemon or lime juice asks for more oil. On the other hand, the flavor of good walnut or hazelnut oil can be quite pervasive, so you might

1 Put the vinegar or other acid in a small bowl with salt, pepper, and ground spices or mustard if using, condiments such as soy sauce, plus chopped garlic, shallot, or other flavorings. Whisk vigorously, 20 to 30 seconds, until the mixture is smooth and the salt dissolves. Gradually whisk in the oil, starting drop by drop so the dressing thickens slightly and forms an emulsion, then continue in a slow steady stream.

The dressing should lightly coat the back of a spoon. Taste and adjust seasoning at this stage, and again after the dressing has been mixed with the salad.

want to cut it with an equal amount of mild vegetable oil. Much depends on the vinaigrette's destination. Cold beef needs the punch of onion, and possibly a bit of garlic and chile, while pork and duck take well to nut oils and balsamic vinegar. Chicken benefits from a shower of fresh herbs. An olive oil and lemon dressing is unbeatable with seafood, whether served warm or at room temperature as a salad (chilling masks flavor and glues the oil).

vinaigrette guidelines

* Salad greens are easily overpowered, so use a gentle dressing and not much of it—a quarter cup of dressing is enough for 6 cups (about 1/2 pound) of greens.

* As well as a dressing for salads, vinaigrette makes a quick marinade for fish and vegetables you plan to grill.

* Vinaigrette keeps well for a week or two at room temperature (if refrigerated the oil sets and the dressing must be warmed to pour); fresh flavorings or herbs should be added just before use.

* Be sure to taste dressing twice: once when it is made, and a second time after it has been mixed with the salad ingredients. Often more salt and pepper are needed after mixing.

Simple Vinaigrette

This dressing will vary dramatically depending on the oil and vinegar that you use.

Makes 1/2 cup dressing

In a small bowl, whisk 2 tablespoons vinegar with 1 teaspoon Dijon mustard, salt, and pepper. Gradually whisk in 6 tablespoons oil in a slow, steady stream so the dressing emulsifies and thickens slightly. Taste the dressing and adjust seasoning, including mustard. If making it ahead, whisk it vigorously to reemulsify it before using.

Citrus Vinaigrette

Delicious with warm poached or grilled fish, and vegetables such as asparagus, artichoke, green beans, and broccoli.

Makes 1/2 cup dressing, enough for 1 1/2 pounds green beans

In the recipe for Simple Vinaigrette, substitute 1 1/2 tablespoons lime, lemon, or blood orange juice for the vinegar, and 1 teaspoon finely chopped fresh ginger for the mustard. Use olive oil and, if you like, whisk in a teaspoon of toasted cumin or sesame seeds. Taste and adjust the seasoning, including citrus juice, ginger, and spices.

Asian Vinaigrette

For grilled fish, chicken, or vegetables.

Makes 3/4 cup dressing

In a small bowl, whisk 1/4 cup lime juice with 2 tablespoons fish sauce (*nam pla*), 1 teaspoon sugar, a pinch of ground red chile pepper, and a little salt. Gradually whisk in 6 tablespoons peanut or vegetable oil in a slow, steady stream so the dressing emulsifies and thickens slightly. Finish with a few drops of dark sesame oil, taste and adjust the seasoning, including flavorings.

Soy and Balsamic Vinaigrette

For tart greens such as spinach or arugula and salads of cooked root vegetables, particularly potatoes and celery root.

Makes 2/3 cup dressing

In a small bowl, whisk 2 tablespoons each of balsamic vinegar and rice wine vinegar, 1 tablespoon soy sauce, and 1 finely chopped garlic clove. Gradually whisk in 6 tablespoons walnut or hazelnut oil in a slow, steady stream so the dressing emulsifies and thickens slightly. Taste and adjust the seasoning, including flavorings.

Leeks Vinaigrette

Leeks with a simple vinaigrette and sprinkling of hard-boiled egg and parsley are a typical winter appetizer in France. The leeks can be served slightly warm.

Serves 4 to 6

6 large leeks (about 3 pounds)
2 hard-boiled eggs, chopped
1 tablespoon chopped fresh parsley

FOR THE VINAIGRETTE
2 tablespoons white wine vinegar
1/2 teaspoon Dijon mustard
1/2 cup olive oil
2 small shallots, finely chopped

Trim the leeks, discarding the green tops. Split them twice lengthwise, almost to the root, and wash thoroughly, fanning them out, as leeks are often very gritty. Reshape them and tie in two bundles with string. Bring a large pan of salted water to a boil, add the leeks and boil, uncovered, until the white bases are very tender when pierced with a knife, 15 to 20 minutes. Drain, rinse with cold water, and drain again thoroughly. Cut the leeks in 3-inch lengths, discarding the strings.

Make the vinaigrette: Whisk the vinegar with the mustard, salt, and pepper. Gradually whisk in the olive oil so the vinaigrette emulsifies and thickens slightly. Stir in the shallots. Taste and adjust the seasoning, including mustard.

To finish: Arrange the leeks on a platter and spoon the dressing over the center of them, leaving the ends uncoated. Sprinkle with the hard-boiled egg and then the parsley. Serve warm or at room temperature.

GETTING AHEAD: The leeks can be cooked and the vinaigrette made several hours ahead of time and kept covered at room temperature. Whisk the dressing with the shallot and assemble the dish just before serving.

HOW TO MAKE MAYONNAISE

Forget the ketchup or the cocktail sauce, make mine mayo and I'll be happy. Most people buy their mayonnaise ready-made in a jar, but once you've tasted the homemade variety, you will find it hard to switch. The basic ingredients—oil and vinegar—are the same as vinaigrette, but the addition of fresh raw egg yolk (see More on Mayonnaise, below) helps form the emulsion that gives mayonnaise its irresistibly rich, satin consistency.

Mayonnaise is reputed to be tricky, but if you start out right, with the ingredients at room temperature, you'll have no trouble. (If the eggs come from the refrigerator, it's a good idea to set the egg yolks and bowl in a warm water bath for a few minutes.) Before adding any oil at all, it also helps to whisk the egg yolks thoroughly with the

more on mayonnaise

* Small quantities of mayonnaise based on just 2 egg yolks are best whisked by hand. With 4 yolks or more, you can use an electric mixer, an upright blender, an immersion blender, or a food processor. Be sure the blades on any machine are running at full speed when you start adding the oil.

* Standard proportions for mayonnaise are 3/4 cup oil per egg yolk, with 1 to 1 1/2 tablespoons of vinegar and a bit less of lemon juice. The more oil you add, the thicker the mayonnaise will become. For a pungent, rustic treat, use olive oil and continue whisking in oil until the mayonnaise is so stiff it will hold a teaspoon upright.

* The egg yolks in homemade mayonnaise are not cooked to a temperature that destroys salmonella bacteria so people at risk should avoid it.

vinegar or lemon and seasonings, including a lit-tle salt, for half a minute so the eggs thicken a bit. Then add the oil drop by drop, whisking briskly so the emulsion forms at once. Take great care that the emulsion forms and the mayonnaise thickens from the very beginning—this is key to the whole process.

White wine, red wine, or cider vinegar are all suitable for mayonnaise. Around the Mediterranean, lemon juice is a favorite substi-tute for the vinegar, often combined with fruity olive oil. With a flavoring of garlic, a lemon, and olive oil, mayonnaise becomes Provençal *aïoli*, perfect with cooked vegetables, cold roast chicken, or hard-boiled eggs. With an injection of red chile, *aïoli* becomes *rouille*, meaning "rusty," a must-have accompaniment to many fish soups and stews. Farther north in Europe, walnut or hazelnut oils are a delectable alternative to olive

oil—near us in Burgundy an artisan presses nut oils in his garage (while his car languishes on the street).

In classic cuisine, a mild, light vegetable oil is preferred for making green mayonnaise fla-vored with herbs to serve with poached fish. Tartar sauce—a derivative of mayonnaise laced with pickles and capers—accompanies deep-fried fish, while in Scandinavia you find sugar and mustard-flavored mayonnaise for gravlax and smoked salmon. American deli sandwiches would fall apart without a layer of mayonnaise or its cousin, Thousand Island dressing, and even the Russians are mayonnaise-crazy, adding it to their favorite salad, *Olivier*, based on diced cooked vegetables. You'll find some of these flavored mayonnaises below. I have to quietly admit that all of them can be made using bottled mayonnaise.

1 Put the egg yolks in a small bowl with a little salt, pepper, and half the vinegar or lemon juice, mustard, and a drizzle of oil. (All the ingredients should be at room temperature.)

2 Whisk the ingredients together until slightly thickened. This will take about 30 seconds. (It helps to set the bowl on a cloth so that it does not move while you are whisking.)

3 Add the oil a few drops at a time, whisking constantly. After adding 2 tablespoons of oil, the mixture should be quite thick. Then you can add the remaining oil more quickly, a tablespoon at a time, or pour it in a very slow stream, whisking constantly.

4 Finally stir in the remaining vinegar or lemon juice, taste and adjust the seasoning. The mayon-naise should be thick and glossy, holding its shape on the whisk.

Homemade Mayonnaise

Take your time when beginning mayonnaise, making sure the egg yolks thicken and emulsify with a little of the oil before you start adding the rest.

Makes about 1 ½ cups mayonnaise

> **2 egg yolks**
> **1 tablespoon white wine vinegar or**
> **   2 teaspoons lemon juice**
> **1 teaspoon Dijon mustard (optional)**
> **salt and white pepper to taste**
> **1½ cups oil, more to taste**

In a small bowl, whisk the egg yolks, half the white wine vinegar or lemon juice, mustard if using, salt, pepper, and a small teaspoon of the oil until slightly thick, at least 30 seconds.

Gradually whisk in the remaining oil, starting with a few drops at a time. After about 1 tablespoon, when the mayonnaise has begun to thicken, you can add the remaining oil more quickly, a tablespoon at a time or in a slow steady stream. Stir in the remaining vinegar or lemon juice. Taste the mayonnaise and adjust seasoning. For extra-rich mayonnaise, so stiff it will hold a teaspoon upright, gradually add 6 to 8 tablespoons more oil.

GETTING AHEAD: The presence of raw egg yolks means that homemade mayonnaise should not be stored for long. A day in the refrigerator (tightly covered) or not more than 2 hours at room temperature are a maximum; freezing destroys the emulsion, so forget it.

Scandinavian Mustard Sauce

This traditional accompaniment to gravlax is also good with hot or cold salmon, baked ham, and cold meats.

Makes about 1 ¾ cups

To 1 ½ cups Homemade Mayonnaise, add 3 tablespoons Dijon mustard, 2 tablespoons brown sugar, and 3 tablespoons chopped fresh dill. Taste, adding more of any of these flavorings to your liking.

Garlic Mayonnaise *(Aïoli)*

Traditional with Provençal fish soup, boiled vegetables, and hard-boiled eggs, *aïoli* is also remarkably good with grilled fish. For a sinful treat, try it with French fries. For a milder flavor, you can substitute vegetable oil for half of the olive oil.

Makes 2 cups aïoli *to serve 4 to 6*

> **3 egg yolks**
> **2 cloves garlic, cut in pieces, more to taste**
> **1 tablespoon lemon juice, more to taste**
> **salt and white pepper to taste**
> **1½ cups olive oil**

In a food processor, put the egg yolks, garlic, lemon juice, salt, and pepper, and add about a tablespoon of the olive oil. Purée until smooth, about 1 minute. With the blades turning, add the remaining oil, starting very slowly, a few drops at a time. Once the *aïoli* starts to thicken and emulsify, you can add the remaining oil in a slow stream. Taste and adjust the seasoning with lemon juice, salt, pepper, and more garlic if you wish. If the sauce is very thick, add 1 tablespoon hot water.

GETTING AHEAD: Like homemade mayonnaise, garlic mayonnaise should not be stored for long. A day, tightly covered in the refrigerator, is a maximum.

Chile and Garlic Mayonnaise *(Rouille)*

A lively accompaniment to fish soups and stews and cooked vegetable salads.

Makes 2 cups

Make Garlic Mayonnaise, adding half the oil. After the mayonnaise has started to thicken and emulsify, add half a cored and chopped chile pepper (more if you want the sauce to be really hot) and 2 to 3 tablespoons tomato paste. Process until the pepper and tomato paste are well incorporated. Finish making the mayonnaise as directed, adding the remaining oil in a steady stream. Taste and adjust seasoning and flavorings.

Green Mayonnaise

Unbeatable with vegetables and fish, particularly salmon.

Makes 2 cups mayonnaise to serve 6 to 8

> **medium bunch of watercress**
> **medium bunch of parsley**
> **large bunch of tarragon**
> **salt and pepper to taste**
> **1½ cups Homemade Mayonnaise**

Strip the leaves from the watercress, parsley, and tarragon. Bring a large pan of salted water to a boil, add the leaves, and blanch them until wilted but still a bright green, about 1 minute. Drain the leaves, rinse them with cold water, and drain them thoroughly. Squeeze them dry with your fists and cut them in pieces with a knife. Put them in a food processor with the mayonnaise and purée until the herbs are very finely chopped. Taste the mayonnaise and adjust the seasoning.

GETTING AHEAD: When made with bought mayonnaise, this herb version can be kept a day in the refrigerator; homemade green mayonnaise should be used within an hour or two.

Santa Monica Chicken Salad

I had great trouble persuading Emma to make homemade mayonnaise, but after she made it once, she was sold. Here she gives traditional chicken salad a Californian twist by replacing walnuts and celery with grapes and almonds. For a lighter version, she sometimes substitutes plain yogurt for half of the mayonnaise.

Serves 4

> **1 cup sliced almonds**
> **3 cooked boneless skinless chicken breast halves (about 1 pound)**
> **small bunch of tarragon**
> **½ pound seedless green grapes, halved**
> **1 cup Homemade Mayonnaise**

Toast the almonds: Preheat the oven to 350°F. Spread the almonds on a baking sheet and bake until crisp, stirring occasionally so they toast evenly, 5 to 8 minutes. Let them cool.

With your fingers, pull the chicken breasts into slivers about 2 inches long. Strip leaves from the stems of the tarragon and chop them, reserving a few sprigs for decoration. Put the chicken, almonds, grapes, and chopped tarragon into a bowl. Stir in the mayonnaise and taste for seasoning. Cover and chill for at least an hour. Serve the salad in individual bowls, decorated with sprigs of tarragon.

GETTING AHEAD: Santa Monica Chicken Salad can be made a day ahead; decorate with tarragon just before serving.

how to save curdled mayonnaise

If mayonnaise fails to thicken when whisked, the oil will separate from the egg yolks in a curdled mess as soon as you stop. This always seems to happen at the wrong time, but luckily mayonnaise can be reconstituted. If the curdled mixture is cold to the touch, warm it to room temperature by setting the bowl in a warm water bath to take off the chill. In a separate bowl, whisk a teaspoon of Dijon mustard with a pinch of salt, then gradually whisk in the separated mayonnaise as if it were oil, adding it drop by drop so that the emulsion starts to form and the mixture thickens. Once this happens, you can add the remaining curdled mixture a bit faster, but take care to whisk as vigorously as possible.

HOW TO MAKE
HOLLANDAISE

Hollandaise is the warm cousin of mayonnaise. Both sauces are emulsions based on egg yolks and a fat (butter in hollandaise, oil in mayonnaise), highlighted by lemon juice or vinegar. Hollandaise is a little lighter, a little fluffier than mayo and shares a similar, addictively voluptuous texture. But nothing is perfect. Hollandaise has a tendency to curdle and cannot be kept for very long. Never mind, it will quickly be consumed.

Picture hollandaise with poached or grilled salmon, sea bass, or halibut. Top poached eggs with hollandaise, serve it with sautéed mushrooms, or with Canadian bacon and toasted muffin as Eggs Benedict. Hollandaise marries ideally with green vegetables such as roast or steamed asparagus, broccoli, artichokes, and many more. You can flavor the sauce with the juice from blood oranges to make *Sauce Maltaise*. If you let the melted butter component in hollandaise toast until nut brown, then whisk it into the egg mousse, you'll have brown butter hollandaise. Note that the better the butter you use, the better your hollandaise will be. The sweet taste of unsalted butter also makes a big difference.

The most reliable way to make hollandaise is to whisk up a mousse of egg yolks with water (a tablespoon per yolk) over low heat, then whisk in melted butter that has been skimmed and cooled to tepid. Lemon juice and seasoning go in last. The secrets of success are a little bit of patience and a heavy-based saucepan. Some cooks like to heat their pan in a warm water bath instead of using direct heat, but it really is not necessary. Recipes also exist for making hollandaise in a food processor or blender, but I've never found them very satisfactory as the egg yolk emulsion is

1 Melt the butter, skim the froth with a spoon, and let it cool until tepid. In a small, heavy saucepan, whisk the egg yolks and water with a little salt and white pepper until mixed and frothy. Set the pan over low heat and whisk for about 3 minutes to make a light, close-textured mousse. It should be just thick enough to hold a ribbon trail for a few seconds when you lift the whisk. Don't be tempted to go too quickly as the mousse will be less stable.

2 Take the pan from the heat and whisk in the tepid butter, a tablespoon at a time, until the sauce thickens slightly and starts to look glossy. You can pour in the remaining butter in a slow, steady stream, whisking constantly. Leave the milky sediment at the bottom of the pan.

3 Stir in lemon juice, salt, and white pepper to your taste. The finished sauce should be light, close textured, and just thick enough to hold a ribbon trail for 5 seconds when you lift the whisk; it should coat the back of a spoon.

unstable unless it is thickened over heat. Nor does a handheld electric mixer help much as the hand whisking involved is not hard work.

The correct temperature for serving hollandaise is "hand-hot," when you can hold your hand on the base of the pan for a couple of seconds. With this in mind, you can keep hollandaise warm in its saucepan in a tepid water bath, or on a rack over a pan of gently steaming water. Give the sauce a whisk from time to time and it will hold for up to an hour. However be careful as too much heat will curdle it. I sometimes store leftovers for up to 24 hours, covered in the refrigerator, but you should be aware that the gentle heat used when making hollandaise is not enough to destroy all harmful bacteria that may lurk in egg yolks. You can reheat the sauce to tepid over a warm water bath, but I don't bother as hollandaise is delicious cold—it sets to form a soft lemon butter.

Classic Lemon Hollandaise Sauce

Hollandaise should be light and smooth, with the butter, egg, and lemon delicately balanced, so don't overdo the lemon juice.

Makes 1 1/2 cups sauce to serve 4 to 6

> 3/4 cup (1 1/2 sticks) butter
> 3 tablespoons water
> 3 egg yolks
> salt and white pepper to taste
> juice of 1/2 lemon, more to taste

Melt the butter, skim froth from the surface, and set the pan aside to cool to tepid. Whisk the water and egg yolks with salt and pepper in a small, heavy saucepan until mixed and frothy, 30 seconds. Set the pan over low heat and whisk constantly, taking the pan on and off the heat so the mousse does not thicken too quickly, until it holds a ribbon trail for a few seconds when the whisk is lifted. This should take at least 3 minutes.

Take the pan from the heat and let it cool 1 to 2 minutes. Whisk in the tepid butter, starting with a tablespoonful or two until the sauce emul-sifies and thickens a bit. Then you can add the rest of the butter, in a very slow stream, whisking vigorously. Leave behind the milky whey in the bottom of the pan.

Whisk in the lemon juice and taste, adding more lemon, salt, or pepper if needed.

GETTING AHEAD: Better a hollandaise sauce that is a bit cool than one that has overheated and curdled, so keep the pan in a tepid water bath. Personally, I try not to keep hollandaise more than about an hour.

how to save curdled hollandaise

Too much heat is the greatest danger when making hollandaise. If you cook the egg yolk mousse too fast, it will form stiff scrambled eggs and you'll need to start again. If the melted butter is too hot, or is whisked in too fast, the sauce may start to separate, or curdle. Stop whisking at once. Plunge the base of the pan in cold water and add an ice cube to the sauce. Wait a minute for everything to cool down (yourself included) and then whisk at the edge of the melting ice cube, catching just a small amount of sauce. With luck you'll see the sauce start to reemulsify and thicken smoothly. Continue whisking, gradually drawing in the remaining curdled sauce and melted ice. If this does not work, you'll need to start again with a second egg yolk mousse, whisking in the curdled butter mixture in place of more melted butter.

Eggs Benedict

Simon's eyes lit up when I mentioned Eggs Benedict. "Of course we must include a recipe," he said, so here we are. You'll need very fresh eggs for poaching so the egg white clings around the yolk, and I often poach an extra egg or two in case a yolk breaks.

Serves 4 as a main course

> **1 recipe Classic Lemon Hollandaise Sauce (page 79)**
> **8 to 10 eggs**
> **1 tablespoon vinegar, for poaching eggs**
> **1 to 2 tablespoons melted butter, for brushing**
> **8 slices Canadian bacon (about ½ pound total)**
> **4 English muffins**
> **4 pitted black olives, halved**

Make the hollandaise sauce. To keep it warm, immerse the base of the pan in a roasting pan of warm but not hot water and set it aside.

To poach the eggs: In a sauté pan or deep frying pan, bring a 2-inch layer of water to a rolling boil, with the vinegar. Break an egg into a bubbling area so the bubbles spin the egg and set the white around the yolks. Add 3 to 4 more eggs, then turn down the heat and poach them so they scarcely bubble, 3 to 4 minutes. To test them, lift an egg with a draining spoon and press with your fingertip: the white should be set with the yolk still soft. Transfer the poached eggs to a bowl of warm water. Trim strings from each one with scissors and leave the eggs in the water. Repeat with the remaining eggs.

Brush a frying pan with melted butter, add the Canadian bacon, and brush the top with butter. Cover it with aluminum foil and warm it over low heat until hot. Toast the muffin halves and lightly brush them also with butter.

To assemble: Set the muffin halves on 4 warm plates and top with a slice of Canadian bacon. Carefully lift an egg out of the warm water, dry it on paper towels, and set it on the bacon. Coat each egg with a large spoonful of warm hollandaise sauce, add a halved black olive, and serve at once.

GETTING AHEAD: If you treat hollandaise carefully and do not let it get too hot, it can be kept warm up to an hour in a water bath, or in a thermos. Poach the eggs ahead, also, and keep them in cold water. Just before serving, warm the bacon and toast the muffins. Warm the eggs for 2 to 3 minutes in a bowl of hand-hot water, drain them, and finish the dish as described.

Blood Orange Hollandaise (*Sauce Maltaise*)

The season for blood oranges coincides with asparagus, and the two are natural partners on the plate.

Makes 1½ cups sauce to serve 6 to 8

Pare the zest of a blood orange, cut it in julienne strips (page 235), and blanch them by boiling in water for 2 minutes and draining. Make Classic Lemon Hollandaise Sauce as directed (page 79), and flavor it with blood orange juice and the orange julienne instead of lemon.

Eggs Benedict

Brown Butter Sauce

This sauce, a variation of hollandaise, is rich and mellow, great with artichokes, broccoli, and shrimp.

Makes 1½ cups sauce to serve 6 to 8

When melting the butter for Classic Lemon Hollandaise Sauce (page 79), skim it as directed. Continue cooking the butter, stirring occasionally. First it will sputter as the moisture boils off. When this stops, the milk solids left in the butter will start to brown. Let them cook to medium brown, stirring until you smell the characteristic aroma, called *noisette* (hazelnut) in French. As soon as the butter smells nutty, plunge the base of the pan into a bowl of cold water to stop browning—as you can imagine, the butter burns easily at this stage. Let it cool to tepid, and use it to make hollandaise sauce as described.

béarnaise

Béarnaise sauce is a feisty version of hollandaise, piquant with shallot, crushed peppercorns, and tarragon, all simmered in white wine or tarragon vinegar. This reduction takes the place of the water in hollandaise. At the end of cooking, the flavorings may be strained out, but it is less work to leave them and they add depth to the sauce. Finished consistency should be slightly thicker and less fluffy than hollandaise.

Blockbuster Béarnaise

Béarnaise is traditional with red meats, particularly grilled steak and lamb chops, and with salmon it's world class.

Makes 1½ cups sauce to serve 4 to 6

> ¾ cup (1½ sticks) butter
> small bunch of tarragon
> 3 tablespoons white wine or tarragon vinegar
> 3 tablespoons dry white wine
> ½ teaspoon crushed peppercorns
> 3 shallots, finely chopped
> 1 tablespoon water
> 3 egg yolks
> small pinch of cayenne pepper
> salt to taste
> 1 tablespoon chopped fresh chervil or parsley

Melt the butter, skim froth from the surface, and set aside to cool to tepid. Pull the tarragon leaves from the stems and chop the leaves. Put the stems in a small, heavy saucepan with the vinegar, white wine, peppercorns, and shallots. Boil until reduced to a glaze, then discard the tarragon stems and stir in a tablespoon of water to cool the mixture to tepid.

Whisk in the egg yolks with cayenne pepper and a little salt. Set the pan back on low heat and whisk constantly until a mousse is formed that just holds the mark of the whisk, slightly thicker than for hollandaise. This should take at least 3 minutes.

Take the pan from the heat and whisk in the tepid butter, starting a tablespoonful at a time until the sauce starts to thicken. Once an emulsion has formed, you can add the butter more quickly in a slow, steady stream. Leave behind the milky whey in the bottom of the pan.

Stir in the chopped tarragon leaves and chervil. Taste and adjust seasoning, including cayenne pepper.

GETTING AHEAD: Keep the sauce warm in the pan in a bath of tepid water, and stir it from time to time. I would not advise leaving it more than an hour.

HOW TO MAKE
BUTTER SAUCES

Emma knows my weaknesses. When I visit her home, she takes care to have a generous stock of butter always on hand, not just for the breakfast muffins and roast chicken, but also for the indispensable white butter sauces that are so good with vegetables and fish, indeed with almost everything. At its most basic, white butter sauce consists simply of butter whisked into a spoonful of water, or sometimes of cream, so it softens enough to pour, yet remains opaque and smooth without melting to oil. A light seasoning of salt and white pepper, and that's it.

From this plain start come dozens of variations. Ancestor of them all is white wine butter sauce, in which a reduction of white wine, white wine vinegar, and chopped shallot takes the place of water. Red wine butter sauce uses a hearty reduction of red wine with shallot, no vinegar. Fish, chicken, or veal stock may be added for body (they are usually first reduced to a glaze [see How to Make a Glaze, page 88]). A butter sauce can also be based on pan juices from roast meat or poultry. Flavorings such as chopped fresh ginger, lemon, and soy sauce, spices like saffron, anise, and coriander, and aromatic herbs like tarragon, chives, or mint add further layers of taste.

Technically, a white butter sauce is an emulsion, with the milk solids and whey in the butter acting as the emulsifier. (That's why butter sauce cannot be made with clarified butter, since the whey has been removed.) As always, the key is to establish the emulsion right from the start by vigorously whisking in a small amount of cold butter. Take it slowly; the pan should never be more than hand-hot, just warm enough to soften but not melt the butter. The fewer the ingredients in a recipe, the more their quality counts, so here's where the very best butter, imported or domestic, can shine. It should be unsalted, as the slight tang of salted butter gives an off flavor to the sauce.

1 In a small heavy pan, boil the flavorings (typically wine, vinegar, shallot, stock and/or meat juices) to a concentrated, slightly sticky glaze. Add cream if using and boil again to a glaze.

2 Take the pan from the heat and let it cool to hand-hot. Add 2 to 3 cubes of cold butter, whisking vigorously so the butter softens and thickens the glaze to a creamy consistency. Add more cubes of butter, several at a time, whisking constantly and if necessary warming the pan over very low heat so the butter softens just enough to pour. Continue until all the butter is added.

If you like, you can strain the sauce at this stage, though I usually prefer to leave in any flavorings such as the shallots you see here. Taste and adjust seasoning with a little salt and white pepper.

how to save separated white butter sauce

If white butter sauce starts to thin, stop stirring and cool the pan at once by dipping the base into cold water. In a separate saucepan, reduce 2 tablespoons heavy cream, whisking constantly until thick, 1 to 2 minutes. Over low heat, whisk 1 teaspoon of the broken butter sauce into the reduced cream so it emulsifies. Whisk in 2 to 3 more spoonfuls, then whisk in the remaining sauce in a slow, steady stream. Taste the sauce and adjust the seasoning. This saved butter sauce does not have the staying power of a perfect sauce, but will hold up to 5 minutes without breaking.

White Wine Butter Sauce

One trick to help stabilize a butter sauce is to add a tablespoon of heavy cream to the flavoring reduction as an additional emulsifier. Purists protest this spoils the flavor, but it works!

Makes 1 cup sauce to serve 6 to 8

> **3 tablespoons white wine vinegar**
> **3 tablespoons dry white wine**
> **2 shallots, finely chopped**
> **1 tablespoon heavy cream**
> **1 cup (2 sticks) cold butter, cubed**
> **salt and white pepper to taste**

In a small heavy pan, boil the vinegar, wine, and shallots to form a glaze. Add the cream and boil again to a glaze. Let the pan cool until the base is hot but not burning to your hand.

Add a small handful of butter cubes to the pan and whisk vigorously over low heat so they soften until smooth without melting completely. Continue until all the butter is added, whisking constantly and taking the pan on and off the heat so the butter softens without melting to oil. This should take only 1 to 2 minutes, but don't risk using too much heat. When finished, the sauce should be very smooth and soft enough to pour.

Taste the sauce, and adjust the seasoning with salt and white pepper.

GETTING AHEAD: Keeping butter sauce at the right temperature is not easy; if too hot it separates in a flash (don't throw it out, there's a remedy, see left), and if too cool it stiffens though it will still be usable. Setting the saucepan on a rack over a pan of gently steaming water is one way to maintain temperature, and another is to use a thermos.

Red Wine Butter Sauce

A fruity red wine such as a Merlot or Beaujolais is best for this sauce, which is delicious with fish, veal, and sweetbreads.

Makes 1 cup sauce

In the recipe for White Wine Butter Sauce, substitute 1/2 cup fruity red wine for the vinegar and wine. If you like, whisk in 1 teaspoon tomato paste to brighten the color of the finished sauce.

Red Wine Sauce for Steak

I always opt for pan-fried rather than grilled steak so I can whisk up this terrific little sauce.

Serves 2

Heat a heavy frying pan or skillet and fry 2 good steaks (page 190) the way you like them. Set them aside to keep warm. Add 2 chopped shallots and 1 chopped garlic clove to the pan and sauté until fragrant, about 1 minute. Add 1/2 cup red wine and boil to a glaze, stirring to dissolve the pan juices. Whisk in 4 tablespoons cold butter, cut in cubes, working the pan on and off the heat so the butter softens creamily to form a pourable sauce. Whisk in a couple of tablespoons of your favorite chopped fresh herbs such as basil, tarragon, thyme, or parsley. Taste, adjust seasoning, and spoon over your steak.

Salmon with a Crispy Skin and Saffron Butter Sauce

Striped bass or any fish with tender skin that sears to be crisp can be substituted for the salmon. Saffron colors butter sauce golden, while a bed of Fennel for Fish (page 269) makes a nice accompaniment.

Serves 4

> 1 to 2 salmon fillets, scaled, with skin
>   (about 1½ pounds)
> 1 to 2 teaspoons olive oil for the pan
>
> FOR THE SAFFRON BUTTER SAUCE
> 2 tablespoons dry white wine
> 2 tablespoons white wine vinegar
> 2 shallots, very finely chopped
> large pinch of saffron threads soaked in
>   1 tablespoon boiling water
> 2 tablespoons heavy cream
> ¾ cup (1½ sticks) cold butter,
>   cut in small pieces
> salt and white pepper to taste

Make the sauce: Put the white wine, vinegar, shallots, and saffron in a small heavy saucepan. Boil until the liquid is reduced to about 2 tablespoons. Add the cream, reduce again to 2 tablespoons, and remove from heat. Add 2 to 3 cubes cold butter, whisking vigorously so the butter softens and thickens the sauce. Add more cubes of butter, several at a time, whisking constantly and if necessary returning the pan to low heat. When all the butter has been added, the sauce should be just soft enough to pour. Do not let the pan get more than hand-warm. Taste the sauce and adjust the seasoning.

Prepare the salmon: Preheat the oven to 425°F. If your frying pan does not fit in the oven, heat a baking sheet. Run your fingers over the flesh and if you feel any bones, pull them out with tweezers. Cut the salmon in 4 portions and season both sides with salt and pepper. Oil the base of a large heavy frying pan or skillet and heat it until very hot. Add the salmon, skin side down. Fry it over high heat without moving the pieces, 2 to 3 minutes, until the skin is crisp. When brown, it

Salmon with a Crispy Skin and Saffron Butter Sauce

will shrink and loosen from the surface of the pan. Turn the pieces skin side up. Transfer them to the oven in the pan or on the heated baking sheet and bake until done to your taste, 1 to 3 minutes for medium salmon, 4 to 5 minutes for well done. The cooking time will vary with the thickness of the fillets.

Set the salmon skin side up on warm plates with the butter sauce spooned around it, and pass any remaining sauce separately. Serve immediately while the skin is crisp.

GETTING AHEAD: You can brown the salmon skin up to 3 hours ahead, though it will soften a bit on standing. Keep the salmon in the refrigerator, then finish cooking in the oven and make the sauce at the last minute.

savory butters

Savory butters for topping hot foods use many of the same flavorings as butter sauces such as chopped herbs, spices, and shallots. They are good with grilled and roasted meats, fish, and vegetables. Boiled potatoes, sliced and topped with slices of Herb and Shallot Butter (page 18), are a perennial favorite—the taste of fresh butter is very different from the hot butter used for frying. Though a savory butter lacks the delicate lightness of a butter sauce, it can be made ahead and keeps well in the refrigerator or freezer.

A savory butter is made by creaming butter, by hand or with an electric mixer, then beating in flavorings, the more vivid the better. Use either salted or unsalted butter, and be sure to taste and adjust the seasonings. The finished butter can be used at once, but it seems to go further after it has been chilled as it melts so much more slowly. Before chilling, I like to shape the butter, for example by rolling in a cylinder inside plastic wrap. For serving, you cut rounds as needed.

Anchovy Butter
For grilled or broiled fish and lamb, and cold canapés.

Enough for 4 servings

Cream $1/2$ cup (1 stick) butter with 6 chopped anchovy fillets, 1 tablespoon lemon juice, and plenty of freshly ground black pepper. Taste and adjust seasoning.

Garlic Butter
For steak, vegetables, and snails.

Enough for 4 servings

Cream $1/2$ cup (1 stick) butter with 2 tablespoons chopped fresh parsley, 1 finely chopped shallot, 2 finely chopped garlic cloves, salt, and pepper. Taste and adjust seasoning.

Mustard Butter
For grilled or broiled steaks and fish

Enough for 4 servings

Cream $1/2$ cup (1 stick) butter with 2 tablespoons Dijon mustard, salt, pepper, and 2 tablespoons chopped fresh parsley. Taste and adjust seasoning.

Tomato and Basil Butter
For fish, poultry, and pasta.

Enough for 4 servings

Cream $1/2$ cup (1 stick) butter with 2 tablespoons coarsely chopped fresh basil, 1 tablespoon tomato paste, salt, and pepper. Stir in 1 medium tomato, peeled, seeded, and chopped, then taste and adjust seasoning.

HOW TO MAKE PAN GRAVY

My mother's method of roasting meat was very odd—she put it in a low-temperature oven and cooked it to death so all the juices (or so it seemed) accumulated in the bottom of the pan. The result was the world's best pan gravy. Gravy can be the outcome of roasting or pan-frying, but it is never any good without dark, caramelized juices from the main ingredient, whether meat, poultry, or game. For extra flavor, you may want to add a sliced onion and carrot, together with any bones you can coax from the butcher, to the pan. If juices start to scorch on the bottom of the pan, add a little stock or water. On the other hand, if juices are not dark enough at the end of cooking, you should reduce them beyond a glaze until they are caramelized.

Gravy can be thick or thin, flavored with wine or stock, or based simply on water. Personally, I think the more taste the better, provided of course that the meat is not overwhelmed. Good stock made from beef, veal, or chicken bones, as appropriate to the main ingredient, adds complexity and no less importantly, rich consistency from the gelatin in the bones. Wine, beer, cider, juice, cream, or small amounts of fortified wines such as Madeira are optional extras. Whatever combination you choose, be sure to boil the gravy down until it is dark and rich. Here's where those caramelized juices make the difference.

Whether you prefer it thick or thin, good gravy depends on the same techniques. The only difference with thickened gravy is that flour is toasted with a bit of the fat in the roasting pan before liquid is added—a mixture technically called a roux. The roux should be golden for poultry, mahogany for red meats, and deep brown for game, but don't overdo it as scorched flour is bitter. Then stir in liquid, whisking briskly so the roux forms no lumps. No sweat if it does, as the next step is to strain the gravy into a saucepan to remove sediment and any vegetables used for flavoring. Just before serving, it's important to taste the gravy and season it just right. All sorts of flavorings, from mustard to chopped herbs, can go in at this stage as you'll see from my recipe suggestions, but I still think it's hard to beat plain old pan gravy, the way that mother made it.

1 For thickened pan gravy, cook the roux until golden for poultry, darker for red meats and game. Then stir in your wine, stock, or water, stirring briskly so the roux does not form lumps.

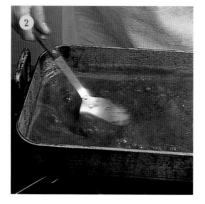

2 Boil the gravy rapidly, stirring until it is reduced to the consistency you want.

3 If you like, strain the gravy: hold the strainer over a saucepan and ladle in the gravy. Push the ladle downward against the mesh in short, sharp strokes, pressing the solid ingredients to extract maximum flavor.

Traditional Thickened Pan Gravy

Use an appropriate stock, whether beef or veal stock for meats, or chicken for poultry. For any gravy, you can use vegetable stock if you prefer it. Even the liquid from boiling potatoes will add more character than water. Quantities are very much up to you, depending on the strength of the liquid you choose and the number of your guests. Three to four tablespoons of gravy is an average serving.

Makes 2 cups gravy to serve 8

> **2 to 3 tablespoons pan drippings**
> **2 to 3 tablespoons flour**
> **2 cups beef, veal, chicken, or vegetable stock**
> **salt and pepper to taste**
> **wine, cider, Madeira, or Cognac (optional)**

When the main ingredient (meat or poultry) is cooked, remove it and set it aside to keep warm, loosely covered with aluminum foil. (This waiting time is helpful, particularly for red meats, as juices are redistributed more evenly throughout the meat and less are lost during carving.) Leave fat and any vegetables in the roasting pan and stir in the flour (use a bit more of both for large quantities). Toast the flour over the heat, stirring constantly, until it is golden for poultry or deeper brown for red meats. Stir in the stock and boil briskly, stirring to deglaze the juices, until the gravy is concentrated and thickened to the consistency you like.

Strain the gravy to remove sediment and any vegetables used for flavoring, then reheat the gravy and season it to your taste, adding a final dash of salt, pepper, and perhaps a drizzle of wine or Cognac.

GETTING AHEAD: I always keep leftovers of gravy as they add all the more flavor to the next batch. They last up to 3 days in the refrigerator, or I store them in the freezer.

Unthickened Gravy

Unthickened gravy is served with all the same roasts as thickened gravy—it is simply a matter of preference.

Makes 2 cups gravy to serve 8

In Traditional Thickened Pan Gravy, omit the flour. Discard any excess fat from the pan, then thoroughly brown the pan juices if not already brown. At this stage I like to add a glass of red or white wine, boiling it to reduce it by half, but that's optional. Add stock and continue as directed.

Cream Gravy

I think of cream gravy as very Southern, classic with chicken fried steak and mashed potatoes.

Makes 2 cups gravy to serve 8

In Traditional Thickened Pan Gravy, substitute light cream or milk for the stock. Simmer the gravy until it generously coats a spoon, strain, and season it well with salt and pepper.

Provençal Herb Gravy

This gravy is designed for lamb chops, and it's also good with pork. The dried mix called herbes de Provence typically includes rosemary, thyme, fennel, savory, and sometimes bay leaf.

Makes 1 cup gravy, enough for 4

Sauté 2 to 3 chops per person in a large frying pan, cooking them in 2 batches. Take out of the pan and keep them warm. Discard all but 2 tablespoons of fat from the pan. Fry a finely chopped onion until lightly browned, stir in a tablespoon of flour and brown it also. Stir in $^1/_4$ cup white wine and boil rapidly, until reduced to a glaze. Stir in $1^1/_2$ cups veal, chicken, or vegetable stock and bring to a boil, stirring until the gravy starts to thicken. Add 2 teaspoons herbes de Provence and $^1/_2$ teaspoon cinnamon, and simmer until the gravy is well flavored and lightly thickened, 5 to 7 minutes. Taste and adjust seasoning, adding more herbes de Provence and cinnamon if you like.

Flashes in the Pan

You'll find the terms *glaze* and *deglaze* used often in this book. They both involve boiling a liquid (often pan juices) down to a concentrated essence, the basis of pan gravy and many butter sauces, thus ensuring the layers of flavor and richness that characterize a good sauce.

how to deglaze pan juices

After roasting and pan-frying, savory juices from the poultry or meat (sometimes fish, too) are left in the pan. Please don't discard them—they form the core of all sorts of imaginative sauces. Pan juices should be reduced until golden brown, then dissolved in liquid—a process called deglazing. Red or white wine, fortified wines such as Port and Marsala, or spirits such as Cognac or whisky are top choices as they add depth of flavor themselves. Stock is good, too, and cider or citrus juice may be used for a few specialty sauces. The liquid from deglazing can be spooned directly over the food as pan gravy, added to an existing sauce, or boiled down to a glaze.

1 Be sure pan juices are thoroughly caramelized before stirring stock or other liquid into the pan, stirring to dissolve the juices. (For thickened gravy, first brown some flour with fat and juices before adding liquid; see page 87.)

how to make a glaze

A glaze is made from well-flavored liquid that is boiled down until it eventually reaches a characteristic glossy, almost syrupy consistency. Typically the liquid contains meat or poultry essences, as found in stock (page 44) or the deglazed juices left after roasting or pan-frying. Wine, vinegar, and other flavorings, often with vegetables added, can also be the foundation of a glaze, as in white butter sauce. In classic cuisine, meat glaze is made by boiling down veal stock, which takes many hours. A glaze made from pan juices is much quicker. Glaze may be enriched with cream or butter to make a sauce, or slightly thinned with stock or another liquid.

1 Discard any fat, and if the juices have not browned, cook them a minute or two until they do. Add your chosen liquid and boil, stirring to dissolve the juices, until the mixture is reduced to a sticky glaze. It will scarcely cover the base of the pan and bubbles will break slowly, with a characteristic fizzing sound.

To make a cream sauce from a glaze

Pour in cream, allowing 2 to 3 tablespoons per person, whisking over medium heat as you bring the sauce just to a boil, then taste and adjust the seasoning. Both cream and butter sauces should be served at once, and I never strain them but simply spoon them over the food.

To make a butter sauce from a glaze

Add cold butter a few cubes at a time, whisking constantly and working the pan on and off the heat so the butter softens and emulsifies without melting to oil. I allow 1 to 2 tablespoons of butter per person, depending on what the sauce will accompany. Don't forget to adjust the seasoning. Unlike a cream sauce, which can be simmered, this type of butter sauce should never be more than warm or it will separate.

tools for sauces

Delicate sauces are much easier to make if you have the right saucepan and whisk. The very best pan is made of lined copper that spreads heat so the sauce warms gently and evenly with less tendency to separate or scorch. If the pan has sloping sides so the whisk reaches into corners, all the better. Next best choice is a stainless pan with a heavy copper or aluminum base to diffuse the heat. Enameled cast-iron pans are acceptable, too, though the enamel tends to be scratched by the whisk. A good whisk is made of stainless steel with a generous number of loops in a plump balloon shape. It should fit the pan easily and feel comfortable in your hand.

water baths

A water bath is a pan of warm or simmering water, large enough to accommodate the smaller pan or baking dish set in it. The bath can be used on top of the stove for cooking or for keeping foods warm in the oven. A water bath controls the temperature of dishes put in it at a maximum of 212°F. I use a water bath when I want the heat to penetrate slowly and thoroughly to the center of the dish, while keeping its contents moist. Always bring the bath to a simmer on top of the stove before putting it in the oven, estimating cooking time from the moment the water boils. I use a water bath for mousses, terrines, and molded custards; some cooks like it for scrambled eggs or delicate sauces like hollandaise, but I rarely bother as I find a heavy pan protection enough provided you keep the heat low. However, I do find that a bath of warm (not simmering) water is useful for keeping fragile sauces and other foods warm on top of the stove.

how to strain sauces

A mesh strainer and small ladle are the best tools for straining sauces, and the finer the mesh the more glossy the sauce will be. You can also use a bowl strainer and a wooden spoon. Straining a sauce removes all the solid ingredients; they should be so thoroughly cooked they have given up all their flavor to the sauce. (See page 86 for a picture of straining.) By contrast, when a sauce is puréed, all the ingredients are left in the finished sauce.

how to coat with sauce

A smooth, even coating of sauce, for example of hollandaise on poached egg or of butter sauce on fish, can seem sleight of hand, but it's simple when you know how. You need a large oval spoon, if possible bigger than a tablespoon. To test consistency of the sauce, dip the spoon in the sauce. Lift it out with the underside of the spoon facing up—it should be quite generously coated. Bear in mind that a hot sauce will tend to set in contact with food, whereas mayonnaise is already cool and slides off easily so it must be thicker. To coat with sauce, hold the spoon handle close to the bowl and fill the spoon with sauce. Hold the spoon at the end of the food nearest you, tip the spoon toward you, and in a fluid motion coat the food, working away from you. Try to avoid stopping as the coating will not be smooth.

how to whisk sauces

No matter how they are put together, all sauces need whisking to give them gloss and a smooth consistency. When inadequately whisked, flour-thickened sauces form lumps and, even worse, emulsified sauces do not thicken at all. Whisking is a primary skill, so please practice a little and you'll save much time in the long run.

If you have the right pan (see Tools for Sauces, page 89) and a whisk to go with it, you're halfway to whisking with the best of the pros. Take a look at what is to be whisked—yolks and water for hollandaise, reduction of white wine and vinegar for white butter sauce, or roux for white sauce. The pan should be large enough to avoid splashing, but small enough for the ingredients to spread generously over the base of the pan so the whisk catches hold of the mixture.

The rest is a matter of quick movement, though not of hard work. Hold the whisk handle like a pencil, and trace a figure of eight rapidly to and fro in the base of the pan so the mixture froths and swirls. (If you turn the whisk constantly in a circle, the sauce forms a vortex and tends to cook too fast on the sides of the pan.) From time to time, take a turn around the sides of the pan with the whisk so sauce does not stick.

HOW TO MAKE WHITE SAUCE

White sauce is quick and easy to make, with none of the tricks of hollandaise and white butter sauces. Almost every kitchen has the ingredients—milk, flour, and butter (or margarine)—on hand. It's basic to macaroni and cheese, moussaka, creamed spinach, cannelloni and lasagne, and many soufflés. With the exception of vinaigrette, white sauce is the most versatile sauce in the kitchen as its mild flavor blends unobtrusively with almost any ingredient. Perhaps its only fault is lack of taste, so be generous with the salt, pepper, and seasonings such as Dijon mustard, nutmeg, or cayenne.

White sauce is based on a roux, a mixture of melted butter and flour that is cooked lightly over medium heat before whisking in milk. Cooking the roux improves the taste of the sauce, but don't overdo it and let the flour start to brown. Then whisk in the milk, which is usually scalded first and cooled to tepid. Don't be timid, but add the milk all at once or the sauce may cook into lumps as you pour. Continue whisking over medium heat—brisk whisking is the key to a smooth, glossy sauce. Just before it boils the sauce will thicken and you can slow down. Lower the heat, add a bit of salt and pepper (preferably white), and leave the sauce to simmer a minute or two to cook the flour. Taste, adjust seasoning, and voilà, that's it. If the sauce has a lump or two, vigorous whisking will often dissolve them, or if not pour the sauce through a strainer.

White sauce is the only sauce that is deliberately made in different consistencies by varying the proportion of flour and butter to milk. A thin white sauce to use as a base for soup calls for a roux made with 1 tablespoon butter and 1 tablespoon flour per cup of milk. A thick white sauce for binding, for example creamed chicken, flaked fish, stuffings, or soufflés, needs 2 tablespoons butter and 2 tablespoons flour per cup of milk. A sauce of medium thickness (see Plain White Sauce) is the most useful, based on a roux of $1\frac{1}{2}$ tablespoons butter and $1\frac{1}{2}$ tablespoons flour per cup of milk.

1 Bring the milk to a boil in a saucepan, then let it cool to tepid. Melt the butter in a second heavy saucepan. Whisk in the flour to make a roux and cook until foaming, 30 seconds to 1 minute.

2 Take the pan from the heat, let the roux cool slightly, then add the warm milk in a rapid, steady stream, whisking vigorously.

3 Return the pan to the heat and bring the sauce to a boil, whisking constantly until it thickens. Let the sauce simmer 1 to 2 minutes, take it from the heat, and taste and adjust the seasoning. A sauce of medium thickness should lightly coat the back of a spoon, and when you draw a finger across it, a clear trail is left.

Plain White Sauce

These proportions make a sauce of medium thickness, right for coating vegetables or mixing with pasta or creamed spinach. Thicker or thinner white sauces are made the same way, using more or less of the butter and flour roux.

Makes 2 cups

> **2 cups milk**
> **3 tablespoons butter**
> **3 tablespoons flour**
> **grated nutmeg to taste**
> **salt and pepper to taste**

First bring the milk to a boil—this saves time when cooking the sauce. In another saucepan, melt the butter, whisk in the flour, and cook until foaming, about 1 minute. Take the pan from the heat to let the roux cool slightly, then whisk in the warm milk. Cook the sauce over medium heat, whisking briskly as it will thicken almost at once and you want to prevent lumps.

Once the sauce has thickened, you can stop whisking. Season it to taste with grated nutmeg, salt, and pepper, and let it simmer over low heat, 1 to 2 minutes, so the flavor mellows.

GETTING AHEAD: If you let white sauce cool without covering it, you'll have lumps, too, so press a piece of plastic wrap on the surface while it is still warm. The sauce will keep in the refrigerator for a couple of days, just be sure to whisk it well when you reheat it.

Cream Sauce

Makes 2 1/2 cups

For a richer sauce, whisk 1/2 cup heavy cream into 2 cups Plain White Sauce, or make the sauce with half milk, half cream.

the way to white sauce

* Take care that white sauce does not scorch—milk burns easily.

* If white sauce is thicker than you want, thin it with more milk. If too thin, simmer to reduce and thicken it, stirring often so it does not stick to the base of the pan.

* Some cooks first infuse the milk with aromatics such as onion and bay leaf, though I rarely bother. A sauce flavored like this is called béchamel.

* Velouté, meaning velvety, is another variation of white sauce in which fish, chicken, or veal stock is substituted for milk. Velouté should be flavored with a squeeze of lemon juice and is normally served with the same main ingredient as the stock.

Béchamel Sauce

Aromatics infuse the milk in Plain White Sauce, useful in soufflés, stuffings, and other recipes where you're looking for layers of flavor.

Makes 2 cups

Before making Plain White Sauce, infuse the milk with aromatic flavorings: For every 2 cups milk, add 2 slices of onion, a bay leaf, 6 peppercorns, and some parsley stems. Cover and heat the milk in a saucepan until almost boiling, then leave over low heat for 10 to 15 minutes. Strain out the flavorings when adding milk to the butter and flour roux.

Kneaded Butter *(Beurre Manié)*

This is a paste of butter and flour that is used instead of a roux to thicken sauces. It is added in small pieces at the end of cooking, rather than at the beginning, and gives rich consistency similar to a roux.

Thickens 1 cup liquid

With a fork, mash 2 tablespoons butter and work in 2 tablespoons flour to make a smooth paste. Drop chunks of kneaded butter into boiling liquid, whisking vigorously so the butter melts and distributes the flour evenly. The liquid will thicken at once. Add pieces of kneaded butter until the sauce reaches the consistency you want.

Spicy Macaroni and Cheese

I call this recipe grown-up macaroni and cheese, though it has long been a favorite of Emma and Simon.

Serves 6

> ³/₄ **pound macaroni**
> **2 tablespoons vegetable oil**
> **2 onions, chopped**
> ³/₄ **pound spicy sausage meat**
>
> **FOR THE CHEESE SAUCE**
> **3 cups milk**
> **6 tablespoons butter, more for the baking dish**
> **6 tablespoons flour**
> ³/₄ **pound sharp Cheddar cheese, grated**
> **salt and pepper to taste**
> **grated nutmeg to taste**
>
> **9 x 13-inch baking or gratin dish**

Preheat the oven to 375°F. Bring a large pan of salted water to a boil. Cook the pasta according to package directions until al dente, tender but still chewy. Drain it in a colander and tip into a bowl. Meanwhile, heat the oil in a skillet and fry the onions until they start to soften, 3 to 5 minutes. Crumble in the sausage meat. Fry it, stirring constantly to break it up, until it is crumbly and brown, 5 to 8 minutes. Remove it with a slotted spoon to paper towels and set it aside.

Make the cheese sauce: Bring the milk to a boil and set it aside. In a saucepan, melt the butter, whisk in the flour, and cook until it foams, about 1 minute. Whisk in the hot milk and bring the sauce to a boil, whisking constantly until it thickens—it will be quite thick. Simmer it for 2 minutes, take from the heat, and whisk in three-quarters of the cheese, stirring just until the cheese melts, ¹/₂ to 1 minute. Taste and adjust seasoning with salt, pepper, and nutmeg.

Stir the sauce and sausage into the pasta and taste again for seasoning. Butter the baking dish. Spread the macaroni in the dish and sprinkle with the reserved Cheddar cheese.

To finish: Bake the macaroni and cheese for 25 to 35 minutes until hot and bubbly. (You may need to turn on the broiler for the last 5 minutes to brown the crust.) Let the dish rest for 5 to 10 minutes before serving.

GETTING AHEAD: Spicy Macaroni and Cheese can be prepared a day ahead and kept covered in the refrigerator. Bake it just before serving.

Cheese Sauce

A full-flavored, fairly dry cheese such as Gruyère, Parmesan, or sharp Cheddar is best for cheese sauce. Never add cheese to the sauce over the heat, nor try to reheat the sauce after adding cheese as it will cook into strings.

Makes 2¹/₂ cups

Off the heat, whisk ¹/₂ cup grated cheese into 2 cups hot Plain White Sauce until the cheese is melted. Stir in 1 to 2 teaspoons Dijon mustard if you like, taste and adjust the seasoning.

Nuts for Sauces

Sauces thickened with nuts come from all over the world, a survival of the days when pounding and grinding by hand with a mortar and pestle (or the local equivalent) was taken for granted. The food processor has brought these sauces into the modern kitchen starting with pesto (the name comes from the Italian *pestare*, meaning to pound). Speaking for myself, I can't have enough of recipes like pungent Georgian Walnut Sauce and savory Mexican Almond Mole, which is packed intriguingly with chiles, banana, and a hint of chocolate. In all of them, the nuts help emulsify and thicken the sauce, adding a characteristic slightly crunchy texture.

Basil Pesto

Pesto can be made with other herbs besides basil, and I'm partial to spearmint (good with pasta and vegetables), and lemon thyme or lemon balm (try either one with fish). If you don't have a food processor, an upright blender works well, too.

Makes 1½ cups sauce, enough for 1 pound pasta

In a processor, combine the leaves from 2 large bunches of basil, 6 peeled garlic cloves, ¼ cup pine nuts, 1 cup grated Parmesan cheese, and 3 tablespoons olive oil. Purée until very finely chopped, using the pulse button and scraping down the sides of the bowl as necessary. With the blades running, work in an additional ½ cup olive oil, adding it very slowly so the sauce emulsifies and thickens. Taste and adjust the seasoning.

1 For an emulsified nut sauce (here Basil Pesto): Combine all the ingredients in a food processor with 2 to 3 tablespoons of oil. Purée until smooth or very finely chopped, scraping down the sides of the bowl as necessary. With the blades turning, add the remaining oil through the feed tube, pouring it in a slow, steady stream so the sauce emulsifies and thickens. Depending on the recipe, it should be quite thick or just fall easily from the spoon.

Mexican Almond Mole

I love this recipe—so very different from the European tradition in which I was raised. Just a little bit of chocolate adds the characteristic depth of flavor to the dark Mexican mole sauces, which are based on roasted chiles. Don't be dismayed by the number of ingredients—they are readily available and puréeing them is easy in the food processor. A traditional accompaniment to cooked turkey, almond mole is also good with cooked chicken or pork chops—for maximum flavor, the meat should be reheated in the sauce.

Makes 3 cups sauce to serve 6

- **4 plum tomatoes**
- **1 onion, cut in chunks**
- **4 garlic cloves, peeled**
- **4 ancho chiles, stemmed, seeded, and cut into strips**
- **3/4 cup sliced almonds**
- **1 banana, sliced**
- **1/4 cup olive oil**
- **1 cup chicken stock, more if needed**
- **1 ounce Mexican or semi-sweet chocolate, cut in pieces**
- **1/2 teaspoon ground cinnamon**
- **salt and pepper to taste**
- **2 tablespoons lime juice**

Heat a skillet over high heat until a drop of water evaporates at once. Add the whole tomatoes, onion, and garlic and roast, stirring frequently. When the garlic and onion start to blacken, after 5 to 6 minutes, transfer them to a food processor. Continue roasting the tomatoes until they are soft and the skin is blistered, 2 to 3 minutes longer. Peel and halve them, squeeze out the seeds, and add the tomato flesh to the processor.

Add the chiles to the skillet and roast briefly until very fragrant, about 1 minute. Remove and add them also to the processor. Reduce the heat and toast the almonds until browned, stirring constantly, 2 to 3 minutes. Put them in the processor with the banana, olive oil, and stock. Purée the mixture until very finely chopped, adding more stock if needed for the mixture to churn easily.

Pour the purée into a saucepan. Stir in the chocolate, cinnamon, salt, and pepper. Simmer the sauce, stirring often (it tends to sputter), until rich but still just thin enough to pour, 10 to 15 minutes. Take from the heat and stir in the lime juice. Taste and adjust the seasoning, including flavorings.

GETTING AHEAD: Mole improves over time—a week in the refrigerator can only do it good.

Georgian Walnut Sauce (*Satsivi*)

From the Republic of Georgia where walnuts flourish, here's a rich sauce to enjoy hot or cold with chicken and fish, or vegetables. The cooked food is best sliced and marinated in the sauce for an hour or two before serving. Color as well as spice is added to the sauce with turmeric, though I like to use saffron—expensive but full of flavor.

Makes 2 cups sauce to serve 6 to 8

Combine in a food processor 1 cup walnut pieces, 3 peeled garlic cloves, $1^1/_2$ teaspoons ground coriander seed, 1 teaspoon ground cinnamon, $^1/_2$ teaspoon ground cloves, $^1/_2$ teaspoon ground fenugreek or aniseed, a pinch of saffron infused for 15 minutes in 1 tablespoon boiling water, 2 tablespoons red wine vinegar, salt, and pepper.

Purée until smooth and thick. Work in about 1 cup warm water until the sauce is thin enough to pour. Taste and adjust seasoning, including spices.

CHAPTER FOUR eggscetera

An egg is surely the most versatile of all ingredients. Eggs thicken sauces, bind stuffings, raise cakes, and give a shine to pastry before even touching on the subject of this chapter: eggs on their own as a main ingredient. Here I've picked my favorites: boiled eggs, scrambled eggs, crêpes, and a wide range of plain and fancy omelets. For all of them, it is worth seeking out the full, fresh flavor of newly laid eggs, and only the taste of butter will do for cooking them. You'll need a little bit of butter for frying crêpes, too, as their lacy texture depends on a generous proportion of eggs.

Boiling an egg is supposed to be the most basic of all kitchen skills, but in fact is not so simple—we've all suffered at one time or another from a so-called soft-boiled egg that turned out to be a rubber ball. Perfect scrambled eggs can be so tricky that they are sometimes set as a test for professional chefs. The reason is that eggs need gentle handling as they set at a quite low temperature (egg whites at 145°F and egg yolks at 150°F). At higher temperatures, eggs harden quickly, becoming tough and dry.

It may seem illogical that an omelet is cooked very rapidly over quite high heat, but here stirring is key, so the eggs keep moving and set lightly and evenly. Watching a master chef cook an omelet has the same fascination as a pizza performance—with a few seemingly simple gestures, a perfect omelet lands on the plate in scarcely a minute. An Italian frittata works in reverse—the eggs are left untouched over very low heat to cook as slowly as possible, achieving the same effect of a soft, fluffy omelet. You can achieve the required level of skill quite quickly as you'll see in the pictures that follow. Another egg technique also begs for your attention—whisking egg whites.

The color of an eggshell, white or brown, is no indication of purity or flavor, but varies with the breed of hen. As a precaution, because of the slight risk of salmonella infection, eggs should be stored in the refrigerator and allowed to come to room temperature only just before use. Note that in many preparations, eggs are not cooked to a temperature that destroys salmonella bacteria, so people at risk such as the elderly, infants, and those with weakened immune systems should avoid them. Hard-boiled eggs and crêpes are an exception.

HOW TO BOIL AND PEEL EGGS

To call an egg boiled is really not correct. The egg should be simmered, not boiled, so it cooks more slowly and evenly and the shell is less likely to crack. I like to put eggs into a saucepan with generous amounts of cold water (a teaspoon of vinegar in the water will help seal any fracture in the shell), then cover and bring the pan slowly to a simmer. Count cooking time from when the water starts to simmer. Hard-boiled eggs take 10 to 12 minutes. If you overdo it, the egg white will turn rubbery and the yolk will develop an ugly black surface tasting of sulfur. The timing of soft-boiled eggs is more tricky, hence those old-fashioned egg timers in the shape of an hour glass. There's an intermediate stage, too, at 6 minutes, when an egg is soft-boiled and closely resembles a poached egg. Called *mollet* in French, it can be peeled if you take care.

To stop further cooking, hard-boiled eggs should be plunged into cold water, then left to cool before you peel them. Sometimes this is easier said than done as the skin clings—this is not your fault, but results from the alkalinity of the egg itself and how the hen has been fed. Just chip away as best you can. In a large batch of boiled eggs, you can reckon on losing one or two during peeling, so I always cook a couple of extras. Hard-boiled eggs can be cooked ahead and shelled a bit later, but if you chill them the whites toughen. I'd advise you to keep them at room temperature, but not for more than a day.

One of the few gadgets I approve of is the hard-boiled egg slicer for cutting wedges or slices—it does a better job than I can by hand. For stuffing, a hard-boiled egg should be halved lengthwise or crosswise so it forms two cups that will sit flat if you cut a little slice from the underside. Then scoop out the yolk and work it though a sieve into a bowl. The pretty fluff that results is called mimosa as it looks like the pretty mimosa blossom. You can bind mimosa with mayonnaise, butter, or sour cream for cold stuffed eggs, or white sauce for hot ones. Popular flavorings include chopped herbs especially chives, crabmeat, shrimp, anchovy, paprika, and cayenne, and the time-honored deviled combination that includes Worcestershire sauce. Mimosa can also be sprinkled over salads as a decoration, with the chopped hard-boiled whites for contrast.

1 To peel a hard-boiled egg, crack the egg on the counter and roll it so the cracks extend all over the shell. Hold the egg under cold running water and detach the egg shell and skin.

2 To make mimosa: Work hard-boiled egg yolks through a sieve, keeping the whites for chopping or stuffing.

Deviled Eggs

A popular egg dish, deviled eggs appear as cocktail hors d'oeuvre, appetizers, sides to main course salads, and in grand presentations such as Whole Roast Salmon (page 121).

Serves 4 as an appetizer

Halve 6 hard-boiled eggs lengthwise or crosswise as you prefer and cut a thin slice from the bases. Scoop out the yolks and sieve them into a bowl. Stir in $^1/_4$ cup mayonnaise or creamed butter with 1 tablespoon chopped fresh chives, 2 teaspoons Dijon mustard, 1 teaspoon Worcestershire sauce, salt, pepper, and a few drops of Tabasco. Taste, adjust seasoning and flavorings, and stuff the egg whites—you can pipe the mixture, or use 2 teaspoons. Top with a caper or 2 crossed chive stems.

Curried Eggs Mimosa

I like to add a bit of curry to the mayonnaise that coats this classic bistro appetizer.

Serves 4

Halve 8 hard-boiled eggs lengthwise and set 3 halves in a triangle, cut side down and points inward, on 4 plates. Sieve yolks from the remaining eggs and chop the whites. Stir 2 teaspoons curry powder, more to taste, into $1^1/_2$ cups mayonnaise, and taste and adjust seasoning. Coat the eggs with the mayonnaise (see How to Coat with Sauce, page 90). (If necessary, thin the mayonnaise with milk to a coating consistency.) Scatter mimosa on top and egg white at the base of the eggs. Add a few leaves of watercress or arugula to the center of the eggs, and serve.

Warm Egg Salad with Tomatoes and Vinaigrette

These eggs are a refreshing change from typical brunch fare.

Serves 4 as a first course

> **6 eggs**
> **3 large tomatoes**
> **$^1/_4$ cup olive oil, more for drizzling**
> **salt and pepper to taste**
> **4 teaspoons red wine vinegar**
> **1 garlic clove, finely chopped**
> **3 tablespoons dry breadcrumbs**
> **1 tablespoon finely chopped fresh parsley**

Put the eggs in a saucepan and cover generously with water. Bring to a boil and simmer them until hard-boiled, 10 to 12 minutes. Plunge the eggs in cold water to cool them and stop the cooking. Peel them under cold running water, dry them, and halve them lengthwise.

Meanwhile, cut each tomato crosswise in 4 thick slices, discarding the ends. Set 3 tomato slices on 4 serving plates, drizzle with olive oil, and sprinkle with salt and pepper. Set them aside.

Stir together the oil, vinegar, pepper, and a large pinch of salt in a frying pan and heat it. Add the egg halves cut side down, and cook over low heat until the vinegar has evaporated, 3 to 5 minutes. Turn the eggs once or twice during cooking. With a slotted spoon, transfer the eggs to the serving plates, putting an egg half, cut side up, on top of each tomato slice.

Add the garlic to the frying pan and sauté over low heat until soft and fragrant, about 1 minute. Stir in the breadcrumbs and cook them until golden brown, stirring constantly, 3 to 4 minutes. Spoon the mixture over the eggs and sprinkle with parsley.

GETTING AHEAD: Boil the eggs and slice the tomatoes an hour or two ahead, then heat the eggs in vinegar and finish the recipe just before serving.

Crab-Stuffed Eggs

A more substantial egg salad to serve as a light summer brunch.

Serves 4

6 eggs
¾ cup cooked crabmeat
2 small celery stalks, chopped
1 teaspoon dry mustard, more to taste
salt and pepper to taste
¼ cup mayonnaise, more if needed
paprika for sprinkling
small head of lettuce

Put the eggs in a saucepan and cover generously with water. Bring to a boil and simmer them until hard-boiled, 10 to 12 minutes. Plunge the eggs in cold water to cool them and stop the cooking. Crack the egg shells and peel them under cold running water. Dry them and halve them lengthwise. Cut a thin slice from the bases so they lie flat. Scoop out and sieve the yolks into a bowl.

Pick over the cooked crabmeat and stir it into the egg yolks with the celery, dry mustard, salt, and pepper. Stir in the mayonnaise to make a firm but creamy mixture, adding more if needed. Taste, adjust the seasoning, including mustard, and pile the filling in the egg whites. Sprinkle them with paprika. Shred the leaves from the lettuce in a chiffonade (page 24), and spread on individual plates. Set 3 halved eggs, points to the center, on top.

GETTING AHEAD: Hard-boil the eggs up to 12 hours ahead and keep them at room temperature. Peel them and make the filling just before serving.

Quail Eggs with Sea Salt

Tiny, pebble-colored quail eggs are available in many gourmet groceries and make a simple, offbeat first course. Allow 4 to 6 eggs per person, and serve them boiled in their shells, with dishes of sea salt and freshly ground black pepper for dipping. Allow 2 minutes' boiling time for raw quail eggs.

soft-boiled and coddled eggs

Surely we were all brought up on soft-boiled eggs with soldiers of buttered toast for dipping—the ultimate comfort food and easy supper for harried Mom. Humpty Dumpty helps it down. In fact, "Broken egg!" was one of the first expressions Simon and Emma ever learned. The degree of cooking for a soft-boiled egg, whether the white should be soft or firm while the yolk remains runny, is a personal matter. For accurate timing, the egg should be lowered into simmering water, allowing 3 minutes for a soft-boiled egg, and 4 minutes for a firmer one.

Coddled eggs are a variant of soft-boiled eggs: put the egg into simmering water, cover the pan, and leave the pan off the heat for 4 to 5 minutes. The egg will be soft-cooked, with a particularly tender white.

HOW TO SCRAMBLE EGGS

When we come back from the farmers' market with day-old eggs, it is a particular treat to scramble them, and butter is the perfect partner. We make scrambled eggs that are creamy, yet lightly thickened, but you may prefer them quite firm. Two eggs per person are a minimum and we often go for broke with three. They need very little flavoring—salt, pepper, and a few chopped herbs can be enough. Scrambled eggs can be used to bind more complex mixtures, for example of smoked salmon, asparagus tips, or corn kernels. For serving, they cry out for a contrasting slice of buttered crisp toast (for Mark), or fried croûte (for me).

Scrambled eggs take barely five minutes to make, but don't let hunger rush you at the stove.

Warming the eggs as gently as possible is key. I find I can control the heat by simply pulling the pan off the burner from time to time, but some cooks like to put the pan in a bath of simmering water. Scrambled eggs need a robust, heavy-based pan that spreads heat evenly. A nonstick pan will save time washing up, as scrambled eggs have a regrettable tendency to stick. Keeping the eggs moving as they cook is vital, so toast and any garnish should be prepared before you start. Recipes may advise adding a spoonful of cream or water, but I regard modern eggs as watery enough already, so I leave them alone. However, if you find that your eggs overcook and stiffen too much, a tablespoon of cream or butter stirred into them will help.

1 Whisk the eggs with salt and pepper (preferably white to avoid black flecks), and continue until the whites and yolks are broken up and slightly frothy. In a heavy pan, melt the butter, about 2 teaspoons per egg, until it melts and froths also. Pour the eggs into the pan and cook very gently, stirring constantly with a wooden spoon (or you can keep going with the whisk if you prefer). After 30 seconds or so, you'll notice curds of egg forming on the sides and base of the pan; keep mixing so they start to thicken the main mass of egg.

2 When the eggs thicken underneath, scrape them with the spoon so they mix with the remaining uncooked eggs. For creamy eggs, you should stir quite briskly, and for fatter flakes, you can let the eggs set a bit on the base of the pan, then scoop them up. Quite soon the eggs will be lightly thickened. Because they will continue thickening in the pan's heat, stop cooking before you think they are done, and keep stirring off the heat for a few seconds until the pan cools and the eggs are creamy-textured and soft. If you prefer them firm, continue cooking a few seconds longer. Serve at once, purists say on unheated plates.

American-Style Scrambled Eggs

Many Americans approach scrambled eggs differently, cooking them until firm in a frying pan. Here's the technique.

Serves 4

Whisk 8 eggs in a bowl with salt and pepper until frothy. Melt 5 tablespoons butter in a nonstick frying pan and add the eggs. Stir with a heatproof spatula or wooden spoon over low heat, letting the egg cook on the base of the pan and scooping it up in large flakes until almost all the egg is set. Take from the heat, letting the egg continue to cook in the heat of the pan until it is firm and set.

Creamy Herbed Scrambled Eggs

Ambrosia, food for the gods!

Scramble your eggs until quite firm. For every 2 eggs, stir in 1 tablespoon crème fraîche and 2 teaspoons of your favorite chopped herb—tarragon would be my choice.

Scotch Woodcock

Woodcock is a zesty game bird and here's the poor man's substitute, piquant with anchovy. You'll be surprised how mild the anchovy is when blended with the eggs.

Serves 4

Soak 10 anchovy fillets in milk for 10 to 15 minutes to remove salt, then drain and finely chop them. Whisk them into 8 eggs and season with plenty of pepper. Toast 4 slices of white bread, trim off the crusts, and spread the bread lightly with butter. Melt 5 tablespoons butter in a frying pan and scramble eggs in the American style. Pile eggs on the toast and serve at once.

Midnight Sun Scrambled Eggs

The Scandinavian lands of the midnight sun are renowned for their smoked fish. Eggs scrambled with smoked salmon and dill will lend an extravagant touch to a weekend brunch.

Serves 4

4 ounces smoked salmon

medium bunch of dill

8 eggs

salt and pepper to taste

5 tablespoons butter

FOR THE CROUTES

½ of a baguette

3 tablespoons butter, softened, more
  if necessary

Make the croûtes: Cut the baguette in 8 diagonal slices about ½ inch thick and toast them in your toaster. Spread them with the softened butter and keep them warm in a low oven.

Cut the salmon in narrow strips about 3/8 inch thick. Pull leaves from stems of the dill and chop them, reserving a few sprigs for decoration. Whisk the eggs with salt and pepper until slightly frothy.

Melt the butter in a heavy pan, add the eggs, and cook over very low heat, stirring constantly, until the eggs start to thicken with some small, soft curds, 2 to 3 minutes. Stir in the salmon and continue cooking until the eggs are cooked to your preference, 3 to 5 minutes longer. Remove from the heat, stir in the chopped dill, and serve garnished with dill sprigs and warm buttered croûtes on the side.

GETTING AHEAD: Prepare the salmon and dill, and whisk the eggs without seasoning an hour before serving; refrigerate both. Season the eggs and scramble them only at the last minute.

Midnight Sun Scrambled Eggs

HOW TO COOK A
FOLDED OMELET

Say "omelet" and I think of supper beside the fire after a long day—it's a solitary treat as the rest of my family does not regard an omelet as a proper meal. Five minutes and I can have the oval, golden yellow package of egg folded and on the plate. The filling is a mere flavoring such as herbs, cheese, or a few sautéed mushrooms that highlights the eggs themselves. In another five minutes, there'll be a salad with vinaigrette on the side. Together, omelet and green salad are the perfect fast foods.

As when making a cake, so also for an omelet: you need to assemble everything before you start to cook. Select the right pan (see Omelet Pans, page 107) and prepare the filling—ingredients such as sliced mushrooms, diced vegetables, fish, or chicken may need cooking ahead. Warm a serving plate to receive the hot omelet from the pan. Just before cooking, whisk the eggs until frothy with a little salt and pepper. Then stir in any chopped flavorings such as herbs or smoked salmon; more substantial fillings come later. I'm never sure whether to add grated cheese at this stage—the omelet will taste better but will be inclined to stick so it's your call.

A folded omelet is cooked fast over quite high heat. Your ear is as important as your eye. Cook butter in the pan until sputtering stops and

1 Whisk eggs with salt and pepper until frothy. Over quite high heat, melt butter in the pan until it stops sputtering. Add eggs and stir briskly with the flat of a fork until they start to thicken, 8 to 10 seconds. Holding the fork upright, quickly pull the egg that sets at sides of the pan to the center, tipping it to pour uncooked egg to the sides. Continue until almost no runny egg is left, 8 to 10 seconds longer.

2 Stop stirring and let the omelet brown on the bottom. Add any filling, reserving a spoonful for topping, and cook the omelet until the top is still runny or lightly set, as you prefer.

3 To fold the omelet, hold the pan handle in one hand and tip the pan away from you. Give the handle a sharp tap with your other hand so the top edge of the omelet flips over, or fold the edge over with a fork.

4 Half roll, half slide the omelet onto the plate, so it lands folded in three with the seam underneath. Pull in the sides of the omelet with a fork to neaten it, brush with butter to give it a shine, and top with reserved filling.

it starts to turn a light gold—this adds delicious nutty flavor. Add the eggs—they should sizzle and will start to thicken at once. How long to cook an omelet is where cooks disagree. I like my omelet soft and runny in the center, and golden brown on the outside. I let it toast underneath a few seconds, and for me it is done. An American-style omelet is allowed to cook until firm but, oh shame!, is not allowed to brown on the outside. If this is what you want, turn the heat down at the end of the runny stage.

Folding an omelet is one of those tricks of the trade that needs a bit of practice. You may not be completely successful the first time, but no one will know if you give a quick push with your fingers or a fork.

omelet observations

* A truly fresh egg can be hard to find, but in an omelet you'll really notice the difference.

* Don't stint on the number of eggs—you'll need at least two per person, three if the omelet is to be a main course. Count on 1 to 2 tablespoons butter per person.

* Do not, however, try to cook too many eggs at once. A personalized omelet just for one, or a larger omelet for two is fine, but when you reach eight eggs for four or more, a folded omelet becomes a jumble, resembling scrambled eggs.

* It is just as quick to make several small omelets as one big one.

* Salt relaxes the protein in egg whites, so you'll have a watery omelet if you mix the eggs with seasoning in advance.

* Just before serving, rub the warm omelet with a lump of butter to give it a shine.

* A spoonful of filling on top of an omelet is a nice touch, and a clue to what is inside.

Monterey Omelet

Depending on what's around, I add just one or all three of these flavorings to a last-minute omelet for supper.

Serves 1

> **2 to 3 eggs**
> **salt and pepper to taste**
> **1 tablespoon butter, more for brushing**
> **1 tomato, peeled, seeded, and chopped**
> **⅓ cup grated Monterey Jack cheese**
> **2 scallions, including green parts, thinly sliced**
>
> **7-inch omelet pan**

Whisk the eggs with salt and pepper until frothy. Melt the butter over quite high heat until it stops sputtering. Add the eggs and stir with the flat of a fork, keeping the raw and cooked eggs moving. As soon as the eggs start to set, stir in the tomato, cheese, and scallions, reserving a teaspoon of each. Once the eggs are lightly set, stop stirring and let the omelet brown on the bottom. When the top is cooked to your taste, soft or lightly set, fold the omelet and slide it onto a warm plate. Brush the top with a little melted butter and sprinkle with reserved tomato, cheese, and scallions.

Goat Cheese and Herb Omelet

Walnuts add texture to this omelet, with herbs for color as well as taste.

Serves 1

Mix 2 tablespoons soft goat cheese with 1 tablespoon chopped walnuts and 1 tablespoon chopped fresh herbs such as chives, parsley, or basil. If necessary, stir in 1 tablespoon cream to soften the cheese so it is easy to spread. Make an omelet using 2 to 3 eggs and 1 to 2 tablespoons butter. Spread the filling in the omelet just before rolling.

HOW TO COOK A
FLAT OMELET

I always think that in a flat omelet it is less the eggs that are important than all the mouthwatering ingredients that combine to make almost a complete meal. Savvy cooks are well aware of this. No American diner menu is complete without a Western omelet, packed with browned onion, green peppers, and ham. France has its *omelette paysanne* with bacon, cubed potato, and parsley, and Spain its tortillas laden with such combinations as onion, tuna, and tomato or pimento, potato, and chorizo. A flat omelet should be moist and juicy, with the eggs firmly set to hold the other ingredients, not overcooked and dry.

All these omelets are made the same way: the filling is cooked separately and the lightly whisked eggs act simply as a binder. The warm filling and eggs are mixed together and cooked quite quickly to a thick cake that is turned over so it browns on both sides. Occasionally the omelet is not flipped, but the soft top is sprinkled with cheese and browned under the broiler. An Italian frittata is different again. Typical fillings include a salty ingredient such as ham, bacon, or cheese, and vegetables play a big role—bell peppers, peas, carrot, the more colorful the better. Crisp fried croutons or potatoes will add a welcome crunch, though a surplus of juice from ingredients such as tomato will make a flat omelet soggy.

A flat omelet, like a folded one, needs the right kind of pan. Here I go for a nonstick surface, given the sticky ingredients that are mixed in with the eggs. Macho chefs flip quite large flat omelets high in the air and catch them in the pan, but not me. I cravenly slide the omelet onto a heatproof plate.

1 Whisk the eggs with salt and pepper until frothy, then stir in the filling (it should be warm). Over medium-high heat, melt butter in the pan until it stops sputtering. Add the eggs—they should sizzle in the hot butter—and stir gently with a fork until they start to thicken.

2 Lift the edges of the omelet so the uncooked egg runs underneath. Continue cooking until the omelet is almost firm on top.

3 Before flipping, shake the omelet loose from the pan, or loosen it with a spatula, and slide it onto a large plate.

4 Place the pan upside down on top and turn the omelet into it. Continue cooking until the bottom of the omelet is browned and set. Slide it again onto a heatproof plate and cut it into wedges for serving.

omelet extras

* For each person I allow three to four heaped tablespoonfuls of filling, a couple of eggs, and a tablespoon of butter for frying.

* Flat omelets are the only type of omelet that can wait around—they are delicious at room temperature, rather like a quiche. Wedges of tortilla or frittata, for example, are a common Mediterranean appetizer.

omelet pans

Whatever the type of omelet, the pan is important. It needs a thick base to distribute the heat evenly and curved, gently sloping sides. The handle should be angled to make transferring the omelet to the plate easier (try it and you'll see what I mean). I incline toward the traditional French pan of cast steel though Emma is always trying to update me with a nonstick pan. An omelet pan should not be washed, but simply wiped after use, if necessary rubbing with a bit of oil and coarse salt to clean it thoroughly.

The size of pan is also important: a small 7-inch pan will hold 2 to 3 eggs to serve one person, while a 9-inch pan is appropriate for a 4- to 5-egg omelet for two. Small omelets are best as attempting an omelet with more than 8 eggs with an 11-inch pan is impractical. Both folded and flat omelets require the same size pan.

French Country Omelet (Omelet Paysanne)

This hearty omelet makes a satisfying meal. If you like, cut wedges of the omelet while still warm and layer in ciabatta or panini bread for an excellent sandwich.

Serves 2 to 3

> **1 tablespoon vegetable oil**
> **4 ounces diced bacon**
> **2 medium potatoes (about 1 pound), peeled and diced**
> **¼ cup chopped fresh flat-leaf parsley**
> **salt and pepper to taste**
> **4 to 5 eggs**
> **1½ tablespoons butter**
>
> **9-inch omelet pan**

Heat the oil in the pan and fry the bacon until brown. Add the potatoes and continue frying until they are brown and crisp, stirring occasionally, 7 to 10 minutes. Stir in half the parsley and season to taste. As the bacon is salty, the mixture will probably not need salt. With a slotted spoon, transfer the mixture to a bowl. Discard the fat and wipe out the pan.

Whisk the eggs with salt and pepper until frothy. Stir in the warm bacon and potato mixture. Melt the butter in the pan and heat until it stops sputtering. Add the eggs and stir with a fork until they start to thicken. Allow the uncooked egg to run underneath the cooked egg by lifting the edge with the fork. When the eggs are almost set, stop stirring and leave the omelet to cook until the top is almost firm.

Take the pan from the heat and slide the omelet onto a heatproof plate. Set the pan over the omelet and flip it back into the pan. Continue cooking until it is browned and set. Slide the omelet onto a serving plate, sprinkle with the remaining parsley and cut it into wedges. Serve warm or at room temperature.

GETTING AHEAD: Flat omelets like this one are good cooked an hour or two ahead to serve at room temperature.

Spanish Omelet

Here's one of the many variations of Spanish omelet.

Serves 2 to 3

Fry a thinly sliced onion in 2 tablespoons olive oil until soft. Add a red or green bell pepper, cored, seeded, and cut in strips, a peeled, seeded, and chopped tomato, 2 chopped garlic cloves, salt, and pepper. Cook, stirring, until the peppers are tender and juice has evaporated. Whisk 4 to 5 eggs with salt and pepper until frothy and stir in the warm filling. Heat 1 to 2 tablespoons butter in a 9-inch nonstick omelet pan until it stops sputtering. Add the egg mixture and stir briskly with the flat of a fork until the eggs are quite thick. Stop stirring and leave the omelet to brown on the bottom, 1 to 2 minutes. Slide it onto a heatproof plate, flip it, and brown the other side.

Flat Mushroom Omelet

Just a few wild mushrooms go a long way in an omelet, and button mushrooms are good, too.

Serves 1

Trim and slice 3 to 4 medium mushrooms (about 2 ounces). Whisk 2 to 3 eggs until frothy and stir in mushrooms. Heat 1 tablespoon butter in a 7-inch omelet pan until it stops sputtering, add egg mixture, and stir with a fork until eggs thicken. Leave omelet to brown on bottom 1 minute. Slide it onto a heatproof plate, flip back into pan, and brown the other side.

frittata

Unlike other flat omelets, a frittata is cooked over the lowest possible heat on the stovetop so the eggs warm gently and puff of their own accord, without any whisking or stirring. Nonetheless, you must keep an eye out as a frittata easily scorches on the bottom. Fifteen to twenty minutes is an average cooking time for an 8-egg frittata. When just set on top it is cooked to perfection, fluffy and light, but if overdone the eggs will be tough. A frittata has similar fillings to other flat omelets, but being Italian in origin, zucchini, tomato, sautéed fennel, and eggplant are favorites, together with spicy sausage, fish such as tuna, shrimp, mussels, and the little clams called *vongole*. Olive oil can be substituted for the butter, and I would advise a nonstick pan.

Melon and Prosciutto Frittata

This combination of sweet juicy melon, salty ham, and eggs is wonderfully refreshing on a hot day.

Serves 3 to 4

Cut the peel from half a small melon and discard seeds. Cut the flesh in $1/2$-inch dice and leave to drain in a strainer about 10 minutes. Whisk 6 eggs with salt and pepper until frothy. Stir in the melon and 2 ounces prosciutto, cut in strips. Melt a tablespoon of butter in a 10-inch omelet pan and pour in the egg mixture, spreading the filling evenly. Cover the pan with a lid and cook very gently, 20 to 25 minutes, until the center of the frittata is set and the base is lightly browned. Rotate the pan from time to time during cooking so the heat spreads evenly. Flip the frittata onto a warm platter, cut in wedges, and serve.

HOW TO MAKE CREPES

Crêpes belong to a worldwide family that includes American breakfast pancakes, Scottish drop scones, Russian blini, and Chinese mandarin pancakes, but crêpes are thinner and more delicate. They are also simpler as they require only three ingredients—flour, milk, and eggs—plus some butter for frying. Most crêpes use wheat flour, though a measure of buckwheat flour will add nutty flavor and lightness, as in the famous crêpes of Brittany. More substantial ones are made with whole wheat flour. Crêpes are primarily used as a wrapper for other ingredients, though they are good on their own, too, sprinkled with sugar or spread with honey or jam.

A good crêpe is pliable as paper, tender, and golden brown, all because of the eggs that bind the batter. For frying, oil or margarine can be used but neither gives the golden color or rich flavor of butter. Only a small amount is needed, but even so, the first crêpe is usually thick and greasy, a gift for the family dog. After that, five or six crêpes will do fine before you need to rebutter the pan. To reduce the danger of scorching and flecking the crêpes with black specks, you may want to clarify the butter (see Clarified Butter, page 128).

Most egg-based dishes cannot be prepared ahead or kept waiting, but crêpes are an admirable exception. I like to make a stack of crêpes and store them for a day or two in the refrigerator, or freeze them for a month or more. Be sure to wrap them tightly so they do not dry out, and before using them, let them come to room temperature so they peel apart easily. Endlessly adaptable, I can have a family dessert on the table in minutes by warming the crêpes a few seconds on each side in a hot pan, then spreading them with warm applesauce or chocolate fudge sauce to serve with ice cream. Savory crêpes are more often rolled like a cigarette or shaped as a parcel with creamy fillings of seafood or wild mushrooms. When coated with a cream or cheese sauce, they keep well in the refrigerator or freezer. (Avoid butter sauces here as they will separate on reheating.)

1 Assemble the batter, a small ladle, a metal spatula, a plate, and a small bowl and brush. Melt 2 to 3 tablespoons butter (preferably clarified) in a crêpe pan, swirl so the pan is coated, and pour the excess into the bowl. Reheat the pan, add a drop of batter, and wait until it spatters, showing the pan is at the right heat. Quickly add a small ladle of batter, rotating and shaking the pan with a turn of your wrist so the base is completely coated in a thin, even layer. With too much batter, the crêpe will be thick, with too little, it will have holes.

2 Fry the crêpe quickly over medium-high heat until it is set on top and brown underneath, 1/2 to 1 minute. Loosen it and flip it with the spatula, or toss it in the air with a flip of your wrist. Continue cooking 20 to 30 seconds, until the crêpe is brown on the other side. As you complete them, pile the cooked crêpes on the plate, one on top of another to keep them moist. After frying 5 to 6 crêpes, or more often if the pan starts to stick, brush the pan again with melted butter to moisten it.

crêpe essentials

* The side of the crêpe that is fried first browns more evenly and so should be folded outward for presentation.
* With a bit of practice and well-seasoned crêpe pans, you can keep two or even three pans going at once.
* A big question when frying is do you toss, or do you flip? It's a question of temperament. Simon tosses crêpes high in the air with macho enthusiasm, and doesn't give a damn if one or two descend to the floor. I flip with a metal spatula, which is safer and just as quick.
* If the finished crêpe is heavy, either the batter was too thick, or you added too much to the pan. If necessary, thin the batter with a bit more milk. Fragile, crumbling crêpes are a sign the batter is too thin; to bind it, whisk in another egg.

crêpe pans

Crêpe pans vary in size, and the most useful measure about 7 inches across the base of the pan. Traditional crêpe pans are made of cast steel, with shallow sides and a flat handle to make flipping easier. You can use a small frying pan, too, provided it is heavy enough to distribute the heat and light enough to handle easily when flipping the crêpes. Nonstick crêpe pans are tempting, but the finished crêpes tend to come out thicker. Like omelet pans, crêpe pans should never be washed. Season them when new by heating with a generous layer of coarse salt and vegetable oil for 5 to 10 minutes, then leave to cool and wipe out for use.

Crêpe Batter

I like to use lots of eggs in crêpe batter so the crêpes are light and easy to fry in the pan.

Makes fourteen to sixteen 7-inch crêpes

Sift 1 cup flour into a bowl with a large pinch of salt and make a well in the center. Break 3 eggs into the well and whisk them until mixed. Add $1/2$ cup milk, in a steady stream, whisking so the flour is gradually drawn in to make a smooth paste. If you add too much liquid at this point, the batter will be lumpy. Thin the paste by stirring in $1/2$ cup more milk. Cover and leave the batter at room temperature, $1/2$ to 1 hour, so starch in the flour expands and thickens the batter lightly. It should be the consistency of half-and-half, so if necessary add a little more milk. Lumps are easily removed by pouring batter through a strainer.

Whole Wheat or Buckwheat Crêpe Batter

Whole wheat crêpes are hearty, while buckwheat crêpes are deliciously light with nutty flavor.

Make Crêpe Batter, substituting $1/2$ cup whole wheat or buckwheat flour for half the all-purpose flour.

Cornmeal Crêpe Batter

These crêpes are a robust foil for pork, turkey, and vegetable fillings such as Rapid Ratatouille (page 248).

Make Crêpe Batter, replacing half the flour with $1/2$ cup fine white or yellow cornmeal.

Curry Crêpe Batter

These crêpes, made with curry powder and chicken stock, are good for wrapping around chicken and vegetables.

Make Crêpe Batter, adding 1 tablespoon curry powder to the flour and salt. Replace the milk with 1 cup chicken stock.

Mushroom Crêpes

If you can fry a crêpe, you can make this deliciously simple mushroom recipe. It's a wonderful vegetarian entrée.

Serves 4 to 8

1 recipe Crêpe Batter
3 to 4 tablespoons butter, for frying the crêpes
3/4 pound mushrooms
3 tablespoons butter, more for the baking dish
juice of 1/2 lemon
salt and pepper to taste

FOR THE WHITE SAUCE
2 cups milk
5 tablespoons butter
1/3 cup flour
grated nutmeg to taste
1 cup light cream
3/4 cup grated Gruyère cheese

Make the crêpe batter, fry the crêpes, and keep them covered at room temperature.

Dice the mushrooms and put them in a saucepan with 2 tablespoons of the butter, lemon juice, salt, pepper, and 1/4 inch of water. Cover and cook over high heat until the liquid boils to the top of the pan and the mushrooms are tender, about 5 minutes. Let them cool. Drain them, reserving the liquid.

Make the white sauce: Bring the milk just to a boil. In another saucepan, melt the butter, whisk in the flour, and cook until foaming, about 1 minute. Whisk in the hot milk and bring the sauce to a boil, whisking constantly until it thickens. Let it simmer 1 to 2 minutes, then stir in the cooking liquid from the mushrooms and season the sauce to taste with nutmeg, salt, and pepper. Stir half the sauce into the mushroom dice. Taste and adjust seasoning again. Pour the cream over the remaining sauce to prevent a skin from forming and set it aside.

Put 2 tablespoons of mushroom mixture on each crêpe and roll them like cigars. Arrange them diagonally in a buttered shallow baking dish. Whisk the reserved sauce to mix in the cream, reheat it, and adjust seasoning again. Coat the crêpes with the sauce and sprinkle with grated cheese. Melt the last tablespoon of butter and sprinkle it on top.

To finish: Preheat the oven to 350°F. Bake the crêpes until they are bubbling and brown, 20 to 30 minutes. If they are already warm, simply broil them until browned.

GETTING AHEAD: The crêpes themselves can be kept in a plastic bag in the refrigerator for up to 3 days, or they can be frozen. When filled, they are fine for 2 days if covered and kept in the refrigerator.

Seafood and Mushroom Crêpes

The addition of seafood lifts mushroom crêpes into the luxury category.

In the recipe for Mushroom Crêpes, substitute 1 cup cooked seafood such as crabmeat, lobster, or shrimp for half of the mushrooms. Make the same amount of crêpes and white sauce.

Parsley Crêpes with Asparagus and Lemon Butter Sauce

A green welcome to spring!

Serves 4

> 1 recipe Crêpe Batter (page 110)
> ¼ cup chopped fresh parsley
> 3 to 4 tablespoons butter, for frying the crêpes
> 1 pound thin asparagus
> salt and white pepper to taste
>
> FOR THE LEMON BUTTER SAUCE
> juice of 1 lemon
> ¾ cup (1½ sticks) cold butter, cut in cubes

Make the crêpe batter, adding the parsley, and fry the crêpes. Wrap the crêpes in aluminum foil to keep them warm. Bring a large pan of salted water to a boil. Trim the asparagus and tie them in bundles with string. Add the asparagus to the boiling water and boil, uncovered, until tender but still firm when pierced with the point of a knife, 2 to 3 minutes. Drain, rinse with cold water, and leave to drain completely.

To assemble the crêpes: Preheat the oven to 325°F and if necessary warm the crêpes, still wrapped in foil. Heat a baking dish. Wrap a warm crêpe around 3 to 4 stems of asparagus and lay them diagonally in the dish. Cover with foil and warm again in the oven, 2 to 3 minutes, while making the sauce.

Make the lemon butter sauce: Heat the lemon juice in a small pan until hot to the touch. Whisk in the cold butter, adding the cubes a few at a time and working on and off the heat so the butter thickens creamily without melting to oil. Taste and adjust seasoning with salt and white pepper. Spoon the sauce over the crêpes and serve at once.

GETTING AHEAD: Make the crêpes up to 3 days ahead and keep them tightly wrapped. Cook the asparagus and make the sauce just before serving.

HOW TO WHISK EGG WHITES

Lots of lovely things depend on whisked egg whites—meringues, marshmallows, soufflés, extra-fluffy omelets, and many sponge cakes. A frothy, smooth, snow white mass of egg whites beaten to just the right stiffness is spectacular. However, almost tasteless, they are not an end in themselves but are always folded into a sweet or savory mixture. Light, fragile, whisked egg whites cannot be kept waiting—so let's get down to business.

First of all, the implements: Whisking egg whites in a traditional unlined copper bowl with a big balloon whisk is hard work. My own copper bowl, badge of the serious cook, hangs in splendor on the wall and yields to my electric mixer, a sturdy model with a balloon whisk and—metal again—a stainless steel bowl large enough to take up to 8 egg whites. The point of the balloon whisk, with its rounded shape and multiple wires, is to incorporate more air into the whites. Hand-held mixers with paddle beaters do poorly in

egg notes

* Egg whites at room temperature can be beaten more quickly and to greater volume than when they are cold.

* Egg whites that have been frozen whisk very well; be sure to use them at room temperature.

* A pinch of salt or cream of tartar added to egg whites before beating slows stiffening and lessens the danger of overbeating.

* In sweet recipes, some sugar is almost always beaten into the whites to make meringue, which is more stable and easier to mix than plain whipped egg whites.

comparison, and glass or ceramic bowls are also unsatisfactory as the whites tend to separate slightly. Plastic bowls are no better—there's no matching metal. Be sure your bowl and whisk are dry, as dampness or even a trace of fat (egg yolk for instance) will prevent whisked egg whites from stiffening. Use nature's tool, a broken eggshell, to scoop out any yellow flecks from the whites.

It is all too easy to over-whisk egg whites so they start to separate, especially in a machine. When you see a telltale roughness at the edge of the bowl, stop at once. To be safe, I usually stop the machine just before I think the whites are ready, then finish whisking by hand. A makeshift remedy to combat separation is to add an extra, unbeaten egg white, and whisk it into the over-whisked whites for just a few seconds. Unfortunately, if the whites are seriously separated you'll need to start again. Remember, whisked egg whites must be used at once or they will deflate rapidly. If you are delayed a minute or two, keep the beater turning very slowly.

how to separate eggs

Eggs are best separated with the help of the shell that cuts easily through the white.

1 Crack the egg at its broadest point by tapping it against a bowl or a sharp edge. With your thumbs, break open the egg, letting some of the white slip over the edge of the shell into the bowl. Tip the yolk from half of the shell to the other, detaching the remaining white from the yolk. If the yolk breaks and some falls into the white, remove it with the eggshell. To remove the white threads, nip them against the side of the eggshell with your fingers.

2 Now apply maximum energy, whether with the mixer or with a strong arm. If working by hand, beat down in the bottom of the bowl, as the aim at this point is to stiffen the egg whites rather than add more air. In about 30 seconds the whites form a stiff, shallow peak.

1 Whether beating egg whites by hand or machine, start slowly until the whisk has broken up the whites so they start to froth. Then increase speed so that the whisk picks up the froth and beats in air until you have a fine, even foam that clings to the sides of the bowl. If you are beating by hand, make a point of lifting the whisk in the bowl so that you incorporate as much air as possible.

Spinach Mousseline

Vegetable purées, particularly of vigorous vegetables like spinach or broccoli, are good lightened with whipped egg white. Excellent with fish, hot spinach mousseline is a good way to liven up frozen spinach.

Serves 6

Thaw 2 packages (10 ounces each) frozen chopped spinach and squeeze out all excess moisture with your fists. Purée it in a food processor with ¹/₂ cup cream. Melt 2 tablespoons butter in a saucepan, add the spinach, salt, pepper, and a grating of nutmeg. Leave it to sauté over low heat. Stiffly beat 2 egg whites. Beat the hot spinach into the egg whites, return the mixture to the pan, and beat it 1 minute over the heat until smooth and light. Taste and adjust seasoning, including nutmeg. Serve hot.

Last-Minute Cheese Soufflé

Last-Minute Cheese Soufflé

Brie or domestic Munster can be substituted for the Camembert in this minimalist soufflé. You'll find the full flavor of the cheese comes through clearly.

Serves 6

> **butter for the ramekins**
> **one Camembert cheese (¹/₂ pound)**
> **6 eggs, separated**
> **3 tablespoons heavy cream or crème fraîche, more if needed**
> **salt and freshly ground black pepper**
>
> **Six ³/₄-cup ramekins**

Preheat the oven to 400°F and butter the ramekins. Chop the cheese, including the rind, and put it in a food processor with the egg yolks, heavy cream, and a generous amount of freshly ground black pepper. Work it until smooth, adding more cream if necessary until the mixture almost falls from the spoon. Transfer it to a bowl.

Stiffly whisk the egg whites in a mixer or by hand, adding a pinch of salt to help stiffen them. If using a mixer, finish whisking them by hand. Stir about a quarter of the egg whites into the cheese mixture to lighten it. Add this mixture back into the remaining whites and fold them together as lightly as possible. Tip the soufflé mixture into the buttered ramekins and smooth the tops with a metal spatula. They should be completely full. Run your thumb around the inside edge of the dishes to detach the mixture from the rim so the soufflés rise straight.

Set the ramekins on a baking sheet and bake until very hot, puffed, and brown, 10 to 12 minutes. When shaken, they should wobble slightly. Do not overbake or the soufflés will be dry. Transfer them to cold plates lined with napkins and serve at once. The center of the soufflés should be slightly soft to provide a sauce for the firm outside.

GETTING AHEAD: The cheese mixture can be made up to 2 hours ahead and kept covered in the refrigerator. The whites must be whisked just before you assemble and bake the soufflé.

Snappy Salmon Mousse

I've always been happy with this mousse, which calls only for salmon, heavy cream, and egg whites. The whites play a double role of thickening and lightening the salmon mixture and the pure flavor of salmon comes right through. The mousse is cooked in a pan of hot water so it emerges light and tender, firmer than a soufflé. A red or white wine butter sauce would be the perfect accompaniment.

Serves 6

> **2 pounds skinless salmon fillet**
> **8 egg whites**
> **1½ teaspoons salt, more for the whites**
> **½ teaspoon white pepper**
> **1¼ cups heavy cream, chilled**
> **butter for the dish**
> **Red or White Wine Butter Sauce (page 83)**
>
> **1½-quart soufflé dish**

Cut the salmon in large chunks, discarding pin bones (see How to Remove Pin Bones from Fish, page 120). Purée the salmon in a food processor. Beat 2 of the egg whites until very frothy, about 1 minute. With the blades turning, gradually work the frothy egg whites into the puréed salmon. Work in the salt and pepper. With the blades turning, gradually work in the chilled cream. Turn the mixture into a chilled bowl and set it over ice so it remains cold.

Preheat the oven to 350°F and bring a water bath (page 89) to a boil on top of the stove. Butter the soufflé dish. Stiffly whisk the remaining egg whites, adding a pinch of salt to help them stiffen. Fold a quarter of the egg whites into the iced salmon mixture, then add this mixture back to the remaining egg whites and fold them together as lightly as possible. Transfer the mixture to the prepared soufflé dish and smooth the top—the dish should be completely full.

Set the mousse in the water bath and bring the water back to a boil on top of the stove. Bake in the water bath in the oven until the mousse is brown and firm in the center, 50 to 60 minutes.

Transfer it to a plate lined with a napkin to stabilize the dish and serve at once, with the warm butter sauce in a separate bowl.

GETTING AHEAD: The salmon mixture can be prepared up to 4 hours ahead if you keep it over ice in the refrigerator. After the whisked egg whites have been added, the mousse must be baked at once.

how to fold egg whites

You'll find I drop the verb "fold" casually here and there in this book. Folding is the technique used to gently combine ingredients, often whisked eggs or eggs whites, so as little air as possible is lost. I like to use a large metal spoon for folding, but wooden spoons and rubber spatulas are also tools of choice. These directions for folding egg whites apply to other mixtures, too.

To fold egg whites: Stiffly whip the whites, then add about a quarter of them to the basic mixture. Stir to combine them thoroughly. Tip this mixture onto the remaining egg whites and, with a spoon or spatula, cut through the center of the ingredients and down to the bottom of the bowl. Drawing the spoon toward you, scoop under the contents with the spoon scraping up against the side of the bowl. Lift and turn them over on top of the mixture at the same time as you rotate the bowl a quarter turn in the opposite direction. Continue folding just until the basic mixture and egg whites are evenly combined into a light and fluffy mixture. It's better to underfold a mixture than to overblend and lose volume.

CHAPTER FIVE fabulous fish and seafood

As a family we've been lucky enough to live near the sea for most of our lives, so fresh fish appears often on the table. We go for quick and easy ways to cook seafood, and in this chapter I've picked just a few of these ideas. Roasting is my first choice—in the steady heat of the oven, the fish cooks evenly and stays moist thanks to basting with all manner of flavorings and marinades. Next, I would choose to sauté fish, particularly delicate white fillets such as sole and catfish. When it comes to broiling or grilling I'm more cautious—not all fish take happily to it. Rich fish such as salmon and tuna do well, but white fish require close attention as they dry out easily in high heat. I find it more rewarding to poach white fish in stock or the aromatic broth known as court bouillon, or best of all to simmer it in a stew with lots of colorful, vibrant flavorings. Lastly, I've included some favorite family shellfish—oysters for Mark, mussels for Emma, and shrimp for us all.

I've learned over the years that rather than look for the particular seafood suggested by a recipe, it's best to buy what looks good in the market. Note that I say "good" not "fresh"—fish that has been correctly frozen and stored is far preferable to a so-called fresh display that has been sitting around at ambient temperatures for goodness knows how long. Good-quality fish and shellfish will look plump, firm, and bright-colored (though iridescence is a bad sign). Your nose is the best guide, as prime fish and shellfish bring a salty whiff of the sea. If you are buying whole fish, be sure it has been cleaned (stomach emptied), scaled, and trimmed to avoid much messy work at home. Depending on head size, you should allow 3/4 to 1 pound of whole fish per person. An ample portion of boneless fish fillets, with or without skin, is generally about 6 ounces.

Back home, fish should be stored in the coldest part of the refrigerator or over a bag of ice. The shorter the wait the better, with a maximum of two days. When it comes to cooking, fish fillets need just a quick rinse in cold water and a pat dry in paper towels. However, when rinsing the gills and stomach cavity, whole fish require a bit more care. Whether large or small, a whole fish should be slashed diagonally two or three times on each side so the heat penetrates and cooks the flesh evenly.

HOW TO ROAST FISH

Let's play it simple. Roasting (a.k.a. baking) is much the easiest way to cook fish, and suits almost any type, whether fillets, steaks, or individual whole fish. The steady heat of an oven is kind to delicate seafood such as swordfish or scallops, while robust fish such as snapper and cod remain succulent. At the farmers' market near Emma in California, a small pickup truck sells the freshest of fish. Even if I arrive early there's not much choice but I grab what I can, baby petrale sole if I'm lucky. I know I'll have the few other ingredients needed for roasting in the cupboard. I oil or butter the roasting dish, add the fish, whole or in pieces, then sprinkle it with salt, pepper, or possibly a spicy or herbal rub (page 56). It's ready to go after I've drizzled the fish with oil or dotted it with butter, and moistened it with lemon juice, white wine, or fish stock (see Simple Marinades for Fish, page 125). A brief pause to allow the fish to absorb the flavorings is beneficial, just enough time to heat the oven. The fish can be prepared for roasting 3 or 4 hours ahead and kept in the refrigerator, but should be cooked just before serving. In summer, an alternative is to roast the fish ahead and serve it, Mediterranean style, at warm room temperature.

Roasting offers enticing possibilities for stuffing, whether it be the cavity of a whole fish, or by folding or layering fillets. A basic herb, lemon, and breadcrumb mixture is hard to beat, with chopped garlic, fresh ginger, shallot, or Parmesan cheese added to your taste. Or you may want to branch out with olives, anchovy, or a crabmeat stuffing. If vegetables such as tomatoes, bell peppers, mushrooms, and eggplant are layered beneath the fish, little or no further accompaniment may be needed. For a quick supper at home, I go for a bed of herb sprigs—we grow rosemary, thyme, oregano, and bay leaf in the garden, all of them good with fish.

Oven temperature for roasting fish depends on what result you are looking for. If you want a golden brown surface and crispy skin, with the

① Preheat the oven to the temperature indicated in the recipe. Line a broiler pan or roasting pan generously with aluminum foil and add the fish. Baste and season the fish (here a salmon) according to the recipe and put it in the oven to roast. A simple rule of thumb for cooking time is to measure the thickest part of the fish and allow 10 minutes per inch plus 10 minutes. Baste every 5 minutes for small fish, every 10 minutes for larger ones.

② To test if the fish is done at the end of the calculated time, pinch the thickest part between your finger and thumb, or press small pieces with a fingertip; if the fish is very soft it will be rare inside, if slightly resilient it is probably done. Tug the back fin—it should pull away easily, and the eye of the fish should be white, no longer transparent. With a fork, flake the fish near the backbone—it should yield easily. You can also check with a meat thermometer, which should register 130°F. Large fish continue to cook from residual heat, so stop cooking when slightly underdone as the temperature will rise a few degrees.

flesh slightly rare and transparent in the center, the temperature can be as high as 425°F; for well-done fish, a lower heat of 375°F does the job. In general, the smaller the pieces of fish, the higher the temperature should be. Scallops, for example, should be roasted in the highest oven heat possible. Timing varies with the type of fish and thickness of the piece.

A bonus when roasting fish is the tasty gravy of juices that often forms in the bottom of the pan. To make the most of this, transfer the cooked fish to a platter and keep it warm. If the pan juices are not already reduced to a brown glaze, boil them further on top of the stove. Add a few spoonfuls of liquid such as fish stock, white wine, dry apple cider, or simply water (what veteran cooks call "stock from the tap"), and stir to dissolve the juices. Spoon it over the fish and serve.

a tip or two

* A heavy pan for roasting is best as fish tends to stick. I often use a cast-iron gratin dish or a traditional glass baking dish.

* Six ounces is an ample portion of boneless fillets or steaks, but allow 3/4 to 1 pound for whole fish on the bone.

* When roasting very thin fish fillets, for example of sole or flounder, they should be folded to increase their density.

* Pictured at left you'll see some tests for when fish is done. Note that the fish will continue cooking for a minute or two in the heat of the baking dish.

* As we all know too well, overcooked fish is dry, tasteless, and chewy. I advise you to play it safe by removing it from the oven too soon rather than too late—it can always be put back to continue cooking.

Roast Sea Bass with Green Olive Tapenade

Halibut is a good substitute for the sea bass here. Be sure to use large, meaty green olives in the tapenade.

Serves 4

1½ pounds sea bass fillets
1 lemon
olive oil, for the dish

FOR THE TAPENADE
1 cup cold water
1 slice of white bread
2 garlic cloves, cut in pieces
½ cup pitted green olives
2 anchovy fillets
⅓ cup flaked almonds
2 tablespoons capers, drained and rinsed
¼ cup olive oil
freshly ground black pepper to taste

Preheat the oven to 375°F. Pour the water over the bread in a small bowl and leave it to soak. Rinse the fish fillets, pat them dry, and cut them in 4 equal portions. Cut 4 slices from the lemon, setting the rest aside.

Make the tapenade: Put the garlic cloves, olives, anchovies, almonds, and capers in a food processor. Squeeze the bread dry, pull it into crumbs, and add it to the other ingredients. Pulse until they are coarsely chopped. With the blades turning, gradually pour in the olive oil. Work in the juice of the rest of the lemon with plenty of pepper. Taste and adjust seasoning—the anchovies will probably add enough salt.

Oil a baking dish and add the fish fillets. Spread the tapenade evenly on top of each fillet and add a slice of lemon. Roast the fish in the oven until it is lightly browned on top and just flakes easily, 12 to 15 minutes. Serve hot or at room temperature.

GETTING AHEAD: Prepare the tapenade up to 2 days ahead and roast the fish at serving time.

Roast Halibut with Herbal Topping

If you like tapenade, you'll like this. The herbal green of parsley takes the place of the olives in Roast Sea Bass with Green Olive Tapenade (page 119), adding a similar punch to roast halibut or any white fish.

Serves 4

Preheat the oven to 375°F. In a food processor, put 2 shallots or a small onion, cut in pieces, a small garlic clove, cut in pieces, 2 anchovies, cut in pieces, 2 tablespoons walnut pieces, a handful of parsley sprigs, 1 teaspoon salt, 1/2 teaspoon pepper, and 3 tablespoons walnut oil. Purée to a coarse paste. Taste and adjust seasoning. Spread the paste on 4 fillets of halibut (about 1 1/2 pounds) and bake as in Roast Sea Bass with Green Olive Tapenade, 12 to 15 minutes.

Hot and Salty Roast Salmon

The heat of horseradish and the salt of bacon perfectly balance the richness of roast salmon. Ginger can take the place of horseradish if you prefer.

Serves 4

Preheat the oven to 400°F. Dice 2 ounces thick-cut bacon. Remove pin bones from 4 thick skinless portions of salmon (about 1 1/2 pounds), poke holes on both sides with a knife point, and insert the bacon dice. Set the salmon in a buttered roasting pan, dot with 2 tablespoons butter, and sprinkle with salt and pepper. Roast in the oven, basting often, until the salmon just flakes easily, 15 to 18 minutes. Remove and keep it warm on a platter. Discard fat from the pan, add 1 cup heavy cream, and bring it to a boil, stirring to dissolve the pan juices. Strain this sauce into a saucepan, stir in 2 tablespoons bottled horseradish, salt, and pepper. Simmer 2 minutes, taste for seasoning, adding more horseradish if you like, and spoon it over the salmon.

how to remove pin bones from fish

Recipes using fish fillets rarely mention that many fish, notably salmon, have a line of pin bones that run from head to tail, perpendicular to the backbone. When the fillets are cut from the backbone, these bones remain in the flesh. They are not hard to remove, but few fishmongers bother unless you ask. Here's how to do it yourself:

1 Run your fingers over the center of the fish fillet from head to tail—you will feel bones sticking up at once. Pull them out with large tweezers or with my secret weapon, needle-nosed pliers from the household tool kit.

Whole Roast Salmon with Piquant Herb Butter

Here's a splendid dish for a party, a showpiece that can be prepared ahead to roast just before serving, or cooked several hours in advance to serve at room temperature. The bigger the fish, the more people it will serve with no extra work involved for the cook. Now that's my kind of food! Watercress, chives, chervil, and tarragon are alternatives to the parsley and arugula that flavor the herb butter, which is also delicious with pasta.

Serves 6 to 8

1 whole salmon (about 5 pounds), with head and fins, scaled and cleaned
3 lemons
8 to 10 thyme sprigs
8 to 10 oregano or marjoram sprigs
2 tablespoons olive oil, more for basting
salt and pepper to taste

FOR THE PIQUANT HERB BUTTER
medium bunch of parsley
medium bunch of arugula
6 anchovy fillets, soaked in milk
2 medium gherkin pickles
2 tablespoons capers, drained
2 garlic cloves, cut in pieces
¾ cup (1½ sticks) butter, cut in pieces
¾ cup olive oil
1 tablespoon Dijon mustard
squeeze of lemon juice

Preheat the oven to 375°F. Wash the salmon inside and out and dry it on paper towels. Cut 4 or 5 diagonal slashes in both sides of the fish so the oven heat can penetrate and cook the flesh more evenly. Cut one lemon in half lengthwise, then crosswise in slices. Cut the remaining two lemons in wedges for serving. Tuck a lemon slice and some herb sprigs into each slash in the salmon. Trim the tail into a neat V shape.

Set the fish on a broiler pan or in a roasting pan on a double layer of aluminum foil and sprinkle it with olive oil, salt, and pepper. (If your pan seems small, stand the fish on its belly

and curve it to fit—it will look as though it is swimming). Measure the thickest part of the fish and allow a cooking time of 10 minutes per inch plus 10 minutes. Roast the fish, brushing regularly with more olive oil, for the calculated time, or until the skin is brown and crisp. The fish eye will have turned white and the flesh should no longer be transparent when you flake a bit loose along the backbone. Check by inserting a meat thermometer into the thickest part of the fish—it should register 130°F.

Meanwhile, make the herb butter: Bring a large saucepan of water to a boil. Strip the leaves from stems of the parsley and arugula. Add the parsley and arugula leaves to the boiling water and blanch them by simmering for 2 minutes. Drain, rinse with cold water, and pat them dry on paper towels. Drain the anchovies and work them in a food processor with the pickles, capers, and garlic until finely chopped, scraping the sides of the bowl with a spatula as needed. Add the butter, puréeing it until smooth. Add the herbs and pulse until they are also finely chopped. With the blades turning, slowly pour in the olive oil. The herb butter will be creamy and a lovely shade of green. Add the mustard and season the butter to taste with lemon juice, salt, and pepper.

When done, transfer the whole fish by lifting it on the foil onto a warm platter. Pull the foil away and decorate the fish with lemon wedges. Serve the herb butter in a separate bowl. At the table, strip the skin off the salmon and cut away fillets of fish, pulling them from each side of the backbone.

GETTING AHEAD: The herb butter can be made 2 days ahead. Let it come to room temperature before serving. If you wish to serve the fish at room temperature, it can be cooked up to 8 hours ahead. Let it cool, store it covered in the refrigerator, then let it come to room temperature for at least an hour before serving.

HOW TO BROIL AND GRILL FISH

I've learned to keep a wary eye when broiling or grilling fish, as in searing heat it can overcook and dry out in literally a minute. Here's where a marinade (particularly one containing some oil) is so helpful in keeping the fish moist and less likely to stick to the grill rack. Nonetheless, I still steer away from delicate fillets of sole, catfish, and other fine-textured white fish. Firm, full-flavored types such as mahi mahi, snapper, cod, and swordfish hold their shape when grilled or broiled and remain so much more juicy. Shellfish such as scallops and shrimp and other firm, rich fish like salmon and tuna also do well.

Occasionally as a family we treat ourselves to a whole fish, a salmon, trout, or sea bass perhaps, or a bream that is easy to carve off the bone. We've never forgotten the house we had one summer on the Delaware Bay, where rockfish, fresh and sometimes flapping, were landed just at dinnertime. A whole fish on the bone makes a fine show, and anything up to five pounds grills well as the bones keep the flesh moist. You'll see shaped metal cages that hold the beast in form—fun, but not a necessity. Leave the fish skin on as it is a protection against fierce heat. Be sure to stuff a bunch of herbs or a couple of lemon halves into the cavity for flavor and plump appearance.

In theory, any broiler or grill can be used for fish, but I find a backyard grill tricky unless it is gas-fired and can be easily controlled. For grilling indoors, I prefer the ridged stovetop griddles that are designed to fit on two burners—one model is actually cast in the outline of a fish. A heavy ridged skillet will also do for steaks and small fillets.

With minimum effort, you can round out a meal of grilled fish with vegetables such as tomatoes, squash, bell peppers, and mushrooms; I marinate them first and then cook them alongside the fish. Other happy partners include green peas, asparagus, or broccoli with hollandaise (page 79) or another butter sauce for white fish, and a chunky tomato salsa for tuna.

2 To test when fish is cooked, poke it with a small knife to see if the center is still translucent (rare), or has become opaque (well done). Or press it with a fingertip: some types, such as tuna, salmon, and scallops, are preferred rare in the center and should still feel soft. Fish that are served well done, such as snapper and cod, should be firm when you press them.

1 Preheat the broiler or light the grill. Brush the hot rack with oil and set the fish on it. Add seasonings or brush the fish with basting sauce and set the rack 3 inches from the heat, or further if the fish is thick. Follow timing in the recipe, basting the fish often and turning it only once after it has browned.

grilling lore

* Choose your grilling fuel with care, as energetic perfumes such as hickory or mesquite will overpower all but the most robust of oily fish.

* You'll find that six ounces is an ample portion of boneless fillets or steaks, while a five-pound whole fish provides six generous servings.

* Before you start to cook, make sure the grill rack is well oiled as fish sticks easily. For broiling, I usually put fish in a baking dish or on a sheet of aluminum foil so I don't have to clean the rack.

* Thin fish should be broiled or grilled about three inches from the heat so the surface browns without the center getting overdone; thick fish will take longer, so a less fierce four to five inches is wise.

* Lastly, be sure to baste broiled or grilled fish generously and often—it won't be a long job as fish cooks so fast.

Grilled Snapper with Mango Tomatillo Salsa

This fruity salsa has plenty of texture, ideal with a hearty fish like snapper.

Serves 4

> **4 portions skinless red snapper**
> **(about 1½ pounds)**
> **olive oil, for brushing**
> **juice of 1 lime**
>
> **FOR THE SALSA**
> **1 jalapeño pepper, cored, seeded, and cut in**
> **small chunks**
> **1 onion, cut in small chunks**
> **4 tomatillos**
> **2 ripe mangos**
> **juice of 2 limes, more to taste**
> **salt and pepper to taste**

Make the salsa: Put the jalapeño pepper and onion in a food processor and work them until coarsely chopped. Remove the husks from the tomatillos, cut them also in chunks, and add them to the processor. Work again until the tomatillo is chopped. Cut the peel from the mangos. Slice on each side of the pit to remove the flesh and coarsely dice it. Add it to the processor with the lime juice, salt, and pepper. Work until the mango is chopped also. Taste and adjust seasoning, including lime juice. Set aside at room temperature for at least 1 and up to 6 hours.

To finish: Light the grill. Brush the red snapper with olive oil and sprinkle with salt, pepper, and lime juice. Grill until brown and the fish flakes easily, allowing 3 to 5 minutes on each side. Serve with the salsa on the side, stirring it before serving.

GETTING AHEAD: Make the salsa up to 6 hours ahead of time, then season and grill the fish just before serving.

Broiled Trout with Almond Brown Butter

Here's a leaner version of the traditional butter-fried trout with almonds.

Serves 2

Wash 2 medium trout (about 3/4 pound each) and dry them on paper towels. Make 3 diagonal slashes on each side so they cook evenly. Sprinkle with salt, pepper, and the juice of 1 lemon. Brush the trout with melted butter and broil or grill them until brown, 4 to 6 minutes. Turn them, brush again with butter, and continue broiling until they just flake easily, 4 to 6 minutes more. Transfer to serving plates and keep warm.

Heat 4 tablespoons butter in a frying pan until sputtering stops. Add 1/4 cup sliced almonds and fry, stirring constantly, until they begin to brown, 2 to 3 minutes. As soon as the almonds start to color, stir in 2 tablespoons of chopped fresh parsley and while the butter is still foaming spoon it over the trout.

Asian Marinade for Grilled or Roast Fish

Rich fish such as tuna, salmon, and mackerel are Asian favorites, excellent with this marinade. It is equally good with grilled vegetables.

Makes 1/2 cup marinade

Put 2 finely chopped garlic cloves, 2 tablespoons chopped fresh cilantro, 1/2 teaspoon dried hot red pepper flakes, and a 1-inch piece of ginger, chopped, in a small bowl. Whisk in 3 tablespoons soy sauce, 1/4 cup sweet rice wine, and 2 tablespoons peanut oil. Taste and adjust the seasoning. Let stand 15 minutes, then pour over the fish and leave to marinate 1/2 to 1 hour before broiling or grilling.

Zesty Caribbean Tuna

In this colorful recipe from the Caribbean, the fish is marinated after grilling rather than before, and the marinade serves also as a basting sauce. The fish is best cooked rare, as the marinade will thoroughly season and lightly pickle it. Try it with grilled vegetables or a tomato salad.

Serves 4

4 tuna steaks (about 1½ pounds)
olive oil, for brushing
4 bay leaves

FOR THE MARINADE
1 large onion
2 garlic cloves
medium bunch of parsley
3/4 cup olive oil
1/3 cup red wine vinegar
pared zest of 1 orange and 2 lemons
2 teaspoons paprika
pinch of cayenne pepper
salt and pepper to taste

Make the marinade: Cut the onion and garlic in chunks and pull parsley leaves from the stems. Combine all the ingredients in a food processor or blender and work until smooth. Taste and adjust the seasoning, including cayenne.

Preheat the broiler or light the grill and brush a rack with oil. Rinse the tuna steaks and pat them dry on paper towels. Season them with salt and pepper and brush them with the marinade. When the broiler or grill is hot, put the steaks on the rack and grill them about 3 inches from the heat, 2 to 3 minutes, basting with the marinade. When brown, turn them over and grill 1 to 2 minutes longer, brushing again with the marinade. Test for doneness with your fingertip—the tuna should be rare and slightly soft.

Remove the tuna from the heat. Pour half of the remaining marinade into a serving dish, add the fish in a single layer, and top with the bay leaves. Pour the rest of the marinade over the fish, cover tightly, and chill at least 8 hours. Let the fish come to room temperature before serving.

simple marinades for fish

In the dry, often fierce heat of roasting, broiling, and grilling, a simple marinade can work wonders for fish. You can soak portions of fish in olive oil with white wine or lemon juice, allowing as little as 15 minutes for fillets or up to an hour for whole fish. The marinade then forms a basting sauce during cooking. Expanding on the theme, I'm fond of grated fresh ginger and chopped shallot in fish marinades, and with a suspicion of garlic, a drizzle of soy, or a splash of Tabasco. Turn to hazelnut, walnut, or dark sesame oils and the field opens further. Spices might include cayenne, paprika, fennel seed, or Chinese five-spice powder. Do not, however, overdo the marinating time as the fish will lose its fresh taste.

Fish is also often marinated to serve raw as in tartare and Latin American seviche. The marinades are similar to those used when roasting or grilling, always with lively flavors and a high acid content, usually of lemon or lime, which "cooks" the fish and turns it white. This happens fast, within 15 minutes when fish is diced or very thinly sliced, so these raw dishes are often prepared just before serving. Seviche, however, may be kept as long as 12 hours and becomes a way to preserve fresh fish in a hot climate. You'll find more marinade ideas on page 52.

Seviche Marinade

Strips of sole or other white fish fillets, or thickly sliced raw sea scallops, are favorites for this Latin American appetizer.

Makes ⅔ cup marinade, enough for 1 pound raw fish or shellfish to serve 6 as a first course

In a bowl mix 1 very finely chopped onion, a finely chopped garlic clove, half a fresh chile pepper, cored, seeded, and finely chopped or a large pinch of cayenne pepper, 6 tablespoons lime or lemon juice, 3 to 4 tablespoons olive oil, salt, and pepper. Taste and adjust seasoning. Add very fresh fish or shellfish, cut in ½-inch strips or slices, with 2 to 3 tablespoons chopped fresh cilantro and a seeded and chopped tomato. Cover and refrigerate ½ hour, or up to 6 hours. Serve chilled.

Balsamic Marinade for Salmon Tartare

A simple first course or main dish for a hot day. Serve tartare very cold, decorated with lime slices and parsley sprigs.

Makes ¼ cup marinade, enough for 1 pound raw salmon to serve 6 as a first course

Stir together in a large bowl 3 shallots, very finely chopped, 2 tablespoons capers, drained, rinsed, and very finely chopped, half a jalapeño pepper, seeded and finely chopped, 1 tablespoon chopped fresh chives, and 1 tablespoon chopped fresh parsley. Stir in 2 tablespoons olive oil, 1 tablespoon lime juice, salt, and pepper. Taste and adjust seasoning. Discard any skin, bone, or membrane from a 1-pound piece of very fresh cold salmon, handling it as lightly as possible. Cut it in ¼-inch slices, then into strips, and finally into dice. Not more than 15 minutes before serving, gently mix the salmon into the flavorings. Taste and adjust seasoning with more olive oil, lime juice, salt, and pepper.

HOW TO SAUTE FISH

Perfect sautéed fish is a joy to behold—colored in butter to an even golden brown, slightly crisp outside, and juicy within. The ideal sautéing temperature is medium high—fish that is pallid and falling apart has been cooked too slowly, while if it is dotted with black spots, the heat was too high. As you would expect, fish with a relatively low fat content such as cod, turbot, halibut, snapper, grouper, striped bass, and flounder are good sautéed, as are shellfish like shrimp and scallops. Sautéed salmon and tuna can be too rich in my opinion.

To provide protection and a light crust, cooks often begin by coating the fish in flour seasoned with salt and pepper. As a child, Emma's job as kitchen helper would be to dip fish fillets in seasoned flour, patting both sides with her hands for an even coating, while I manned the frying pan. It helps to have a pan with a thick base that spreads heat evenly; its surface should be just large enough for the fish to lie flat. You don't need much fat, just enough to thoroughly moisten the bottom of the pan. In a nonstick pan, you can use less fat but the fish will not brown as well (nor will it taste so good). Sautéing is sometimes called pan-frying, though to me this term implies the use of more fat, sometimes as much as $1/2$ inch deep. Deep-frying (page 64) is yet another way to cook fish in fat.

Fish is best sautéed in butter, and perfectionists maintain that the butter should be clarified to raise its scorch point. I've included instructions but frankly, for similar effect, I add a tablespoon or two of vegetable oil and nobody notices the difference. Olive oil is a pleasant-tasting alternative to butter when sautéing—it does not brown the fish so well but is less likely to burn. Sautéed fish is usually served with its cooking juices (unlike deep-fried fish, it should not be drained on paper towels) and a simple garnish of lemon wedges. A coating of oatmeal gives a crunch to rich fish such as mackerel, while diced bacon or sliced sautéed mushrooms go with more robust fish such as bream. Scallops do particularly well sautéed with garlic and tomato in classic Provençale style. Traditional accompaniments are equally simple—pasta or boiled small potatoes and a green vegetable such as broccoli, zucchini, green peas, or sautéed cucumber. And that's really all there is to it.

1 Spread some flour on a plate or sheet of parchment paper and mix with salt and pepper. Dip each side of the fish (here sole fillet) in flour, then pat to coat the fish evenly and dust off the excess. This should be done just before frying so the flour does not absorb fish juices. Heat butter with a little vegetable oil just until it stops sputtering—do not let it brown. Add the fish, cut side down in the case of fillets, and sauté over medium-high heat 1 to 2 minutes, or longer for thick pieces of fish. Shake the pan—if the fish slides on the pan surface, you can be sure it is brown and ready to turn; if it sticks, loosen it with a metal spatula. Turn it and brown the other side. When done, the fish should just flake easily when tested with a fork.

Sole as Little Fish *(Goujonettes)*

Any delicate white fish fillets can be used for gou-jonettes, which are named for the minnows swimming in French rivers. The fillets are cut in diagonal strips to resemble little fish. Serve them with lemon wedges or with Scandinavian Mustard Sauce, *Aïoli,* or Rouille (page 76).

Serves 4

Rinse and dry 1 $^{1}/_{2}$ pounds skinless white fish fillets and cut them in diagonal strips. Put $^{1}/_{2}$ cup flour seasoned with $^{1}/_{2}$ teaspoon salt and $^{1}/_{4}$ teaspoon pepper in a plastic bag, add the fish, and toss until well coated. Spread strips on a plate so they do not stick. Heat 1 tablespoon butter and 1 tablespoon vegetable oil in a frying pan until foaming, add half the strips, and sauté briskly, stirring often, until the fish is browned and just flakes easily, 3 to 4 minutes. Transfer to a platter and keep warm while frying the remaining fish with more butter and oil. Pile fish on the platter and serve lemon wedges or a sauce separately.

Scallops Provençale

Garlic and tomatoes give this recipe a Mediterranean flavor that in no way overwhelms the sweet scallops. Boiled rice is the best accompaniment.

Serves 4

Rinse and dry 1 $^{1}/_{2}$ pounds sea scallops and remove the tough crescent-shaped muscle. Toss to coat them in $^{1}/_{4}$ cup flour seasoned with $^{1}/_{4}$ teaspoon salt and a pinch of pepper. Heat 2 tablespoons vegetable oil and 2 tablespoons butter in a large frying pan until it stops sputtering. Add the scallops and cook until browned, 1 to 2 minutes. Turn and brown the other side—they should still be translucent in the center. Remove them, melt 2 tablespoons more butter, add 4 chopped garlic cloves, and cook until fragrant, about a minute. Stir in 2 large tomatoes, peeled, seeded, and cut in strips, 1 teaspoon each chopped fresh oregano and thyme, salt, and pepper. Sauté 2 to 3 minutes, replace the scallops, and stir to mix. Taste and adjust seasoning. Serve at once.

Mackerel in Oatmeal

To coat fish with rolled oatmeal is an ancient Scottish custom. Mustard sauce makes a piquant contrast.

Serves 6

> 6 mackerel fillets (about 1 $^{1}/_{2}$ pounds)
> $^{1}/_{2}$ cup flour seasoned with $^{1}/_{2}$ teaspoon salt
>   and $^{1}/_{4}$ teaspoon pepper
> 2 eggs, beaten to mix
> 2 cups rolled oats
> 2 tablespoons oil, more if needed
> 2 tablespoons butter, more if needed
> 1 lemon, cut in wedges
>
> FOR THE MUSTARD SAUCE
> 4 tablespoons butter
> 2 tablespoons flour
> 1 $^{1}/_{4}$ cups boiling water
> juice of $^{1}/_{2}$ lemon
> 1 tablespoon Dijon mustard
> salt and pepper to taste

Make the mustard sauce: Melt half the butter in a saucepan and whisk in the flour. Cook until foaming then whisk in the boiling water and simmer until the sauce thickens. Take it from the heat and stir in the lemon juice, Dijon mustard, salt, and pepper. Whisk in the remaining butter, cut in pieces, taste and adjust seasoning, adding more lemon juice or mustard if you like. Keep the sauce warm.

Rinse and dry the mackerel fillets. Spread the seasoned flour on a plate. Put the beaten eggs and oats also on plates. Dip the fish fillets in flour, then in egg and oatmeal, and arrange on parchment or wax paper so they do not overlap. Heat the oil and butter in a frying pan until it stops sputtering. Add half the mackerel fillets and sauté until browned, 2 to 3 minutes. Turn and brown the other side, another 2 to 3 minutes. Fry remaining fillets, using more oil and butter if needed. Arrange them on a platter, add lemon wedges, and serve mustard sauce on the side.

GETTING AHEAD: The mustard sauce can be made ahead, reheated, and finished with butter.

Sole with Lemon and Parsley Butter *(Sole Meunière)*

Sole meunière is one of the great classics of French cuisine (*meunier* in French means miller). A whole sole or sole fillets are coated in flour, sautéed in butter, and finished with pan juices deglazed with lemon juice and parsley. Almost any flat fish fillets, such as turbot, flounder, and pompano, take kindly to a similar coating of flour and gentle browning in butter. Note that thin fillets should be sautéed quickly over quite high heat.

Serves 4

1½ pounds sole fillets
½ cup flour seasoned with ½ teaspoon salt and
    ¼ teaspoon pepper
4 tablespoons butter
2 tablespoons vegetable oil

FOR THE BUTTER
juice of 1 lemon
salt and pepper to taste
3 tablespoons butter
2 tablespoons chopped fresh parsley

Rinse the sole fillets and pat dry with paper towels. If large, cut them in portion-sized pieces. Coat them with the seasoned flour. In a heavy frying pan, heat half the butter and oil until they stop sizzling. Add half of the fillets, cut side down. Sauté them over medium heat until golden brown, 1 to 2 minutes. Turn the fillets and brown the other side, 2 to 3 minutes depending on thickness of the fish. The fillets should just flake easily when tested with a fork. Be careful not to overcook the fish as it will flake into pieces, particularly if the fillets are small. Transfer it to a hot platter and keep it warm while frying the remaining fillets in the rest of the butter and oil.

Make the lemon and parsley butter: Season the lemon juice with salt and pepper. Wipe out the frying pan with paper towels, add the butter, and heat until it stops sputtering. When it starts to brown, turn down the heat and continue cooking until the milk solids at the bottom have browned and the butter has developed a characteristic nutty aroma, 15 to 30 seconds. At once add the lemon juice and swirl the pan to mix the butter and juice. Add the parsley, and while still sizzling, pour the butter over the fish. Serve immediately.

clarified butter

Clarified butter is excellent for sautéing as it can be heated to a high temperature without scorching. If used in hollandaise (page 79) or béarnaise (page 81), it adds richer flavor. It can be kept longer than regular butter.

To clarify butter, melt it over low heat until it gradually separates into three layers: a thin topping of foam, a thick yellow middle layer that is pure butterfat, and a milky-white bottom layer. Both the upper and lower layers must be removed. Skim off the frothy top layer with a metal spoon. Gently pour the yellow clarified butter into a bowl, leaving behind the milky sediment (whey). Alternatively, cover and refrigerate the melted butter until solid. Scrape off the thin top layer and pry away the clarified butter, leaving the sediment.

HOW TO POACH FISH

It was the 18th-century essayist Jonathan Swift who said that a fish should swim three times, first in the sea, then in butter, and lastly in good red wine. I might not go quite so far, but I would strongly recommend poaching as a way to develop the intrinsic flavor of a fish while respecting its texture. Poaching means to simmer very gently in an aromatic broth, a technique that babies the fish along so there's little danger of overcooking. Delicate white fish such as sole, flounder, trout, and snapper are good poached, whether as fillets, steaks, or occasionally left whole.

The liquid used for poaching fish may be fish stock (page 45) or a court bouillon. Court bouillon means quick boiling, and my own version takes only 10 minutes, while still packing a flavor punch. All sorts of seasonings can be introduced to the liquid such as onion, carrot, and celery not to mention herbs such as parsley, thyme, and bay leaf. Asian cooks might include sliced fresh ginger, star anise, or lemon grass. Wine, lemon juice, vinegar, or some other acid is almost obligatory as it stiffens texture as well as sharpening taste. After poaching, the infused liquid from cooking is never discarded but may be served as a broth with the fish, as in Golden Fish Stew with Shrimp and Mussels, or go toward a lush, velvety sauce as in Turbans of Turbot.

1 Rinse the fish fillets (here turbot), dry them, and lay them in a buttered flameproof baking dish, coiling them into "turbans" or folding them so they cook more evenly. You can add a bed of vegetables to the dish such as chopped shallot, thinly sliced fennel, or even seaweed, depending on the recipe. Pour fish stock or court bouillon and wine over the fish to cover it by half or three-quarters, and top with a sheet of buttered parchment paper.

2 Poach the fish on top of the stove or in a preheated 350°F oven for the time given in the recipe. It won't take long, from 3 to 8 minutes on top of the stove, or 10 to 15 minutes in the oven, depending on the thickness and density of the fish pieces. Test the fish with a fork to see if it flakes and has changed from translucent to opaque in the center, showing it is well done. It should feel springy to your touch. Some fish, for example salmon and scallops, may be less cooked, leaving a translucent line in the center.

Court Bouillon

Court bouillon is an aromatic cooking liquid used for poaching fish, and sometimes for meats or vegetables. It is based on water with generous amounts of flavorings and an acid such as lemon juice, wine, or vinegar. I find it very useful as a replacement for fish stock when I don't have any on hand.

Makes 2 cups bouillon

In a medium pan, combine 2 cups water, a few slices of carrot and onion, 6 peppercorns, $^1/_2$ teaspoon salt, a few parsley stems, and a bay leaf. Add the juice of 1 lemon, or $^1/_2$ cup dry white wine, or $^1/_3$ cup of any vinegar. Bring to a boil and simmer, uncovered, for 20 to 30 minutes. The bouillon may be strained, or not, depending on the recipe.

Sole in Cider

In this simple Breton recipe that uses dry apple cider or tart apple juice, any white fish fillets such as flounder or tilapia can replace the sole.

Serves 4

Melt 2 tablespoons butter in a shallow flameproof baking dish, add 2 chopped shallots, and sauté until soft, 2 to 3 minutes. Wash and dry $1^1/_2$ pounds sole fillets and fold them in half, skinned side inward. Lay them on the shallots, sprinkle with salt and pepper, and pour 2 cups dry apple cider or tart apple juice over the fish. Cover with foil and poach on the stove until the fish just flakes easily, 3 to 5 minutes. Remove the fillets and drain them on paper towels.

For the sauce: Stir 2 teaspoons potato starch with 2 tablespoons cider to form a paste. Bring cooking liquid to a boil and whisk the starch paste into the boiling sauce so the sauce thickens. Whisk in 1 tablespoon chopped fresh parsley and taste and adjust seasoning. Arrange the fish on plates, spoon over the sauce, and serve.

Turbans of Turbot in a Mushroom and Tomato Sauce

Fillets of sole or flounder make fine substitutes for the turbot. The rich creamy sauce cries out for an accompaniment of mashed or small boiled potatoes.

Serves 4

> $1^1/_2$ pounds turbot fillets
> salt and white pepper to taste
> 1 tablespoon butter, more for parchment paper
> 2 shallots, finely chopped
> $^1/_2$ pound button mushrooms, thinly sliced
> 2 tomatoes, peeled, seeded, and
>   coarsely chopped
> $1^1/_2$ cups fish stock
> $^1/_2$ cup white wine
>
> FOR THE SAUCE
> 4 tablespoons butter
> 3 tablespoons flour
> $^1/_4$ cup heavy cream
> 2 tablespoons chopped fresh parsley

Rinse and dry the fish fillets, and season them with salt and pepper. If large, cut them in half lengthwise. Coil them in a spiral, skinned side inward, beginning at the head end and wrapping the thin tail to seal the turban shape. Butter a sauté pan and sprinkle with the shallots, mushrooms, tomatoes, and salt and pepper. Top with the fish turbans, spiral side upward. Pour the fish stock and wine over the fish, cover with buttered parchment paper, and simmer gently until opaque in the center and just flaky, 6 to 8 minutes. Let cool slightly, then lift out the turbans, drain on paper towels, cover, and keep them warm.

Make the sauce: Boil the cooking liquid with the vegetables until reduced to about $1^1/_2$ cups. With a fork mash 3 tablespoons of the butter with the flour until smooth. Whisk the butter-flour mixture into the liquid piece by piece, until the sauce thickens slightly. Simmer for 2 minutes, add the cream, and bring just back to a boil. Take the pan from the heat and whisk in the remaining butter, cut in pieces. Add the parsley and taste for seasoning. Arrange the turbans in 4 heatproof dishes or one large dish. Spoon the sauce over to coat the fish completely. Preheat the broiler and brown the fish about 5 inches from the heat, 2 to 3 minutes. Serve immediately.

GETTING AHEAD: Turbans of Turbot is a great dish to make ahead. Store it, covered, in the refrigerator up to 2 days, and reheat it in a 350°F oven until very hot and browned, 12 to 15 minutes.

Poached Scallops with Pernod

The anise flavor of Pernod is an ideal foil for the sweetness of scallops. Find fresh dry-pack scallops if you can as they will brown much better than scallops that have been frozen. Serve with fresh green fettuccine.

Serves 4 as a main dish

> **1½ pounds fresh sea scallops**
> **1 recipe Court Bouillon made with white wine (see opposite)**
> **3 tablespoons Pernod or other anise liqueur**
>
> **FOR THE SAUCE**
> **1 shallot, finely chopped**
> **½ cup heavy cream**
> **6 tablespoons cold butter, cut in pieces**
> **1 tablespoon Pernod, more to taste**
> **1 tablespoon finely chopped fresh parsley**
> **salt and white pepper to taste**

Discard crescent-shaped muscle from the side of each scallop, rinse them, and dry on paper towels. Put the scallops in a saucepan and strain Court Bouillon over them—they should be almost covered. If necessary, add a bit of water. Bring them scarcely to a simmer and poach until they are somewhat firm but still translucent in the center, 2 to 3 minutes. Lift them out with a slotted spoon and set them aside. Boil the cooking liquid so it reduces to about 2 tablespoons of glaze, 5 to 10 minutes.

Replace all the scallops in the pan, pour the Pernod over them, and flambé it, setting it alight with a match and standing back as the flames may rise high (see How to Flambé, right). Remove the scallops and set them aside again.

Make the sauce: Sauté the shallot in the pan until soft but not brown, about 1 minute. Whisk in the cream and bring it to a boil. Take the pan from the heat and gradually whisk in the butter, working the pan on and off the heat so it melts and thickens the sauce creamily. Whisk in the remaining tablespoon of Pernod with the parsley, taste and adjust seasoning, adding more Pernod if you like.

Replace the scallops in the sauce and warm gently, 1 minute. Arrange them on warm plates and spoon over the sauce. Serve at once.

GETTING AHEAD: Cook the scallops up to an hour ahead and make the sauce but do not add the butter. Just before serving, reheat the sauce, whisk in the butter, and then reheat the scallops in the sauce.

how to flambé

Flambéing brings drama to the kitchen as well as toasting and browning the food. Don't be intimidated—it's as simple as pouring 1 to 2 tablespoons of spirits or liqueur per serving into the hot pan then lighting the side of the pan with a match or carefully tipping the edge of the pan to catch the gas flame. Do not add too much liqueur at one time as the flames can be fierce. To be sure the alcohol flames, the recipe may tell you to warm it first. When lit, stand back as the flames may rise high. Spoon the flaming alcohol over the food until the flames die away naturally, indicating the alcohol has evaporated. What's left behind is concentrated flavor.

Cognac complements many savory dishes, such as Five Pepper Steak, page 191. Fruit brandies also come into use, for example apple brandy lends a fruity intensity to pork dishes, while whisky suits fish and beef. Anise-flavored liqueurs are perfect with fish, and the sweet pungency of rum is usually reserved for desserts.

Fish Stews

A variation on the poached fish theme is a stew where you combine fish in one pot with generous amounts of flavorings and vegetables, the more the better. Chowder, seafood gumbo, and bouillabaisse are all versions of fish stew, and there are dozens of other regional recipes. A typical mix might include white fish such as snapper, rockfish, and cod; a rich fish like mackerel; onions, garlic, tomatoes, and saffron for color; or potatoes and cream in a white stew. Fennel and anise-tasting herbs such as tarragon go well in fish stew, as do thyme and bay leaf. In fact, you don't need a set recipe at all, simply combine any fish and vegetables that take your fancy. Shellfish, particularly shrimp and mussels, add a further dimension with their salty taste and glistening shells.

The guiding principle when making fish stew is to layer slowly cooked ingredients such as onion and potato at the bottom of the pot, adding more delicate items like tomato on top, sometimes later in the cooking process. Cut ingredients into pieces that will cook in more or less the same time frame. And add a cooking liquid (often wine or fish stock) with lots of taste, making sure it is reduced and concentrated before adding it to the stew; if you try to reduce it later, the fish will be overcooked.

Golden Fish Stew with Shrimp and Mussels

Served on its own, or with sliced baguette, this fish stew is an easy one-pot supper and generous meal in itself. Any firm white fish such as snapper, halibut, or mahi mahi is suitable. Often the fish breaks up and helps thicken the broth, highlighting the shellfish.

Serves 6

2 tablespoons butter

1 large fennel bulb (about 3/4 pound), sliced

1 onion, chopped

salt and white pepper to taste

4 large firm potatoes (about 2 pounds), peeled and cut in 1-inch cubes

large pinch of saffron threads

2 cups fish stock

1 bay leaf

2 pounds mussels

1 pound white fish fillets, skinned and cut in 1½-inch pieces

2 cups milk

½ pound cooked peeled medium shrimp

1 cup heavy cream

2 tablespoons chopped fresh parsley

Melt the butter in a large casserole and add the fennel, onion, salt, and pepper. Sauté gently, stirring occasionally, until the vegetables are translucent but not brown, 7 to 10 minutes.

Spread the potatoes over the fennel. Mix the saffron with the fish stock and pour it over the potatoes. Add the bay leaf, cover, and bring to a boil, then reduce the heat and simmer until the potatoes are almost tender, 12 to 15 minutes. Meanwhile, clean the mussels thoroughly (see page 136).

When the potatoes are tender, spread the fish over them and add the milk. Stir to mix the ingredients and spread the color of the saffron. Add the mussels, cover tightly, and simmer until the mussels have opened and the fish is just tender when flaked with a fork, 5 to 7 minutes. Note that the milk should simmer, not boil, or it may curdle.

Add the shrimp, cream, and parsley and bring just to a boil. Discard the bay leaf and taste and adjust the seasoning. Serve the stew from the casserole or in individual bowls.

GETTING AHEAD: Ingredients can be prepared and chilled several hours ahead, but I try to cook the stew just before serving so as to keep the fresh aroma of the fish.

Spicy Catfish Stew with Coconut Milk

This looks like a long list of ingredients, but many of them you'll have in your cupboard and all chopping is done in the food processor. Any white fish fillets such as perch or tilapia can replace the catfish. Serve the stew with boiled rice.

Serves 4

2 medium onions, cut in chunks

4 garlic cloves, peeled

2 stalks lemon grass, outer husks removed and inner core cut in chunks

2-inch piece of ginger, peeled and sliced

1 fresh jalapeño chile pepper, seeded and sliced

1 tablespoon coriander seed

2 teaspoons fennel seed

1 teaspoon cumin seed

1 teaspoon ground turmeric

1/2 teaspoon ground nutmeg

1 teaspoon salt, more to taste

1 2/3 cup unsweetened coconut milk (a 13.5-fluid-ounce can)

1 1/2 pounds catfish fillets

1 pound tomatoes, peeled and thinly sliced

juice of 1 lime, more to taste

2 to 3 tablespoons chopped fresh cilantro

Put the onion, garlic, lemon grass, ginger, chile pepper, and coriander, fennel, and cumin seeds in a food processor and purée until finely chopped. Transfer the purée to a saucepan and stir in the turmeric, nutmeg, salt, and coconut milk. Bring to a boil and simmer 10 minutes, stirring often. Taste, adding more of any of the spices as you prefer.

Rinse the fish, dry it, and cut it in diagonal strips. Put it in a medium saucepan and top with the tomatoes. Pour the spice broth over the fish and bring just to a simmer, stirring once or twice. Simmer until the fish just flakes, 3 to 5 minutes. Just before serving, stir in the lime juice and cilantro, and taste and adjust seasoning.

GETTING AHEAD: The spicy broth can be prepared up to 2 days ahead and refrigerated. Reheat it, cook the fish, and add lime juice and cilantro just before serving.

Spicy Catfish Stew with Coconut Milk

HOW TO SHUCK OYSTERS

An oyster's habitat governs its taste. Oysters are raised in brackish waters at the mouth of rivers where fresh and sea waters meet, and it is these waters that give them their essential character and taste, and often their names such as Long Island, Olympia, Malpecque, or Blue Point. Oysters also vary enormously in size and shape—round or elongated, flat, or hollow and full of juice. For most of us, oysters are a luxury, with prices varying with the season and place of origin. They are carefully graded by size, the larger being usually (though not always) more expensive. Rely on your supplier to find you the best. When shucking (opening) oysters, discard any shell that is not tightly shut or smells unpleasant. Oysters are remarkably resilient and provided they are kept damp and cold, preferably near but not actually on ice, they can survive for a week or two out of water. Shucked oysters are good for two days if refrigerated in an airtight container.

Habitual shuckers of oysters have their favorite tools. The traditional knife is short and pointed, often with a guard. Always wear a tough glove or use a thick cloth to protect your hand if the knife slips. The trick in opening an oyster is to insert the knifepoint very near the hinge of the shell with a decisive push and sharp twist. If you hesitate, the oyster tenses up and clings all the more—or so they say. Everyone has their own ruse. James Beard, who came from oyster country in Oregon, was a hands-on man, spurning protective gloves, and I've seen Julia Child use a beer can opener.

Once opened, raw oysters on the half shell should be bedded flat on platters of crushed ice and sent to table at once with their trimmings—there's quite a choice, as you'll see listed here. For baking, oysters are sauced or stuffed, and then perched on rock salt to keep them steady in the oven. Given the risk that salt crystals may fall into the shells, why not substitute rounds of baguette, cutting out the middle to accommodate the shells? Scalloped oysters, served with crusty bread, are a very American treat. Europeans are less imaginative: they prefer their oysters straight from the shell—salty, cold, and spiked with a trickle of lemon.

1 First scrub oysters in cold water to remove any grit or weed on the shells. Take a short, pointed oyster knife in one hand and cover your other hand with a thick cloth or glove. Grip the oyster shell in your palm, flat side upward and hinge toward you. Keeping the oyster level with the knife, insert the point of the blade into the hinge and twist to pry open the shell.

Sliding the knife across the top shell, cut the muscle of the oyster loose and discard the shell. With the knife, loosen the oyster meat in the lower, hollow shell. If shucking the meat, tip it with the juice (often called the liquor) into a bowl.

Maryland Scalloped Oysters

These oysters can be baked in ramekins or in one large baking dish, where they will take about 10 minutes longer to cook. Serve them with plenty of crusty bread to soak up the juices.

Serves 4

> **1 pint shucked oysters, with juices**
> **5 tablespoons butter**
> **3 celery stalks, chopped**
> **1 large onion, chopped**
> **salt and pepper to taste**
> **3 to 4 tablespoons chopped fresh parsley**
> **16 to 20 unsalted soda crackers**
> **¼ cup light cream**
> **1½ teaspoons Worcestershire sauce**
> **½ teaspoon Tabasco, more to taste**
>
> **4 ramekins or custard cups (1 cup each)**

Preheat the oven to 350°F. Melt 2 tablespoons of the butter in a frying pan. Stir in the celery and onion with salt and pepper. Sauté over low heat, stirring often, until soft but not brown, 5 to 7 minutes. Remove the vegetables, add the parsley, and set aside. Melt the remaining butter in the pan.

Put the crackers in a plastic bag and crush them with a rolling pin to medium crumbs. There should be about 1 cup. Stir them into the melted butter with salt and pepper. Drain the oysters, reserving juices. Stir the cream, Worcestershire, Tabasco, salt, and pepper into the juices. Taste and adjust seasoning—the cream should be quite spicy—then add it to the oysters.

Spoon half the oysters with some cream into the ramekins. Spread reserved vegetables on top and add remaining oysters and cream. Sprinkle with the buttered crumbs.

To finish: Set the ramekins on a baking sheet and bake 25 to 30 minutes, until the crumbs are brown and sauce is bubbling. Serve at once.

GETTING AHEAD: The oysters can be prepared up to 4 hours ahead and kept in the refrigerator. Bake them just before serving.

Oysters on the Half Shell with the Works

I don't need to tell you how many oysters on the half shell to eat—if you're an aficionado, six is a tease, a dozen is for starters, and you'll take it from there. Condiments are also a matter of personal taste. For me, a squeeze of lemon juice does the job, with pumpernickel bread on the side, but you and your friends may pick and choose from among the following.

Serves 2

> **A dozen or more oysters**
>
> **FOR THE MIGNONETTE SAUCE**
> **1 teaspoon cracked black pepper**
> **1 shallot, very finely chopped**
> **⅓ cup red wine vinegar**
> **pinch of salt**
>
> **FOR THE CONDIMENTS**
> **lemons, cut in wedges**
> **shallots, very finely chopped**
> **fresh horseradish, coarsely grated**
> **red wine or sherry vinegar**
> **Worcestershire sauce**
> **Tabasco**
> **pumpernickel bread, thinly sliced**
> **butter, softened**

Make the mignonette sauce: Whisk the ingredients together and put them in a small bowl. Prepare the condiments: Put the lemons, shallots, horseradish, vinegar, and sauces in small bowls. Spread the bread thinly with butter and arrange it overlapping on a plate.

Scrub the oysters. Open them, working over a bowl to catch any juices. Discard the flat top shells. Slide the knife under each oyster to loosen the meat, leaving them in the shell. Set the oysters on a platter of crushed ice and spoon the reserved juices over them. Pass the condiments and bread separately.

GETTING AHEAD: The condiments can be readied ahead of time, but the oysters should be kept chilled and served as soon as they are opened.

HOW TO CLEAN AND
STEAM MUSSELS

We once had a beach house near Dieppe, on the northern coast of France. Swimming was chilly, it rained rather often, but the seafood was divine. Glittering piles of little black mussels appeared each morning in the market and would be gone by noon, bringing the scent of the sea straight into the kitchen. Emma and Simon were small then, and loved mussels as a legitimate excuse to eat with their fingers, using an empty shell as pincer to pry out the meat.

Fresh, live mussels are an imperative. Even when kept damp and cold, they will last only a few days out of the water. They are particularly subject to contamination, so it can be risky to gather mussels (or indeed any shellfish) in the wild. Always buy cultivated varieties that come from a reliable source. Since they are grown on ropes so the tide can wash through them, you'll see a string-like "beard" that needs to be removed clinging to many shells. Mussels should be steamed in a deep pan with enough room for the shells to expand as they gape open. Herbs, peppercorns, a finely chopped shallot or onion, a dried chile, or a cup of wine added to the pan will flavor the mussels and the juices. This juice, with or without cream or other additions, forms a broth for the mussels. The broth and mussels may be served together in a bowl, or the mussels may be taken from their shells for a soup based on the broth.

Mussels are not nearly as varied as oysters, but they do come in several sizes. Small mussels are more piquant and tingling on the tongue, good for soup and for serving steamed in big bowls with French fries on the side. Larger mussels are plump and rich, delicious in zesty Mediterranean salads or stuffed on the half shell. The meat inside a mussel may range from beige to bright orange, but color is not an indication of taste.

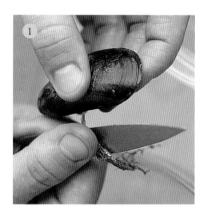

1 Clean mussels not more than an hour before cooking. Rinse them under cold water and drain in a colander (they will quickly die if left to soak in fresh water). Shells that gape open are suspect, so tap them on the counter and discard any that do not close or are damaged; also discard any mussels that are still closed after steaming. With a small knife, pull off the "beard" and scrape the mussels clean of any barnacles.

2 To steam mussels open: Put them in a deep pan with any flavorings according to the recipe. Cover and cook over high heat 2 to 3 minutes. Stir with a big spoon (the bottom shells will already have opened) and continue 2 to 3 minutes more until all the shells are open. Lift the mussels from the pot, leaving the sea-imbued juices. You'll likely see sediment, so strain the juice or carefully pour it off leaving grit behind. This juice makes a broth for the mussels.

Brussels Stuffed Mussels

In a popular quarter of Brussels, the streets are lined with restaurants specializing in mussels stuffed in a dozen styles. This recipe with tomato and cheese is my favorite. (Note that the bread is for stabilizing the mussel shells, not for eating!) Large mussels are usually sold by the count, but I'm giving the weight as well.

Serves 4

2 to 3 dozen large mussels (4 to 6 pounds)
¼ cup dry white wine
baguette of bread
oil for the baking sheet

FOR THE STUFFING
3 tablespoons butter, more for sprinkling
1 onion, finely chopped
2 garlic cloves, finely chopped
4 tomatoes, peeled, seeded, and chopped
1 teaspoon chopped fresh thyme
freshly ground black pepper to taste
1 cup grated Gruyère cheese

Clean the mussels under cold running water and remove their beards. Discard any that are open and do not close when tapped on the counter. Put them in a large saucepan, pour the wine over them, and add the lid. Cook over high heat, stirring once, until the shells open, 5 to 7 minutes. Discard the top shell from each mussel and remove the rubbery ring around each one; discard any shells that do not open. Pour off and reserve the mussel broth, leaving sediment behind.

Make the stuffing: Melt the butter in a frying pan and fry the onion until soft, 4 to 5 minutes. Stir in the garlic, tomatoes, thyme, and pepper and simmer until pulpy, stirring often, 5 to 8 minutes. Add ½ cup of the mussel liquid and simmer until very thick, 1 to 2 minutes. Taste and adjust seasoning—as the mussels are salty, more salt may not be needed.

Thinly slice the baguette and lay the slices on an oiled baking sheet. Set the mussels in their shells on the bread rounds so they are level. Spoon filling on the mussels and sprinkle with grated cheese and more melted butter.

To finish: Preheat the broiler. Broil the mussels until very hot and browned, 2 to 3 minutes. Transfer them, with bread rounds, to large plates. Serve at once.

GETTING AHEAD: Prepare the mussels up to 2 hours ahead and refrigerate them. Broil them just before serving.

Mussels with White Wine and Herbs *(Moules Marinière)*

It's hard to beat a great classic. For a richer broth, stir in some cream just before serving.

Serves 4

4 to 6 pounds mussels
½ bottle (375 ml) white wine
3 shallots, very finely chopped
1 garlic clove, finely chopped
bouquet garni of 2 bay leaves and a few sprigs
   of thyme and parsley
freshly ground black pepper to taste
2 tablespoons coarsely chopped fresh parsley

Clean the mussels under cold running water and remove their beards. Discard any open ones that do not close when tapped on the counter.

Put the wine, shallots, garlic, bouquet garni, and plenty of freshly ground black pepper in a large pot. Bring to a boil and simmer for 2 minutes. Add the mussels, cover, and steam them over high heat, stirring once, until they open, 5 to 7 minutes. Discard any that do not open.

Stir in the parsley and taste the broth for seasoning. As the mussels are salty, the broth may not need salt. Serve the mussels in soup bowls with the liquid spooned over them. Note that the sand and grit from inside the mussels will have fallen to the bottom of the broth, so spoon the liquid carefully so as to leave the grit behind. (Or strain the broth through cheesecloth.)

GETTING AHEAD: Clean the mussels and refrigerate them. Assemble and simmer the wine broth, leaving it on the stove to cook mussels at the last minute.

HOW TO PEEL AND DEVEIN SHRIMP

My first paid job as a child was peeling baby shrimp for my father at a dime a shrimp—he hated to do it himself and I could quickly earn enough for an ice cream cone. My small fingers found it easy to pull the shrimp shell apart under the tail, stripping it away along the back so a quick nip of the thumbnail detached the meat (some cooks leave the tail flanges for decoration.) I was excused removal of the dark intestinal vein that runs along the back of shrimp, as that involved a knife. This vein can be bitter, particularly in large shrimp.

Whole shrimp equipped with head, body, and handsome antennae are rarely seen on sales counters here in the U.S. Usually the tail (the meaty part) has already been separated before shipping. These tails are marketed four ways: cooked in the shell; cooked and peeled; raw in the shell; and very occasionally raw and peeled. They are sold by count—medium shrimp with shell range from 25 to 50 per pound, large plump ones come as low as a dozen, and jumbos, often called gambas, can be as few as 6 to the pound. A pound of medium or large shrimp serves three people, but jumbos do not go so far—

you should allow at least three tails per person. When choosing raw or cooked shrimp, a salty sea smell is the clue to freshness. Store shrimp on ice and use them within two days.

You can make most recipes with almost any type of shrimp, but cooking time will vary. Depending on size, raw peeled shrimp cook in one to three minutes, and you should allow only one minute more if they are in the shells. Overcooking is all too easy. When done just right, shrimp shells should be opaque and still clinging to the meat, not white or calcified. Shrunken flesh and tails contracted in a tight circle are further signs of overcooking. Peeled shrimp need to be watched even more closely on the stove. In less than a minute, small ones lose their translucency and turn pink, showing they are done. When shrimp are already cooked, reheating can take as little as a minute, especially if they are already peeled.

We all know what flavorings are good with shrimp—butter, olive oil, Provençale herbs, garlic, a dash of black pepper or chile, lemon, lime, saffron, almonds, coconut, sesame—need I say more?

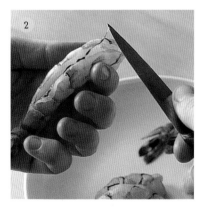

1 With scissors, cut between the legs of the shrimp to the tail. With both thumbs, pry open and pull off the shell to release the meat.

2 To remove the dark intestinal vein, make a shallow cut along the back of the shrimp with a small knife and pull out the vein. (Sometimes the vein is scarcely visible and does not need cleaning.)

Pan-Fried Salt and Pepper Shrimp

Here's the place to use your special sea salt and the very best freshly ground black pepper, reputed to come from Tellicherry in India. Serve the shrimp as an appetizer, and they will vanish all too fast!

Serves 4 as a first course

Peel and devein 1 1/2 pounds large raw shrimp. In a medium bowl, mix 1/4 cup cornstarch, 1 tablespoon coarse sea salt, and 2 teaspoons freshly ground black pepper. Add the shrimp and toss until coated. Heat 2 tablespoons vegetable oil in a skillet or large frying pan over medium heat. When almost smoking, add half the shrimp, spreading them flat. Press them down with another heavy pan on top. Fry until lightly browned, 1 to 2 minutes. Remove the pan, turn the shrimp, press again, and brown the other side, 1 to 2 minutes longer. Repeat with remaining shrimp, adding more oil if necessary. Serve very hot.

how to butterfly shrimp

When I butterfly shrimp, I like to leave the tail flange to hold the meat together.

1 Peel the shrimp and set it flat on the work surface. Make a full-length cut along the back about three-quarters of the way through the flesh, so the meat opens to lie almost flat but is still attached at the tail. Discard the intestinal vein. When cooked, the meat will curl prettily into crescents.

Shrimp on Shrimp

The original Renaissance recipe for these stuffed shrimp calls for verjuice, the sour grape juice still made today by a few discriminating vineyards. Lemon juice is a good substitute.

Serves 4

> **1 1/2 pounds large cooked shrimp**
> **1/2 cup chopped blanched almonds**
> **1/2 cup grated Parmesan cheese**
> **2 tablespoons chopped fresh parsley**
> **1 tablespoon chopped fresh oregano**
> **2 tablespoons verjuice or lemon juice, more to taste**
> **salt and pepper to taste**
> **4 egg yolks**
> **2 to 3 tablespoons olive oil, more for the baking dish**

Oil a baking dish. Peel and butterfly 1 pound of the shrimp. Set them backs down in the baking dish and spread the halves flat. Peel the remaining shrimp and put them in a food processor. Add the almonds, Parmesan cheese, parsley, oregano, verjuice, salt, and pepper. Pureé until the mixture is coarsely chopped. Taste and adjust seasoning, adding more verjuice if you like. Add the egg yolks to bind the mixture and pureé briefly to mix.

To finish: Preheat the broiler. Using a tablespoon, pile the stuffing on the shrimp and moisten them with the olive oil. Broil until very hot and browned, 4 to 5 minutes. The time will vary depending on the size of the shrimp. Serve hot or at room temperature.

GETTING AHEAD: Prepare the dish up to 6 hours ahead, cover, and store in the refrigerator. Moisten with olive oil and broil the shrimp just before serving.

Shrimp Kebabs with Cherry Tomatoes and Cucumber

Shrimp Kebabs with Cherry Tomatoes and Cucumber

A rice pilaf is all that's needed with these kebabs.

Serves 4

> 1½ pounds large raw shrimp
> 1 pound cherry tomatoes
>
> FOR THE MARINADE
> ⅓ cup vegetable oil
> juice of 1 lime
> 2-inch piece of cucumber
> 1½-inch piece of ginger, grated
> 1 tablespoon soy sauce
> 1 garlic clove, finely chopped
> ½ teaspoon sugar
> ½ teaspoon salt
> pinch of dried hot red pepper flakes
> 2 tablespoons chopped fresh coriander
>
> 8 wooden skewers, soaked in water

Peel the shrimp and remove the veins. Put the shrimp in a bowl and add the cherry tomatoes.

Make the marinade: Whisk the oil with the lime juice. Grate the cucumber, including peel, and stir it into the lime juice mixture with the remaining marinade ingredients. Taste and adjust the seasoning, including flavorings. Add the marinade to the shrimp and tomatoes and toss well to coat them. Cover the bowl and chill 2 to 4 hours, stirring occasionally.

To finish: Preheat the broiler or light the grill. Drain the shrimp and tomatoes, reserving the marinade. Drain the kebab skewers and thread shrimp and tomatoes onto them. Broil or grill the kebabs about 3 inches from the heat, turning once, 4 to 6 minutes, until the shrimp are no longer transparent and the tomatoes are split and charred. Baste the kebabs often during cooking with the reserved marinade.

GETTING AHEAD: An extra hour or two of marinating will do no harm.

Stir-Fried Shrimp with Water Chestnuts and Soba Noodles

Soba noodles are made with buckwheat, giving them nutty flavor and light texture.

Serves 4

> 1½ pounds medium raw shrimp, peeled
>   and deveined
> salt to taste
> 5 scallions
> 3 tablespoons soy sauce, more to taste
> 1 teaspoon Thai red chile paste, more to taste
> ¾ pound soba noodles
> 3 tablespoons vegetable oil
> 2 garlic cloves, chopped
> 1 tablespoon chopped fresh ginger
> 8-ounce can sliced water chestnuts, drained
> 1 teaspoon dark sesame oil

Bring a large pan of salted water to a boil. Peel and devein the shrimp. Trim the scallions, cut the green part in thin diagonal slices, and chop the white. Stir together the soy sauce and chile paste in a small bowl. Add the noodles to the boiling water, stir, and simmer for 1 to 2 minutes, until they are tender but still chewy. Drain and set aside.

Meanwhile, start stir-frying: Heat a wok over high heat for about 30 seconds. Drizzle the oil around the sides, add the chopped white scallion, garlic, and ginger and stir-fry until fragrant, ½ to 1 minute. Add the shrimp and stir-fry until pink and no longer translucent, 1 to 2 minutes. Stir in the chestnuts and heat briefly. Add the noodles to the wok and stir-fry until mixed and hot. Add the soy sauce mixture and continue tossing until well mixed, about 30 seconds. Take from the heat, add the sliced green scallion and sesame oil, and toss well. Taste and adjust seasoning with soy sauce and chile paste. Serve at once.

GETTING AHEAD: Stir fries must be cooked at the last minute, but the shrimp can be peeled and the flavorings chopped and sliced up to 2 hours ahead and refrigerated.

CHAPTER SIX from the farmyard

This chapter is an indulgence. I enjoy a whole roast bird more than any other dish, and here there are three of them: chicken, duck, and a Thanksgiving turkey. Feasting is the name of the game—simple though it is, a whole roast chicken adds a sense of occasion to the table. Chicken can be seasoned in many different ways and offers a choice of white meat, dark meat, crispy skin, and tidbits like the oyster meat to suit a variety of tastes. A whole roast duck is even more of a treat, whether aromatic with dry spices or sweet with orange and caramel, or with cherries. As for a whole roast turkey, you'll find a complete array of traditional stuffings, accompaniments, and gravy, along with detailed instructions for roasting and carving.

Chicken breast is our most popular cut—everyday fare—but there's no need for it to be routine. Once you know how to debone and trim a breast yourself (you can save a bit of money that way), you can easily cut a pocket for holding a savory stuffing. Alternatively, the meat can be butterflied and flattened to form an escalope, a wonderfully versatile item that can be sautéed as one piece or cut into smaller ones called piccata. A whole turkey breast, once trimmed, will yield not just one but a dozen or more escalopes, ready for the pan.

Mark and I are the dark-meat lovers of the family, preferring legs and thighs to the white breast. We reckon that dark meat is moister and tastier, and it shrinks less as it includes a bone. I've strong opinions about chicken pieces cut from a whole bird, too. Supermarkets tend to cut them into awkward pieces, some with over-generous amounts of meat, others consisting mainly of backbone. When you want a variety of pieces for old favorites such as coq au vin, I urge you to buy a whole bird and cut it into even portions of meat yourself.

One advantage of today's poultry is its consistent, if unexciting, quality. However, if you are lucky enough to find an artisan producer of free-range birds, they will be worth every extra dollar in terms of flavor and texture. Note that washing poultry only makes it harder to brown and does not destroy harmful salmonella. Heat is the key to that. When poultry is cooked to well done, a temperature of 165°F, with no trace of pink juices, it's fine.

HOW TO ROAST A CHICKEN

When we get together as a family, whether with Simon in Russia, Emma in California, or at home in France, roast chicken is how we celebrate. Even on our own, Mark and I have roast chicken at least once a week. I rarely do anything fancy, just truss the chicken and put some herbs inside for flavor, top it with butter, salt, and pepper and into the oven it goes. Not only do we have a delicious dinner for up to four but any leftovers are useful the following day, while the carcass goes to make stock for soup or gravy. A bargain.

Trussing the chicken keeps it in a neat shape. It cooks more evenly, looks attractive for serving, and holds together well for carving. Trussing string will also hold aromatic herbs and seasonings in place in the cavity. I find that mixtures of parsley, bay leaf, and sage or thyme add so much character to the cooked bird; in Italy sprigs of rosemary are customary. In a British chicken, you might find a halved onion stuck with a clove, and in Mediterranean climates, some garlic cloves or a whole lemon pricked with a skewer to release a bit of juice. The skin of the bird also needs seasoning, possibly with a spiced or herbal rub, or simply with salt and pepper.

Cooks often debate whether to roast a chicken quickly in high heat, or slowly for a longer time. As so often, I follow the French and begin with high heat, then lower the temperature to cook the meat more slowly and thoroughly.

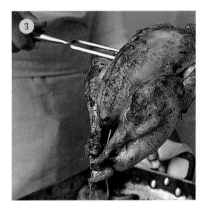

1 After seasoning the cavity, truss the chicken so it maintains a compact shape (see How to Truss a Bird, page 146), and set it in a buttered roasting pan so it does not stick. Spread the skin with butter and sprinkle it with salt, pepper, and any seasoning called for in the recipe. If you like, add an onion and carrot, cut in pieces, to flavor the gravy.

2 To keep the meat moist during cooking, turn the chicken from one leg to another, then breast down and finally breast upward again to crisp the skin. Most important of all, you must baste often.

3 A chicken should be thoroughly cooked with no trace of pink at the joints. There are several tell-tale signs for when it is done: The meat will start to shrink from the end of the leg and the drumstick will be slightly flexible when you pull it. The skin should be evenly golden and crisp. Lift the bird with a two-pronged fork and tip the juices from the cavity—they should run clear, not pink. This last test is infallible. I rarely bother with a thermometer, but if you like to cross-check, insert it in the thickest part of the chicken's thigh: it should register about 165°F.

Our family is convinced that only butter will do for succulent brown skin. You may want to experiment with olive oil or a basting sauce, but keep it simple so the chicken flavor is not masked. Yet another joy of roast chicken is the pan gravy. Thick or thin, flavored with wine or other condiments, whatever you do, don't pass up those delicious caramelized juices in the bottom of the pan.

chicken checkpoints

* I allow about one pound of chicken per person, so a five-pound chicken serves four to five, but much depends on appetites.

* For a self-basting chicken, insert softened butter underneath the skin, gently easing skin away from the breast and top of the legs with your fingers, then spreading the meat with butter. (Add chopped herbs, garlic, lemon juice, hot chile, or whatever seasoning you fancy to the butter.) You will need to baste much less often during cooking.

* When a chicken is cooked, cover it with aluminum foil and let it rest 10 to 15 minutes before carving. Juices will be redistributed throughout the meat so it is easier to carve.

* You'll find substantial stuffings for roast birds based on toasted white bread or wild rice on pages 166 to 167, but they are best cooked separately rather than inside the bird.

Mom's Roast Chicken with Herbs and Butter

For chicken I like an unthickened pan gravy, but if you prefer a traditional thickened gravy, you'll find out all about it on page 87. A few little potatoes, fried in butter or boiled in their skins, are the best accompaniment.

Serves 4

> **1 large chicken (4 to 5 pounds)**
> **salt and pepper to taste**
> **2 medium bunches of herbs, such as thyme, rosemary, or sage**
> **4 tablespoons butter, softened**
> **3 cups chicken stock**

Preheat the oven to 450°F. Wipe the inside of the chicken with paper towels and season both inside and outside with salt and pepper. Put the herbs inside the cavity and truss with string (see page 146). If you like, put some herbs under the skin of the breast. Spread it with the butter and set it on its back in a roasting pan. Roast the chicken until it sizzles and starts to brown, 12 to 15 minutes.

Lower the oven heat to 375°F and turn the chicken on one leg. Continue roasting, basting every 10 minutes and turning the bird onto its other leg, then onto its breast. Finally, after about 30 more minutes, turn the bird onto its back so the breast skin crispens. Continue roasting, 15 to 30 minutes, basting often, until the juices run clear, and the leg joint feels pliable.

Transfer the chicken to a carving board and cover it loosely with foil. For the pan gravy, pour off all but a tablespoon of fat from the pan. Set the roasting pan on a burner and add the stock. Bring to a boil and scrape to dissolve the pan juices. Boil rapidly for 10 to 15 minutes, until it thickens slightly and the bubbles break more slowly. Taste and adjust seasoning. I rarely bother to strain pan gravy, but you may like to do so at this point. Carve the chicken, discarding trussing strings and herbs from the cavity, and serve with the gravy.

GETTING AHEAD: Roast chicken can wait up to half an hour, in a warm place, covered loosely.

how to truss a bird

Chicken, duck, and other smaller birds cook much more evenly in the oven if they are trussed, so the bird is compact. With this method, all you need is string, no trussing needle or skewers. The breast of the bird emerges smooth and golden brown from roasting, with no disfiguring string stretched across it.

2 With the legs pointing away from you, take the strings along the sides of the body, inside the legs.

1 So the bird is easier to carve, remove the wishbone, inserting a knife under the skin and cutting around the bone to loosen it. Tie a long piece of string around the tail of the bird and knot it over the leg joints to hold them together.

3 Flip the bird toward you, back upward. Fold the neck skin along the back of the bird and twist the wing pinions to hold it in place. Pull the strings into the center of the triangle formed by the wing bones. Pull the string tight, knot it, and trim. Turn the bird onto its back. It will sit firmly in a compact shape.

Chicken with Lemon and Parmesan

Cooking chicken in a closed casserole keeps it moist, ideal for small birds of 3 to 4 pounds. Fettuccine is the perfect accompaniment.

Serves 2 to 3

Preheat the oven to 375°F. Truss a 3- to 4-pound chicken and sprinkle it with salt and pepper. Heat 2 tablespoons butter in a heavy casserole and brown the chicken on all sides over medium heat, taking 8 to 10 minutes. Add the pared zest of 2 lemons, cover the pan, and pot roast in the oven until very tender, 30 to 40 minutes. Test by lifting the chicken with a two-pronged fork; the juice from the cavity should run clear not pink.

Transfer the chicken to a carving board and keep it warm. Discard any fat from the pan. Add ³/4 cup chicken stock and bring it to a boil, stirring to deglaze the pan juices. Strain juices into a saucepan. Add 3 to 4 tablespoons heavy cream and bring this gravy just back to a boil. Mix 1 teaspoon arrowroot to a paste with 1 tablespoon water. Whisk the paste into the hot gravy—it will thicken at once. Take it from the heat, whisk in ¹/4 cup grated Parmesan cheese, and taste for seasoning. Discard trussing strings and carve the chicken (see How to Carve a Chicken, opposite page). Serve it with the lemon and Parmesan gravy.

Drunken Chicken

A day-long soak in a wine marinade gives roast chicken a spectacular golden glaze as well as adding punchy flavor!

Serves 4

Combine the following ingredients in a heavy-duty plastic bag set over a bowl: 2 cups dry white wine, $1/4$ cup brandy, 1 grated carrot, 1 grated onion, 2 bay leaves, 2 to 3 sprigs thyme, and 2 to 3 sprigs parsley. Truss your chicken (any size), put it in the bag and seal it, pushing out as much air as possible. Marinate the chicken in the refrigerator for a day, turning it from time to time. Before roasting, drain and dry it with paper towels, discarding the marinade. Roast as for Mom's Roast Chicken with Herbs and Butter (page 145), omitting the herbs.

Chicken Casserole with Forty Garlic Cloves

Don't be nervous about the quantity of garlic here, you'll be amazed how garlic mellows in the oven's heat. I avoid the work of peeling the cloves and leave guests to squeeze out the soft pulp.

Serves 4

Follow the recipe for Mom's Roast Chicken with Herbs and Butter (page 145), seasoning the chicken and trussing with herbs. Melt the butter in a deep casserole and brown the chicken on all sides, ending on its back. Add 40 unpeeled garlic cloves with chicken stock to cover them, about 2 cups. Cover and roast the chicken in a preheated 375°F oven, turning it from time to time, until done, 50 to 60 minutes (use the same tests as for Mom's Roast Chicken). Transfer the chicken and half the garlic to a platter and keep warm. Push the remaining garlic and cooking juices through a sieve to extract the garlic pulp and make a sauce. Reheat the sauce, taste it, and adjust the seasoning.

how to carve a chicken or duck

A chicken of 4 pounds or more should be carved with the breast in slices so everyone has some dark and some white meat (in our family, competition is keen). A smaller chicken is usually cut in 4 pieces, with breast and legs left whole. A duck is carved much the same way, with long, thin slices cut from the breast of a large bird. You'll find that the leg joints of a duck can be hard to locate as they are tucked farther under the bird.

1 Let the bird stand for 10 minutes, covered, in a warm place. Discard the trussing string and set the bird, back down, on a carving board. Cut the skin between the leg and breast. With a carving fork, turn the bird on its side. Cut carefully around the nugget of meat (the oyster) that lies halfway along the backbone so that it remains attached to the thigh.

2 With the flat of the knife, force the leg forward to snap the joint, then cut through the joint. Continue cutting to remove meat from the front of the carcass. After detaching the leg, halve it by cutting through the joint, using the white line of fat on the underside as a guide.

3 To detach the white meat: Cut just above the wing bone, down through the joint and remove it on both sides. Carve the breast in slices parallel to the rib cage. Remove leg and breast meat on the other side. You'll have 4 pieces of dark meat from the leg, 2 wings, and white meat from the breast cut in slices.

HOW TO CUT AND COOK CHICKEN PIECES

When we were first married, it was perfect. Mark liked the white meat of chicken and I preferred the dark. But time changes everything and now we compete for the succulent dark meat, with the white breast leftover for chicken salad the next day. Recipes that call for a whole chicken to be cut in pieces satisfy us both. They supply at least two pieces of dark meat on a small chicken, and four when the legs of a larger bird are cut in two.

Packaged whole chicken parts are easy to find in the supermarket, but results are far better (and cheaper) if you cut up a whole bird yourself. This way you can divide the bird in even pieces, each with some bone and more or less the same amount of meat. All the pieces will be done at the same time, which is not the case with irregular precut parts. What is more, leftover trimmings from the backbone are good for stock. If you do prefer to pick up chicken parts at the market, I'd advise you stick to one kind: leg, thigh, wings, or breast, rather than buying an entire precut bird. A raw chicken can be cut into four, six, or eight pieces, depending on its size and the dish you are making. Larger birds are best for dishes that, like coq au vin, call for marinating and cooking in generous amounts of liquid. A small chicken divided into four to six pieces is good for grilling, or for a sauté in which the pieces are browned, in butter, then gently cooked in their own juices on top of the stove, covered with a lid.

Chicken is an amenable bird, inviting all kinds of company. Vegetable combinations include Basque Country Chicken with bell peppers and Mexican Almond Mole with dried ancho chile peppers darkened with a touch of chocolate. Chicken pieces can be fried Southern-style in shortening, they can be cooked quickly on the grill for instant gratification, or simmered at the back of the stove to serve in a few days' time.

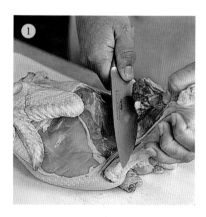 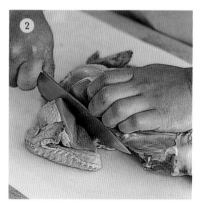 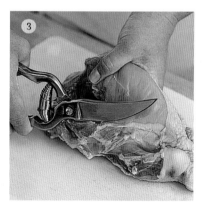

1 To remove the legs: With a medium knife or a boning knife, cut the skin between the leg and the breast. With the tip of the knife, locate the oyster meat lying under the backbone. Cut around it so it is attached to the thigh joint. Twist the leg sharply outward to break the thigh joint, then cut through it, severing it from the carcass so the oyster meat is attached. Repeat with the other leg.

2 To remove the wing with some breast meat, cut down at an angle to the ribs and when you reach the bones, slide the knife, cutting down to the wing joint. Cut through the joint to release the wing.

3 Using poultry shears, cut through the rib bones on each side of the bird, including the wishbone. This separates the remaining breast meat from the backbone, which has no meat on it.

④ Cut the breast in half along the bone using the shears. The bird is now divided into six pieces.

⑤ Turn the legs cut side up and locate the white line of fat that shows the joint. Cut down through the joint with a knife.

⑥ The bird is now divided into eight. Before cooking, cut off the wing pinions and trim excess fat and skin from all pieces.

Virginia's Southern Fried Chicken

Every Southern cook adds a personal twist to fried chicken, but soaking in buttermilk, coating with flour, and frying in shortening rather than oil are essential to all. Georgia-born Virginia Willis adds cayenne pepper to the flour as well as salt and pepper. Pan gravy is the classic accompaniment.

Serves 4

> **1½ cups buttermilk**
> **8 pieces of chicken (a whole bird or**
>   **single parts)**
> **2 cups flour**
> **2 teaspoons salt**
> **1 teaspoon pepper**
> **large pinch of cayenne pepper**
> **3 cups shortening**

Pour the buttermilk over the chicken pieces. Cover and refrigerate at least 2 and up to 8 hours. Drain the chicken. Put the flour, salt, pepper, and cayenne pepper in a brown paper bag and shake until mixed. Add half the chicken pieces and shake until well coated. Remove them and coat the rest.

Heat the shortening in a large skillet or sauté pan until a piece of chicken bubbles vigorously when lowered into the pan. Add all the pieces skin side down and fry over high heat until the undersides start to brown, about 5 minutes. (Take care as the shortening may spatter.) Turn the chicken, lower the heat to medium, and continue frying until it is evenly browned and tender when pierced with a two-pronged fork, 10 to 15 minutes longer. Transfer to a rack or paper towels to drain.

GETTING AHEAD: The chicken will stay crisp for an hour or two at room temperature.

Sauté of Chicken with a Friendly Bite

A cousin of coq au vin, this chicken takes half the time, ending with just a few spoonfuls of sauce per person flavored with the tang of vinegar instead of wine. Don't be concerned about the amount of vinegar—after cooking it is very mild.

Serves 4

> 1 chicken (about 3½ pounds)
> salt and pepper to taste
> 3 tablespoons butter
> 1 large head of garlic
> 1 cup red wine vinegar
> 1 pound tomatoes
> 1 tablespoon tomato paste
> bouquet garni of 2 bay leaves and a few sprigs
>   of thyme and parsley
> 1 cup chicken stock, more if needed
> 1 tablespoon chopped fresh parsley

Cut the chicken in 8 pieces and season them with salt and pepper. Melt half the butter over medium heat in a sauté pan, skillet, or deep frying pan with a lid, and heat until it stops foaming. Add the chicken pieces, skin side down, and sauté them over medium heat until brown, about 10 minutes. Turn them over and brown the other side for 1 to 2 minutes. Separate the garlic cloves and add them, unpeeled, to the pan. Cover and cook over low heat for 10 minutes.

Holding the lid on the pan so the chicken pieces do not fall out, drain off the excess fat. Return the pan to the heat, add the vinegar, and simmer it, uncovered, until very well reduced, 10 to 15 minutes. Chop the tomatoes—there's no need to seed or skin them as the sauce will later be strained. Stir them into the chicken with the tomato paste and the bouquet garni. Cover and simmer again until the chicken is tender, 10 to 15 minutes more—the pieces should fall easily from a two-pronged fork. If some pieces are cooked through and tender before others, remove them.

Transfer the chicken pieces to a serving dish and keep them warm in a low oven. Add the stock to the pan and simmer the sauce, uncovered,

until it is concentrated and lightly thickened, 5 to 8 minutes. Work the sauce through a sieve into a saucepan, pressing hard to extract the garlic pulp. Bring the sauce just to a boil, take it from the heat, and whisk in the remaining butter in small pieces. Taste it and adjust the seasoning. Spoon the sauce over the chicken and top with chopped parsley.

GETTING AHEAD: Sauté of chicken is excellent reheated, so keep it up to 2 days, covered in the refrigerator.

Asian Grilled Chicken Legs

These gutsy chicken legs invite eating with your fingers. You'll need to allow two or three per person.

Serves 4

In a shallow dish, mix 6 tablespoons soy sauce, ¼ cup fish sauce (*nam pla*), 6 chopped garlic cloves, 4 tablespoons chopped fresh ginger, 2 teaspoons dried hot red pepper flakes, and ¼ cup vegetable oil. Slash each leg 2 to 3 times so the marinade can penetrate. Roll 8 to 12 chicken legs (about 2 pounds) in the mixture to coat them, and refrigerate 30 minutes or up to 2 hours. Light the grill and brush the rack with oil. Grill the legs, turning them often and brushing with the remaining marinade, until browned and tender, 15 to 20 minutes. Serve hot or at room temperature.

Basque Country Chicken Sauté

Feisty Espelette pepper, a type of chile that comes from the Basque country bordering Spain, flavors this recipe. Espelette is available in gourmet stores; paprika is an alternative though the flavor is less hot.

Serves 4

- **1 chicken (about 3½ pounds)**
- **salt and pepper to taste**
- **1 tablespoon vegetable oil**
- **1 tablespoon butter**
- **1 tablespoon dried Espelette chile pepper**
- **2 garlic cloves, halved**
- **½ pound tomatoes, peeled, seeded, and coarsely chopped**
- **2 red bell peppers (about 1 pound), cored and cut in strips**
- **2 green bell peppers (about 1 pound), cored and cut in strips**
- **¼ pound raw ham, such as prosciutto or serrano, diced**
- **1 cup chicken stock, more if needed**
- **1 tablespoon chopped fresh parsley**

Cut the chicken in 8 pieces and season them with salt and pepper. Heat the oil and butter in a sauté pan or deep frying pan with a lid until foaming. Add the leg pieces, skin side down, and sauté over medium heat until they begin to brown, about 5 minutes. Add the breast pieces and continue cooking gently until they are all very brown, 10 to 15 minutes longer. Turn them, brown the other side, then remove and set them aside.

Sprinkle the Espelette pepper in the pan and sauté it, stirring 1 minute to mellow the flavor. Add the garlic and sauté 30 seconds until fragrant. Stir in the tomatoes, red and green peppers, and ham. Sauté the vegetables, stirring often, until they start to soften, 2 to 3 minutes. Stir in the chicken stock and replace the chicken, pushing the pieces well down into the vegetables and liquid.

Cover and cook over medium heat, stirring occasionally, until the chicken is tender, 25 to 35 minutes. Test by piercing the pieces with a two-pronged fork: they should fall away easily without clinging. If some pieces cook before others, remove them and keep them warm in a low oven.

Transfer the chicken to a platter or individual plates and keep warm in a low oven. There should be a small amount of sauce in the pan (2 to 3 tablespoons per person). If necessary, add a bit more stock. Stir the parsley into the vegetable mixture, taste and adjust the seasoning—salt may not be needed as the ham is salty. Spoon the garnish over the chicken and serve.

GETTING AHEAD: Basque Country Chicken Sauté reheats well. Make it ahead and store it in the refrigerator for up to 3 days, or freeze it.

Basque Country Chicken Sauté

HOW TO DEBONE AND TRIM CHICKEN BREASTS

French chefs always know when they are on to a good thing. The breast of a chicken was (and is) called the *suprême*, the best bit of meat around. Deboning and trimming a chicken breast is easy, well worth the effort, and besides, you save a bit of money on the supermarket price for prepared breasts. Another bonus is the chicken tenderloin, sometimes called the fillet, a sliver of meat that is prized by restaurateurs and often missing from precut breasts.

You'll find bone-in chicken breasts sold as doubles, with the whole breastbone and two pieces of meat, or as singles, with only a few bits of rib remaining. A single boneless chicken breast is regarded as an average serving, though its size can vary from a modest five ounces to jumbos of seven ounces or even more. My recipes assume single breasts, unless stated otherwise. Preparing a breast is simply a matter of cutting out the bones, removing the skin if you wish, and stripping out the tough tendon underneath the loose bit of tenderloin meat.

Once trimmed, you've a pristine chunk of tender white meat. You can leave it whole, or cut it in thin slices on the diagonal, pounding them flat in imitation of Italian veal piccata. More opportunities open when a pocket for stuffing is cut in the whole breast, or it is butterflied to lie flat. Mild and adaptable, chicken breast meat is an ideal foil for salty foods like bacon and olives, for Indian dry spices, and Asian flavorings like sesame and soy. It marries well with mushrooms, tomato, bell peppers, dried fruits, citrus, and a multitude of herbs.

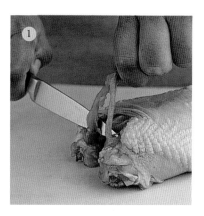

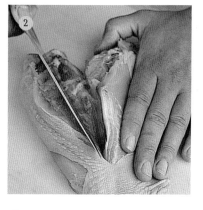

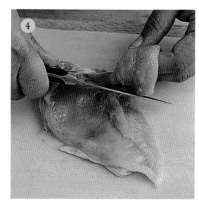

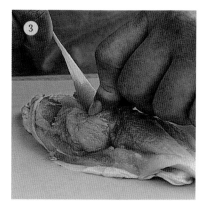

1 If using a double breast, place it skin side up on a chopping board. Cut out the wishbone.

2 Crack down sharply with the heel of your hand to snap the breastbone. Discard the skin if you wish. With a knife, cut along the breastbone, cutting and scraping the meat from the breastbone until it is free. Continue cutting the meat from the rib bones until the breast meat is released in one piece. Repeat on the other side.

3 To strip out the tendon: Turn the breast cut side up and locate the white tendon. Loosen one end with the tip of the knife. Grasp it tightly and strip it out with the finger and thumb of your other hand.

4 To remove the tenderloin: With your fingers, pick up the loose piece of meat lying on the breast and detach it with a knife.

Chicken breast may sound like the perfect ingredient, but if not properly cooked, the mild meat can be tough. Freezing does not help, so if you can find fresh breasts, go for them. Marinating before cooking is beneficial, but you must choose your cooking method carefully. Poaching in liquid or simmering gently in a stew helps keep the meat moist, and if you are sautéing chicken breasts, use gentler heat than usual. I find there is no way that a grilled chicken breast can be made tempting, but that is my personal prejudice.

There's a narrow line between thorough cooking—no trace of pink—and overcooking a chicken breast. When pressed in the center with a fingertip, it should feel resilient, but still slightly pliable. If in doubt, poke the chicken breast with the point of a knife to inspect the juices. If they are pink, keep cooking a bit longer.

Hungarian Paprikash Chicken Breasts

Here's my quick version of an old favorite. Be sure to serve it with noodles or spätzle to soak up the generous quantities of sauce. You can be sure there won't be a drop left!

Serves 4

Preheat the oven to 375°F. Heat 3 tablespoons vegetable oil in a skillet or large frying pan with an oven-proof handle, add 3 large onions, thinly sliced, with salt and white pepper and sauté them, stirring often, until they are golden brown. Stir in 3 to 4 tablespoons paprika and cook until very fragrant, about 1 minute. Stir in 1 cup chicken stock. Bury 4 skinless, boneless chicken breasts underneath the onions. Cover with aluminum foil and bake in the oven until the chicken breasts are very tender when pierced with a two-pronged fork, 25 to 30 minutes. Remove them to a platter and keep warm. Stir 3/4 cup sour cream into the onions and heat gently to make a sauce. (If the cream boils it will curdle.) Taste, adjust seasoning, including paprika, and spoon the sauce over the breasts.

Cashew Chicken Stir Fry

Use raw or cooked chicken, turkey, even fish for this dynamite stir fry. Increase the chiles if you like it hot, or for milder flavor with more vegetable, thinly slice some bok choy or white cabbage and add it just before the snow peas, stirring until wilted.

Serves 4

> 3 raw or cooked boneless chicken breasts
>   (about 1 pound total)
> 2 tablespoons soy sauce, more to taste
> 2 tablespoons rice wine
> pinch of sugar
> 2 teaspoons cornstarch
> 2 tablespoons vegetable oil
> 6 scallions, including green parts, thinly sliced
> 2 small whole dried red chile peppers,
>   more to taste
> 1 tablespoon chopped fresh ginger
> 1 garlic clove, chopped
> 1/2 cup cashews
> 8 ounces snow peas, trimmed

Cut the chicken breasts in thin strips. Mix the soy sauce, rice wine, sugar, and cornstarch in a bowl and mix with the chicken until coated. Leave it to marinate.

Heat a wok over high heat, about 30 seconds. Drizzle oil around the sides, add the scallions, chile peppers, ginger, and garlic and stir-fry until fragrant, about 30 seconds. Drain the chicken, reserving the marinade, and stir-fry until whitened and very hot, about 1 minute for cooked chicken, 2 minutes if the chicken is raw. Add the cashews and snow peas and continue frying for 2 minutes.

Finally, add the marinade to the wok and continue stir-frying until the marinade thickens and coats the chicken, about 1 minute. Discard the chiles, taste, and adjust seasoning with soy sauce.

GETTING AHEAD: Cover and marinate the chicken 1/2 to 1 hour in the refrigerator, then stir-fry it to serve fresh from the wok.

Warm Spiced Chicken Breasts with Pan Chutney

Chinese five-spice powder is one of my secret weapons—it adds a warmth and depth of flavor that is quite different from curry powder. The key flavorings are cinnamon, star anise, fennel, clove, and Sichuan peppercorns, but like curry powder the exact mix varies.

Serves 4

4 chicken breasts (2½ to 3 pounds total)
1 tablespoon five-spice powder
salt to taste
2 to 3 tablespoons butter
2 tablespoons port wine or balsamic vinegar
1 cup chicken stock
1 medium mango or half a melon, diced
2 tablespoons dried fruit (dates, apricots, cherries, or cranberries), chopped

Debone, skin, and trim the chicken breasts. Pat them dry on paper towels and roll them in the five-spice powder and a little salt, patting with the palms of your hands so the mixture adheres. Melt the butter in a large frying pan, add the breasts, and sauté until browned on all sides, 3 to 4 minutes. Turn the heat to low, cover the pan, and continue cooking, 10 to 15 minutes, until the chicken is firm to the touch and no pink juice is left when you poke it in the center.

Meanwhile, put the port wine in a small saucepan and boil, stirring, until reduced by half. Add half the chicken stock and continue boiling until reduced again by half. Add the mango and heat gently for 1 minute. Stir in the dried fruit then taste and adjust the seasoning.

When the chicken is done, transfer it to a serving dish and keep warm. Add the remaining stock to the frying pan and bring it to a boil, stirring to dissolve pan juices. Boil about a minute, stir it into the chutney, and check the seasoning again. Spoon the chutney over the chicken.

GETTING AHEAD: Make the chutney a day ahead and, if you like, coat the chicken breasts with spice and leave them to marinate in the refrigerator. Sauté them in butter just before serving.

Warm Spiced Chicken Breasts with Pan Chutney

Poaching Chicken

The meat from a whole poached chicken is always welcome, good served with mayo in chicken salads, as a filling for pot pie, or simply in soup.

Chicken Pot Pies

Nothing says comfort food like chicken pot pie, and no accompaniment is needed. If you prefer to make a large pie rather than individual ones, spread the filling in a baking dish and top with rounds of biscuit dough. A large pie will take 10 to 15 minutes longer to bake.

Makes 6 generous pot pies

> **1 Poached Whole Chicken (below), or about 1½ pounds cooked chicken meat, cut in slivers**
> **1 quart chicken stock**
> **3 carrots, sliced**
> **3 celery stalks, sliced**
> **2 medium potatoes, diced**
> **1 cup shelled peas**
> **4 tablespoons butter**
> **1 onion, chopped**
> **¼ cup flour**
> **½ cup heavy cream**
> **½ teaspoon grated nutmeg**
> **salt and pepper to taste**
> **3 tablespoons chopped fresh parsley**
> **1 recipe Plain Biscuit dough or Herbed Biscuit dough (page 279)**
> **1 egg**
>
> **6 heatproof bowls (2 cups capacity)**

Bring the stock to a boil. Add the carrots, celery stalks, and potatoes. Simmer 3 minutes. Add the peas and simmer until the vegetables are tender, 5 to 8 minutes. Drain the vegetables, reserving the stock. If using a whole chicken, remove the cooked meat from it, discarding the skin. Pull the meat into slivers and put it in a bowl. Add the vegetables and set aside.

Melt the butter in a small saucepan. Add the onion and cook until soft but not brown, 3 to 5 minutes. Sprinkle the flour over the onion and cook, stirring, 1 to 2 minutes.

Stir in 2 cups of the stock and heat, whisking, until the sauce comes to a boil and thickens. Simmer for 2 minutes then add the cream and nutmeg. Taste and adjust the seasoning—the sauce should be highly seasoned. Pour the sauce over the chicken and vegetables and stir in the parsley.

Preheat the oven to 425°F. Divide the filling evenly among the bowls. Make the biscuit dough and pat it out. Cut out rounds and put one on top of each pie. Beat the egg with ½ teaspoon salt and brush the biscuits with this glaze. Bake the pies for 15 minutes, then reduce the heat to 350°F. Continue baking until the crust is browned and the filling is hot, 7 to 10 minutes.

Poached Whole Chicken

After taking the chicken meat from the bones, for the world's best chicken stock I put the bones back in the broth and keep simmering for another hour before straining it.

Serves 4, and makes about 1½ quarts chicken stock

Truss a 4-pound chicken (see page 146) and put it in a deep pot with 1 quartered onion, 1 quartered carrot, 1 celery stalk, cut in pieces, a bouquet garni (a bay leaf and a few sprigs of thyme and parsley), 1 teaspoon salt, 1 teaspoon peppercorns, and enough water to cover. Bring to a boil, skimming often, and simmer, uncovered, until the chicken is very tender and juice runs clear, not pink, when the thigh is pierced with a two-pronged fork, 3/4 to 1 hour. Turn the bird once during simmering and add more water if needed to keep it covered. Let the chicken cool to tepid, then drain and refrigerate it. For stock, skim fat and boil the cooking liquid until flavor is concentrated.

Poultry Breast Possibilities

Admit it, a plain chicken breast looks pretty dull sitting there on the plate. Luckily, all sorts of surprises can be fashioned from the even, close-textured meat. Most versatile of all are chicken escalopes, created by splitting breasts in half in a butterfly cut, then pounding them flat to an even $^1/_4$-inch thickness. Turkey escalopes are even easier to cut from a whole breast, needing only to be flattened. The thinly sliced meat can also be cut in smaller pieces, then pounded as thinly as possible for piccata, three or four to a serving. Read on!

how to butterfly and flatten chicken breasts

After chicken breasts are split and folded open, they can either be pounded flat to cook as an escalope, or cut into piccata.

board and press your hand on top to hold the meat steady. With a large knife, slit the breast horizontally almost in two, leaving it joined at the long straight edge. Open it.

1 Bone and trim the chicken breasts (page 152). If the tenderloin was included, reserve it for another use. Lay a breast flat on a chopping

2 Set the meat between two sheets of plastic wrap, and pound it flat with the base of a heavy pan or a rolling pin to obtain flat, even escalopes that are about $^1/_4$ inch thick.

Chicken alla Cacciatore

Cacciatore, hunter's style, can mean almost any flavoring that includes mushrooms, so here I'm keeping the ingredients to a minimum. There will be very little sauce as the chicken and mushrooms absorb the juices, making them wonderfully moist.

Serves 2 to 3

Butterfly 2 chicken breasts and pound them flat. Mix 2 to 3 tablespoons flour with salt and pepper and dip the escalopes in it, patting so they are evenly coated on both sides. Heat 2 tablespoons butter and 2 tablespoons oil in a large frying pan and sauté the escalopes in 2 batches, browning them 1 to 2 minutes on each side. Set them aside. Add 4 ounces sliced mushrooms and 2 chopped garlic cloves to the pan. Sauté, stirring, until tender, 2 to 3 minutes. Stir in 3 to 4 tablespoons each of white wine and water and heat, stirring to dissolve the pan juices. Taste, adjust seasoning, and replace the escalopes. Sprinkle them with a tablespoon of chopped fresh parsley and warm, 1 to 2 minutes.

Escalopes with Roquefort Cheese Sauce

Any tasty cheese does well in this weeknight special, including Parmesan or aged Cheddar. Serve it with green fettuccine to soak up the sauce.

Serves 4

> **4 chicken, turkey, or veal escalopes (about 1¼ pounds total)**
> **½ cup flour seasoned with ½ teaspoon salt and ¼ teaspoon pepper**
> **1 tablespoon oil**
> **2 tablespoons butter**
> **¾ cup crème fraîche or heavy cream**
> **3 ounces Roquefort cheese, finely crumbled (¾ cup)**
> **pepper to taste**

Flatten the escalopes. Spread the seasoned flour on a plate and coat the escalopes, patting them so they are evenly coated. In a large frying pan, heat the oil with 1 tablespoon of the butter until it stops sputtering and add 2 escalopes. Sauté them until browned, 1 to 2 minutes, then turn them and brown the other side. They should still be juicy in the center if you poke them with the point of a knife. Set aside and keep them warm. Melt remaining butter and fry the remaining escalopes, setting them aside also.

Pour excess fat from the pan, add the crème fraîche, and bring to a boil, stirring to dissolve pan juices. Simmer 1 minute, add the Roquefort cheese off the heat, and whisk over the heat until melted—do not let the sauce boil or it will separate. Taste and adjust the seasoning of the sauce with pepper. Salt may not be needed as the cheese is salty. Replace the escalopes and warm them in the sauce over very low heat, about 1 minute.

GETTING AHEAD: By all means flatten the escalopes up to 12 hours ahead and keep them in the refrigerator, but they are best freshly cooked.

how to make chicken breast piccata

Butterflied chicken breasts cook quickly and stay moist when cut and pounded in small flat slices called piccata in Italian.

1 If necessary, bone and trim the breast (page 152). If the tenderloin is included, first pull it off. Butterfly the breast and cut it in quarters. Lay the pieces, including the tenderloin, between sheets of plastic wrap and pound them as thinly as possible.

Piccata al'Limone

Add a lemon-friendly green vegetable such as broccoli or beans.

Serves 2

Make piccata from 2 chicken, turkey, or veal escalopes, about 10 ounces total, (see How to Make Chicken Breast Piccata, page 157). Mix the grated zest and juice of 1 lemon in a bowl with 3 tablespoons olive oil and plenty of freshly ground pepper. Add the piccata, toss, and leave to marinate, 15 to 30 minutes. Heat 2 tablespoons olive oil in a large frying pan. Drain the piccata, reserving marinade, and sauté the meat briskly until browned, 1 to 2 minutes. Turn and brown the other side, 1 to 2 minutes longer. Transfer to 2 serving plates. Add the reserved marinade and 3 tablespoons water to the pan and cook, stirring to dissolve juices, about 1 minute. Stir in 1 tablespoon chopped fresh parsley, taste and adjust the seasoning. Spoon sauce over the piccata and serve.

Saltimbocca

Saltimbocca means "jump in the mouth" and this lively little Italian recipe, which combines veal, chicken, or turkey with sage, prosciutto, and red wine, does just that.

Serves 4

**4 chicken, turkey, or veal escalopes
(about 1¼ pounds total)
16 sage leaves, more for garnish
4 thin slices prosciutto (about 3 ounces)
4 tablespoons butter, more if needed
1 cup full-flavored red wine
salt and pepper to taste**

Cut each escalope in 3 or 4 pieces and pound them flat to make piccata. Trim fat from the prosciutto slices and cut each in 4 pieces. Top each piece of escalope with a sage leaf and then a piece of prosciutto. Cover with plastic wrap, pound to press the prosciutto into the meat, then peel off the wrap. Prepare the remaining saltimbocca in the same way.

Heat half the butter in a frying pan and when it has stopped sputtering, add a few of the saltimbocca to the pan, prosciutto side down. Sauté over medium heat until brown, about 1½ minutes. Turn and brown the other side, about 1 minute longer. Don't overcook them or they will be dry. Transfer the saltimbocca to a warm platter and keep warm while frying the rest (if the pan becomes dry, add more butter).

When all the saltimbocca are cooked, add the red wine to the pan and bring to a boil, stirring to dissolve the pan juices. Reduce for 3 to 5 minutes, until slightly thickened to form a glaze. Add the remaining 2 tablespoons butter in small pieces, swirling the pan over low heat so the butter softens and thickens the sauce slightly without melting to oil. Taste, adjust the seasoning, and spoon it over the saltimbocca. Decorate the platter with sage sprigs for serving.

GETTING AHEAD: The saltimbocca can be prepared up to 6 hours ahead and refrigerated, ready to sauté at the last minute.

how to cut turkey escalopes

It's even easier to cut escalopes from a breast of turkey than from a chicken breast. Each escalope will weigh around 5 ounces, so you'll get at least 6 to 8 escalopes from the average single bone-less breast weighing around 2 1/2 pounds. Turkey escalopes are cooked just like veal, taking well to herbs, tomato, and the tang of fruit. In fact, turkey and veal escalopes taste so much alike that I bet no one can tell the difference at table.

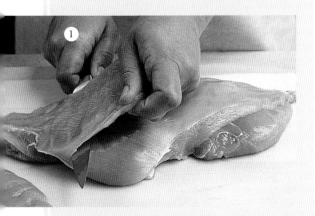

1 Trim a boneless, skinless turkey breast of any fat and sinew, and remove the tendon as for chicken (page 152). Lay the turkey breast cut side down on a chopping board. With a flexible-bladed knife, cut slices on the diagonal, angling the knife so the slices are as large as possible. Before using them, set the escalopes between sheets of plastic wrap and pound them flat as for butterflied chicken breasts.

Party Escalopes with Pomegranates and Pistachios

This eye-catching dish looks great for guests and, be assured, the 10 minutes of work needed to extract the pomegranate kernels is worth it. Pomegranates are in season in autumn and early winter.

Serves 4

> **1 small pomegranate**
> **4 turkey, chicken, or veal escalopes**
>   **(about 1¼ pounds total)**
> **olive oil for brushing**
> **salt and pepper to taste**
> **¼ cup blanched and peeled pistachios**
> **1 tablespoon melted butter**

To extract the pomegranate kernels: Cut the flower end from the pomegranate and with a sharp knife, score the skin in quarters, taking care not to puncture the juicy kernels inside. With your hands, break the fruit into quarters following the score lines. Bend the skin back-ward so the fruit kernels pop out, letting them fall into a bowl. Discard any membrane.

Brush the escalopes on both sides with olive oil and sprinkle with salt and pepper. Heat a stovetop grill and when a drop of water sizzles on it, add the escalopes. Press down so they cook evenly and grill until browned, about 2 minutes. Turn and brown the other side, 1 to 2 minutes longer. Transfer the escalopes to 4 warm plates. Stir the pomegranate seeds and pistachios into the hot butter. Spoon over the escalopes and serve.

GETTING AHEAD: Prepare the pomegranate and blanch the pistachios a few hours ahead. The escalopes must be cooked at the last minute.

HOW TO SPLIT AND COOK SMALL BIRDS

The belief that the sweetest meat is on the bone could well have come from eating small birds. The little meat they have is wonderfully succulent and juicy. If the backbone is cut out and the carcass anchored flat with skewers, a small bird cooks evenly and is easy to handle and flip on the fire. The Brits call this technique spatchcock, and the French have a word for it too: *en crapaudine*, meaning "like a toad." You can see why—the flattened bird does look very much like a crouching amphibian.

Half a dozen birds come to mind for this treatment, from quail to pigeon, dove, pheasant, and baby chicken, all available in gourmet stores and even on the Internet. Even easier to find are Cornish game hens. To add flavor, a quick soaking in marinade (make it short as the meat is not dense) or a rub with some dry spices can be helpful. During cooking, a small bird needs generous brushing with melted butter, a flavored oil, or a light barbecue sauce. Two other quick ideas include a vigorous Texan barbecue mix, or Emma's yogurt marinade. Simplest of all is a brush with Dijon mustard.

Once the birds are split and flattened, you can choose your favorite cooking method, whether on an indoor or outdoor grill, under the broiler, or in the oven. Seasonings are the same, but cooking times vary somewhat depending on the heat source. Small birds cook quickly, so check them often. As a very rough guide, a one-pound bird needs about 10 minutes on each side and a larger bird of up to two pounds will take up to 30 minutes total; it may need turning two or three times so the meat cooks more evenly.

Small birds are done when both sides are browned, lightly charred in places, and the meat starts to pull from the leg joint. Poke the breast with the point of a knife: chicken and Cornish hen should be well done, but game birds are served rare, or at most faintly pink, so they do not dry out. You should allow at least one bird per person, possibly two or three for tiny ones like quail. And no carving is needed—chewing on the leg bones at table is part of the fun.

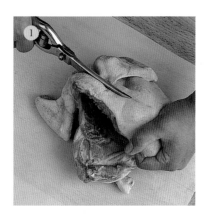

1 Trim off the wing pinions with poultry shears and set the bird breast side down. Cut along each side of backbone and remove it.

2 Clean inside the bird with paper towels and trim any loose skin. Set the bird, breast side up, with the legs turned in. Using the heel of your hand, push down sharply on the breast to break the breastbone and flatten the bird.

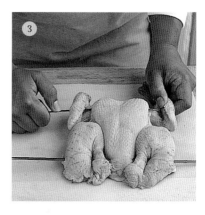

3 Make a small cut in the skin between the leg and breastbone, and tuck in the leg knuckles so they do not char and look ugly when cooked. Thread 2 skewers through the bird to hold the wings and legs flat.

Deviled Cornish Game Hens

These game hens cook to a dark, glowing brown due to the paprika and Worcestershire sauce. Baby chickens (weighing about 1 pound) are delicious here, too, and I like to serve either with fresh pasta.

Serves 2

> **2 small Cornish game hens (about 1 pound each)**
> **2 tablespoons butter, softened**
> **2 tablespoons paprika**
> **pinch of cayenne pepper**
> **pinch of salt**
> **3 tablespoons Worcestershire sauce**
> **1 tablespoon red wine vinegar**
>
> **4 metal skewers**

Light the grill or preheat the broiler. Split and flatten the game hens. Skewer them, threading each with 2 skewers to hold the legs and wings flat and level with the breast. Spread the butter all over them. Mix the paprika, cayenne, salt, Worcestershire sauce, and vinegar in a small bowl and brush the mixture over the birds.

Put the game hens on an oiled rack—skin side down for a grill, up for a broiler. Grill or broil them about 3 inches from the heat, basting them often, 12 to 15 minutes, or until very brown. Turn them over, baste them, and continue cooking, 8 to 10 minutes, on the other side.

Turn the birds over a last time, skin side toward the heat, and continue cooking until they are tender when pierced with a two-pronged fork, 5 to 10 minutes longer. If they brown too quickly at any point during cooking, move the rack farther from the heat. When done, pull skewers from the game hens and arrange them on a serving dish.

GETTING AHEAD: Brush the birds with the spicy sauce an hour before cooking—the flavor will be all the more pungent.

Deviled Cornish Game Hens

Garlicky Mustard Cornish Game Hens

I tuck garlic-herb butter under the skin and brush these tasty birds with Dijon mustard, serving them with a salad of peppery greens.

Serves 2

Light the grill or preheat the broiler. Cut the backbone from 2 baby chickens or Cornish game hens (about 1 pound each). Cream 2 tablespoons softened butter with 2 finely chopped garlic cloves, 2 tablespoons chopped fresh parsley, the juice of ¹/₂ lemon, salt, and pepper. With your fingers, gently loosen the skin from the breast and legs of the birds and spread garlic butter under the skin. Thread the birds on skewers and cook as for Deviled Cornish Game Hens, basting with the butter as it melts. Before turning the birds a final time, brush the skin side with 2 tablespoons Dijon mustard and sprinkle with 2 tablespoons dry breadcrumbs.

Spicy Texan Quail

To be savored with a large margarita!

Serves 4 generously

Light the grill or preheat the broiler. Cut the backbone from 8 quail, flatten them, and thread them on skewers. In a small bowl, whisk 1/2 cup olive oil, 3 tablespoons lemon juice, 1 teaspoon cracked black pepper, and 1/2 to 1 teaspoon dried hot red pepper flakes. Brush the sauce on the quail and sprinkle with a little sea salt. Set the birds on an oiled rack, 2 to 3 inches from the heat. Grill or broil them, breast toward the heat, 5 to 6 minutes, until brown and lightly charred. Turn and brown the other side, 3 to 8 minutes, depending on the plumpness of the quail. Poke a breast with the point of a knife—it should remain juicy and slightly pink. Serve the quail in a basket lined with a paper napkin.

Emma's Yogurt Chicken

There's always a container of plain yogurt in Emma's refrigerator (mine too) so this recipe appears regularly at the table, accompanied by green beans or a rice pilaf. In a pinch, simply marinate birds (or chicken pieces) in yogurt with no added spices, and you'll be surprised at the tasty results.

Serves 2

In a food processor, purée 1 small onion, cut in chunks, and 2 garlic cloves with 1 cup plain yogurt, 1 tablespoon ground coriander, 1 teaspoon paprika, salt, and pepper until smooth. Taste and adjust seasoning. Split, flatten, and skewer 2 baby chickens or Cornish game hens, set them in a baking dish, and spoon the yogurt marinade over them. Cover and refrigerate at least 1 and up to 4 hours. Just before cooking, scrape off the marinade and dry the birds with paper towels. Light the grill or preheat the broiler. Cook them as for Deviled Cornish Game Hens (page 161), brushing once with marinade.

HOW TO ROAST THE THANKSGIVING TURKEY

No meal is more traditional than family Thanksgiving with turkey cooked by Mom. When we are in the U.S. with Emma and Todd, we celebrate together. Since every Mom has her personal way of doing things, here, stage by stage, is mine. Well in advance, I order the turkey from a local farm if I can find one, consulting with the producer about size and freshness. (I have no confidence in frozen birds, especially for an important occasion.) Ideally, I collect the turkey only the day before Thanksgiving, but a wait of a couple of days in the refrigerator is all right.

A day or two ahead, cooking preparations begin. I make stock for the gravy using chicken wings and the giblets from the turkey, and I start assembling accompaniments. Here I hardly dare

turkey tips

* The bigger the bird, the more people it serves proportionately, so that an 8-pound bird is enough for 8, a 10-pound bird feeds 10 to 12, a 15-pound bird is ample for 18, even 20, and so on.
* When storing the turkey in the refrigerator, wrap it loosely in butcher paper, not plastic, and keep giblets separately.
* I use a single string for trussing (see How to Truss a Bird, page 146), but if you find that awkward with an extra-large bird, secure the legs and wings in place with wooden skewers.
* For basting a large bird, I use a pastry brush to mop up the pan juices and spread them over the skin. I can reach easily this way without lifting the hot, heavy pan out of the oven.
* When we make our turkey gravy, we have a little ceremony, adding a glass of Champagne to the pan.

make suggestions as every family has its time-honored favorites. You would probably find our customary sides of wild mushrooms, glazed wild chestnuts, Brussels sprouts, and toasted buck-wheat (kasha) very surprising, but Mark, Simon, and Emma would think American-style oyster stuffing and baked pumpkin with brown sugar equally odd.

As a compromise, I'm suggesting a time-honored stuffing based on toasted bread, celery, and apple handed down from Todd's grand-mother, plus a more contemporary wild rice, mushroom, and pecan combination. Stuffings like these are best baked in a separate dish so they develop a crusty brown top. This way there's no risk of salmonella bacteria, which can develop during the long cooking time needed for a fully stuffed turkey. Another way to be sure the stuffing is fully cooked is to fill it under the neck skin, outside the actual cavity of the bird (see pictures of carving turkey, page 165). Under no circumstances should a bird be stuffed ahead of time.

So we're ready for the big day, with stuffing made and accompaniments chilled and ready to bake. Action begins at least four hours before we sit down to table. My kitchen has two ovens, but with a single one you may need to do more cooking ahead to make room for the turkey. It's not long before tempting aromas waft through the house, so that by the end everyone has gravitated to the kitchen to assist with the finale. The turkey is transferred to a platter, covered with a tent of aluminum foil, and left to keep warm. The gravy is put to simmer, side dishes are reheated. Mark sharpens the carving knife to a final edge. Simon hefts the platter and the rest of us follow on. That's it, Thanksgiving dinner is ready for the Cherniavsky family table (in case you were wondering, my father-in-law was Russian).

1 Preheat the oven to 350°F. Set the trussed turkey in a buttered roasting pan that is big enough to maneuver when basting but not so large that the juices scorch. Spread the turkey with softened butter and sprinkle with seasoning. Put it in the oven to roast, basting as soon as the butter has melted. For best results and aromatic brown skin, it must be basted every 15 minutes or so. When the turkey is thoroughly browned, halfway or more through cooking, cover it with a loose tent of aluminum foil and continue cooking.

2 Turkey is done when meat starts to pull from the leg bones. Snip the trussing string and rotate the leg bone with your fist. If it feels pliable the bird may be done. Prick the thickest part of the thigh with a fork—the juice should run clear and not pink (like all white poultry, turkey must be served well done). Finally, test the temperature of the thickest part of the breast—the thermometer should register 165°F (the temperature will continue to rise for 5 to 10 minutes in retained heat).

Traditional Roast Turkey

For me, a whole turkey is best kept simple, so here is my unbeatable plainly roasted bird. I like to add a bit of symbolic sparkle with Champagne or a dry white wine for the gravy, but it's optional.

Serves 8 to 10

> **1 turkey (8 to 10 pounds)**
> **½ cup (1 stick) butter, softened, more for the pan**
> **salt and pepper to taste**
>
> **FOR THE GRAVY**
> **½ cup Champagne or sparkling white wine (optional)**
> **3 cups chicken or veal stock**

Preheat the oven to 350°F. Wipe the turkey inside and out with paper towels and truss it (see How to Truss a Bird, page 146)—you'll find that even a big bird can be effectively tied with a single string. Butter a large roasting pan and set the turkey in it, breast side up. Spread the bird generously with butter and season with salt and pepper. Roast the turkey for a total of 3 to 3½ hours, basting often. When the breast is well browned, cover it loosely with aluminum foil and continue cooking. Baste very often, every quarter hour.

The turkey is done when the juices run clear, the leg joint is pliable, the skin is browned and crisp, and a meat thermometer inserted in the thickest part of the thigh reads 165°F. Test the breast, too, just to be sure. Transfer the turkey to a serving platter and keep it warm.

Make the gravy: Discard all but about 2 tablespoons of fat from the pan. (We like a bit of butter in our gravy, but you may prefer to discard all the fat.) Pour the Champagne into the pan if using; alternatively add a bit of stock. Heat the liquid on top of the stove, scraping to dissolve the pan juices, until they are sticky and brown, 2 to 3 minutes. Pour in the stock, still stirring, and simmer until the gravy is concentrated and reduced by half, 10 to 15 minutes. Taste, adjust the seasoning, and strain the gravy into a bowl.

GETTING AHEAD: Devoting time to your turkey is all part of the festivity, so don't count on preparing it ahead beyond trussing the bird an hour or two before it goes in the oven.

how to choose a roasting pan

A roasting pan is usually rectangular, sometimes oval, and has sides high enough to partly shield the roast as well as retain pan juices. The base should be thick enough to deter scorching, and the pan should have two handles that are easy to grasp. Ideally the pan is 2 inches larger all around than the food and, if you roast often, it is good to have at least two sizes. For poultry you'll need a roasting pan of chicken size, and a giant pan if you plan on roasting a turkey. In too small a pan, food is awkward to handle and tends to steam rather than dry-roast to a crispy brown. In too large a pan, juices from the food scorch on the bottom.

For me, the best material for roasting pans is sturdy, anodized aluminum, thick enough not to warp in the heat. Regular aluminum is not suitable as it may react with wine or other acids. For the same reason, cast-iron roasting pans must be coated with enamel and I find them heavy and clumsy. Stainless-steel pans look attractive but the food tends to stick. In a nonstick roasting pan, by contrast, pan juices do not brown well for gravy.

turkey timing

When roasting turkey at 350°F:

* For an 8- to 10-pound bird, allow 20 minutes per pound plus 20 minutes

* For a 10- to 14-pound bird, allow 18 minutes per pound

* For anything bigger, allow 16 minutes per pound

Maria's Spicy Turkey

In case plain roast turkey seems unadventurous, here's an inspired recipe from our Portuguese housekeeper, Maria. She finds that turkey has no taste and as a remedy she marinates it with an exuberant mix of garlic, chile pepper, wine, and olive oil, declaring that she hardly needs to baste it as a result. I'd recommend the same tonic for any white-fleshed bird.

Serves 8 to 10

> **1 turkey (8 to 10 pounds)**
> **2 lemons, halved**
> **2 garlic cloves, chopped**
> **2 teaspoons salt**
> **1½ teaspoons ground red chile pepper**
> **1 teaspoon ground black pepper**
> **¾ cup dry white wine**
> **¾ cup olive oil**

A day ahead, wipe the turkey inside and out with paper towels. Rub the skin of the bird with the cut lemons. Whisk the garlic in a bowl with the salt, chile pepper, black pepper, and white wine. Whisk in the olive oil. With your hands, rub the inside of turkey with the marinade and truss it with string. Put it in a heavy-duty plastic bag, pour in the remaining marinade, and tie the bag closed, pressing to exclude air. Keep it in a bowl in the refrigerator for 24 hours.

Preheat the oven to 350°F. Set the turkey in a roasting pan and pour the marinade over it. Roast the bird as for Traditional Roast Turkey, allowing 3 to 3½ hours, basting every half hour.

how to carve a turkey

Be sure to leave the turkey to rest in a warm place, covered loosely with aluminum foil, for at least 15 minutes so the juices are redistributed before carving. This is a handy pause for making gravy (page 86).

1 Discard the trussing string and hold the bird steady with a carving fork. With a sharp knife, make a horizontal cut just above the wing joint to cut through the breast meat to the bone. Cut the skin between the leg and the breast and push the leg outward so the breast meat is exposed. Carve the breast in slanting slices (including any stuffing), starting at the wing end and working toward the cavity.

2 Holding the leg firmly, carve horizontal slices, working parallel to the leg bone. When you have sliced off as much meat as you can, locate the knee joint with the knife and cut through the joint, freeing the drumstick. Slice the remaining meat from the drumstick. To remove the thigh, force it outward with a fork, then locate the thigh joint with a knife and cut through it. Cut meat from the thigh in slices.

Turkey Tidbits

Emma never forgives me for telling this story. She was 16, Simon 18, when they were left alone to cook the Thanksgiving turkey. Calling trans-Atlantic, I had delivered all the advice I could think of but it proved not to be enough. Simon, with Emma at his side, had proudly carried the golden roast bird to the table to the acclaim of assembled friends. He seized the carvers and set to: impossible to do more than penetrate the skin. It was several minutes before he identified the problem—the turkey had been roasted upside down!

Wild Rice Stuffing

Rich pecans and wild mushrooms bring a luxurious depth of flavor to this wild rice stuffing.

Makes 5 cups stuffing, enough to accompany a 10-pound turkey

> **1 cup wild rice**
>
> **1 quart chicken stock**
>
> **salt and pepper to taste**
>
> **1 pound wild mushrooms**
>
> **2 tablespoons vegetable oil**
>
> **6 tablespoons butter**
>
> **3 tablespoons Marsala or sweet sherry**
>
> **2 shallots, chopped**
>
> **2 tablespoons chopped fresh parsley**
>
> **1 tablespoon chopped fresh sage**
>
> **3/4 cup pecan pieces**

In a medium saucepan, stir the rice with the chicken stock, salt, and pepper. Cover, bring to a boil, and simmer for 40 to 50 minutes, until all the stock is absorbed and the rice is tender—it will remain chewy. Meanwhile, trim the stems of the wild mushrooms and brush them to remove any grit. If they are very dirty, rinse them briefly in cold water and drain them. Cut them into chunks. Heat the oil in a frying pan, add the mushrooms with salt and pepper, and cook, stirring often, until the liquid evaporates, 5 to 12 minutes. Cooking time will vary with type of mushroom. Cream the butter and beat in the Marsala, shallots, parsley, and sage.

When the rice is cooked, stir the butter into the warm mushrooms so that it melts. Stir mushrooms into the wild rice with the pecan pieces. Taste and adjust seasoning.

GETTING AHEAD: Make the stuffing a day ahead. Reheat it in a buttered baking dish for 10 to 15 minutes in a 350°F oven.

Trio of Roasted Root Vegetables

Potatoes and sweet onions are always part of this trio, but the choice of a third vegetable—sweet potato, turnip, parsnip, or celery root—depends on what is around. Here, I'm suggesting rosemary as the herb but thyme or sage would be just as good. To get ahead, cook the vegetables in advance then broil them just before serving to heat and brown them.

Serves 10 to 12

Preheat the oven to 375°F. Cut 8 medium unpeeled potatoes (about 2 pounds) and 4 unpeeled sweet potatoes (about 3 pounds) in 1 1/2-inch chunks. Put them in a roasting pan. Peel 6 medium Vidalia or other sweet onions (about 1 1/2 pounds) and quarter them through the root and stem so they hold together. Add them to the potatoes. Stir to mix with 1/2 cup olive oil, salt, and pepper—the vegetables should be quite crowded as they will shrink during cooking. Tuck 4 to 6 rosemary branches among them. Roast in the oven, stirring occasionally, until the vegetables are tender and well browned, 1 to 1 1/2 hours. Discard the rosemary before serving, and taste and adjust seasoning.

Grandma Esther's Traditional Turkey Stuffing

This recipe dates back 70 years in the family of Emma's husband Todd. If you like your stuffing crispy, add only 1/2 cup stock—more if you prefer it moist.

Makes about 5 cups stuffing, enough to accompany a 10-pound turkey

> 1-pound loaf of dry white bread
> 4 tablespoons butter, more for the baking dish
> 1 onion, chopped
> 2 celery stalks, chopped
> 2 tart apples, peeled, cored, and diced (about 2 cups)
> 1/2 cup raisins
> 1 tablespoon chopped fresh thyme
> 1/2 teaspoon freshly grated nutmeg
> salt and pepper to taste
> 2 eggs, beaten to mix
> 1/2 cup turkey or chicken stock, more for a moist stuffing

Preheat the oven to 350°F. Discard crusts from the bread. Cube the bread and lightly toast it on baking sheets in the oven, 8 to 12 minutes. Melt the butter in a skillet and fry the onion and celery until lightly browned, 8 to 10 minutes. In a large bowl, mix the onion and celery with the toasted bread squares, apples, raisins, thyme, nutmeg, salt, and pepper. Stir in the eggs and turkey stock, adding more stock for a moist stuffing. Butter a baking dish and spread the stuffing in it. Bake it in a 350°F oven beside the turkey until hot and browned, 35 to 45 minutes.

GETTING AHEAD: The stuffing can be baked up to 6 hours ahead and reheated for serving.

Baby Onions in Cream Sauce

Baby onions in cream sauce are lovely with roast chicken, veal, and pork, as well as with roast turkey.

Serves 4 to 6

> 2 pounds baby onions, peeled
> 2 tablespoons butter
> 1/2 cup water, more if needed
> 1 teaspoon sugar
> salt and pepper to taste
>
> FOR THE WHITE SAUCE
> 2 cups milk
> 2 tablespoons butter
> 2 tablespoons flour
> grated nutmeg to taste

Trim tops of the onions, leaving a bit of root to hold them together. Melt the butter in a sauté pan or deep frying pan and add the onions, water, sugar, salt, and pepper. All of the onions should be touching the base of the pan. Cover the pan tightly and simmer over medium heat, shaking often, until almost tender, 10 to 15 minutes. If necessary, add more water during cooking so the onions do not brown.

Make the white sauce: Scald the milk. In another saucepan, melt the butter, stir in the flour, and whisk in the hot milk, off the heat. Bring the sauce to a boil, whisking constantly until it thickens. Season it to taste with salt, pepper, and nutmeg and simmer for 1 minute. Pour the sauce over the onions, stir, and simmer without the lid until the onions are tender and generously coated in sauce, 5 to 7 minutes.

GETTING AHEAD: Refrigerate the onions in their sauce for up to 2 days, then reheat them on top of the stove using very low heat so the sauce does not curdle.

HOW TO ROAST DUCK

Duck with cornbread stuffing, spiced roast duck, duck with orange, duck with cherries—how tempting they all sound! No wonder duck is a treat appreciated worldwide; served Peking-style with pancakes, plum sauce, and scallions, roast duck transports me to Asia, and with sauerkraut simmered in Riesling wine, I fancy I'm in the vineyards of Alsace. You'll notice that most of these famous dishes involve accompanying sauces or vegetables. The duck itself is usually left quite plain to ensure that the skin is crisp and the meat is done just right. Whether duck should be served pink or well done is your choice (mine is for juicy, lightly pink meat). The difference is simply a matter of a few extra minutes of cooking. A whole roast duck unfortunately does not go far—the average duck weighing five pounds serves at most three people and sometimes only two.

There are several common breeds of domestic duck, but you'll find only fatty Peking duck (also known as Long Island duck) in most stores. Before cooking, wipe the duck thoroughly dry inside and out (it is likely to be soggy after freezing) and pull out and discard any chunks of fat you find in the cavity. Possible seasonings to go in the cavity include a whole onion stuck with a clove, or herbs such as thyme, sage, and bay leaf. I truss a duck the same way as chicken, with a single long string (see How to Truss a Bird, page 146). Always rub the duck skin with salt, but do this only just before roasting to avoid extracting juices.

① Pricking the skin of a duck during cooking is important as fat runs out in surprising quantities, literally shrinking the carcass. As roasting progresses, the pan should contain only enough fat for basting; pour or spoon off any buildup so the duck does not wallow in fat. Some cooks raise the duck above the fat in the roasting pan by perching it on a rack, but removing fat from time to time is equally effective. The fat drained from the pan is a bonus, perfect for frying the world's crispest potatoes (see Petite Potato Cake, page 233).

Roast Duck with Apples and Calvados

I picked up a taste for apples in savory dishes when we lived in Normandy, and this recipe has remained a favorite.

Serves 2 to 3

Prepare and roast the duck (see opposite). Peel, core, and slice 4 tart apples in eighths. Melt 2 tablespoons butter in a frying pan, add the apples, and sprinkle with 1 tablespoon sugar. Turn the apples and sprinkle with a tablespoon more sugar. Sauté them until caramelized, 2 to 3 minutes. Turn, brown the other side, and reserve them. When the duck is done, transfer it to a platter and make gravy, flavoring it with 1 to 2 tablespoons Calvados or Cognac. Reheat the apples, and when very hot, add 3 to 4 tablespoons Calvados or Cognac. Flambé them (see How to Flambé, page 131), standing back from the flames. Pile apples around the duck and serve.

Plain Roast Duck

High oven heat is important to dissolving fat and browning the skin when roasting duck.

Preheat the oven to 500°F so cooking will start at once. Wipe the duck thoroughly dry inside and out (it is likely to be soggy after freezing) and pull out and discard any chunks of fat in the cavity. Season the duck inside and out with pepper and, if you like, a teaspoon or two of ground allspice. Rub the duck skin with salt, but do this only just before cooking to avoid extracting juices. Truss the duck and set it in an oiled roasting pan, breast side up.

Roast the bird until it begins to brown and sizzle, 25 to 30 minutes. Lower the heat to 400°F. Prick the skin all over to release fat and turn the duck breast downward. Continue roasting, basting often, until the duck is very brown, about 45 minutes longer. During cooking, spoon off excess fat from the pan and reserve it for another use. Turn the duck onto its back and continue roasting 10 to 20 minutes longer, until it is medium or well done, depending on your taste.

A duck is done when the meat starts shrinking from the leg joints and the skin is very brown and crisp. Best test is to lift the bird with a two-pronged fork and pour out juices that will have accumulated in the cavity. If they are red, the bird is not cooked, if pink the bird is medium done, and if clear, it is well done. If you like, you can take the bird's temperature as well, inserting the thermometer in the thickest part of the thigh: for medium meat it should register 160°F and about 170°F for well-done meat.

Transfer the duck to a platter or carving board, cover it loosely with foil, and keep in a warm place about 10 minutes so juices are reabsorbed. Meanwhile make a pan gravy (page 86) or sauce with cherries (see right). Carve the duck in the kitchen, or at the table (page 147).

Roast Duck with Cherries

Duck with cherries is a special summer treat when fresh cherries are in season. As a cold-weather alternative, substitute 1/2 cup pitted dried cherries, soaking them and then simmering in port wine until they are tender, 10 to 15 minutes.

Serves 2 to 3

> **1 duck (about 5 pounds)**
> **1 pound tart cherries**
> **1 cup port wine**
> **1 tablespoon sugar**
> **1 tablespoon red currant jelly**
> **salt and pepper to taste**
> **1 tablespoon flour**
> **1 cup chicken stock**

Pit the cherries. Put the port wine, sugar, and red currant jelly in a medium pan and heat, stirring, until the jelly melts and the sugar dissolves. Stir in the cherries, take from the heat, and leave to soak while roasting the duck (see opposite).

Meanwhile, simmer the cherries in their liquid until just tender, 5 to 7 minutes. When the duck is done, make the gravy: Discard all fat from the roasting pan and stir in the flour. Cook it, stirring until brown, 1 to 2 minutes. Add the stock and bring the gravy to a boil, whisking until it thickens. Simmer until it generously coats a spoon, 4 to 5 minutes. Taste and adjust seasoning. Strain the gravy into the cherries and syrup and reheat it if necessary. Serve the duck with the cherries and sauce spooned over it.

GETTING AHEAD: The cherries can be cooked up to 2 days ahead and refrigerated with their liquid. Roast the duck, make the gravy, and finish the sauce just before serving.

Orange Glazed Duck

This is my quick version of the grand classic, delicious with wild rice. The orange sauce is based on a pan gravy that's flavored with caramel dissolved in vinegar, giving it a characteristic sweet-sour bite.

Serves 2 to 3

> **1 duck (about 5 pounds)**
> **salt and pepper to taste**
> **2 oranges**
>
> **FOR THE SAUCE**
> **3 tablespoons sugar**
> **3 tablespoons red wine vinegar**
> **2 tablespoons flour**
> **1 cup chicken stock**
> **2 tablespoons Grand Marnier, more to taste**

Prepare the duck as for Plain Roast Duck (page 169), putting the pared zest of 1 orange inside the duck before trussing. Roast it as directed. While it is roasting, pare zest from the remaining orange, and with a large knife, cut it into the thinnest possible julienne strips (see How to Cut Vegetable Julienne, page 235). Simmer the strips in boiling water for 2 minutes, drain, and set them aside. Cut the pith and skin from the 2 oranges, scoop out the segments with a knife, and reserve them in a medium saucepan with their juice.

When the duck is done, transfer it to a platter and keep it warm. Make the sauce: Spread the sugar in a small saucepan and cook over moderate heat. When the sugar starts to melt, reduce the heat to very low and continue cooking, swirling occasionally, until it is a deep golden brown caramel, 3 to 5 minutes. When the sugar is caramelized (watch carefully as it can scorch quite fast), remove it from the heat at once and add the vinegar, standing back as the vapor will sting your eyes. Drain the juice from the segmented oranges into the pan, stir, if necessary warming the mixture over the heat to dissolve the caramel, and set aside.

Pour all but 2 tablespoons fat from the roasting pan. Stir in the flour and cook until brown, $1/2$ to 1 minute. Whisk in the stock and bring the sauce to a boil, scraping to dissolve pan juices. Strain it into the pan of caramel mixture and simmer until the sauce is well flavored and generously coats a spoon. Taste and adjust seasoning.

Add a few spoonfuls of sauce to the orange segments and heat gently, 1 to 2 minutes. Spoon them with the sauce over the duck. Add the orange julienne and Grand Marnier to the remaining sauce, bring just to a boil, and adjust the seasoning, adding more Grand Marnier if you like. Serve the sauce separately from the duck.

GETTING AHEAD: The orange segments and julienne can be prepared ahead, but the sauce can be made only after the duck has been roasted.

Spiced Roast Duck

This recipe cuts across the centuries, adding an Asian twist to medieval European roast duck. A luscious honey glaze colors the bird's skin to rich mahogany. Serve it with a compote of quince or tart apples.

Serves 2 to 3

Make a spiced basting sauce by melting 3 heaping tablespoons honey with 2 tablespoons red wine vinegar, 1 tablespoon five-spice powder, and 1 teaspoon ground ginger in a small saucepan. Preheat the oven and prepare a duck as for Plain Roast Duck (page 169). Set it in a roasting pan and brush with spiced sauce. Roast as directed, basting often and taking care not to let the honey pan juices scorch—if they start to brown, add some duck or chicken stock to the pan. When the duck is cooked (it will be deep golden brown), transfer it to a platter and keep warm. For gravy: Discard fat from the roasting pan, add 1 cup stock and boil, stirring to dissolve juices, until reduced by half. Taste and adjust seasoning.

Duck Magret

Magret refers to the boneless breast meat of a domestic duck, and you'll find it in gourmet stores and via producers of foie gras (fattened duck liver). These magrets are meaty and plumper than the breast you'll find on the average roasting duck. Think of magret as a sophisticated steak and you can't go wrong. It says to me bold flavor, rich, juicy meat, and individual servings (sometimes one breast is enough for two). Watch out—magret toughens dramatically when overcooked so it is best served rare, or at most pink. The meat is sold with the skin, and I would advise leaving it on for moisture during cooking. After that, you can discard it if you wish but what a pity!

Magret of Duck with Ginger and Scallions

This simple little ginger and scallion glaze adds an Asian touch to magret. Personally, I find that a plump magret, weighing ten ounces or more, is enough for two, but as with beef steak, serving size depends on personal taste.

Accompaniments can go in several directions such as fruit chutney, rice pilaf (page 222), or a salad of bitter greens.

Serves 1 to 2

1 large duck magret (about ¾ pound)

FOR THE GLAZE
1-inch piece of ginger, sliced
1 scallion, including green parts,
   cut in pieces
2 tablespoons hoisin sauce
2 tablespoons mirin rice wine or
   medium sherry
1 tablespoon soy sauce, more to taste
1 teaspoon chile oil or a pinch of
   cayenne, more to taste

Preheat the oven to 350°F. Combine the ginger and scallion in a food processor and work them until coarsely chopped. Add the hoisin sauce, mirin, soy sauce, and chile oil and work to a purée. Taste and adjust seasoning, including soy sauce and chile oil. Crosshatch the skin of the magret with the point of a knife, cutting almost through to the meat so fat is released during cooking. Heat a dry frying pan over medium heat, add the magret, and fry until the skin is thoroughly brown and crisp, 3 to 5 minutes, or longer if necessary to extract a maximum of fat. Turn and brown the other side, 2 to 3 minutes. Pour off excess fat.

Transfer the magret to a shallow baking dish and pour the ginger and scallion sauce over it, basting well so the magret is coated. Roast it in the oven, allowing 8 to 12 minutes for rare meat, or 12 to 15 minutes if you prefer it well done—much depends on the thickness of the meat. Test by pressing the meat with a fingertip: it should feel resilient for medium done meat or firm for well done, just as for a beef steak.

To finish: Reheat the magret if necessary. Transfer the magret to a chopping board and leave 4 to 5 minutes for juices to be reabsorbed. Carve the magret on the diagonal, as for steak, and spoon the pan juices over it. Personally I like thin slices, but thicker ones are fine, too. Note that the seasoned, spicy skin is the best part!

GETTING AHEAD: Magret can be roasted an hour or so ahead. Wrap it in aluminum foil, reheat it in a very hot oven for 1 to 2 minutes (in restaurant-speak, "flash it"), then slice it for serving.

CHAPTER SEVEN mastering meats

I like to take my time to pick and choose my meat. Just occasionally I find a friendly butcher who can direct me to the best cut for the dish I want to make. If you find a good guy behind the counter, don't hesitate to ask questions. The array in the market can be bewildering, especially in the beef section, and it's very important to find the right piece. However, if you look closer you'll find groupings: whole roasts are in one place, steaks and more tender cuts in another, stew meats and other less familiar pieces in a third. There are characteristic cooking methods for each.

Large cuts for roasting are easy to eyeball. They may come on the bone, which adds flavor and helps keep the meat moist; typical are beef rib roast, rack of lamb, or pork ribs. When the children come home, one of our family treats is roast leg of lamb on the bone laced with garlic and herbs. More common are cuts that are boneless or have been boned, such as beef tenderloin, lamb leg and shoulder, pork loin and sirloin, and veal round. If you take a bit of time to carefully trim and tie them before roasting, as I explain on page 179, you'll be amply rewarded. Always make sure that a large cut of beef or lamb for pan roasting, which calls for high, dry heat, is well marbled with fat. Lean cuts such as beef chuck and round may look temptingly meaty, but they are best pot roasted with liquid at a lower temperature. If in doubt, play it safe and pot roast.

The steak section probably needs no introduction. Again marbling is the key to a steak that will grill or broil to be juicy and tender. The same is true of lamb, with chops cut from the rack or the loin the best choice for grilling; shoulder chops are less expensive, but more chewy. Alas, in this section of the meat case you get what you pay for, particularly with the red meats, lamb and beef. To be economical you may do better with a plump pork chop (it should not be cut too thin), sautéing it with a bit of fat rather than exposing it to the heat of the grill or broiler.

Last section of the supermarket meat case will include stew meat and ground meat. Quality here can vary a lot, so inspect the package with care. Stew meat should be thoroughly trimmed of connective tissue, with a bit of fat (but only a bit) left for flavor. The meat should not look wet and its color should be clear, not faded. With ground meats, freshness is all-important: a big stack of unsold packages can be a bad sign, as is discoloration of the meat.

HOW TO ROAST MEAT

When I think big for Christmas or a family birthday, I go for roasting a grand cut of meat. We all know the most famous: tenderloin, rib, and sirloin of beef; tenderloin, loin, and rack of pork; and rack, saddle, and leg of lamb. These are the pampered parts of the animal that don't do much work and so don't develop tough sinews. For roasting, I'm a firm believer in buying top-quality meat, marbled with fat (see Choosing and Storing Meat, opposite). Some cooks also roast less luxurious cuts, such as beef rib eye and lamb shoulder, but I find them better cooked more slowly in moist heat as a pot roast or braise (page 181). The same is true of veal—as a young meat, it dries out easily and I don't recommend oven roasting it.

Let's face it, roasting is hard on meat as it is cooked uncovered in searing oven heat to create a tasty brown crust and a moist interior. Bigger cuts acquire a succulent crust in the oven during the long cooking time. To ensure a crisp outside on smaller cuts—beef tenderloin, for example—first I brown them on top of the stove, then I roast them fast, at high heat, so the center remains juicy. Beef should be roasted until rare, medium, or well done, while lamb and veal may be medium or well done. Pork is the only meat that should always be thoroughly cooked, to a stage where the roast loses all but the faintest pink color. You'll see how to judge this in the pictures, and in the box on Roasting Times and Temperatures, page 178.

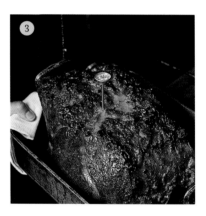

① Preheat the oven as called for in the recipe, and season the meat (here a rib roast with a mustard topping). For added crispness, sprinkle the surface of the roast with flour. Score any surface fat in a diamond pattern with the tip of a knife. Set the meat in the roasting pan and moisten it with a tablespoon or two of vegetable oil.

② Once in the hot oven (be sure to heat it well ahead), the roast will start to sizzle and need basting with the pan drippings. Drippings on their own are fine, or for moisture and taste, you may like to add a liquid such as stock, red or white wine, or cider. But none of these will do much good unless you baste often—it's the key to everything. If the shape of the cut is cylindrical, turn it from time to time so it browns evenly. When done, the meat should be well browned, crispy, and starting to pull away from any bones. The pan juices should be well reduced.

③ To test if a roast is done: Press the meat with your finger; if very soft it is still rare. When springy it is medium done, and when firm it is well done. The most accurate test is to insert a meat thermometer in the thickest part of the meat. For rare roast beef, as here, it should measure 125°F. A large roast will continue cooking because of retained heat for up to 10 minutes after you take it from the oven, so allow for this in your calculations.

When taken from the oven, your roast meat will improve if you cover it loosely with aluminum foil and leave it for 10 to 15 minutes in a warm place. This helps its internal temperature to stabilize so fewer juices are lost during carving. While waiting, make the pan gravy (page 86) that is half the pleasure of a grand roast. Other accompaniments are enormously varied and depend on family tradition. We always enjoy Gratin Dauphinois and green beans with roast lamb, fresh fruit chutney with pork, and potatoes roasted in pan drippings plus Yorkshire pudding for roast beef (I am from Yorkshire after all!).

roasting rules

* When roasting, a half pound of boneless meat is an average serving.

* Let meat come to room temperature before roasting.

* To flavor the meat before roasting, rub the surface with pepper, dry mustard, and spices such as paprika or allspice, or aromatic herbs such as thyme and rosemary. Leave the seasoned meat to mellow an hour or two in the refrigerator.

* The roasting pan should be a couple of inches larger all around than the meat itself (see How to Choose a Roasting Pan, page 164).

* Rolling and tying meat with string before roasting holds it in shape so it cooks evenly (see How to Roll and Tie a Roast, page 179).

* To prevent the meat from stewing in fat at the bottom of the pan, you can lift it on a rack or set it on some sliced onion and carrot.

* Roast meat should not wait longer than a quarter hour. It will overcook if you try to keep it warm.

* If reheated, roast meat tends to be dry and tough, so leftovers are best served at room temperature with a cheerful chutney or salsa. You'll find a few in this book.

choosing and storing meat

The top three grades for USDA-inspected beef, lamb, and veal are prime, choice, and select (pork is not graded). Prime meat is sold only by specialty butchers, so the choice grade is the best you'll find in most supermarkets. Beef and lamb should be well marbled with fat and trimmed of sinew and excess surface fat. I find that color is a good indicator—beef should be a clear, deep crimson rather than bright red; lamb will be paler, particularly when very young, but should always be rosy.

Good veal is pale, creamy pink—a red tinge to the veal indicates it is no longer milk fed and is likely to be tough. In pork, I look for a fine grain in the meat; the color of good-quality pork may vary from pink to beige depending on the breed. All meats should look moist and fresh with no discolored edges; wet meat is a sign of poor handling.

Storage time for meat depends a good deal on the size of the piece and how it is wrapped. You should always keep meat in the coldest part of the refrigerator, wrapped a bit loosely, preferably in traditional butcher paper so air can circulate. Look for the sell-by date on the package: a large roast can usually be kept at home for three to five days, and steaks and chops for two to four days. Ground meat deteriorates much faster and is best used within a day, or two at the most.

Roast Rib of Beef with Pan Gravy

At least one world-class dish has come out of England and that's roast beef. At my mother's house, roast beef was always a celebration, the centerpiece of the family Sunday lunch or a winter dinner for friends. Our home was in Yorkshire, the region famous for the best accompaniment to roast beef, Yorkshire pudding. The crisp cup of batter pudding, resembling a popover and filled with gravy, was at least as good as the meat itself. Other side dishes would invariably include crisp potatoes, roasted golden in drippings from the meat, and horseradish sauce made from the freshly grated root and stirred into whipped cream (opposite page).

Serves 6 to 8

1 standing rib roast with 3 to 4 ribs
(about 7 pounds)
2 teaspoons dry mustard
2 teaspoons Dijon mustard
2 teaspoons sugar
salt and pepper to taste
2 tablespoons vegetable oil

FOR THE GRAVY
2 tablespoons flour
2 cups beef stock or water

Cut away any excess fat from the meat, leaving a thin layer. Combine the mustards and sugar and rub the mixture over the meat. Refrigerate the roast for 2 to 12 hours.

Let the meat come to room temperature and preheat the oven to 450°F.

Sprinkle the beef with salt and pepper, score the fat in a lattice pattern with the tip of a knife, cutting almost through to the meat, and set it rib side down in a roasting pan. Drizzle it with oil and roast it for 15 minutes, then lower the heat to 375°F. Continue roasting, basting often with pan juices, until the beef is done as you like it, 1 3/4 to 2 1/2 hours total. It should be well browned and pulling away from the bones. A meat thermometer should read 125 to 130°F for rare meat, 140 to 145°F for medium, and 160 to 165°F for well done.

Transfer the roast to a cutting board and, before carving, let it rest 15 minutes, loosely covered with aluminum foil. Meanwhile, make the gravy: Pour off all but 2 tablespoons of fat from the roasting pan, leaving the caramelized juices. Set the pan over medium heat and stir in the flour. Cook, scraping up the caramelized bits, until the flour is a deep golden brown, 1 to 2 minutes. Stir in the stock and bring to a boil, stirring until the gravy thickens. It should lightly coat the back of a spoon. If necessary, simmer a few minutes to reduce it. Taste and adjust the seasoning. Strain the gravy into a sauce boat and keep it warm while carving the meat.

GETTING AHEAD: By all means marinate the meat up to 12 hours ahead, but a grand roast like this must arrive at table fresh from the oven.

how to carve roast ribs of beef

The best way to carve rib roast depends on how many ribs are included. In any case, the bones are first cut away, and diners like me will ask for a bone to scrape as well as sliced meat.

For a two- to three-rib roast: Set the meat fat side upward and, holding it steady with a two-pronged fork, cut away the rib bones at the base in a single piece. Turn the meat on its side and carve it across the grain into diagonal slices, thin or thick as you prefer.

For a four- to seven-rib roast: Hold the meat steady with a two-pronged fork and cut along the rib bones to remove them completely in a single sheet. Set the meat on a board, boned side down, and cut vertically to form thin or thick slices.

Sides for Roast Beef

Two of the traditional accompaniments to roast beef—Yorkshire pudding and potatoes roasted in pan drippings—are cooked in the oven with the meat, so you'll need two oven shelves, the lower one for the beef, the other for the puddings and potatoes.

Oven-Roasted Potatoes

If you enjoy potatoes roasted in pan drippings, be sure to add a few extra tablespoons of oil when you start roasting the beef. The oil will be flavored with beef juices—perfect for cooking the potatoes. Start the potatoes about 1¼ hours before you expect the roast to be done.

Serves 6 to 8

Scrub 4 to 6 baking potatoes (about 3 pounds) and cut them in 3 to 4 pieces. Put them in a large pan of salted water, cover, and bring to a boil. Simmer the pieces 5 to 7 minutes and drain them. Let them cool slightly, then peel them and scratch the surface with a fork (this makes for a crisper potato). Heat 4 to 6 tablespoons pan drippings from the roast in a separate roasting pan on the stove. Add the potatoes and stir to coat them with drippings. Roast the potatoes in a preheated 375°F oven, or in the oven on a rack above the beef, until tender, crisp, and very brown, about 1 hour. Stir and baste them occasionally. Just before serving, sprinkle them with salt.

Fresh Horseradish Sauce

Horseradish root looks innocuous but will sting your eyes, so stand back when you are grating it. If substituting bottled horseradish, allow 3 tablespoons.

Makes 1¹/₂ cups sauce to serve 6 to 8

Peel a small horseradish root and grate 1 to 2 tablespoons on the medium grid of a grater. Whisk ³/₄ cup heavy cream in a bowl until it holds soft peaks. Stir in the horseradish, juice of ¹/₂ lemon, salt, and pepper. Taste and adjust seasoning. Horseradish sauce can be refrigerated up to 24 hours.

Yorkshire Pudding

Yorkshire puddings resemble popovers, and I find they rise best in large muffin tins. The puddings are best served at once, but can be kept warm in a low oven while you make gravy.

Makes 12 puddings

> **1 cup flour**
> **¹/₂ teaspoon salt**
> **freshly ground black pepper to taste**
> **2 eggs**
> **1¹/₂ cups milk, more if needed**
> **6 to 8 tablespoons drippings from the roasting pan**
>
> **twelve 1-cup muffin tins**

Put the flour, salt, and pepper to taste in a bowl and make a well in the center. Add the eggs and about a quarter of the milk and whisk until mixed. Stir in the flour from the sides of the well until you have a smooth stiff batter. Stir in the remaining milk, cover the batter, and let it stand for at least 30 minutes at room temperature so the starch in the flour expands.

About half an hour before the beef is done, bake the puddings: Using a bulb baster or spoon, pour about 2 teaspoons of drippings from the roasting pan into each of the muffin tins. Put the tins in the oven on a rack above the beef. Stir more milk into the batter if necessary to make it the consistency of heavy cream. When the drippings in the tins are very hot, pour in the batter, filling them about one-third full. The batter should sizzle in the hot fat. Bake the puddings in a preheated 375°F oven, or in the oven above the beef, until puffed, browned, and crisp, 25 to 30 minutes.

roasting times and temperatures for meat

BEEF AND LAMB

I like to start a beef or lamb roast in high heat (450°F) for 15 minutes, then I turn down the temperature to 375°F. Note that beef tenderloin is cooked very fast at high heat.

* For rare meat (beef only)

Minutes per pound: 12 to 15 minutes

Temperature on meat thermometer: 125°F

* For medium done

Minutes per pound: 15 to 18 minutes

Temperature on meat thermometer: 140°F

* For well done

Minutes per pound: 18 to 20 minutes

Temperature on meat thermometer: 160°F

PORK AND VEAL

Pork and veal roasts are best begun at 425°F for 15 minutes, then cooked at 350°F. I cover veal, and often pork, too, loosely with aluminum foil so the roast stays moist. Both veal and pork should be served well done, or very lightly pink.

* For lightly pink meat

Minutes per pound: 18 to 22 minutes

Temperature on meat thermometer: 150°F

* For well done

Minutes per pound: 22 to 25 minutes

Temperature on meat thermometer: 160°F

Roast Pork with Cabbage, Potatoes, and Plums

"Saturday dinner!" this recipe says to me. Pork takes happily to the tart sweetness of plums, while potatoes and cabbage make it a complete meal.

Serves 4 to 6

> **2 pounds boneless pork loin**
> **6 tablespoons butter, more for the pan**
> **2 pounds potatoes, peeled and cut in**
>   **1-inch chunks**
> **1/2 head of cabbage (about 1 pound)**
> **1 tablespoon caraway seeds**
> **salt and pepper to taste**
> **large bunch of sage**
> **1 pound purple plums, halved and pitted**
> **1 cup chicken stock**

Preheat the oven to 425°F. Melt half the butter in a large frying pan and add the potatoes. Brown them over medium heat on all sides, stirring often, 15 to 18 minutes. Quarter the cabbage, discard the core, and cut it crosswise in 1/2-inch slices. Stir the cabbage, caraway seeds, salt, and pepper into the potatoes. Continue cooking until both vegetables are browned and tender, 10 to 12 minutes longer.

Meanwhile, tie the pork in a neat cylinder (see opposite). Pull sage leaves from the stems, reserving a few sprigs for decoration. Chop the leaves. Spread the pork with the remaining butter and sprinkle with half the sage, salt, and pepper. Put it in a large buttered roasting pan and roast in the oven. After 15 minutes, lower the heat to 350°F and continue roasting, basting often, until the meat is tender and the juices run clear when the meat is pierced with a skewer, about 1 1/2 hours total. About 20 minutes before the pork is done, stir the plums into the potatoes and cabbage, and spread them around the pork. Continue roasting until the pork is done and the vegetables are tender and very brown. A meat thermometer should read 160°F when inserted in the center of the pork.

Transfer the pork and vegetables to a platter and keep warm. Discard fat from the roasting pan, add the stock, and stir to dissolve the pan juices. Stir in the remaining chopped sage and boil the gravy briefly, until concentrated, then taste and adjust the seasoning. Carve the meat in generous slices, discarding the strings, and serve with the vegetables, plums, and gravy. Decorate with the reserved sprigs of sage.

GETTING AHEAD: I would not roast the pork and vegetables ahead, but they can be covered loosely with foil and kept warm in a low oven for up to half an hour without harm.

how to roll and tie a roast

Rolling and tying a roast is one of the most popular techniques when I give a cooking class. With its honor guard of string and tidy knots, the meat looks almost gift-wrapped. However, tying a roast is not just for show. Meat that has been carefully bundled into a cylinder cooks more evenly and can be carved into neater slices, particularly after it has been boned. To moisten a tougher cut, the surface can be covered with sliced bacon or barding fat (thinly sliced pork fat that you'll find at specialty butchers), though the meat underneath will not then brown to a crust. Herbs, shallots, and chopped garlic can be tucked under the fat, or you can spring a surprise inside, for example, prunes stuffed in a pork roast.

I have a special double knot for tying meat (Christmas parcels, too) that you'll see at right. The circular strings discipline cylindrical cuts such as beef tenderloin and improve the shape of uneven pieces such as beef round and veal breast. The floppy profile of the average veal roast is also much improved by

tying. Slicing between the strings produces hearty tournedos steaks from beef tenderloin, medallions from pork loin, and noisettes from rack and sirloin of lamb (see How to Cut Tournedos, Medallions, and Noisettes, page 198).

1 Cover the meat with bacon or barding fat if you wish. Wrap two strings lengthwise around the meat (here a pork roast) so it does not curl during cooking, then knot and tie the strings. Wrap a string around one end of the meat, giving a second turn to the knot. Pull it tight and give a sharp twist—it will hold just long enough to add a second knot to secure the first. Snip the string. Repeat at the other end of the meat, then fill in with more strings, spacing them evenly so the meat is tied in a neat cylinder.

Leg of Lamb with Garlic and Herbs

From Turkey to southern Spain, here's how lamb is roasted in the Mediterranean. A layer of sliced onions and potatoes cooks underneath the meat, absorbing the juices.

Serves 6 to 8

1 leg of lamb on the bone (5 to 6 pounds)
4 to 5 garlic cloves, peeled
medium bunch of rosemary
medium bunch of thyme
salt and pepper to taste
2 tablespoons olive oil
8 medium potatoes (about 3 pounds),
**   peeled and sliced**
6 medium onions (about 1½ pounds),
**   thinly sliced**
2 cups brown stock, more if needed

Preheat the oven to 450°F. Cut 1 garlic clove in slivers and chop the rest. Trim the skin and all but a thin layer of fat from the lamb. Poke several holes in the meat with the point of a knife and insert the garlic slivers. Pound the rosemary and thyme with a rolling pin to release the aromas, rub the lamb with a sprig of each, and sprinkle it with salt and pepper. Put the leg in a baking dish or roasting pan large enough to hold it and the potatoes and onions, and spoon the olive oil over it. Roast the lamb in the oven for 15 minutes.

Meanwhile, mix the potatoes, onions, chopped garlic, salt, and pepper in a large bowl. After 15 minutes, take out the lamb leg and set it aside. Lower the oven heat to 375°F. Spread the potato mixture in the roasting pan, tucking rosemary and thyme sprigs down among the vegetables. Add the stock—it should almost cover the vegetables—and if necessary add more.

Replace the lamb and continue roasting, basting often with stock, until it is done to your taste, 1½ to 2 hours. A meat thermometer should register 140°F for medium done meat or 160°F for well done. The vegetables should be very tender, browned, and moist but not soupy. If they are not browned, remove the meat and continue roasting at high heat until done. If they are soupy, boil the pan on top of the stove until the juices are reduced. Taste and adjust seasoning.

To finish: If necessary, reheat the lamb in the oven. Cover it loosely with aluminum foil and leave it for 10 to 15 minutes before serving it with the potatoes in the baking dish. I like to carve the lamb at the table: Hold the leg by the shank, rounded muscle upward. Cut horizontal slices lengthwise, working away from the shank, until you reach the thigh bone. Turn the leg over and set the cut side downward. Carve more horizontal slices on this side until you reach the thigh bone again. Finally, carve slices from the meat left on each side of the bone.

how to roast a beef tenderloin

Beef tenderloin should be roasted at very high heat. Cooking time is gauged by measuring the thickness of the meat, not by its weight.

Preheat the oven to 500°F. Trim any sinew, membrane, or excess fat from the tenderloin and fold under the tapered end to give the roast an even shape. Tie it with string. Measure the diameter of the meat with a ruler: allow 8 to 9 minutes per inch for rare meat, 9 to 10 minutes for medium done, and 10 to 12 minutes for well done.

Season the beef with salt and pepper. Heat a tablespoon or two of oil in a roasting pan and brown the meat on all sides over high heat, allowing 5 to 7 minutes. Transfer it to the oven and roast, basting often, for the measured time. Take the internal temperature with a meat thermometer; it should register 125°F for rare meat, 140°F for medium done, and 160°F for well-done meat. Take the roast from the oven, cover it loosely with aluminum foil, and leave it for 10 to 15 minutes, or until cool if you are serving it cold. Discard strings just before carving.

HOW TO POT ROAST MEAT

You might be surprised by how many famous recipes are closely related to homey American pot roast. German *sauerbraten* (marinated in spiced vinegar), Italian *stufato Milanese* (red wine and spices), French *daube* (beef or lamb with olives), Jewish *tzimmes* (beef with prunes), and English breast of veal with lemon, sage, and breadcrumb stuffing all belong to the pot roast family. Pot roasting is best for lean cuts of beef such as round or chuck, as well as veal shoulder, breast, and shank, lamb shoulder and breast, and pork shoulder,

ribs, and leg. These are the hard-working parts of the animal, full of flavor and tough—sometimes very tough. They need plenty of liquid and long, slow cooking.

When pot roasted, a large piece of meat stays moister than a small one. In gentle heat, the meat softens to be meltingly tender, falling from any bones, while gelatinous tissue dissolves to enrich the sauce. Traditionally, pot roast should be soft enough to cut with a spoon. At least as beguiling as the meat of a pot roast is the sauce. It should be

1　Preheat the oven to 325°F, or a bit lower, as indicated in the recipe. Season the meat (here pork loin for Italian Pot Roast Pork with Milk) with salt, pepper, and possibly aromatics such as allspice, cloves, cinnamon, and nutmeg. Brown the meat on all sides in a bit of fat on top of the stove, then discard any excess fat. Add any flavorings called for in the recipe—few cooks, certainly not me, can resist adding an onion or two, garlic, and some carrot and other roots such as celery, turnip, or whatever happens to be on hand. (Here is an herb and garlic mixture.)

2　Add enough liquid to half cover the meat, often wine, beer, beef or veal stock, milk as here, or simply water. Cover the pot and, to speed cooking, bring it to a boil on top of the stove before putting it in the oven. Turn the meat from time to time so it stays moist on all sides, and add more liquid if the pan seems dry.

3　To test that the meat is thoroughly cooked, insert a metal skewer into the roast for about 30 seconds, then hold it against your wrist: it should be hot to the touch and juices should run clear. The temperature on a meat thermometer inserted in the thickest part of the meat should be 160°F. (No matter what the meat is, a pot roast should always be well done.)

4　When done, a pot roast is firm to the touch when you press it, and feels tender if you pierce it with a two-pronged fork. When carved, it should be meltingly tender and almost falling apart.

concentrated, lightly thickened, and dark or chestnut brown, depending on the recipe. If it looks and tastes a bit thin, remove the meat and boil the sauce to reduce it; if the sauce is thick and sticky, thin it with stock or a little water.

There's sometimes confusion between the terms pot roasting, stewing, and braising. For me a pot roast involves a large piece of meat and a stew uses smaller ones. A braise takes another, mainly French, route. Strictly speaking, a braise is flavored with a mixture of diced carrot, onion, and celery (called a *mirepoix*) that is strained out of the sauce before serving. However the term braise is often applied to both pot roasting and stewing. Let's not be picky; in practice, when braising most cooks serve the *mirepoix* with all manner of other ingredients in the finished dish.

pot roasting essentials

* You should allow 6 to 8 ounces of boneless meat per person.

* For pot roasting, you need a heavy flameproof casserole that holds the meat easily without touching the sides.

* During cooking, the liquid should simmer very gently. If the sauce boils the meat will toughen.

* An oven temperature of 300°F is ideal.

* Since pot roasts and braises come with their sauce, and often with vegetables as well, the only accompaniment needed is boiled or mashed potatoes, pasta, or a boiled grain.

* In contrast to roast meat that should be served as soon as it is cooked, pot roasts benefit from resting a day or two in the refrigerator so flavors blend and mellow.

* Leftovers of pot roast, whether sliced or in one piece, reheat deliciously in the gravy—on top of the stove or in the oven.

* Pot roasts also freeze well up to 6 months.

Pot Roast of Beef with Red Wine

To make this a complete meal, add some vegetables to the casserole 1 1/2 hours before the end of cooking. I'd suggest quartered carrots with celery root or turnip, cut in chunks. The vegetables will color deep red in the wine gravy and taste delicious.

Serves 4 to 6

1 piece of beef chuck or round (about 3 pounds)
3 tablespoons flour
1/2 teaspoon ground cloves
1/2 teaspoon ground cinnamon
salt and pepper to taste
2 tablespoons vegetable oil
1/4 pound thickly sliced bacon, cut in
    1/4-inch dice
1 onion, chopped
3 garlic cloves, chopped
bouquet garni of 1 bay leaf, 2 to 3
    sprigs basil, and 2 to 3 sprigs marjoram
1 bottle (750 ml) red wine

Preheat the oven to 300°F. Roll and tie the roast neatly with string (see How to Roll and Tie a Roast, page 179). Mix the flour on a plate with the cloves, cinnamon, and a half teaspoon each of salt and pepper. Coat the meat in the flour mixture, patting with your hands so it adheres.

Heat the oil in a casserole, add the meat, and brown it very thoroughly on all sides over medium heat, 10 to 15 minutes. Remove the meat and wipe out the pan if there are black specks. Add the bacon and fry it until the fat runs, 3 to 5 minutes. Add the onion and fry, stirring, until the bacon and onion are browned, 5 to 7 minutes longer. Put the meat back with the garlic and bouquet garni. Pour in the wine, cover the casserole, and bring it to a boil. Transfer it to the oven and cook until the meat is so tender it can almost be cut with a spoon, 3 1/2 to 4 1/2 hours. Turn the beef from time to time during cooking, adding water if the wine evaporates—the meat should always be half covered.

Transfer the beef to a serving platter and keep it warm in a low oven. Strain the cooking juices and taste them. If necessary, boil the gravy to reduce and concentrate it, up to 15 minutes. Taste again and adjust the seasoning. Discard the bouquet garni and trussing strings and carve the meat in generous slices. Spoon some gravy over the meat and pass the rest separately.

GETTING AHEAD: Pot roast improves on reheating, so make it up to 2 days ahead.

Beef Pot Roast in Sweet-Sour Sauce (*Sauerbraten*)

The sour in *Sauerbraten* comes from vinegar, with sweetness from raisins and the ginger cookie crumbs that thicken the sauce. You must start well ahead as the beef should be marinated at least a day before cooking. Round or chuck roast is a good cut, and be sure to use an aged red or white wine vinegar. When it comes to serving, noodles are a good foil for the sauce.

Serves 6 to 8

1 beef pot roast (3 to 4 pounds)
2 tablespoons vegetable oil
½ cup raisins
½ cup crumbled ginger cookies
½ cup sour cream
salt and pepper to taste

FOR THE MARINADE
3 cups water, more as needed
1 cup red or white wine vinegar
1 tablespoon honey
5 to 6 star anise
1 teaspoon black peppercorns
1 teaspoon juniper berries

Make the marinade: Combine the water, vinegar, and honey in a saucepan and bring to a boil. Put the anise, peppercorns, and juniper berries in a plastic bag, crush them with a rolling pin, and add to the marinade. Simmer it for 10 minutes, then cool and chill it.

Marinate the beef: Roll and tie the roast neatly with string (see How to Roll and Tie a Roast, page 179). Put it in a plastic bag and set it, open, in a bowl. Pour the marinade over the roast, seal the bag, excluding air so the meat is covered with marinade, and refrigerate, 1 to 2 days.

Preheat the oven to 300°F. Drain the beef, reserving the marinade, and pat it dry with paper towels. Heat the oil in a casserole and brown the meat very well on all sides, 10 to 15 minutes. Pour the marinade over the meat, cover, and bring it to a boil. Put the roast in the oven and cook until the meat is very tender when pierced with a two-pronged fork, 3 to 4 hours. A skewer inserted in the center of the meat should be hot to the touch when withdrawn after 30 seconds. Baste the meat and turn it from time to time during cooking. Add water if the pan gets dry—the meat should always be half-covered by liquid.

Transfer the beef to a carving board and cover it with aluminum foil to keep warm. Strain the cooking juices into a saucepan—you should have about 2 cups. If not, boil them down or add water. Stir in the raisins, crumbled cookies, and sour cream then bring the sauce to a boil on top of the stove. If necessary, simmer it until quite thick, taste, and adjust seasoning. Discard strings from the beef, carve generous slices, and arrange them overlapping on a platter. Moisten the meat with sauce, serving the rest separately.

GETTING AHEAD: The flavor of *Sauerbraten* mellows temptingly on standing for 2 to 3 days in the refrigerator, so I usually make a generous quantity.

Glazed Ham with Apples

Country ham needs fruit to balance the salt, and for me apples are just right. A delicious syrupy caramel gravy brings it all together.

Serves 4 to 6

> **1 shank or butt end of cooked country ham on the bone (about 4 pounds)**
> **2 cups dry cider, more for gravy**
> **¾ cup dark brown sugar**
> **1 teaspoon ground ginger**
>
> **FOR THE STUFFED APPLES**
> **6 to 8 small tart apples (about 2¼ pounds)**
> **4 tablespoons butter, softened**
> **¼ cup dark brown sugar**
> **2 tablespoons chopped candied ginger**

Preheat the oven to 325°F. Stuff the apples: Wipe the apples, core them, and cut a circle around the equator of each so they do not burst. Cream the butter, stir in the sugar and ginger, and fill the apple cavities with the stuffing.

Trim any skin from the ham and all but a thin layer of fat. Score the fat in a lattice pattern with the point of a knife, cutting almost through to the meat. Put the ham in a casserole and pour the cider over it. Cover the pot, bring it to a boil, and cook in the oven for 20 minutes. Arrange the apples around the ham and continue cooking 30 to 40 minutes longer. A skewer inserted in the center of the ham should be hot to the touch when withdrawn after 30 seconds. Remove the ham and set it aside. Test the apples also with the skewer: if they are not tender, let them continue cooking until done; if they cook more quickly than the ham, remove them first.

Boil the cooking liquid on the stovetop until it begins to caramelize. Let it caramelize for 1 minute, then remove from the heat. Mix the brown sugar and ginger in a bowl and stir in the caramelized pan juices to make a very stiff paste. Spread the paste over the ham, return it to the oven, and continue cooking until it melts into a rich dark brown glaze, 25 to 35 minutes, basting occasionally. About 10 minutes before the end of

Glazed Ham with Apples

cooking, replace the apples in the casserole to reheat them.

Transfer the ham and apples to a serving platter and keep warm in a low oven. Stir the caramel gravy in the pan: if it is very thick, add a few tablespoons of cider and simmer, stirring to melt the caramel. The gravy should be very syrupy. Pour it over the ham and apples. Carve the ham in generous slices at table, and serve it with gravy and apples.

GETTING AHEAD: Glazed ham is delicious cold as well as hot, so making it ahead is no problem.

Italian Pot Roast Pork with Milk (Arista)

Roasting pork with milk, an ancient trick for whitening the meat, also produces a pleasant gravy the color of a café latté. Don't be alarmed if the sauce separates slightly—it usually does. If this bothers you, purée it until smooth with an immersion blender, or in an upright blender. I like to serve this pork with roasted shallots (page 29) and a green vegetable such as zucchini or green beans.

Serves 6

> **2 pounds boneless pork loin**
> **small bunch of rosemary**
> **small bunch of chives**
> **head of garlic, separated into cloves and peeled**
> **1 tablespoon crushed black peppercorns**
> **1 teaspoon salt**
> **⅓ cup olive oil**
> **2 cups milk, more if needed**

Preheat the oven to 325°F. Tie the pork loin in an even cylinder (see How to Roll and Tie a Roast, page 179). Pull leaves from the rosemary, reserving a few sprigs for decoration. Cut the chives in short lengths. Work the rosemary and chives to a paste in a food processor with the garlic, peppercorns, salt, and 3 tablespoons of the olive oil.

Heat the remaining oil in a casserole and brown the meat thoroughly on all sides, 8 to 10 minutes. Pour off any excess fat. Spread the herb and garlic paste on top of the meat and pour the milk into the casserole. The meat should be half covered by the liquid. Cover loosely with aluminum foil and roast in the oven, basting occasionally, until a skewer inserted in the center of the meat comes out hot when withdrawn after 30 seconds. You should allow 1 to 1¼ hours and a meat thermometer should register 160°F. If the sauce reduces rapidly during cooking, add more milk.

To finish: If necessary, reheat the pork in the pot. Transfer it to a carving board, cover it loosely with aluminum foil, and leave it for 5 to 10 minutes. Whisk the sauce vigorously to smooth the texture and simmer until it is well flavored and reduced by about half. Taste and adjust the seasoning. To serve, carve the pork into thick slices, discarding strings, and arrange them overlapping on a platter. Spoon the sauce over the pork and decorate with rosemary sprigs.

GETTING AHEAD: Pot roasts reheat wonderfully. When done, leave meat and juices in the pot and store in the refrigerator up to 2 days. Reheat it in a 350°F oven, allowing 25 to 35 minutes.

HOW TO MAKE A MEAT STEW

There's a school of thought that claims a rich, aromatic meat stew, packed with vegetables, herbs, spices, and wine, is the equal of any roast or grilled meat. I totally agree. For me, slowly simmered casseroles of beef with carrots, dark ragoûts of game, and sweet-sour mixes of pork and dried fruits outrank a juicy steak any day. The international competition also includes *boeuf bourguignon*, Irish stew, Indian curries, and the perfumed tajines that emanate from Morocco.

Stewing is a broad term, covering any dish in which the meat (or poultry) is cut in pieces, whether browned or not, and cooked slowly in a good deal of liquid. In brown stews the meat and vegetables, typically onions and other roots, are sautéed to caramelize their surface then combined with dark, intense flavorings such as brown stock, red wine or beer, garlic, cinnamon and other aromatic spices, and herbs such as thyme and bay leaf. As you can imagine, there are hundreds, even thousands of brown stews but most follow the pattern you'll see here in Indian lamb curry. White stews are simpler, often a matter of layering the chosen ingredients and covering them with veal stock or water, and perhaps some white wine or cider. The finished dish—Winter White Veal Stew is a typical example—is fresher and lighter than a brown stew.

Stews offer so many possibilities and they don't need much equipment or technical skill. A single, heavy-based pot that is flameproof as well as ovenproof is all that most recipes require. A wide range of inexpensive cuts of meat can be used, and other ingredients can follow availability and the seasons. A stew is often a one-pot meal, needing at most an accompaniment of boiled

1 For a brown stew (here Indian lamb curry), first dry the meat thoroughly or juices will be drawn out and the meat will steam instead of browning. In a casserole, brown the pieces of meat in fat over high heat, turning them so they color on all sides. Do not crowd the pan, so the meat cooks rapidly and does not leak juices.

2 Remove the meat, add onions or other vegetables, and brown them over medium heat, stirring often. Stir in flour if called for in the recipe and brown it also; spices should be lightly fried at this point. Stir in liquid and other seasonings such as garlic and shallots. Whole spices are tied in cheesecloth and herbs are knotted with string so they can be removed later.

3 Mix in the meat—it should be generously covered with liquid. Cover the casserole and bring the liquid to a boil. Stews may be cooked on top of the stove at a gentle simmer or in the oven at 350°F. At the end of cooking, the meat should be very tender when you pinch a piece between your finger and thumb. The sauce should be dark, rich, and thickened enough to lightly coat the back of a spoon. If it seems thin, boil it down to achieve the right consistency.

rice, potato, or pasta. What is more, almost all stews are better when reheated because the sauce mellows on keeping. In the refrigerator, they can be stored, covered, up to 2 days.

When choosing the cut of meat for stew, I'll risk saying go for the tougher parts of the animal. Tough cuts have more taste and so invite long gentle simmering, allowing the other ingredients to blend to tempting effect. And tough cuts, often from the shoulder or leg, are much, much cheaper than the so-called prime cuts. Don't waste your money stewing beef fillet—its virtue is tenderness, not flavor. For stew I think of beef chuck, round, and brisket, or veal shoulder, breast, and shank. For lamb, good stewing cuts are shoulder, neck, and breast, and for pork they include shoulder, ribs, fresh ham (pork) butt, and shank.

clues on stews

* The longer a stew is to be cooked, the larger the pieces of meat should be cut. One-inch cubes are right for the tender meat in a veal stew, for example, but cubes should be up to three inches for a dark beef stew such as *Carbonnade*.

* Meat for stew must be carefully trimmed of tendons, though it is good to leave a little fat and gelatinous connective tissue that will dissolve during cooking.

* Six ounces is an average allowance of boneless meat per serving.

* Careful seasoning is important in a stew. At the start, you should add only a little salt as it will be concentrated when the sauce reduces during cooking. Always taste and adjust seasoning before serving.

* Typical temperature for cooking a stew is 350°F. The liquid should simmer gently and never boil or the meat will be tough.

Indian Lamb Curry

Curry invites a multitude of accompaniments, for example boiled rice, fresh fruit chutney, chopped peanuts, garlic, and Chile Cilantro Relish (page 40).

Serves 4 to 6

> **2 pounds boneless leg or shoulder of lamb**
> **¼ cup oil**
> **4 onions, chopped**
> **3 tablespoons ground coriander**
> **1 tablespoon ground cumin**
> **2 teaspoons ground red chile pepper, or to taste**
> **1 teaspoon ground cinnamon**
> **½ teaspoon ground nutmeg**
> **1⅔ cups unsweetened coconut milk**
> **(a 13.5-ounce can)**
> **salt and pepper to taste**
> **2 pounds canned tomatoes, drained and**
> **coarsely chopped**

Trim the meat, discarding all but a few bits of fat. Cut it in 1½-inch cubes. In a large casserole, heat 2 tablespoons of the oil and brown the lamb on all sides, a few pieces at a time, using quite high heat, 3 to 4 minutes. Remove the meat, lower the heat, and add the onions. Sauté them, stirring often, until golden brown, 8 to 10 minutes. Add the remaining oil and stir in the coriander, cumin, chile pepper, cinnamon, and nutmeg. Cook gently, stirring constantly, 3 to 5 minutes, until the spices are fragrant and the onions are thoroughly browned. Do not scorch.

Stir in the coconut milk, salt, and pepper. Replace the meat, stir to mix, cover, and bring to a boil. Simmer the meat on top of the stove until tender, or if you prefer, cook it in a 350°F oven. It will take 1¼ to 1½ hours and you will need to stir it quite often. If the pan gets dry, add some water. At the end of cooking, you should be able to crush the meat easily. Stir in the tomatoes and cook 10 minutes longer. Taste and adjust seasoning, adding more chile pepper if you like.

GETTING AHEAD: You can make this recipe up to 3 days ahead.

Beef with Beer and Onions (*Carbonnade*)

Carbonnade is a hearty Flemish recipe, just right for cold winds and wet weather. Serve it with mashed potatoes and braised red cabbage.

Serves 4 to 6

> 2 pounds beef chuck
> salt and pepper to taste
> 2 tablespoons vegetable oil
> 1 tablespoon butter
> 4 large onions, thinly sliced
> 1 tablespoon sugar
> 2 tablespoons flour
> 3 cups dark beer
> 1 cup beef or veal stock, more if needed
> 1/2 teaspoon grated nutmeg
> bouquet garni of 2 bay leaves and a few parsley stems and sprigs of thyme

Preheat the oven to 350°F. Trim the beef of all but a little fat and cut it in 2-inch cubes. Sprinkle them with salt and pepper. Heat 1 tablespoon of the oil with the butter in a heavy casserole, add half the beef cubes, and fry them until well browned on all sides. Remove them, add the rest and brown them also. Set the beef aside.

Add the onions to the pan with salt, pepper, and the remaining oil and cook over low heat, stirring often, until the onions are very soft, 15 to 20 minutes. Turn up the heat, add the sugar, and continue frying until the onions are caramelized, 3 to 5 minutes. Stir in the flour and cook for 1 minute. Add the beer and bring to a boil, stirring constantly. Stir in the stock, nutmeg, and bouquet garni. Add the beef, pushing it well down into the liquid, and bring just to a boil.

Cover the casserole and cook in the oven, stirring occasionally, until the beef is very tender when you pinch it or poke it with a two-pronged fork, 2 to 2 1/2 hours. Stir from time to time during cooking and add more stock if the pan gets dry. At the end of cooking, the sauce should be well reduced, dark, and concentrated. If it is thin, boil it on top of the stove. Discard the bouquet garni, taste, and adjust the seasoning. The longer you keep *Carbonnade*—refrigerate for up to 3 days—the better it will be.

GETTING AHEAD: *Carbonnade* can be refrigerated up to 3 days and it freezes well. Reheat it on top of the stove.

Tajine of Lamb with Eggplant and Olives

A tajine is the Moroccan earthenware cooking pot with a characteristic conical cover, designed to retain steam but not soak the food. The premise is that the ingredients should cook in their own juices, and they do that fine in any heavy casserole. You'll find preserved lemons at a good gourmet store, or the juice and grated zest of 1 lemon can be substituted. Couscous or boiled rice is the appropriate accompaniment.

Serves 4 to 6

> 1 1/2 pounds boneless lamb shoulder
> 2 garlic cloves, chopped
> 2 teaspoons ground cinnamon
> 1 teaspoon ground ginger
> 1 teaspoon salt, more for sprinkling
> 1/2 teaspoon ground black pepper
> 1/4 cup olive oil, more for the baking sheet
> 2 large onions, sliced
> 2 medium eggplants (about 1 1/2 pounds)
> 1 preserved lemon, rinsed very well
> 1/2 cup pitted oil-cured green olives
> juice of 1 lemon

Preheat the oven to 350°F. Trim the lamb shoulder, leaving some fat, and cut it in 1-inch pieces. Mix the garlic in a medium bowl with the cinnamon, ginger, salt, pepper, and oil. Add the lamb and toss until coated. Spread half the lamb in a small casserole, top with the onions, and cover with the remaining lamb. Add the lid and bake in the oven 1 hour, stirring once halfway through cooking.

Meanwhile, trim the eggplants, cut them lengthwise in half, and then crosswise into 1/2-inch slices. Set them on a tray, sprinkle with salt, and leave for 30 minutes to draw out the juices.

Rinse and dry them. Set eggplant slices on an oiled baking sheet and sprinkle them with pepper. Bake them in the oven on a rack above the casserole until browned and quite dry, turning once, 12 to 15 minutes. Cut the preserved lemon in quarters and then dice it.

When the lamb has cooked for an hour, stir in the browned eggplant, preserved lemon, olives, and lemon juice. Continue cooking until the lamb is very tender when you pinch a piece and the other ingredients are blended and aromatic, 15 to 30 minutes.

GETTING AHEAD: Any tajine reheats well; simply store it in the cooking pot and reheat it on top of the stove.

Winter White Veal Stew (Blanquette de Veau)

This famous French stew, with its light, creamy sauce, is the perfect showcase for veal, which is naturally tender with a delicate flavor. Traditionally all the ingredients are white—veal, baby onions, button mushrooms, white wine, and cream—but I've slipped in a few carrots to brighten it up. The best cut to use is meaty veal shoulder, plus some pieces of breast including rib bones for richness. The stew should be accompanied by rice or noodles—white again.

Serves 4 to 6

2 pounds veal shoulder
1 pound veal breast including rib bones
1½ quarts water, more if needed
1 cup dry white wine
bouquet garni of 2 bay leaves and a few
   parsley stems and sprigs of thyme
1 garlic clove, chopped
salt and white pepper to taste
1 pound baby carrots, or medium carrots,
   quartered
24 to 30 baby onions (about 10 ounces), peeled
½ pound button mushrooms, quartered

FOR THE SAUCE
4 tablespoons butter
¼ cup flour
¾ cup crème fraîche or heavy cream

Cut the veal shoulder in 1-inch cubes, leaving fat and connective tissue, which will dissolve during cooking. Cut the breast into portions of 1 to 2 ribs. Put the veal in a large saucepan with the water and bring slowly to a boil, skimming often, 10 to 15 minutes. Add the wine, bouquet garni, garlic, salt, and pepper, cover, and simmer the veal, skimming and stirring occasionally, ¾ to 1 hour.

Add the carrots with more water to cover if needed and continue simmering until the veal is nearly tender when you pinch a piece, 10 to 15 minutes. Stir in the onions and mushrooms—all the ingredients should be just covered with water. If there is too little water, add more, and if too much, remove the lid. Continue simmering until the veal and all the vegetables are tender, 20 to 25 minutes.

Transfer the meat and vegetables to a bowl, discarding the bouquet garni. Boil the liquid down to 1 quart—this may take up to 20 minutes. Crush the butter with a fork and work in the flour to make a paste. Whisk the paste, a piece or two at a time, into the simmering liquid so it melts and thickens lightly. Whisk in the crème fraîche or cream, bring the sauce back to a boil, and simmer for 1 minute. Taste and adjust the seasoning. Stir the veal and vegetables back into the sauce and taste again. Reheat the stew on top of the stove.

GETTING AHEAD: Veal stew is much improved by at least a day in the refrigerator and can be kept up to 2 days.

HOW TO COOK A STEAK

Grilling calls for direct, searing heat, the highest you'll probably ever use. In a restaurant, the grill station is the toughest of the lot, fast moving and fierce, but at home you can relax. There's time to get organized and you may want to season your steak ahead of time with a rub (page 56) or marinade (page 52). You'll also want to plan accompaniments in advance, from the classic baked potato to grilled tomatoes, mushrooms, and possibly caramelized onions or Cotton Onions. After grilling, the steak itself may be topped with a pat of Herb and Shallot Butter (page 18), or better still a spoonful of béarnaise sauce (page 81).

No matter how you like your steak, at the start of cooking you need the highest possible heat, reducing it later if the cut is large or very thick. Some home ranges are fitted with stovetop grills for grilling indoors, and you'll also find portable grills that fit over two burners. An outdoor grill can be fun but more difficult to control. If you choose to pan-fry your steak, you need a heavy pan—a traditional cast-iron skillet is ideal. Avoid pans and grills with a nonstick surface as the steak will not brown so well. A bonus when pan-frying are the succulent pan juices that caramelize in the bottom of the pan, invitation to a little pan sauce. If you have a good broiler that heats to searing hot and is capable of creating that slightly charred surface that makes fine steak so tempting, by all means use it. Otherwise, broiled meat is best at a restaurant where they have super-hot salamander broilers.

To gauge the heat of an outdoor or stovetop grill, Emma has an amusing test. She holds her hand about 3 inches above the heated rack and recites the word "California" (she lives in Los Angeles). If she snatches her hand away halfway through, the grill is too hot; if she has time for "Los Angeles" as well, the heat is not yet fierce enough. Just in our small family of five, we have five different preferences on seasoning, whether plain, spicy, marinated, or brushed with a barbecue sauce. Degree of cooking, rare, medium-rare, or medium varies, too—can you believe that my daughter likes her steak well done? A death sentence so far as I am concerned!

1 Always preheat a broiler or grill to the highest possible temperature and set the rack about 3 inches from the heat. Season the steaks as indicated in the recipe, adding salt only at the last minute to avoid losing juices. When very hot, brush the grill rack or pan with olive or vegetable oil and add the steak, taking care not to stretch the surface of the meat. It should sizzle briskly. Let it cook for 2 minutes undisturbed—at first it will stick to the grill rack or pan, then it will detach as the surface browns and a crust forms. Lift one corner with tongs to see the color. If brown, turn it and brown the other side. For rare steak, you should leave the meat on high throughout cooking unless it is cut very thick. For medium and well-done meat, turn down the heat after a minute on the second side and continue cooking. Very large or thick steaks should also finish cooking on lower heat. Alternatively, you can transfer the steaks briefly to a 400°F oven until done.

Five-Pepper Steak

This classic French bistro dish is best made with individual New York strip, entrecôte, or filet mignon. Serve it with Scrumptious Sautéed Potatoes (page 247).

Serves 2

> **2 steaks, cut 1 inch thick (about 1 pound total)**
> **1 tablespoon Szechuan peppercorns**
> **1 tablespoon black peppercorns**
> **1 tablespoon white peppercorns**
> **1 tablespoon dried pink peppercorns**
> **1 tablespoon dried green peppercorns**
> **salt to taste**
> **1 tablespoon vegetable oil**
> **2 to 3 tablespoons brandy**
> **¾ cup heavy cream**

Toast the Szechuan peppercorns in a dry skillet over low heat until fragrant, tossing and stirring, 3 to 5 minutes. Put them in a heavy-duty plastic bag with the other peppercorns and crush them finely with a rolling pin. Spread the pepper in a shallow dish, add the steaks, and coat both sides with pepper, pressing so it adheres. Cover and refrigerate up to 6 hours.

If you like strong flavor, leave the peppercorns; for milder taste scrape most of them from the meat. Sprinkle both sides of the steak with a little salt. Heat the oil in a heavy pan and add the steaks. Fry over high heat until they are browned, 3 to 4 minutes. Turn and brown the other side, allowing 3 to 4 minutes longer for rare steak. If you prefer steak cooked further, lower the heat and continue frying until done to your taste, 2 to 5 minutes longer. Test the steaks by pressing with your finger (page 196). Add the brandy to the pan and flambé the steaks (see How to Flambe, page 131). Transfer them to serving plates and keep warm.

Add the cream to the pan and bring it to a boil, stirring to dissolve the pan juices. Simmer until the sauce thickens slightly, 1 to 2 minutes. Taste the sauce, adjust seasoning, and spoon it over the steaks. Serve at once.

Steak Pizzaiola

Imagine steak with a pizza topping of tomato and melted mozzarella and you have luscious Steak Pizzaiola, a real treat. This is a good recipe for sirloin steak that will serve several people. You can cut corners by using canned chopped tomatoes, provided they are a good brand. As accompaniment, how about some focaccia?

Serves 4

> **1 sirloin steak, cut 1½ inches thick**
> **(about 2 pounds)**
> **1 tablespoon olive oil**
> **salt and pepper to taste**
> **4 ounces very thinly sliced mozzarella**
> **small bunch of oregano**
> **2 bay leaves**
> **3 tomatoes (about 1 pound), peeled, seeded, and**
> **chopped, or 1 cup chopped canned tomatoes**
> **2 garlic cloves, chopped**
> **½ cup red wine**
> **2 tablespoons olive oil**

Make the topping: Strip oregano leaves from the stems and tie stems with the bay leaves. Put the tomatoes, garlic, wine, olive oil, and bunch of herbs in a saucepan with salt and pepper. Simmer, stirring, until thickened and the spoon leaves a trail on the base of the pan, 7 to 10 minutes. Chop the oregano leaves and stir them into the topping. Discard the bunch of herbs, taste, and adjust seasoning.

Cook the steak: Preheat the broiler. Brush the steak with olive oil and sprinkle with salt and pepper. Broil about 3 inches from the heat until the steak is browned, 3 to 4 minutes. Turn and brown the other side, 3 to 4 minutes more. Lower the broiler rack to 5 inches from the heat and continue cooking until the steak is done to your taste, 5 to 10 minutes longer. Test it with your fingertip (page 196).

Reheat the tomato topping. When the steak is almost done, cover it with the topping and add mozzarella slices. Broil until the mozzarella is melted, ½ to 1 minute. Cover the steak loosely with aluminum foil, let it stand for 3 to 5 minutes, then carve it in thick diagonal slices.

selecting your steak

The more generously a steak is marbled with fat, the juicier and tastier it will be. Color can be deceptive: well-aged, tender beef is dark red, but so are the tougher cuts from older animals. Look for beef of cardinal rather than fire-engine red, with no tinge of purple. As you might expect, pale meat tends to be bland.

By no means are all cuts suitable for grilling or broiling. Chuck steak cut from the hard-working shoulder is lean, full-flavored, and chewy; I keep it for braises and stews. At the other end of the scale is the lazy tenderloin muscle that hardly moves at all, since it's tucked under the ribs. That's where filet mignon and tournedos steaks come from—meltingly tender and expensive, but for me they lack taste.

In between these extremes come the celebrity steaks: boneless rib-eye, French entrecôte, T-bone, and porterhouse. They are part of the loin of the animal and include firm strip on one side of the bone and buttery tenderloin on the other. Strip or shell steaks, also known as New York strip or Kansas City strip, come from this part of the animal, too. Sirloin steaks, cut from near the hind quarters, offer good value, while boneless, thin and lean flank steaks provide great flavor at a lower price but can be tough.

Serving size is another matter, with portions ranging from a diet-sized filet mignon of 6 ounces to a pound of T-bone steak on the bone for macho appetites. I find that 3/4 inch is a minimum thickness to ensure a juicy steak with a crisply browned surface. Thinner steaks are too easily overcooked. Small steaks, notably filet mignon and tournedos, may be cut up to 1 1/2 inches thick and still serve one person, but a thick-cut New York strip or entrecôte may be enough for two, and a generous slice of sirloin serves three to four.

Upper Crust Steak Sandwich

Upper Crust Steak Sandwich

Sirloin, top round, and flank steak all work well for this sandwich. Sirloin gives a good beefy flavor but somewhat irregular slices, top round provides very even slices, and flank steak can be counted on for great flavor. The meat is marinated in a simple mixture of garlic, mustard, and lemon juice, then grilled, sliced, and piled onto crusty bread with spicy arugula and meltingly soft onions.

Makes 4 hearty sandwiches

2 pounds sirloin, top round, or flank steak

1 tablespoon vegetable oil, more for brushing

2 onions, thinly sliced into rings

8 slices crusty bread

mayonnaise or mustard (optional)

large bunch of arugula, washed and trimmed

FOR THE MARINADE
2 garlic cloves, finely chopped

2 teaspoons Dijon mustard

1 tablespoon Worcestershire sauce

¼ cup fresh lemon juice

¼ cup olive oil

salt and pepper to taste

Make the marinade: Whisk together the garlic, mustard, Worcestershire sauce, lemon juice, olive oil, salt, and pepper. Put the steak in a shallow dish, pour the marinade over it, cover, and chill the steak for 2 to 12 hours, turning occasionally.

Light the grill or heat a heavy skillet until very hot. Drain the steak and pat it dry, discarding the marinade. Brush the grill rack or pan with oil and add the steak. Grill or fry the steak over high heat until brown, 2 to 3 minutes. Turn and continue cooking until the steak is done to your taste. Allow 2 to 3 minutes longer for rare meat, 4 to 5 minutes longer for medium done, and test cooking with your fingertip (page 196). Transfer the steak to a cutting board and let it rest for 10 minutes.

Heat the oil in a frying pan (if using the same skillet, wipe it out first). Add the onions with salt and pepper and sauté gently, stirring occasionally, until softened and brown, 10 to 15 minutes. Toast the bread.

Slice the steak on the diagonal as thinly as possible, cutting across the grain.

If you like mayonnaise or mustard, lightly spread them on the slices of bread. Layer the meat, arugula, and onions on top and add another slice of bread. Cut the sandwich in half and serve while the steak and onions are warm.

GETTING AHEAD: Cook the steak ahead of time and assemble a cold steak sandwich at serving time.

steak wisdom

* An advantage of grilling and pan-frying is the minimal amount of fat needed for cooking. In addition, high heat draws fat from the meat.

* Steak must be cooked to order as it should not be reheated.

* Let a steak come to room temperature before cooking so its temperature is uniform and it cooks evenly.

* Individual steaks should be served with the first-cooked side upward.

* Large steaks for more than one person are normally cut off the bone, trimmed of fat, and carved in thick diagonal slices.

More Great Grills

Great steak is just the start of the grilling story. Other favorite cuts include pork and lamb chops and the many kinds of sausages that vary from fresh to spicy. If you're a lover of sausages like me, it's well worth looking in ethnic and specialty butchers for varieties beyond the familiar sweet or spiced Italian links. Spearing together your own kebabs at home is another way to go. The many names we have for kebabs—brochettes, shish kebab, shashlik, satay—are witness to their popularity. You can choose your own main ingredient, whether beef, pork, chicken, veal, or even a bit of goat. What makes each kebab different is less the meat than the seasoning, barbecue sauce, or marinade (page 52) that goes with it.

Another idea is to butterfly boned leg of lamb—this takes less than 5 minutes—so it sits flat on the grill and cooks evenly. Just recently I've been lured away from my customary herbal red wine marinade for lamb by an exotic *Mechoui,* the Moroccan version of barbecue. Dry rubs (page 54) are good on lamb, too.

how to make kebabs

The meat you choose for kebabs must be a tender cut as it will be grilled or broiled fast over high heat, just like steak. Pieces are usually cut small and should be trimmed carefully of fat. Add color to the kebabs with vegetables such as cherry tomatoes, button mushrooms, and segments of bell pepper. The skewers can be prepared several hours ahead and benefit from marinating in oil and spices—you'll find ideas on page 52.

Metal skewers for kebabs come in large and small sizes. I find Asian-style wooden skewers easier to handle when hot—to avoid scorching, they should be soaked in water first. I also prefer a grill to a broiler as the kebabs are easier to baste and turn. High heat is key: hold your hand three inches above the grill rack—if you do not have to snatch your hand away within a count of one, two, three, the grill is not hot enough. A kebab is done when it is brown and the meat within is still pink and juicy. (Chicken and pork should be thoroughly cooked and therefore cut in quite small pieces.)

Randall's Spiced Beef Brochettes

When Randall Price was chef at the American Embassy in Budapest, he discovered the delights of paprika and its versatility in all kinds of recipes. Here's one of them.

Serves 4 to 6

> 1½ pounds boneless beef sirloin or top round
> 1 pound button or cremini mushrooms, trimmed and halved or quartered
>
> FOR THE MARINADE
> 2 tablespoons olive oil
> 2 garlic cloves, chopped
> 2 tablespoons chopped fresh marjoram or oregano
> 2 tablespoons sweet paprika
> 2 teaspoons ground cumin
> 2 teaspoons caraway seeds
> 2 teaspoons salt
> 1 teaspoon ground black pepper
> zest and juice of 1 lemon
> ¾ cup white wine
>
> 12 skewers

Make the marinade: Combine the olive oil, garlic, marjoram, paprika, cumin, caraway seeds, salt, pepper, and lemon zest and juice. Whisk in the wine, taste, and adjust the seasoning. Trim fat from the meat, cut it in 1-inch cubes, and mix well with the marinade. Cover and chill, 4 to 6 hours. If using wooden skewers, soak them in water so they do not scorch.

To finish: Light the grill. Drain the beef and thread it onto skewers, alternating with the mushrooms. Grill the kebabs about 3 inches from the heat, turning once, until the beef and mushrooms are browned and the beef is rare or better done, to your taste, 5 to 8 minutes.

GETTING AHEAD: Marinate the beef up to 6 hours ahead, but make the kebabs and grill just before serving.

how to butterfly and grill a leg of lamb

Leg of lamb, particularly a small one of not more than 4 to 5 pounds, is ideal for grilling after it has been boned and butterflied so the meat is more or less of even thickness.

1 To butterfly a boned leg of lamb: Set your palm flat on top of the meat and partially slit open the cavity left by the leg bone, cutting horizontally through one side of the meat, leaving the long edge attached. Turn the flap outward, like the page of a book, and lay the meat flat. Repeat on other side so the lamb lies flat and the meat is of fairly even thickness.

Moroccan Grilled Lamb with Mint (*Mechoui*)

Middle Eastern stores carry their own special ground hot red pepper for recipes like this, or 2 teaspoons of paprika and 1/2 teaspoon of cayenne can be substituted. I like to serve the lamb with couscous flavored with dried fruits, or a cracked wheat pilaf.

Serves 6 to 8

> 1 leg of lamb (4 to 5 pounds)
> 1/2 cup chopped fresh mint
> Grated zest and juice of I lemon
> 4 garlic cloves, finely chopped
> 2 tablespoons ground coriander
> 2 teaspoons ground cumin
> 2 teaspoons ground black pepper
> 2 teaspoons ground red chile pepper
> 1/4 cup olive oil

Butterfly the lamb. Mix the mint, lemon zest and juice, garlic, coriander, cumin, black and red peppers, and olive oil in a bowl and rub the mixture all over the lamb. Wrap it in plastic wrap, set it in a dish, and marinate in the refrigerator, 6 to 12 hours.

Light the grill. Brush the grill rack with oil. Sear the lamb over the highest possible heat, turning it so it browns on both sides, 10 to 15 minutes. Lower the grill heat to medium or move meat farther from heat so it cooks less quickly. Cover and let the lamb cook, allowing 15 minutes for rare meat, 10 to 15 minutes longer if you prefer it well done.

When done, open the grill, turn off heat, and wrap the leg loosely in aluminum foil. Let it rest on the side of the grill for 15 minutes so juices are reabsorbed before carving.

GETTING AHEAD: Marinate the lamb as short or as long as you like before grilling.

Red Wine Lamb Butterfly

Here's my marinade for butterflied leg of lamb—as you can see, I'm crazy for garlic and herbs!

Serves 6 to 8

Substitute this marinade in the recipe for Moroccan Grilled Lamb with Mint (page 195): Mix 1 bottle fruity red wine, 5 to 6 chopped garlic cloves, the leaves from a large bunch of thyme and a large bunch of rosemary, chopped, 3 crumbled bay leaves, and ¹/₂ cup olive oil. Soak the butterflied lamb in the marinade for at least 2 and up to 12 hours, and then use it for basting when you grill the meat.

to test cooking of grilled meats

When meat is on the grill, you'll see chefs poke it with a knowing fingertip to decide when it is done just right. This finger test is the most accurate, good for chicken and fish, too.

1 To test when steak and other grilled meats are done: Make a circle with your first finger and thumb and press the ball of your thumb: it will feel soft. Press the center of the meat with your fingertip: if it has the same soft texture, it is rare. Move your thumb to the middle finger and test the ball of your thumb again: food with the same resilience will be medium done. Finally test with your little finger: the ball of your thumb will be firm, and so will well done food.

to grill a lattice

In restaurants, flat pieces of meat such as steaks, medallions, and chops often have an attractive browned lattice marked on the surface. It is quite easy to do. The parallel bars of a stovetop or outdoor grill will sear food in lines and, if you rotate the food and continue browning, it will acquire a lattice pattern. This trick is used for steak and also for grilled fish, chicken breast, and vegetables such as sliced eggplant, squash, and onions.

1 To create a lattice pattern on a grill: Heat a ridged stovetop or outdoor grill. When very hot, brush the grill rack or pan with olive or vegetable oil and add the steak, taking care not to stretch the surface of the meat. It should sizzle briskly. Let it cook for 1 minute undisturbed. Lift one corner with tongs to see if ridges are clearly marked on the meat.

If so, lift and rotate it almost 90 degrees so the grill ridges will form lattice markings on the meat surface. Continue cooking a minute longer, then turn the steak. Continue cooking, again rotating 90 degrees after 1 minute. For rare steak, you should leave the meat on high throughout cooking unless the meat is very thick. For medium and well done meat, turn down the heat after a minute on the second side and continue cooking. Test with your finger.

HOW TO HANDLE HAMBURGER AND GROUND MEATS

At one stage in my life I was a regular patron of the best burgers in New York City, hot off the grill of a now-defunct Irish pub. Weighing in at one-half pound and at least an inch thick, they were crusty brown on the outside and explosively moist within. They tasted of plain, hearty beef with no fancy seasonings, and the slices of juicy tomato and sweet onion were equally spartan. The bun was also exemplary—tender, slightly chewy, and toasty brown on top. Those hamburgers have been my benchmark ever since.

By no means everyone agrees with me. Take Julia Child and Jacques Pepin. In *Julia and Jacques Cooking at Home*, Julia goes for a thin burger, weighing around 4 ounces, that fits neatly in the bun while Jacques is like me, big is better. Steven Raichlen, grilling guru, tucks a disk of herb butter insides his patties to keep them moist, brushes them with a little butter, and seasons with salt and pepper before grilling. Tyler Florence livens up his ground beef by gently folding in horseradish and chives. I take a middle way, seasoning the burger patty with salt and pepper just before I put it in the pan.

There's also debate about the perfect beef for hamburger. Just how lean should it be? You don't need a prime cut, which is wasted if ground up. Chuck, cut from the shoulder, has rich flavor but more fat. I prefer round or leg that has an average fat content of 20 percent (much less than that and your hamburger will be dry and tough). What's really important with all ground meat, whether lamb, pork, or veal, is that you buy it freshly ground from a trusted source. Keep ground meat in the refrigerator, tightly sealed, and use it as soon as you can, definitely within two days.

To cook hamburger, I get out my trusty cast-iron skillet that dates from way back when. You may prefer an indoor or outdoor grill. However, your broiler is unlikely to be hot enough to sear the meat and create a crusty surface, mark of the first-class burger. For hamburger accompaniments, see next page—if you have a hamburger party in the backyard, you'll need them all.

1 Press the patty with a finger to test its resilience. If soft, the meat is rare, if springy it is medium, and if firm it is well done. Pink juices running from the burger indicate the meat inside is medium done, with clear juices for well done. Note that cooking hamburger until well done eliminates any risk of contamination with the toxic *E. coli* bacteria.

The Unbeatable Burger

Hamburger calls for a more personal approach than almost any other dish. With this in mind, I'm listing possible accompaniments for your guests to build their own burger from the patty—large or small, thick or thin—that you'll provide.

Serves 4

> 1½ pounds freshly ground beef, more if needed
> salt and pepper to taste
> 4 buns, split
>
> OPTIONAL CONDIMENTS
> 1 very finely chopped onion
> Worcestershire sauce
> Tabasco
> fresh breadcrumbs
> 1 to 2 eggs, beaten to mix
>
> FOR SERVING
> 4 thin slices of Cheddar, Monterey Jack, Swiss,
>   or other melting cheese
> Dijon or hot mustard
> ketchup
> mayonnaise
> lettuce leaves
> slices of tomato
> thin slices of red onion
> sliced pickles
> ½ pound sliced bacon, cooked until crisp

Heat a stovetop or outdoor grill until very hot. Add condiments, if any, to your taste to the ground beef, stirring it as lightly as possible with a wooden spoon. (If overworked, the meat will be stringy.) Breadcrumbs or beaten egg help bind the meat but the burger will not be so light. Divide the meat into mounds, large or small, depending on your audience, and gently shape each one into a thick or thin patty. Season it generously with salt and pepper.

If using a skillet, heat it now. Brush the hot grill or pan surface with oil and add the burger, pressing down lightly with a spatula. Cook for 2 to 3 minutes, until brown. Turn and brown the other side, still over high heat, 2 to 3 minutes.

If making a cheeseburger, top the burger with the cheese just after flipping it. If you like your meat well done, after 1 to 2 minutes turn down the heat and continue cooking 1 to 2 minutes, or longer depending on the thickness of the burger. Test for doneness by pressing the burger with a finger: if soft, the meat is rare, if springy it is medium, and if firm it is well done.

Meanwhile, toast the buns on the grill or in a toaster. If you like, spread the bun halves with mustard, ketchup, or mayonnaise. Layer your choice of lettuce, tomato, onion, and pickles on the bottom half of the buns and top with the burger. Add bacon, more lettuce and tomato, and finally the top bun.

GETTING AHEAD: Prepare your condiments so they're ready to go, but season and grill the burgers at the last minute.

other ground meats

Ground meat dishes from other nations always seem so tempting. Many a neighborhood restaurant thrives on British shepherd's pie of ground lamb topped with mashed potato, Lebanese *kibbeh* of ground lamb with bulghur, nuts, yogurt, and parsley, or Italian meatballs and spaghetti. Don't neglect *pojarski*, the Russian version of a hamburger made with ground veal and topped with a mushroom cream sauce, and American chili, subject of so much debate. Like hamburger, all these recipes deserve top-quality meat, gentle handling, and close attention to seasoning. The more freshly ground the meat, the better.

Spaghetti and Meatballs

Spaghetti and meatballs so often come from a can—fine for the tomato sauce but I draw the line when it comes to the meatballs and pasta. Here's what it should really taste like.

Serves 4

> 1 pound lean ground beef
> 2 slices white bread
> 1 cup milk, more if needed
> 1 small onion, grated
> 2 egg yolks
> ¼ teaspoon ground nutmeg
> ¼ teaspoon ground allspice
> 1 teaspoon salt, more to taste
> large pinch of pepper, more to taste
> 3 tablespoons butter
> 1 jar (28 ounces) marinara-style tomato sauce
> 1 pound spaghetti

Pull the bread into pieces and soak it in the milk, about 5 minutes. Using a fork, stir the onion, egg yolks, nutmeg, allspice, salt, and pepper into the ground beef in a bowl. Squeeze the excess milk from the bread, pull it apart into crumbs, and stir it into the meat mixture. Add 1 to 2 tablespoons more milk if the mixture is dry. Brown a small piece in a frying pan and taste it, adding more salt and pepper if needed.

Dampen a chopping board and roll the meat mixture to a loose cylinder about 12 inches long. Cut it in 16 portions. Dip your hands in a bowl of cold water and roll the meat into even balls.

Heat the butter in a frying pan until sputtering stops. Add the meatballs and sauté them over medium heat until they are evenly browned, turning them often, 6 to 8 minutes. Add the tomato sauce, cover, and simmer the meatballs, stirring often, 5 to 7 minutes. A skewer inserted in the center of a meatball should come out warm to the touch when withdrawn after 30 seconds.

To finish: Bring a large pan of salted water to a boil. Add the spaghetti, coiling it into the pan as it softens. Stir once and boil until al dente, 8 to 10 minutes or according to package directions. If necessary, reheat the meatballs.

Drain the pasta, return it to the pan, and toss it over the heat with about 1 cup sauce from the meatballs. Pile the pasta in bowls and top with the meatballs and remaining sauce.

GETTING AHEAD: Cook the meatballs up to 24 hours ahead and refrigerate them. Boil the pasta and gently reheat the meatballs and sauce just before serving—if overcooked the meatballs will be tough.

Andrew's Chili

I asked a Texan friend what he puts in his chili and he rolled his eyes: "Almost anything," he said. "That's chili!" Chili can be served with accompaniments such as kidney beans or corn kernels (James Beard's favorite) on the side, or the cooked beans or corn may be mixed into the chili and simmered, 15 minutes before serving.

Serves 4

Heat 3 tablespoons vegetable oil in a large sauté pan or skillet and, over medium heat, fry 2 thinly sliced onions until lightly browned, stirring often, 10 to 12 minutes. Stir in $1\frac{1}{2}$ pounds ground beef and cook until light brown, stirring and breaking up the meat with two forks. Stir in a 15-ounce can of diced tomatoes, $\frac{1}{4}$ cup tomato paste, 1 cup beer, 2 tablespoons chili powder, 2 teaspoons salt, and $\frac{1}{2}$ teaspoon Tabasco. Cover and simmer, stirring often, until the chili is dark and rich in flavor, $\frac{3}{4}$ to 1 hour. Adjust seasonings, adding more chili powder and Tabasco to your taste. Chili is one of those dishes that the longer you keep it (3 days is a maximum), the better it is.

HOW TO PAN-FRY CHOPS AND MEDALLIONS

"A good fry up" is the way many of us start out cooking. Simon and Emma could produce competent fried bacon, sausage, eggs, and tomato by the time they were 10. However, when they applied the same general principles—hot pan, a bit of fat—to frying steak, or pork and lamb chops, they soon found that more skill was required. The meat needed seasoning at the very least with salt and pepper, and possibly with dried herbs or a Caribbean-style hot dry rub. If the pan was not hot enough, the meat turned gray and stewed in its own juices instead of sizzling to an appetizing, caramelized brown. With too much fat the meat would be soggy, and with too little it tended to scorch.

Pan-frying is fast, but it does need attention. High heat is fine for pan-fried steaks, small lamb chops, and other red meats served rare, but for more delicate items like veal medallions, the heat should stay at medium-high. In fact, at this temperature you are sautéing, a precise term that implies there's just enough fat to moisten and flavor the meat while browning it at the same time. The food should cook briskly, and every now and again steam builds up inside causing a little hiccup (*sauter* in French means "to jump").

Sautéing is kinder to meats than the dry heat of grilling or broiling. Pork chops, veal medallions, and lamb noisettes and cutlets are all best sautéed, especially if you want them well done. I like to sauté in butter because of its rich taste, but olive oil is an alternative, with bacon fat and lard appearing in ethnic dishes. If you're using only butter for frying, you may want to clarify it (see Clarified Butter, page 128) so it burns less easily, or add a tablespoon or two of oil to raise the scorch point, as I do. At the end of pan-frying or sautéing, you can make a quick little sauce or pan gravy from the juices browned in the pan (page 86).

2 For medium or well-done meat, turn down the heat and continue cooking to the stage you want, testing the resilience of the meat with your fingertip (page 196). Rare meat will feel soft, when medium-done it will be springy, and when well done it will be firm. Check by pulling away meat from the bone with the point of a knife to be sure the flesh is no longer pink, but remains juicy.

1 Season the meat according to the recipe. Heat the fat and fry the meat (here stuffed pork chops) over medium-high heat until well browned, 2 to 3 minutes. Turn and brown the other side. The darker the meat, the more thoroughly it should be browned. Fried steak and game medallions should be a dark mahogany color, white meats should be golden, and lamb chops halfway between.

Pork Chops with a Cornbread Surprise

Bell peppers, cornbread, and goat cheese are lively flavorings for stuffed pork chops.

Serves 4

> 4 center-cut pork chops, about ³⁄₄ inch thick
>   (about 2 pounds total)
> 4 tablespoons butter
> ¹⁄₂ onion, chopped
> 1 garlic clove, chopped
> ¹⁄₂ green bell pepper, cored, seeded, and
>   chopped
> ¹⁄₂ red bell pepper, cored, seeded, and chopped
> pinch of dried hot red pepper flakes
> salt and pepper to taste
> 1 cup coarse crumbs of cornbread
> 1 tablespoon oil
>
> **FOR THE PAN GRAVY**
> 1 cup chicken stock
> 3 ounces soft goat cheese, cut in pieces

Make the stuffing: Melt 3 tablespoons of the butter in a medium skillet. Stir in the onion, garlic, bell peppers, and hot red pepper flakes with salt and pepper and sauté until they are soft, 5 to 8 minutes. Remove from the heat and stir in the cornbread crumbs, salt, and pepper. Taste, adjust the seasoning, and let the stuffing cool.

Lay each pork chop flat on a board and cut a pocket. Season the chops with salt and pepper and stuff a quarter of the cornbread mixture into each chop. Close them and secure with toothpicks. Sprinkle them with salt and pepper.

Wipe out the frying pan and melt the remaining butter and oil. Fry the chops until well browned, 2 to 3 minutes. Flip them and brown the other side, 2 to 3 minutes. Turn down the heat, cover the pan, and continue cooking until the chops are just firm when pressed with a fingertip, 3 to 5 minutes. Check by poking a knife point near the bone—there should be no trace of pink. Remove the chops to a plate and keep them warm. Discard the fat from the pan and deglaze with the chicken stock, stirring to dissolve the pan

juices. Boil to reduce this pan gravy until concentrated, 3 to 5 minutes. Whisk in the goat cheese and simmer, whisking constantly, just until the cheese is melted. Take the gravy from the heat, taste, adjust the seasoning, and spoon it over the chops.

GETTING AHEAD: The chops reheat quite well if you cook them up to 12 hours ahead and keep them in the refrigerator. Reheat them with the pan gravy over very low heat.

how to cut a pocket and stuff chops

A stuffing for lamb, pork, or veal chops can range from a simple combination of chopped herbs and garlic or the cornbread and bell peppers I suggest here, to meat or vegetable-based mixtures, or fillings bound with breadcrumbs.

1 Trim any excess fat from the chop and lay it flat on the board. Set your hand on top and cut a deep pocket through to the bone, leaving the meat attached at the sides.

Fill the pocket with stuffing (take care, if overstuffed it will burst) and secure it closed with two toothpicks.

Veal Medallions with Mushrooms and Marsala

Whether you use wild or button mushrooms, the combination of veal and mushrooms in a Marsala cream sauce is magical.

Serves 4

2 pounds boneless veal loin

2 tablespoons vegetable oil, more if needed

salt and pepper to taste

1 tablespoon flour

¾ cup Marsala

¾ cup veal or chicken stock

½ cup crème fraîche or heavy cream

FOR THE MUSHROOMS

½ pound wild or button mushrooms

2 tablespoons olive oil

1 tablespoon butter

2 garlic cloves, chopped

2 shallots, chopped

2 to 3 tablespoons chopped fresh
   flat-leaf parsley

Veal Medallions with Mushrooms and M[...]

Tie the meat as for a whole roast, spacing 8 strings at even intervals. Cut between the strings to form 8 even medallions.

Prepare the mushrooms: Trim the stems and brush mushrooms to remove any earth, or wipe them with a damp cloth. Rinse them with cold water only if they are gritty as soaking softens them. Cut them in large chunks. Heat the oil and butter in a large frying pan and fry the garlic and shallots just until fragrant. Stir in the mushrooms with salt and pepper and cook over medium-high heat until tender and any moisture has evaporated, up to 10 minutes, depending on the type. Set aside 4 attractive pieces for garnish. Stir parsley into the remaining mushrooms, taste for seasoning, and set them aside.

Cook the veal: Sprinkle the medallions with salt and pepper. Heat half the oil in a large frying pan, add the veal, and sauté over high heat until brown, 2 to 3 minutes. Turn and brown the other side. Reduce the heat and continue cooking until the medallions are cooked to your liking.

Allow 1 to 2 minutes for veal that is pink in the center, or 2 to 3 minutes for well done. Remove them and keep warm in a low oven.

Make the sauce: Over moderate heat, add the remaining oil to the pan and stir in the flour. Cook until browned, 1 to 2 minutes. Add the Marsala, stirring to dissolve the pan juices, and boil until reduced by half. Stir in the stock and any juices from the medallions, and simmer until the sauce lightly coats a spoon. Finally, whisk in the crème fraîche, bring to a boil, and simmer, stirring constantly, until the sauce again coats a spoon, 2 to 3 minutes. Taste and adjust seasoning.

Reheat the mushrooms on top of the stove. Arrange the veal on 4 warm plates, discarding the strings and overlapping the medallions with the mushrooms alongside. Spoon the sauce over the medallions and top each with a reserved mushroom.

GETTING AHEAD: The mushrooms can certainly be cooked several hours ahead, but personally I like to sauté the veal and make the sauce just before serving.

how to cut tournedos, medallions, and noisettes

Beef tournedos steaks, lamb noisettes, and pork or veal medallions are cut from large pieces of meat that are tied so they hold their shape. The individual pieces of meat are cooked with the strings on, which are discarded at the end of cooking.

1 Tie the meat (here a pork loin) as for a whole roast (page 177), omitting the lengthwise strings. The strings should be as far apart as the width of the slices you will cut. Slice between the strings to form even medallions or tournedos, trimming ends neatly.

Lamb Noisettes with Tarragon

A noisette of lamb is a nugget of boneless meat that has been tied in a neat round (*noisette* means hazelnut); you'll find them at specialty butchers. You can also do it yourself using a boned sirloin or rack of lamb that has been rolled and tied. Simply slice the meat between the strings. Noisettes are so good by themselves that I like to serve them simply, with this little pan gravy flavored with tarragon. Green peas or lima beans are the ideal accompaniment.

Serves 4

Allow 2 noisettes cut $3/4$ inch thick per person (about $1^1/2$ pounds total). Mix $1/4$ cup dry white vermouth, 2 tablespoons olive oil, and 2 to 3 tarragon stems in a shallow dish and add the noisettes, turning to coat them. Leave for 15 to 30 minutes. Drain them, reserving marinade, and sprinkle with salt and pepper. Heat 1 tablespoon olive oil in a frying pan and sauté noisettes until brown, 3 to 4 minutes on each side for pink lamb, 5 to 6 minutes for well done. Remove and keep warm. Discard excess fat from the pan, add reserved marinade, and boil to a glaze. Whisk in 1 cup veal or chicken stock and simmer, 2 to 3 minutes, stirring to dissolve pan juices. Strain the sauce, whisk in 1 tablespoon chopped fresh tarragon, and adjust seasoning.

perfect pan-frying

* Delicate meats, notably veal, may take a coating of flour or egg and breadcrumbs when they are pan-fried or sautéed, but more robust lamb and pork chops do not need it.

* Large items like veal chops may need to be sautéed in more than one batch.

* Use just enough fat for pan-frying and sautéing to moisten and flavor the food. (Dishes like Southern fried chicken are really deep-fried as they require such a generous layer of fat.)

* To drain any excess fat, hold a lid over the food in the pan and pour fat into a bowl. Food should remain moist and not be dried on paper towels.

CHAPTER EIGHT perfect pasta and rice

Emma's the pasta cook. She once had a summer job on the island of Elba cooking for a dozen hungry American academics. Mountains of easy, inexpensive pasta were standard at every meal but breakfast, where its place was taken by hot oatmeal. She became adept at dressing up spaghetti and other dried pastas, and even made fresh pasta from time to time using the food processor and a pasta rolling machine.

So, following her lead, we begin with dried commercial pasta, taking a look at how to boil, drain, and serve it with creative toppings, many of which you'll recognize at once. In Italy where they originated, toppings like carbonara and tomato-laden *arrabbiata* are the backbone of everyday eating, hardly regarded as recipes at all. Moving on to fresh pasta, the second great field of exploration, we'll investigate fresh pasta dough, learning how to knead it, roll it, and finally stuff it as ravioli and tortellini, the packages that are the pride of home and professional cooks alike. If it sounds like a lot of work, be assured that I'm a modernist and it's machines all the way. I mix dough in the processor, then knead and roll it with a hand-cranked pasta machine.

Truth be told, I'm the rice fan of the family, particularly of the many variations that can be made from plain boiled rice. I think of Iranian pilafs with pistachios and dried fruits, Indian-inspired *kedgeree*, and Chinese fried rice. European pilafs are cooked differently, but achieve similar savory results. A glance at the supermarket shelf shows that the world of rice is complex. We'll be concentrating on three basic groups of white rice: long-grain, short-grain, and round-grain or risotto rice, ignoring the many commercial mixes and flavorings. We can do better than that at home!

HOW TO BOIL PASTA

First lesson in the kitchen used to be how to boil an egg, but now it's how to cook pasta. Here in the U.S., we grow up with the dried commercial kinds—spaghetti, lasagne, and macaroni, then graduate to the fresh pasta that is quite widely available in markets and restaurants. And now, more and more cooks put aside weekend time to prepare hundreds of yards of fresh pasta as a special feast for friends.

Just in case you don't already know, pasta is almost always boiled in salted water, although broth is occasionally used, too. You need a large quantity of liquid so the pasta pieces swim without touching and sticking together—large pasta such as lasagne and cannelloni may need cooking in batches. For small shapes or string pasta such as fettuccine, you'll find one of the special pasta boilers fitted with a strainer useful. The pasta is cooked inside the strainer, which makes it easy to lift out and drain after cooking, leaving the hot water to be used again for another batch or two. (After that, the water becomes saturated with starch.) For larger pasta, a shallow pan such as a sauté pan is better, so the pieces can float freely. To avoid damaging large pieces, such as lasagne sheets or ravioli, lift them out with a slotted spoon and drain them on paper towels or a dish towel.

Cooking times vary with the dryness and shape of the pasta. Fresh pasta is done in just a minute or two, as soon as the strands rise to the surface of the water, which may scarcely have come back to a boil. Dried commercial pasta takes longer and the guidelines on the package are a good starting point. As soon as pasta is cooked, drain it. I like to rinse it in hot water so it is less sticky (or in cold water if it is for a salad). However many Italians disagree; they leave their pasta unrinsed as a bit of starch helps bind the sauce or dressing. Either way, cooked pasta must be served at once because it glues together if left to stand. Is it okay to follow the restaurant practice of almost-cooking pasta, then reheating it in a strainer dipped into boiling water? Not really. Do so if you must, but the wonderful flavor of freshly cooked pasta will be lost.

1 Bring a large, deep pan of water to a boil and add a tablespoon of salt and a tablespoon of oil. Dried long pasta (here spaghetti) must be slowly bent and stirred into the water until it softens enough to be completely submerged. Stir it once or twice to prevent sticking.

2 To test when pasta is done, pinch it with a fingernail—if you feel a hard, undercooked core, it's not ready. Best test is to taste it: it should be tender but still chewy or al dente, so it is firm to the bite with no hard center or raw taste. Take care not to overboil pasta such as cannelloni, lasagne, and macaroni that you are pre-cooking before baking.

tttttttttt1tttttttttttt1ttttttttttttt1ttttttttttttt1ttttttttttttt1ttttttttttttt1tttttttttttt1tttttttttt

perfect pasta

* A pound of pasta is generally reckoned to serve four as a main course, but much depends on sauces and other accompaniments, not to mention diners' appetites.
* Start with at least five quarts of water for the first pound of pasta, increasing the quantity of water by a quart for each additional half pound. You'll need a tablespoon of salt for each pound of pasta; add it after the water has been brought to a boil.
* I like to add a tablespoon of oil to the boiling salted water as it helps keep the pasta from sticking and the water from boiling over.

Spaghetti Carbonara

Bacon and egg, what could be better! In Italy, pancetta is used in *carbonara*, but I think that plain American bacon is just as good.

Serves 4

Make the sauce before cooking the pasta: Melt 2 tablespoons butter in a frying pan and stir in 1/2 pound diced thick-cut pancetta or bacon with 2 chopped garlic cloves. Fry, stirring often, until the bacon starts to brown, 2 to 3 minutes. Add 3 to 4 tablespoons dry white wine, boil to reduce by half, and set aside to keep warm. Whisk 4 eggs in a large bowl with 3/4 cup grated Parmesan cheese and some freshly ground black pepper. Boil 1 pound spaghetti until al dente when you taste a piece, following timing on the package. Drain and at once add the pasta to the eggs, tossing so the eggs cook and coat it evenly. Add the warm bacon mixture and toss again. Taste and adjust seasoning—you may not need the salt as the bacon and cheese are salty. Pile the spaghetti on 4 warm plates and serve at once.

Herb and Ricotta Fettuccine

Emma put together this simple combination of herbs and cheese for supper one night and it has become a family standby.

Serves 4

Bring a large pan of salted water to a boil, add 1 pound fettuccine, stir, and boil, following timing on the package. Assemble 2 generous handfuls of fresh herbs such as parsley, basil or oregano, and chives and chop them. Reserve 4 sprigs for garnish. Crumble 2 cups fresh or dry ricotta and stir it into the herbs with 1/2 cup grated Parmesan cheese and 2 chopped garlic cloves. Test the fettuccine and when cooked, drain them. Heat 1/2 cup olive oil in the pot and add the pasta, herb mixture, and 1/2 cup white wine. Season generously with freshly ground black pepper and toss over the heat for about 1 minute. Pile into bowls, top each with an herb sprig, and serve with a bowl of grated Parmesan cheese if you like.

Penne all'Arrabbiata

Penne is a typical hollow pasta that's perfectly complemented by robust *arrabbiata* tomato sauce. *Arrabbiata* means angry, and this sauce is red with tomato and hot with chile, as fiery as you like to make it. I find that a good brand of canned tomatoes is fine, so the sauce takes no longer to cook than the pasta.

Serves 4 to 6

Bring a large pan of salted water to a boil, add 1 pound penne, stir, and boil until al dente, following timing on the package. Heat 2 to 3 tablespoons olive oil in a saucepan, add a sliced onion, and fry briskly until starting to brown, 3 to 5 minutes. Stir in 2 cups chopped tomatoes, 2 chopped garlic cloves, and a pinch, medium or large to your taste, of dried hot red pepper flakes. Simmer the sauce, stirring often, for a few minutes until the penne is done. Drain the penne, return it to the pan, and toss with 2 to 3 tablespoons olive oil. Pile the penne in bowls, make a hollow in the center, and spoon in the sauce. No cheese needed!

Pasta with Red Wine and Olive Sauce

This dark assertive sauce parades so many favorite Italian ingredients—tomatoes, garlic, capers, olives, and of course some red wine. Best with a string pasta such as fettuccine, it takes me straight to Italy!

Serves 4

1 pound fresh or dried spaghetti or fettuccine

FOR THE SAUCE
1/4 cup olive oil
1 onion, chopped
1 tablespoon flour
1 cup fruity red wine
2 cups boiling water
1 pound tomatoes, peeled, seeded, and chopped
3 garlic cloves, chopped
8 walnut halves, chopped
1 teaspoon fennel seeds
2 whole cloves
salt and pepper to taste
4 to 6 sprigs each of thyme, rosemary, and parsley
3 tablespoons capers, rinsed and drained
1/3 cup oil-cured black olives, pitted and coarsely chopped

Heat the oil in a saucepan, add the onion, and cook over medium heat until browned, 5 to 7 minutes. Whisk in the flour and cook until foaming. Stir in the wine, water, tomatoes, garlic, walnuts, fennel seed, cloves, pepper, and a little salt (the olives will add salt later). Chop the leaves from the thyme, rosemary, and parsley and reserve them. Tie the herb stems together and add them to the sauce. Bring it to a boil and simmer, uncovered, over low heat, stirring occasionally, until reduced by two-thirds and the flavor is concentrated, 3/4 to 1 hour.

Discard the cloves and bundle of herbs. Stir in the capers, olives, chopped herbs, and plenty of pepper. Taste and adjust seasoning.

To finish: Bring a large pot of salted water to a boil. Boil the pasta until it is al dente, testing by tasting or with your fingernail. Drain and toss with the sauce.

GETTING AHEAD: This sauce keeps in the refrigerator for at least 3 days and the flavor improves. It freezes well, too, so you can make a double or triple batch for emergencies.

pasta shapes

Dried pasta can be every conceivable shape—long, short, thin, wide, flat, curly, ribbed, or circular, you name it. Hence names like *farfalle* (butterflies), *ruoti* (wheels), *fusilli* (twists), and *penne* (quills). Each type tends to be associated with a particular sauce and dish, and not without reason, as you can't mix and match a pasta and a sauce at will. String pastas such as fettuccine, tagliatelle, linguine, and spaghetti may be served simply tossed in butter or olive oil, with a few chopped herbs or tomato dice. A more complex sauce needs body so that it clings to the slippery pasta strands: the bacon and egg for Spaghetti Carbonara, and cream and Parmesan for Fettuccine Alfredo are good examples.

Hollow dried pastas and many of the fancy shapes such as fusilli are specifically designed to absorb a maximum of rich sauce. Think of Macaroni and Cheese or the pesto sauces in pasta salads. Similarly, flat sheets of lasagne and big tubes of cannelloni and manicotti do best with thick, rich sauces like meaty Bolognese and chunky tomato that are sometimes so thick as to be almost a stuffing.

HOW TO MAKE FRESH PASTA DOUGH

Here's where pasta advances from being a quick supper dish to a gourmet treat. It's only recently that many of us have started going into the kitchen to make pasta from scratch, thanks to machines that help with mixing and take the hard work out of kneading and rolling. The dough itself can be mixed with an electric mixer using the dough hook, or in a food processor, or by hand. All take about the same length of time. Dough made in the mixer clings together in a mass on the hook, while dough made in the processor forms grainy crumbs. (When you press the crumbs together on the work surface, they will reform into a stiff, tough dough.) Dough mixed by hand shapes into a ball ready to knead. With all three methods, the finished dough will look rough and uneven until it is kneaded through the rollers of a pasta machine.

Pasta dough calls for at most four ingredients—flour, water, eggs, and salt—so getting the right balance is important. Much depends on the flour: for a chewy al dente finish to pasta you need plenty of gluten, the protein that makes dough elastic. American unbleached all-purpose flour is good in this respect, while European flours tend to have less gluten. As when making pastry, the amount of liquid your flour will absorb varies from batch to batch, and also depends on the temperature and humidity of the kitchen. Remember, for pasta the dough should be drier than pastry dough, mixed to a point where it only just holds together. Kneading develops the gluten, so the dough becomes elastic and satin-smooth.

To bind the flour, either water, egg, or a mixture of both, is used. Eggs also enrich the dough so (you might have guessed it) that's what I and most cooks prefer. On the question of salt, however, opinions differ. Personally, I think that salt in the dough itself adds depth of flavor, but some Italian cooks disagree, maintaining that salted boiling water is sufficient. A tablespoon of oil will make the dough a bit easier to work, but this is unnecessary if you use a machine for kneading and rolling. If you want to color or flavor the dough, several additions are possible. The simplest is tomato paste or freshly ground black pepper, with puréed spinach for green. Proportions of the ingredients in the dough must be adjusted to allow for extra liquid, particularly when using spinach.

1 To mix fresh pasta dough: Add the dough ingredients to the food processor and work until they form small, even crumbs. Press a few crumbs together with your fingers: if they are too dry to hold together, work in about a tablespoonful of water. If sticky, work in 2 to 3 tablespoons flour.

2 Tip the crumbs onto a work surface and press them into a ball, kneading them lightly so they hold together in a rough ball. If you are not kneading the dough at once, cover it with an upturned bowl so it cannot dry out.

Fresh Pasta Dough

Basic quantities for pasta dough are very simple: for each person you should allow 1 egg and 3/4 cup flour. I usually make a 4-egg quantity. You can decide by feeling the dough with your fingers whether more flour or liquid is needed to achieve the ideal consistency.

Makes 1 pound dough to serve 4

> **3 cups flour, more if needed**
> **4 eggs**
> **1 teaspoon salt**
> **water, if needed**
>
> **pasta-rolling machine**

Put the flour, eggs, and salt into the bowl of a food processor and work them until the mixture forms quite coarse crumbs, 1 to 2 minutes. Press a few crumbs together with your fingers. If the crumbs are sticky, work in more flour until they are dry, only lightly tacky. If the crumbs are very dry, work in a tablespoon or more of water.

Turn the crumbs onto a board and press them into a ball. It will look rough and uneven.

GETTING AHEAD: Personally, I prefer to shape pasta dough while it is very fresh, storing it after it has dried, but I know at least one cook who wraps balls of dough tightly and refrigerates them up to 2 days before kneading and rolling them.

Spinach Pasta Dough

This dough can be tricky unless the cooked spinach is very thoroughly dried. When making it, you may need to work in up to 1/2 cup of extra flour. Spinach pasta dough needs longer kneading, and sometimes holes form when rolling the dough if the spinach is not finely chopped.

Serves 4

Thaw 1/2-pound frozen chopped cooked spinach. Squeeze it as dry as you can with your hands, then put it in the corner of a dish towel and squeeze it even drier. Finely chop the spinach and add it to the recipe for Fresh Pasta Dough with the eggs and 1/4 cup more flour. Add more flour as needed when testing the crumbs of dough after mixing.

Tomato Pasta Dough

Tomato paste colors pasta an agreeably rusty red. Make 3 batches of dough in red, green, and white and you'll have Pasta Tricolore, the colors of the Italian flag.

Serves 4

When making Fresh Pasta Dough, add 2 tablespoons tomato paste to the eggs and increase the flour by 1/4 cup.

Black Pepper Pasta Dough

Freshly cracked black pepper adds kick to pasta dough and a speckled appearance that is great with cheese sauces or simply tossed in melted butter.

Serves 4

Put 2 tablespoons black peppercorns in a double thickness of plastic bags and pound with a rolling pin until they're as finely cracked as possible. In the recipe for Fresh Pasta Dough, add the pepper to the flour.

how to mix fresh pasta dough by hand

In Italy a marble slab, cool and with a slippery surface, is part of even a modest kitchen, but any smooth work surface will do for mixing and rolling pasta dough.

Tip the flour onto a work surface and make a well in the center. Add the eggs to the well with the salt and any coloring ingredient such as tomato paste or spinach, and mix them with the fingertips of one hand. Gradually mix in the flour from the sides, drawing in more as the dough thickens. Using the fingers of both hands, tear the half-mixed pieces of dough into crumbs. If they are dry, sprinkle them with a tablespoon of water; if sticky, add 2 to 3 tablespoons more flour. When the dough is evenly mixed, press the crumbs together and shape into a ball.

HOW TO KNEAD PASTA DOUGH BY MACHINE

Kneading pasta by hand can be fun and folkloric, but buy a $50 machine and your timing will be halved. Once you have a ball of dough, kneading is simply a matter of cutting off a manageable piece, pressing it to a rectangle, and working it through the machine. Then it is folded in three, given a quarter turn, and the action is repeated. In 2 to 3 short minutes, a rough uneven lump of dough will have been disciplined to a satin-smooth, velvety ribbon that is ready to roll to the thickness you want.

fresh pasta pointers

* A pasta machine attaches to the counter and consists essentially of two rollers operated with a crank handle. A few electric mixers have a pasta rolling attachment that is wonderfully easy to use.

* During kneading and rolling, the sheets of dough need regular dustings of flour to prevent them from sticking together.

* A pound of fresh pasta dough (a four-egg quantity) serves four as a main course, six as an appetizer.

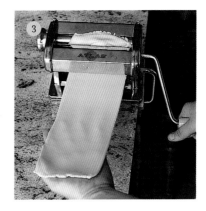

1 Set the pasta machine rollers on the widest setting. Cut the ball of dough in 3 pieces. Cover 2 with an upturned bowl and lightly flour the third. Press it into a rectangle and feed it through the rollers.

2 Fold the dough strip in 3 to make a square, give it a quarter turn, and feed it again through the rollers, dusting it with flour if it sticks.

3 Continue rolling and folding until the dough is elastic, very smooth, and does not crack at the sides, 6 to 8 times.

HOW TO ROLL AND CUT PASTA DOUGH

Now we're at the final stage of making fresh pasta: rolling and cutting it to shape. Using the pasta machine, the ball of fresh dough has been kneaded to a short, flexible ribbon, the same width as the rollers. To roll the ribbon to the thinness you want, simply continue feeding the dough through the machine, narrowing the rollers each time. The settings of machine rollers vary slightly, but in general the second-narrowest setting is right for lasagne, fettuccine, and other noodles, while the narrowest setting is appropriate for stuffed pastas such as ravioli.

Making pasta is a friendly affair. With one or two people to help, it is far easier to handle the ever-lengthening sheets of dough as they emerge from the rollers. After rolling, I have two approaches to keeping pasta sheets apart until they dry and are no longer sticky. Either I suspend a broom or large wooden spoon over two chair backs so I can drape the pasta sheets or noodles over them, or I line trays or racks with parchment paper, sprinkle them with flour (some cooks like to use semolina flour or fine cornmeal), and lay the pasta on top. A little pasta spreads a

long way and even a modest four-egg dough will decorate your kitchen from wall to wall.

If rolled pasta dough is to be stuffed (see The Ravioli Family, page 216), it should be used at once. To store homemade pasta such as noodles, let them dry 15 to 30 minutes (much depends on humidity) until they are no longer sticky, but still pliable. Then dust them with flour and toss until coated, working in small batches. Twist them loosely in nests, arrange them on a paper-lined tray, and leave to dry further until brittle. Now the pasta can be layered with paper, wrapped loosely, and stored for up to three days at room temperature. Flat sheets of pasta for lasagne or cannelloni should be left until dry and stiff before storage.

Homemade pasta is such a treat in itself that the simplest of toppings or sauces is appropriate—like the all-time favorites such as the Alfredo and Primavera that you see here. Feel free to substitute any string pasta except ultra-fine angel hair. My own top choice might be Emma's specialty of hot olive oil infused with shredded sage or basil and tossed with the just-cooked pasta (page 25).

1 To roll pasta dough: Tighten the pasta machine rollers 1 notch and feed the dough through them. Continue rolling, tightening the rollers 1 notch each time and flouring the dough as necessary so it does not stick. The dough ribbon will lengthen with each rolling and when it is quite long, seal the ends together to form a continuous band. Continue rolling the band, narrowing the roller settings, until the dough is the thickness you want.

2 To cut noodles: Roll dough through the rollers to the right thickness (usually the second-thinnest setting), snip the band, and detach the long ribbon of dough. Cut the ribbon in 12-inch lengths and let them dry, draped over broom handles or on parchment paper sprinkled with flour, until no longer sticky, at least 15 minutes. Add the noodle attachment to the machine and run the dough sheet through it to cut it in fettuccine or narrower tagliatelle. Twist them in loose nests of portion size so they are easy to handle for cooking or for storage.

recommendations for rolling

* As rolling proceeds, the ribbon of dough becomes quite long. A neat trick is to seal the ends together to make a circular band. Carry on rolling the band, narrowing the rollers until you arrive at the thickness you want. You'll find a band of pasta much easier to handle than a long ribbon.

* Fresh noodles and lasagne can be cooked after just a few minutes of drying, though personally I find them pasty. I prefer the firmer al dente texture of pasta that has been dried beyond the sticky stage, until it starts to lose flexibility but is still pliable. This can take as little as 15 minutes or up to an hour or two, depending on humidity.

* Fresh pasta freezes well and can be boiled directly out of the freezer.

Linguine with Olives and Capers

A piquant sauce that marries well with fresh or dried pasta.

Serves 4

Bring a large pan of salted water to a boil. Chop 3 garlic cloves and 1/2 cup pitted black olives. Add 1 pound fresh or dried linguine to the boiling water, stir, and boil until al dente when you taste a piece, 1 to 2 minutes for fresh pasta, 8 to10 minutes if dried. Drain the pasta. Heat 1/2 cup fruity olive oil in the pasta pan, add the garlic, olives, and 1/4 cup drained capers and heat, stirring, until fragrant, about 1 minute. Add the linguine and toss until coated. Season with plenty of freshly ground black pepper.

Fettuccine Alfredo

Alfredo is a legendary character, maître d' of the Alfredo alla Scrofa restaurant in Rome, where he cooked up cheese and cream topping on a table burner for his guests.

Serves 4

Bring a large pan of salted water to a boil. Add 1 pound fresh fettuccine and boil until al dente when you taste a piece, 1 to 2 minutes. Meanwhile melt 4 tablespoons butter in a small pan, add 1 cup heavy cream, and bring almost to a boil. Drain and rinse the fettuccine and return it to the pan. Pour the cream mixture over it and heat gently, tossing until the pasta is coated, about 1 minute. Add 1/2 cup grated Parmesan cheese and toss again until very hot, about 30 seconds. Pile the fettuccine on 4 plates and grind black pepper generously on top. Serve at once with more grated Parmesan.

Tagliatelle with Lemon and Parsley

Another of Emma's quick ideas using ingredients that are often around.

Serves 4

Bring a large pan of salted water to a boil. In a bowl, stir together 1/2 cup heavy cream, 2 egg yolks, 1/2 cup grated Parmesan cheese, the juice and grated zest of 1 lemon, and some freshly ground black pepper. The lemon juice will thicken the cream slightly. Chop a handful of parsley sprigs. Add 1 pound fresh tagliatelle to the boiling water and boil until al dente when you taste a piece, 1 to 2 minutes. Drain the pasta, melt 4 tablespoons butter in the pan, and put back the pasta. Add the lemon mixture and toss over medium heat until coated and hot, 1 to 2 minutes. Add the parsley and toss again. Taste, adjust seasoning, adding a little salt if necessary, and serve at once.

Fettuccine Primavera

In Italian, *primavera* means spring, epitomized by the glowing green and orange of these vegetables. Bulb fennel, green bell pepper, snow peas, broccoli, and asparagus tips can be substituted or added as you like.

Serves 4

2 medium zucchini
2 medium carrots
1½ cups shelled peas
3 tablespoons butter
¾ cup heavy cream
1 recipe Fresh Pasta Dough (page 210)
¼ cup grated Parmesan cheese, more to taste
salt and pepper to taste

Trim the ends from the zucchini, cut them lengthwise in half, then quarter them. Cut the quarters across into ¼-inch chunks. Cut the carrots into ¼-inch dice. Bring a medium saucepan of salted water to a boil. Add the carrots and peas and cook for 5 minutes. Add the zucchini and cook 2 to 3 minutes longer, until the vegetables are just tender. Drain, rinse with cold water, and leave to drain thoroughly. Make the pasta dough, then roll and cut it into fettuccine. Let it dry for 15 minutes, or longer if you wish.

Cook the pasta: Bring a large pot of salted water to a boil. Add the fresh pasta and simmer until it rises to the surface of the water, 1 to 2 minutes after coming back to a boil. It should be tender but still chewy or al dente. Stir it occasionally to keep from sticking. Drain the pasta, rinse with hot water, and drain again.

While the pasta is cooking, finish the sauce: Heat the butter in a large saucepan, add the vegetables, and sauté 1 minute. Add the cream, stir well to mix, and heat until simmering. Remove from the heat, add the pasta, and toss to mix with the vegetables and cream. Finally, add the Parmesan and toss gently so the fettuccine is coated. Taste and adjust the seasoning, adding more Parmesan if you like. Serve it at once so it does not stick together.

GETTING AHEAD: The fettuccine can be made up to 3 days ahead and stored at room temperature. Boil and drain the vegetables for the Primavera topping an hour or two before serving so that while the pasta is boiling all you have to do is finish the sauce.

Fettuccine Primavera

The Ravioli Family

Ravioli, tortellini, and other members of the stuffed pasta family take fresh pasta a big step beyond flat shapes such as fettuccine and lasagne. Stuffings should be finely chopped and firm so they do not burst easily from their pasta covering. Simple mixtures do best, based on cheese, vegetables such as pumpkin, and more rarely shellfish or meat, made vivid with herbs or a backing of spice. All fillings should be highly seasoned to compensate for the bland pasta dough. Ravioli and crescent turnovers are easy to shape, and even tortellini require only a quick twist of the fingers. Simplest of all is layered pasta created by "quilting" two layers with flat-leaf parsley.

Let stuffed pastas dry 1 to 2 hours until quite firm before boiling them in salted water. Because the filling is moist, they do not keep well and should be stored in the refrigerator and cooked within 4 to 6 hours. Simmer them gently so they do not break up, and stir from time to time. Do not cook too many packages at once as they swell during cooking. Cooking time varies from 2 to 5 minutes, depending on the dryness and thickness of the pasta. If overcooked, the packages will burst. Stuffed pasta is generally served plain, tossed in a bit of oil or melted butter, with or without grated Parmesan cheese. Another simple idea is the classic cream-based Alfredo sauce.

To shape ravioli, roll the dough as thinly as possible and trim it to strips about 5 inches wide, discarding ends and rough edges. Cut the strips in half. Brush 1 piece of dough very lightly with water and arrange mounds of filling on the moistened dough, spacing them about 1 1/2 inches apart and leaving a 1/2-inch border. Lay the other piece of dough on top. With your fingers, press down between the mounds of filling to seal the dough, pushing out any pockets of air. Seal the dough firmly by pressing down with the upper side of a small cookie cutter or a blunt shot glass. Cut them into squares with a fluted pasta wheel or large knife. Set the ravioli, not touching each other, on a floured dish towel, dust them with flour, and leave to dry, 1 to 2 hours.

1 To shape turnovers *(mezzalune):* Roll the dough as thinly as possible with the pasta roller. Stamp out 2-inch rounds (or larger) with a fluted pastry cutter. Mound a half teaspoonful of filling (more if you have cut a larger round) in the center and brush the edge lightly with water. Fold the dough to make a half moon and seal the edges, pressing firmly first with your fingers and then with the blunt upper edge of the pastry cutter or a shot glass.

2 To shape *tortellini:* Brush one point of a dough half moon with water. Bend the half moon around the first finger of one hand, pinching the points of dough together to seal them. Set the tortellini, not touching each other, on a floured sheet of parchment paper or dish towel, dust them with flour, and leave to dry, 1 to 2 hours.

Red Pepper and Ricotta Stuffing for Pasta

A tasty stuffing that is vivid with roasted red pepper.

Makes 2 cups stuffing, enough to fill 1 pound fresh pasta dough to serve 8 to 10 people

Roast 2 red peppers under the broiler (see How to Roast and Core Bell Peppers, page 255) so they cook slightly. Peel them, discard core and seeds, chop them finely, and put them in a bowl. Chop $^1/_2$ cup pitted black Kalamata olives and add them to the peppers. Stir in $^1/_2$ cup ricotta cheese with 1 teaspoon ground cumin and $^1/_2$ teaspoon ground black pepper. Taste and adjust seasonings.

Goat Cheese and Chive Stuffing for Pasta

Basil, thyme, or oregano may be used instead of chives.

Makes about 2 cups stuffing, enough to fill 1 pound fresh pasta dough to serve 8 to 10 people

Beat $1^1/_2$ cups grated Parmesan cheese into 2 cups soft goat cheese (if necessary soften the cheese with a little milk). Stir in 2 large bunches of chives, chopped, 2 finely chopped garlic cloves, 1 teaspoon grated nutmeg, a little salt, and plenty of black pepper. Taste and adjust seasoning.

Asian Shrimp Stuffing for Pasta

Packages with this wonton-style shrimp stuffing are delicious for dipping in Asian Vinaigrette (page 73).

Makes 2 cups stuffing, enough to fill 1 pound fresh pasta dough to serve 8 to 10 people

Heat 2 tablespoons vegetable oil in a frying pan or wok, add 2 thinly sliced scallions, 2 finely chopped garlic cloves, and a 1-inch piece of ginger, finely chopped. Stir-fry until fragrant, about 1 minute. Stir in $^1/_2$ pound raw peeled shrimp, the grated zest of 1 lemon, and 1 table-spoon soy sauce and stir-fry until very hot, about 1 minute. Transfer stuffing to a food processor and work until finely chopped. Brown a small piece of stuffing in a frying pan and taste it, adjusting the seasoning with soy sauce as needed.

quilted pasta

Blanched leaves of parsley can be enclosed between two layers of pasta dough to make a random or carefully contrived pattern. The dough is then cut in squares or wide strips for boiling and served simply tossed in melted butter or oil so the pattern shows at its best.

Detach leaves of flat-leaf parsley, discarding the stems. Blanch the parsley in boiling water for 30 seconds until just wilted, drain, and rinse it with cold water. Drain again on paper towels. Roll the dough as thinly as possible and trim it to 4-inch-wide strips, discarding ends and rough edges. Cut the strips in half. Brush one strip lightly with water and arrange the parsley leaves, spacing them quite wide apart. Set the other strip on top and press it down firmly with a rolling pin. Dust the dough with flour and run it once more through the pasta roller at the second-widest setting. Cut the dough in strips or squares and set them, not touching each other, on a floured dish towel. Dust them with flour and leave to dry for at least 1 to 2 hours. When completely dry, the pasta keeps well for up to 48 hours before cooking.

HOW TO BOIL AND STEAM RICE

In the West, we like our rice fluffy, with each grain separate and slightly chewy to the teeth. A similar style is followed in Iran and India. To get this fluffy effect, rice is boiled quite rapidly in lots of salted water so as to keep the grains apart and wash off starch. Asians prefer rice that is softer and clings together, making it easy to lift in a loose ball with chopsticks. It is more often gently simmered, without stirring, in a limited amount of water so it half-steams to a tender and slightly sticky consistency.

A quick rinse with cold water before cooking helps get rid of starch, and many Indian recipes call for rice to be soaked so the grains are flexible enough to withstand long cooking. Cooking time varies with the type of rice and its dryness. The best test is to nibble a few grains—they should be chewy with no trace of crunch. You can test with a fingernail, too. As soon as it is done, Western-style boiled rice is rinsed with hot water if it is to be served hot, or with cold water for rice salads, then left to drain. When Asian-style rice is done, it is left a few minutes for the grains to contract before stirring with a fork. Cooked rice can be kept warm in a colander over a pan of gently steaming water for an hour or more. Or you can spread it in an oiled or buttered baking dish, cover it tightly with oiled or buttered aluminum foil, and heat it in a 350°F oven for 10 to 15 minutes. Plain boiled or steamed rice provides the perfect background for many other dishes.

types of rice

The type of rice you use makes a big difference. Large, long-grain varieties including fragrant basmati cook to be fluffy and separate when boiled. That's the kind we Western cooks use for boiled rice and pilaf. Asian rice grain varieties are smaller and more compact, with a high starch content that makes them cling no matter how they are cooked. For pilaf, the rice must hold its shape when cooked so long- or medium-grain rice is best again, in particular the deliciously fragrant varieties such as basmati, jasmine, and texmati. Short-grain rice is often called pudding rice as it softens easily and almost falls apart as it sheds starch for thickening puddings. Asian cooks use a type of short-grain rice for their sticky rice. Another group consists of plump round-grain types of rice for risotto and paella. Risotto rice absorbs at least four times its own volume of liquid and should still hold its shape. Brown rice is not a different variety, but includes the nutritious bran layer that has been stripped from white rice. Wild rice, botanically speaking, is a grass rather than a grain, but it looks and behaves like rice in the kitchen, taking longer to cook than most types.

1 To test when long-grain rice is done, lift out a few grains on a fork. Pinch a few between your fingers—they should squash quite easily with no hard white starch at the center. Alternatively, taste a few grains to be sure they are not crunchy. If the ends of the grains have burst, the rice is overcooked. A table fork is useful when cooking rice as the tines are narrow enough to trap a few grains for testing; a fork also fluffs the cooked grains.

Fluffy Boiled White Rice

Check your package of rice; if it is "converted," it will cook more quickly than regular white rice as some of the starch has been removed. Brown rice is boiled the same way as white rice and takes up to 40 minutes.

Serves 3 to 4

Bring a large pan of salted water to a boil, allowing at least 5 quarts of water and a tablespoon of salt. If you like, add a half lemon to whiten the rice and add flavor, squeezing it to extract the juice. Stir in 1 cup long-grain rice. Boil rapidly without the lid, stirring once or twice, until the rice is just tender, 10 to 12 minutes. Drain in a colander and rinse with hot or cold water. Leave to drain about 5 minutes, then stir with a fork.

Asian Steamed Rice

If you steam long-grain white rice, the grains will emerge fluffy, while small-grained Asian rice tends to cling.

Serves 4

Soak 1 cup rice in a bowl of water for 5 minutes, stirring once or twice. Drain and rinse it in a colander. Put it in a saucepan with 1 1/2 cups water and 1/2 teaspoon salt. Cover, bring to a boil, and simmer gently, 8 to 10 minutes, until the water is absorbed and small craters show on the surface of the rice (you'll see at once what I mean). Leave the rice covered in a warm place 10 minutes longer, so the grains steam until tender. They will contract slightly so that long-grain types will separate and fluff when you stir them with a fork.

rice reminders

* When boiling rice, a slice of lemon in the water whitens the rice and adds pleasant flavor, especially to cold rice for salads.
* Rice swells enormously during cooking and you can reckon that one cup of dry rice will yield three cups when cooked, and serve four people.

Fried Rice

This basic recipe for fried rice is a foundation for all sorts of other ingredients. For a more substantial vegetable dish, for instance, you could add 1 or 2 cups of cooked broccoli florets or some diced carrot, red peppers, or squash. Cooked fish, particularly shrimp, chicken, or pork can be included, too, and should be finely shredded. Leftover cooked rice is best for fried rice as freshly cooked rice is heavy with moisture.

Serves 4

> 3 eggs
> salt and pepper to taste
> 2 tablespoons vegetable oil
> 1-inch piece of ginger, chopped
> 1 garlic clove, chopped
> 3 cups cooked rice
> 1 cup frozen peas, thawed
> 3 scallions, including green parts, sliced
> 1½ tablespoons soy sauce, more to taste
> 1 teaspoon dark sesame oil, more to taste

Whisk the eggs with salt and pepper until mixed. Heat a wok over high heat for about 30 seconds. Drizzle half the oil around the sides. Add the egg, swirling the pan so the sides are coated, then stir-fry it, cutting and turning so the egg is shredded. When firm, remove and set it aside.

Add the remaining oil to the wok with the ginger and garlic and stir-fry until fragrant, about 1 minute. If adding any cooked fish, poultry, or meat, add it now and stir-fry to heat it for 1 minute. Add the rice and fry until very hot, 1 to 2 minutes. Lastly add the peas and scallions with any other vegetables and continue stir-frying until the rice is again very hot, about 1 minute. Stir in the egg. Add the soy sauce and mix well. Take the rice from the heat, sprinkle the sesame oil over it, and taste for seasoning, adding more soy sauce or sesame oil if you like.

GETTING AHEAD: By definition, fried rice involves reheating boiled rice. You can also cook the shredded egg an hour or two ahead.

Southern Dirty Rice

This is my simplified version of dirty rice—it might be scorned by a true Southern cook, but it's delicious.

Serves 4 to 6

> 1 cup long-grain rice
>
> 1 cup chicken livers
>
> 1 onion, thinly sliced
>
> 2 tablespoons bacon fat or vegetable oil
>
> 2 garlic cloves, chopped
>
> salt and pepper to taste
>
> 4 scallions, including green parts, sliced
>
> 2 cups water
>
> 1 to 2 whole dried red chile peppers
>
> 2 teaspoons chopped fresh thyme leaves
>
> 3 to 4 tablespoons chopped fresh parsley

Soak the rice in a bowl of water, stirring once or twice. Trim the chicken livers, discarding any membrane, and chop them. In a large skillet, fry the onion in the bacon fat until it starts to brown, 5 to 7 minutes. Stir in the garlic and cook 1 minute. Add the chicken livers with salt and pepper and cook over high heat, stirring constantly, until they start to brown, 2 to 3 minutes. Add the scallions and continue cooking until they are tender and the livers are very brown, 2 to 3 minutes. Add ¹/2 cup of the water, cover, and set aside.

Drain the rice and rinse it in a colander. Put it in a saucepan with the remaining water, dried red chile pepper, thyme, and ¹/2 teaspoon salt. Cover, bring to a boil, and simmer gently, 8 to 10 minutes, until the water is absorbed. Discard the chile pepper. Stir the chicken liver mixture so juices on the bottom of the pan are dissolved in the water. Spread the mixture over the rice, stir with two forks, and cover the pan again. Leave over very low heat for 10 minutes, then turn off the heat and leave for 10 minutes more. Stir in the parsley. Taste and adjust the seasoning.

GETTING AHEAD: Dirty rice improves if you make it ahead, keeping it in the refrigerator up to 2 days. Warm it over low heat on top of the stove.

Curried Rice with Smoked Haddock *(Kedgeree)*

As a child I found boiled rice boring until I discovered *kedgeree*, an English version of Indian *khichri*, boiled rice mixed with hard-boiled eggs, smoked haddock, and a bit of curry. Salmon can be substituted for the haddock, adding even more color. Great brunch stuff!

Serves 6 to 8

> 2 pounds smoked haddock fillet
>
> 2 cups milk
>
> 1¹/2 cups rice
>
> 1 slice of lemon
>
> 4 tablespoons butter, more for baking dish
>
> 2 tablespoons curry powder
>
> 6 hard-boiled eggs, coarsely chopped
>
> ¹/2 cup cream
>
> salt and pepper to taste
>
> 6 tablespoons chopped fresh parsley

Cook the smoked haddock: Preheat the oven to 350°F. Butter a baking dish, add the smoked haddock, and pour the milk over it. Cover with aluminum foil and bake until the fish flakes easily, 20 to 25 minutes. Let it cool.

Bring a large pan of salted water to a boil. Add the rice and lemon and cook until just tender, 10 to 12 minutes. Drain, discard the lemon, and rinse the rice with hot water. Drain it in a colander for 5 minutes. Drain the smoked haddock and flake it, discarding any skin and bones.

To finish: Melt the butter in a large casserole, stir in the curry powder, and cook gently until fragrant and toasted, 1 to 2 minutes. Add the fish and chopped hard-boiled eggs. Stir in the rice and toss with two forks over high heat until very hot, 1 to 2 minutes. Add the cream, salt, pepper, and parsley, and continue heating 1 minute. Taste, adjust seasoning, and serve at once.

GETTING AHEAD: Almost all the cooking for *kedgeree* can be done the day before, including boiling the rice, boiling the eggs, and cooking and flaking the fish. To finish, reheat the rice in a 350°F oven for 10 to 15 minutes, then finish the dish.

Foolproof Polenta

Polenta is the Italian name for cornmeal, usually made from yellow corn. It can be of fine, medium, or coarse grind and is cooked by simmering in salted water to a soft porridge. Like risotto, making polenta is a full-time occupation: at the start of cooking, an occasional stir will do, but once the polenta starts to thicken it needs stirring constantly. Be sure to use a heavy pan to spread the heat and lessen sticking.

1 At the end of simmering, polenta should be creamy and soft enough to fall easily from the spoon, as here. For grilled polenta, it is simmered a few minutes longer until stiff enough to hold a shape.

Soft Polenta

Serve soft polenta in shallow individual soup or pasta bowls, making a well in the center and adding a savory stew or sauce of poultry, meat, or vegetables.

Serves 4 to 6

Bring a quart of water to a boil and add a teaspoon of salt. Slowly pour 1 cup polenta into the rapidly boiling water, stirring vigorously with a wooden spoon so it does not form lumps. Lower the heat and simmer gently, stirring often, 30 to 40 minutes, until the polenta is soft, creamy, and just falls easily from the spoon. Finished consistency of polenta, whether soft and almost runny or stiff enough to hold a shape, depends on your taste and its final use, but it should never be sticky. Toward the end of cooking you will need to stir constantly to prevent sticking. Take the polenta from the heat and beat in 2 to 3 tablespoons butter, cut in pieces, and if you like up to $^1/_2$ cup grated Parmesan cheese.

Grilled Polenta

Soft polenta can also be spread on an oiled baking sheet, left to set, and then cut in shapes to grill or fry.

Make Soft Polenta and cook until it pulls away from the sides of the pan and is stiff enough to hold the spoon upright. Pour it onto an oiled baking sheet to form a $^1/_2$-inch layer. Let cool and then chill it, uncovered, at least 2 hours until firmly set. Light the grill and oil the rack. Cut the polenta in squares or triangles, set them on the hot grill, and toast, 3 to 5 minutes. Turn and brown the other side.

HOW TO SIMMER RICE PILAF

Plain boiled rice is useful stuff, but to me pilaf is far more tempting. Rice pilaf is flavored with onion and all manner of spices, then simmered with stock to a savory finish. Other more substantial ingredients, such as mushrooms and smoked sausages, can be included, and vegetables like carrots and green peas add color. Taken further, a pilaf develops into an alternative appetizer to pasta. When seafood, particularly shrimp, clams, and mussels top up the pot, pilaf expands to become a main course. Best known in this genre is paella, with its multiple layers of ingredients simmered together in a sea of rice.

① When rice pilaf is done, put back the lid and let it stand 8 to 10 minutes before fluffing it with a fork to separate the grains. Herbs, nuts and other ingredients that need little cooking are added at this stage. Aim for glistening rice with grains that separate when stirred with a fork. Color will be light beige and flavor should be mellow, well rounded without overwhelming the rice itself.

The best rice for pilaf is long- or medium-grain, especially basmati and other fragrant varieties. You'll find a heavy saucepan is very helpful in spreading heat so the rice does not scorch. Pilaf is a pleasure to prepare ahead. When done it waits happily in a warm place for a half hour or more. You can keep it up to 3 days in the refrigerator. Just leave it in the cooking pot, and reheat it in that same pot on top of the stove or in the oven. It freezes well, too.

intriguing grains

Each time I go to a certain world-famous grocery store in New York, I look at the lineup, from ancient varieties of wheat such as kamut and spelt, to buckwheat and quinoa that, botanically speaking, do not qualify as grains. Couscous, for example, is a cereal made from wheat. Whole grains such as brown rice and pearl barley appeared in supermarkets long ago, and you may also find cracked grains that include bulghur and cracked wheat.

Though these grains may be unfamiliar, you'll be glad to know that they behave just like rice, though cooking times and the amount of liquid needed vary widely. Kasha (which is wholegrain buckwheat that has been parboiled and dried) takes only 10 minutes to cook and absorbs no more than its own volume of liquid. Wheat berries can take hours to become tender and will need moistening with up to five times their own volume of liquid.

Plain Rice Pilaf

This simple pilaf is an alternative to boiled or steamed rice, particularly with stews and meats in sauce.

Serves 4

Measure 1 cup of long-grain rice: As with boiled rice, this will make about 3 cups of pilaf. In a heavy casserole, heat 2 tablespoons olive oil or butter and sauté a chopped onion until translucent, 3 to 5 minutes. Stir in 1 teaspoon ground coriander and 1/2 teaspoon pepper. Sauté, stirring, 30 seconds, then stir in 1 cup long-grain rice. Continue sautéing 1 to 2 minutes, until the fat is absorbed and the grains look shiny. Stir in 1 1/2 cups vegetable stock or water with salt to taste. Cover the pan and bring to a boil. Simmer until all the stock is absorbed, 18 to 20 minutes. Taste the rice, and if it is not tender, stir in 1/2 cup more stock and continue cooking, 3 to 5 minutes. Taste again and, when tender, put back the lid and leave the rice 8 to 10 minutes. Fluff the rice with a fork, taste and adjust the seasoning.

Herbed Pilaf

This basic pilaf is a good accompaniment to fish, poultry, or meats, and should be cooked with the matching stock. For vegetarian pilaf, use vegetable stock.

Serves 4

In a heavy casserole, melt 2 tablespoons butter and sauté a chopped medium onion until transparent, 3 to 5 minutes. Stir in 1 cup long-grain rice and sauté, stirring, until the butter is absorbed and the grains look shiny. Add 1 1/2 cups stock with 1 teaspoon fresh thyme leaves, 2 bay leaves, salt, and pepper; cover and bring to a boil. Simmer until all the stock is absorbed, 18 to 20 minutes. Taste the rice to see if it is tender. If not done, add more stock and continue cooking. If done, put back the pan lid and leave the rice for 10 minutes. Using two forks, stir in 2 tablespoons chopped fresh parsley, discard bay leaves, and adjust the seasoning.

Suleiman's Pilaf with Pistachios

This main course pilaf is excellent with cooked turkey or chicken as well as lamb. Toasted almonds or pine nuts can be substituted for the pistachios. For a vegetarian pilaf, simply leave out the lamb and use water or vegetable stock.

Serves 4

> **6 ounces lean cooked lamb**
> **2 tablespoons olive oil**
> **2 onions, chopped**
> **2 garlic cloves, chopped**
> **1 cup basmati or long-grain rice**
> **1 1/2 cups veal stock or water**
> **1/4 cup currants**
> **1/4 cup dried apricots, chopped**
> **2 tomatoes, peeled, seeded and chopped**
> **2 teaspoons chopped fresh thyme**
> **1 teaspoon chopped fresh rosemary**
> **1/2 teaspoon ground cinnamon**
> **salt and pepper to taste**
> **1/2 cup blanched pistachios**
> **small bunch of dill, chopped**
> **2 tablespoons chopped fresh parsley**
> **1/2 cup plain yogurt**

Trim any fat or sinew from the lamb and finely shred it. Heat the oil in a heavy casserole and fry the onions until soft, 5 to 7 minutes. Stir in the garlic and fry, stirring until fragrant, about 1 minute. Stir in the rice and cook until it looks translucent and the oil is absorbed. Stir in the stock with the lamb, currants, apricots, tomato, thyme, rosemary, cinnamon, salt, and pepper. Cover, bring to a boil, and simmer until liquid is absorbed and rice is tender, 18 to 20 minutes.

Let the rice stand 10 minutes, then remove the cover and, using a fork, stir in the pistachios, dill, and parsley. Add enough yogurt to moisten the pilaf, then taste and adjust the seasoning.

GETTING AHEAD: Reheated rice pilaf is even better. Keep it in the pot up to 2 days in the refrigerator, then warm it over low heat on top of the stove, stirring in the pistachios, herbs, and yogurt just before serving.

Sausage and Lentil Pilaf

An aromatic, spicy pilaf that is delicious as an appetizer or side dish with grilled chicken and lamb.

Serves 6

Simmer 1 cup any type of lentils in generous amounts of water for 20 minutes, then drain them. In a heavy casserole, heat 2 tablespoons vegetable oil and fry a chopped small onion until soft, 3 to 5 minutes. Stir in ½ teaspoon ground allspice and ½ teaspoon ground cinnamon and cook until fragrant, about 1 minute. Add 1 cup basmati or long-grain rice and fry, stirring, until the rice looks translucent, 1 to 2 minutes. Add 1½ cups chicken or veal stock and stir in the lentils with ½ cup cooked spiced sausage, chopped, salt, and pepper. Cover, bring to a boil and simmer until the liquid is absorbed and the rice is tender, 18 to 20 minutes. Let stand 10 minutes. Stir the pilaf with a fork, taste and adjust the seasoning.

Pearl Barley Pilaf

The chewy texture of barley is a welcome change from plain rice.

Serves 4

> 1 cup pearl barley
> 2 tablespoons butter
> 1 onion, chopped
> 2 cups chicken stock, more if needed
> salt and pepper to taste
> 2 tablespoons chopped fresh marjoram or parsley

Melt the butter in a heavy pan, add the onion, and sauté, stirring occasionally, until it is soft but not brown, 5 to 7 minutes. Stir in the barley and sauté 2 to 3 minutes, until the grains look transparent. Add the stock with salt and pepper, cover, and bring to a boil. Simmer until all the liquid is absorbed, 30 to 40 minutes. Taste, and if the barley is not tender, add more stock and continue simmering. When the barley is cooked, add marjoram, stir to mix all the ingredients, and taste for seasoning.

GETTING AHEAD: Barley pilaf reheats perfectly on top of the stove and keeps well up to 3 days in the refrigerator.

Paella by the Beach

When Emma and I welcome friends in Los Angeles, we're very near the ocean and fine seafood. We both agree that a good paella is unbeatable as a one-pot meal. Key is a good mix of ingredients—fish, chicken, and vegetables, plus the smoke of ham, a spicy chorizo sausage, and a couple of pinches of genuine saffron.

You might expect paella to be made with long-grain rice like other pilafs, but in fact the rice should be round-grain, either Spanish paella rice or Italian risotto rice such as arborio. A purpose-designed shallow, two-handled paella pan helps, too, but is not essential. Traditionally, paella is cooked outdoors on a barbecue; on a domestic stove, you should use two burners and turn the pan often so the heat spreads evenly.

Serves 10 to 12

> ⅓ cup olive oil
> 10 to 12 chicken thighs or legs (about 3 pounds)
> salt and pepper to taste
> 3 onions, chopped
> 3½ cups risotto or paella rice
> 1½ quarts chicken stock or water,
>   more if needed
> 2 pinches saffron threads soaked in 1 cup
>   boiling water
> 1 pound cleaned squid, sliced
> 1 pound sliced raw smoked ham, cut in strips
> 1 pound chorizo sausage, sliced
> 1½ pounds tomatoes, peeled, seeded,
>   and chopped
> 2 red bell peppers, cored, seeded, and
>   cut in strips
> 1 cup fresh or frozen green peas
> 1 pound cod or other white fish fillets,
>   cut in chunks
> 1½ pounds raw shrimp, in their shells
> 1½ pounds mussels, cleaned
>
> 20-inch paella pan or large shallow flameproof
>   casserole

Paella by the Beach

Heat half the oil in the pan, season the chicken pieces with salt and pepper, and brown them on all sides over medium heat, 10 to 12 minutes so they are partially cooked; remove them and set aside. Add the remaining oil to the pan and fry the onions until soft but not brown, 5 to 7 minutes. Add the rice and cook, stirring, until the grains are transparent and the oil is absorbed, 2 to 3 minutes. Add the stock, saffron with soaking liquid, and salt and pepper.

Add more ingredients in the following order, pushing them down into the layer of rice: browned chicken, squid, smoked ham, chorizo, tomatoes, peppers, and peas. The fish and shrimp should be spread on top so they cook more slowly; reserve the mussels. Bring the liquid to a boil and cook the paella for 15 minutes,

adjusting the heat so it simmers gently. Shake the pan from time to time to discourage sticking.

After 15 minutes, set the mussels on top of the pan and continue cooking, 15 to 20 minutes, until the mussels are opened, the rice is almost tender, and most of the liquid is absorbed. Turn off the heat, cover the pan, and leave, 5 to 10 minutes, for flavors to mellow and the rice to become tender and absorb all the liquid. Taste the paella and adjust the seasoning.

GETTING AHEAD: All the prep can be done ahead, but the paella must be assembled and freshly cooked for serving.

HOW TO SIMMER RISOTTO

Special varieties of rice are important in certain traditional preparations, and nowhere more so than in risotto. Risotto rice—the most common is called arborio—is fat and round, so absorbent and full of starch that it takes four times its own volume of liquid, sometimes more. No wonder risotto is famous for its intensity of flavor and rich, creamy texture! The essential ingredients are four in number: butter, rice, a few spoonfuls of wine, and a light broth that is usually made from veal or a bit of beef or chicken, though vegetable stock is useful, too. This plain risotto doesn't amount to much, but add a star ingredient such as porcini mushrooms, baby shrimp, spring greens, or the first asparagus of the season, and it's transformed. In the fall, warmer flavors of pumpkin or butternut squash and spicy sausage come into play. Most famous of all is Risotto Milanese, flavored with saffron, classic accompaniment to osso buco. In general, however, risotto is served as a separate course.

Making risotto is a peaceful occupation, a matter of standing by the stove and stirring gently, more or less constantly, for up to half an hour. When Emma and I make supper together, that's my job. Famous chefs have tried to invent microwave or stop-and-go risotto methods that match the original, but in vain. You'll need two saucepans, one for the risotto itself, the other to keep the simmering broth ready to ladle, little by little, into the bubbling rice.

1 In a large, heavy saucepan, sauté onion in a tablespoon or two of butter. Stir in the rice and toast it a minute or two. Pour in a few tablespoons of wine (usually white)—they will hiss and bubble, starting the rice steaming and opening the surface of the grains.

Add the first ladleful of hot broth and stir gently. As soon as the broth has been absorbed and the risotto looks dry, add another ladleful of hot broth and keep going. The purpose is to draw starch from the surface of the rice so the grains cook through to the center and the starch thickens the cooking broth.

2 The rice will continue to absorb broth (about four times its own volume) until, after 25 minutes or so, it will seem saturated. Go slower now—if the rice is smooth, creamy, and holds the trail of the spoon, you may want to stop. If you prefer risotto Venetian-style as I do, *all'onda* or "on the wave," stir in a bit more broth. Now taste the rice—it should be meltingly smooth with a hint of chewiness.

3 Take the pan from the heat and stir in at least a tablespoon of butter. This process, called *mantecare*, marries the ingredients together. Stir in any flavorings (here wild mushrooms). The flavorings are often cooked separately and should be reheated before adding so they do not cool the hot risotto. Adjust seasoning, and serve your risotto at once. It will amply reward your care and attention.

Broth for Risotto

The broth used in risotto reduces and intensifies during cooking; it should be mild and unobtrusive in flavor so it does not overwhelm the rice and other ingredients. For risotto, the veal, fish, or chicken stock (page 45) that adds great taste to stews and sauces is too strong. I find if I add an equal quantity of water to any of these stocks and simmer with a thinly sliced onion and carrot for 20 minutes, I get a much better result. Vegetable stock (page 45) is less assertive and can usually be used as is. When starting from scratch, here is a simple broth that accommodates most risottos.

Makes 1 quart broth

Sauté a thinly sliced onion and a thinly sliced carrot in 1 tablespoon vegetable oil until very soft, 5 to 7 minutes. Add 6 cups water, 2 bay leaves, 3 to 4 sprigs thyme, 3 to 4 sprigs parsley, 1 teaspoon peppercorns, and ¹/₂ teaspoon salt. For a full-flavored broth for Red Wine Risotto, or Risotto Milanese, crumble in 2 to 3 ounces ground beef.

For chicken risotto, add 3 to 4 chicken wings or necks. For a fish or shellfish risotto, add a fish bone or a handful of shrimp shells. For vegetable risotto, add trimmings, for example of asparagus or mushrooms. Bring to a boil, simmer the broth uncovered for 30 minutes, and strain.

Risotto Milanese

Risotto Milanese is traditional with osso buco, or it may be served as a separate course with shavings of Parmesan cheese on top. In Italy you may find it topped with luscious slices of bone marrow, too, but at home I make this simple version.

Serves 4

1 quart meat or vegetable broth
large pinch of saffron threads
4 tablespoons butter
1 onion, finely chopped
1 cup risotto rice, preferably carnaroli or arborio
¹/₂ cup dry white wine
¹/₂ cup grated Parmesan cheese
salt and pepper to taste

Bring the broth to a boil and pour a few tablespoons over the saffron threads. Heat 2 tablespoons of the butter in a heavy pan and fry the onion until very soft, 5 to 7 minutes. Stir in the rice and sauté until it is translucent, about 2 minutes. Stir in the wine and boil until almost dry. Add a ladleful of hot broth and simmer the risotto, stirring constantly and adding more broth as needed, until it is tender and creamy, 25 to 35 minutes. Take risotto from the heat and stir in the saffron and liquid. Cut the remaining butter in pieces and add it to the risotto, stirring it into the rice as it melts. Stir in the Parmesan cheese, taste and adjust seasoning. Serve the risotto as soon as possible.

the right way to risotto

* A heavy pan that spreads heat evenly is a boon, so here's the place for your copper saucepan if you have one.

* Risotto is done when the grains of rice are tender and still slightly chewy. I hate the recent fashion for undercooked, crunchy risotto, and the uncooked starch will give you indigestion.

* If kept waiting more than a few minutes, risotto will stiffen to a heavy paste, especially if you try to keep it hot.

* Freshly grated Parmesan cheese is the mandatory accompaniment to vegetable risottos, but Italians do not countenance mixing cheese with fish.

Red Wine Risotto

A rich, lusty risotto that is served, with a wink, at weddings! It calls for a Chianti or other robust red wine.

Serves 4

Omit the saffron and white wine in the recipe for Risotto Milanese (page 227). In two separate pans, heat a half bottle (375 ml) red wine and 3 cups meat or vegetable broth. Make the risotto as for Risotto Milanese, adding the wine alternately with the broth. Finish the risotto with butter and Parmesan cheese.

Risotto with Pumpkin

The appearance of pumpkin risotto flavored with rosemary on Venetian menus heralds the fall. The most popular Italian pumpkin for risotto is the dark, rich zucca that you'll find in a few specialty markets, or look out for the American variety Small Sugar. Butternut squash is also good in risotto.

Serves 4 to 6 as an appetizer

   1 quart vegetable broth, more if needed
   3 tablespoons butter
   1 small onion, very finely chopped
   1 shallot, very finely chopped
   1 cup risotto rice, preferably carnaroli or arborio
   ½ cup dry white wine
   ⅓ cup grated Parmesan cheese

   FOR THE PUMPKIN
   1-pound pumpkin
   2 tablespoons olive oil
   2 tablespoons butter
   1 onion, chopped
   2 garlic cloves, chopped
   4 to 5 sprigs rosemary
   salt and pepper to taste

Cook the pumpkin: Peel the pumpkin and cut it in ³/₄-inch cubes. Heat the oil and butter in a large heavy-based pan, add the onion, and cook until lightly browned, 3 to 5 minutes. Stir in the pumpkin with the garlic, rosemary, salt, and pepper. Moisten with 3 to 4 tablespoons water,

cover, and cook over low heat, stirring occasionally, until the pumpkin is very tender and begins to fall apart, 12 to 15 minutes. If the pumpkin gets too dry, add a bit more water during cooking. Set it aside to keep warm, discarding the rosemary.

Make the risotto: Bring the broth to a boil, reduce the heat, and leave it to simmer. Heat all but a tablespoon of the butter in a large heavy-based saucepan. Add onion and shallots and cook, stirring with a wooden spoon, until soft but not brown, 3 to 4 minutes. Add the rice and sauté, stirring, until the rice is translucent, 2 to 3 minutes. Stir in the wine and reduce until almost dry. Ladle in about a cup of broth and simmer, stirring, until the rice is almost dry. Ladle in more broth, and continue cooking, adding more broth as needed, until the rice is very tender, creamy, and falls very easily from the spoon, 25 to 35 minutes.

Take the risotto from the heat and fold in the warm pumpkin, with the remaining butter and half the cheese. Taste and adjust seasoning. Spoon the risotto into warmed bowls, sprinkle with remaining cheese, and serve at once.

GETTING AHEAD: You can cook the pumpkin 3 to 4 hours ahead, but the rice is best cooked at the last minute.

Asparagus Risotto

Pumpkin brightens risotto in the fall, and asparagus announces that spring has finally arrived. Flavors differ but the method of cooking is the same.

Serves 4

In the recipe for Risotto with Pumpkin, omit the pumpkin. Peel 1 pound white or green asparagus, cut the stems in ½-inch lengths, and set aside the tips. Sauté the asparagus stems with the onion and shallots until tender, 3 to 4 minutes. Make the risotto as directed, adding the asparagus tips with the last ladleful of broth.

Wild Mushroom Risotto

Fragrant porcini mushrooms are classic in risotto, and other intensely flavored types such as chanterelles do well, too. Dried mushrooms are an alternative (you'll need about 2 ounces for this recipe), or you can supplement expensive fresh wild mushrooms with some cultivated ones. For example, portabellas, peeled and cut in wedges, make a nice color contrast with the white rice. This risotto is a hearty vegetarian entrée.

Serves 4 to 6

1 quart chicken or vegetable broth
3 tablespoons butter
1 small onion, finely chopped
1 cup risotto rice, preferably carnaroli or arborio
½ cup dry white wine
¼ cup grated Parmesan cheese
2 tablespoons chopped fresh parsley

FOR THE MUSHROOMS
1 tablespoon olive oil
1 tablespoon butter
1 garlic clove, peeled
½ pound wild mushrooms, such as porcini or
**   chanterelles, trimmed and cut in ¼-inch slices**
salt and pepper to taste

Cook the mushrooms: Heat the oil and butter in a skillet and add the whole clove of garlic. Add the mushrooms with salt and pepper and sauté them, stirring often, until they are tender and all liquid has evaporated, 5 to 8 minutes, depending on the type of mushroom. Take from the heat and discard the garlic clove. Taste, adjust seasoning, and set the mushrooms aside.

Make the risotto: Heat the broth in a saucepan and keep it warm at the side of the stove. In a heavy-based saucepan, melt half the butter. Stir in the onion and sauté it until transparent, 3 to 5 minutes. Stir in the rice and sauté it, stirring constantly, until it absorbs the butter and looks translucent, about 2 minutes. Add the wine and simmer until reduced by half. Add about 1 cup of the broth and simmer, stirring, until the rice starts to dry, 5 to 7 minutes. Continue cooking, stirring constantly and adding more broth in batches to keep the rice moist. At the end of cooking, the rice should be tender, still slightly al dente (chewy), and creamy from the starch that has begun to leach from the grains. This will take 25 to 30 minutes and don't hesitate to use plenty of broth.

Meanwhile, reheat the mushrooms in the skillet. When the risotto is ready, stir them into the rice. Take it from the heat and stir in the remaining butter, the Parmesan, and the parsley. Taste, adjust the seasoning, and serve the risotto in shallow bowls or on deep plates.

GETTING AHEAD: Risotto is best eaten at once, hence the wait in a good Italian restaurant while your risotto is prepared from scratch. It can be kept warm for up to 15 minutes with the pan in a water bath, but it will stiffen so you will need to stir in a little more broth just before serving.

CHAPTER NINE the vegetable story

French cooks have had great influence on the way we look at vegetables. We blanch vegetables, we refresh them, we cut them in julienne strips—all French terms. We take Gallic advice on how to hold knives when slicing and dicing them. However, when it comes to cooking vegetables, France has plenty of competition. Just in this chapter, from Italy we have minestrina soup and a peppery sweet salad of arugula with balsamic dressing. From the U.S.A. come corn dollars, roasted garlic mashed potatoes, and colonial roast squash. There's a summer parsley and sesame salad from Asia and a mushroom salad from the Mediterranean.

With so many ideas, so many vegetables, and so many different seasonings to choose from, you can imagine how hard it is to decide what to include. So I start with the basics of peeling, slicing, and dicing, then move on to boiling and steaming root vegetables, with special attention to everyone's favorite, mashed potatoes. You might think that boiling greens is quite similar to cooking root vegetables, but not at all. Green vegetables overcook so easily that they need careful handling. I maintain that they are equally unpleasant when undercooked and almost raw. Finding the perfect balance is tricky.

After the basics come the frills, with first of all a quick look at three vegetables that originated in the New World: bell peppers, corn, and squash. A couple of others—eggplants and artichokes—traveled in the opposite direction, from the Old World to the New. Given my own love of mushrooms, I could not leave out ham-stuffed portabellas, mushroom soup from family friend Emily, and the duxelles mushroom purée that is so delicious in stuffings and pies. That leaves how to wash salad greens, with a few handy tips on choosing and storage. And let's not forget sautéed vegetables, another love of mine. I'm a firm believer that a little bit of butter (or olive oil) does you and me—and our vegetables—good.

HOW TO SLICE AND DICE ROOT VEGETABLES

As with so many simple food techniques, slicing, dicing, and even peeling vegetables is a matter of a little practice. Be guided by the shape of the vegetable. Long ones such as leeks and asparagus sit placidly on the chopping board, awaiting the stroke of the knife, but round ones such as potatoes and onions (page 32) are not so compliant. Either you should halve them or cut a thin slice off the bottom so you have a flat surface that gives them a base. For neat slices and dice, the sides and top of the vegetable should also be squared or trimmed; for a rough dice, they can be left on.

Diced vegetables, notably carrot, are very useful in a mix to provide depth of flavor and a contrast of color. A classic combination of carrot, onion, and celery (called a *mirepoix* in French), is used in braises, soups, and stews. A recipe is usually specific on how small or large the sliced or diced pieces should be. As a rough guide, I think of $1/2$-inch slices as thick and $1/2$-inch dice as large. Medium slices and dice measure about $3/8$ inch,

and small dice can be anything from $1/4$ inch to the minuscule cubes that are used to garnish consommé. I would like to say that some of this handwork can be done by a food processor, but no. However, you will have excellent results using a mandoline (see How to Use a Mandoline, page 22) for thinly slicing vegetables and cutting julienne strips. For many of these tasks, a few knife skills make all the difference (page 20).

When you cut slices and cubes evenly as directed, you will have gone a long way toward making the recipe work. The vegetables in the Minestrina you see here, for instance, are carefully cut to different shapes and sizes so they cook evenly and look their best in your bowl at table. If the root vegetables for a gratin are sliced too thin, they fall apart, but if too thick the gratin will be clunky and dull. Beware of introducing beets into the vegetable equation—their color makes them tempting, but they bleed distressingly when mixed with other ingredients!

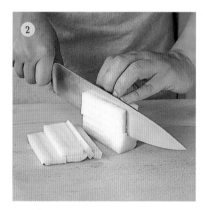

1 To slice a root vegetable: Peel the vegetable (here a turnip) if indicated in the recipe. Square off the sides and set the vegetable firmly on the chopping board. Slice it vertically into thick or thin slices.

2 To dice a root vegetable: Slice the vegetable, cutting thickly for large dice, thinly for small ones. Stack the slices and cut them into even sticks.

3 Gather the sticks into a pile and slice them crosswise into even dice of the size you want.

Petite Potato Cake

Need I say that potatoes fried in butter—or duck fat, even better—go with almost any main dish? When I'm making just a single potato cake to serve 2, I usually slice the potatoes by hand, but for more people I get out the mandoline. I like to use floury baking potatoes that absorb butter and brown nicely—by all means arrange the potatoes in an attractive pattern if you have time, or simply spread them flat in the pan as I do. Don't be tempted to rinse the slices as you'll wash away starch that holds the cake together.

Serves 2

Spread a 6- to 7-inch nonstick frying pan (an omelet pan is perfect) generously with 2 table-spoons butter or duck fat. Peel and cut 1 pound of baking potatoes in 1/8-inch slices. Arrange half of them in a layer, or simply spread them flat and sprinkle with salt and pepper. Add the remaining potatoes, spread them flat, and press a generously buttered piece of aluminum foil on top. Press the potatoes down with a heatproof plate and a weight, and cook over quite low heat until the potatoes are tender and the edges are brown, 25 to 30 minutes. You will smell browned butter. Remove the plate and weight and loosen the cake with a spatula. Slide it onto a plate and flip it back into the pan. Brown the other side of the cake over medium heat, 10 to 12 minutes, and serve.

Blushing Red Radish Relish

Thinly sliced radishes turn a delicate pink when marinated in salt and lemon juice—a striking accompaniment to a lunch of cold chicken and green salad.

Serves 4 to 6 as a condiment

Trim 1 pound red radishes. Slice them as thinly as possible, using a mandoline if you like. (Much depends on the size of the radishes, and small ones are easier to slice by hand.) Put them in a bowl with 1/2 teaspoon salt and the juice of 1 lemon. Mix well and chill at least an hour. Stir to combine, taste for seasoning, and serve. The longer you keep them, the pinker they will be.

Italian Beet Salad

The Italian flavoring of fresh mint for beets perfectly offsets the fruity juice of the vegetable.

Serves 4 to 6

> 1 pound small or medium beets
> 3 tablespoons chopped fresh mint
> 1 sweet red onion, cut in thin rings
>
> FOR THE VINAIGRETTE
> 2 tablespoons red wine vinegar
> 1/2 teaspoon Dijon mustard, more to taste
> salt and pepper to taste
> 6 tablespoons olive oil

Trim the leaves of the beets, leaving the root and some stem so the beets do not bleed. Wash but do not peel them. Bring a large pot of salted water to a boil and boil the beets until they are tender to the touch and the skins rub off easily, 30 to 60 minutes, depending on size. Drain and let cool.

Make the vinaigrette: Whisk the vinegar with the mustard, salt, and pepper. Gradually add the oil, whisking vigorously so the dressing emulsifies and thickens slightly. Taste and adjust the seasoning, including mustard. Rub peel from beets with your fingers. Square off sides and cut the beets in 1/2-inch dice. Put them in a bowl and toss with the vinaigrette and mint. Pile in a shallow serving bowl and top with the red onion slices. Adjust seasoning again before serving.

GETTING AHEAD: The salad improves if kept 2 to 3 hours before serving.

Minestrina with an Accent

A crisp croûte spread with basil pesto picks up this minestrina, a young cousin of minestrone. Pass more pesto to stir into the soup and you have a version of pistou, from Provence. Serve the soup hot in the winter or at room temperature in the summer.

Serves 6

2 tablespoons olive oil

3 small carrots, sliced on the diagonal

2 medium onions, sliced

2 celery stalks, sliced

6 cups water, more if needed

1 bay leaf

salt and pepper to taste

1/2 cauliflower, divided into florets

2 small potatoes, cut in 3/8-inch dice

1/4 pound green beans, trimmed and cut
  in 1-inch lengths

2 tomatoes, peeled, seeded, and chopped

1 garlic clove, crushed

1 tablespoon chopped fresh parsley

3/4 cup grated Parmesan cheese

FOR THE PESTO CROUTES

1/2 baguette or other crusty bread

1 recipe Basil Pesto (page 94)

In a large soup pot, heat the oil. Add the carrots, onion, and celery and sauté until they just begin to soften and brown, stirring occasionally, 5 to 7 minutes. Stir in the water, bay leaf, salt, and pepper. Cover and simmer, 15 to 20 minutes.

Add the cauliflower and simmer 10 minutes longer. Finally, add the potatoes, green beans, tomatoes, garlic, and parsley and simmer 5 to 10 minutes longer, until all the vegetables in the soup are tender.

Meanwhile, cut the baguette in 6 diagonal slices about 1/2-inch thick and toast them. Spread the croûtes generously with pesto. Taste the soup for seasoning and ladle it into 6 warm soup bowls. Sprinkle with Parmesan cheese and plenty of freshly ground pepper, and top with a pesto croûte. Pass the remaining Parmesan and pesto separately.

GETTING AHEAD: Fresh minestrina made at home has instant, sprightly appeal. When you reheat the soup, the flavor is just as attractive but different—deeper and more soothing.

Minestrina with an Accent

how to cut vegetable julienne

Julienne are fine strips of vegetables cut when raw to the size of a matchstick, sometimes a bit longer. A surprising number of vegetables qualify, but don't get carried away and mix too many together. Three or at most four julienned vegetables are sufficient, otherwise flavors will conflict. Roots come to mind first as they are so easy to trim to size, slice thinly, then stack and cut into matchsticks. As in diced vegetable mixtures, carrots are a favorite because so many other roots, including turnips, parsnips, celery root, and jicama are white. An appealing touch of green can be added with leek or zucchini, with strips cut to include the dark skin. A small quantity of vegetable julienne is easy to cut by hand, but for large quantities a mandoline is quicker (see How to Use a Mandoline, page 22).

1 Peel the vegetable (here a carrot) and cut a thin strip from one side so it sits flat on the chopping board. Cut the vegetable crosswise into 2-inch-long cylinders. Then cut each cylinder lengthwise into thin vertical slices.

2 Stack the slices and cut them lengthwise again into thin strips.

Garden Julienne

For a classic julienne you need the color of carrot and the outer peel of zucchini, as well as your choice of white turnip, celery root, or parsnip. They are cooked gently together in their own juices ("sweated" is the vivid term) with a very little butter, or oil, salt, and pepper. Julienne is the perfect garnish for white fish, chicken breasts, veal, and pork chops.

Serves 4

Peel 3 medium carrots and cut them in julienne strips. Trim 3 medium zucchini and cut them in julienne strips, including the peel and discarding the soft inner seeds. Peel 2 medium turnips, 1 medium celery root, or 3 medium parsnips. Quarter the turnips or celery root if using, then cut them or the parsnips in julienne. Spread 1 tablespoon butter in a saucepan and add the julienne with salt and pepper. Press a piece of aluminum foil on top, add the pan lid, and cook over low heat until the vegetables soften in their own juices and are tender, 15 to 20 minutes. Stir them once or twice, and take care they do not brown. Taste and adjust seasoning before serving.

Glorious Gratins

In the kitchen, the French noun *gratin* means a dish with a savory brown topping, often of cheese or breadcrumbs, but the word has a wider meaning: *le gratin* is the aristocracy, the upper crust! More prosaically it is also the name of a shallow dish specifically shaped to deliver as much golden crust as possible. Macaroni and cheese is in effect a gratin; top of the charts perhaps is Gratin Dauphinois, potatoes baked with cream and Gruyère cheese. Typical gratins are made of sliced or coarsely diced vegetables such as zucchini, squash, turnip, broccoli, or cauliflower coated with white or cheese sauce. As a change from white sauce, tomato sauce or a nut-based pesto are also delicious on vegetables, especially when they are sprinkled with a topping of grated cheese, breadcrumbs, or chopped nuts or herbs. As they bake in the oven they brown to a savory, scrumptious topping. Almost all gratins can be prepared ahead and baked later, another reason for their popularity. They are versatile, too, making a warming appetizer, a light main course, or an accompaniment to roast and grilled meats and poultry. Here are a few of my favorites.

Gratin of Parsnip and Potato

If you've ever made scalloped potatoes, you'll have noticed that the milk used to cook them often curdles. This gratin evades the problem by first cooking the vegetables in milk, then finishing them luxuriously in cream!

Serves 6

> **2 to 3 medium baking potatoes**
> **(about ¾ pound)**
> **¾ pound parsnips**
> **3 cups milk, more if needed**
> **pinch of grated nutmeg, more to taste**
> **salt and pepper to taste**
> **1¼ cups heavy cream, more if needed**
> **1 garlic clove, finely chopped**
> **½ cup grated Gruyère cheese**
>
> **9 x 13-inch gratin or shallow baking dish**

Peel the potatoes and cut them in ¹/₈-inch slices, preferably using a mandoline. Peel the parsnips, quarter them if large and slice them. Put each vegetable in a separate saucepan with half the milk, nutmeg, pepper, and a little salt. Stir to mix and bring them to a boil. If necessary, add more milk to cover. Simmer both vegetables, stirring occasionally, until they are just tender, 10 to 15 minutes.

Drain both vegetables, reserving the milk for another use such as soup. Wipe out one of the saucepans and return both vegetables to the pan with the cream and garlic. Heat gently and simmer, stirring occasionally, until the vegetables are very tender, 10 to 15 minutes. The slices break up easily, so stir carefully. The mixture should be quite creamy and liquid, not stiff, so if necessary stir in more cream. Taste and adjust the seasoning, including nutmeg. Pour the vegetables with the cream into the baking dish, spreading them evenly, and sprinkle the top with the grated cheese.

To finish: Preheat the oven to 375°F. Bake the gratin until the top is golden brown and the edges are bubbling, 15 to 20 minutes.

GETTING AHEAD: A perfect dish for a party, parsnip and potato gratin can be prepared up to 2 days ahead and refrigerated, ready to bake and brown just before serving. Allow up to 30 minutes to give the vegetables time to reheat as well as brown.

Gratin Dauphinois

The grand classic at its very best—a wily old chef gave me this recipe, which was so popular that he made it by the bucketful. I'm not surprised!

In the recipe for Gratin of Parsnip and Potato, simply replace the parsnips with an equal weight of potato.

Gratin of Peppery Greens

Any robust greens such as kale, Swiss chard, or spinach are good in this recipe.

Serves 6 to 8

> 2 pounds greens
> 1 cup grated Gruyère cheese
>
> FOR THE WHITE SAUCE
> 3 cups milk
> 6 tablespoons butter, more for the baking dish
> 6 tablespoons flour
> salt and pepper to taste
> freshly grated nutmeg

Bring a large pot of salted water to a boil. Discard stems from leaves of greens and coarsely shred the leaves. Boil them until nearly tender, 2 to 5 minutes, depending on type. Drain, refresh the greens in cold water, and drain thoroughly.

Preheat the oven to 375°F. Make the white sauce: Scald the milk. Melt the butter in a heavy-based pan and whisk in the flour. Cook 1 to 2 minutes until foaming but not browned. Add the hot milk, whisking, and bring to a boil, stirring constantly. Simmer 2 to 3 minutes, taste and adjust seasoning with salt, pepper, and nutmeg. Take from the heat. Butter a large, shallow, ovenproof dish and spread the greens in it. Spoon the white sauce on top and sprinkle with the grated cheese. Bake for 15 to 20 minutes, until very hot and browned.

Jessica's Garden Gratin

A La Varenne trainee made this delicious gratin one evening when we needed a first course and had nothing but a tomato or two from the garden and rather a lot of zucchini. It immediately became a favorite recipe—we have it at least once a week during the summer.

Serves 4

> 2 tomatoes (about $1/2$ pound)
> 1 tablespoon olive oil, more for drizzling
> 3 tablespoons chopped fresh herbs,
>   such as basil, oregano, or parsley
> salt and pepper to taste
> 2 medium zucchini (about $3/4$ pound)
> 2 tablespoons butter
> 4 ounces feta or dry goat cheese, crumbled
>
> 4 small (6-inch) gratin dishes

Preheat the oven to 350°F. Seed and finely chop the tomatoes but do not peel them. Toss them with the olive oil, 2 tablespoons of the chopped herbs, salt, and pepper. Trim the zucchini and slice it very thinly, preferably on the mandoline.

Cut the butter in 4 pieces and put 1 piece in the bottom of each gratin dish. Layer half the zucchini in each dish followed by half the tomatoes and the remaining zucchini. Pile the remaining tomatoes on top and sprinkle with the feta cheese and remaining herbs. Drizzle a little olive oil on each one. Bake for 25 to 30 minutes, until the cheese is browned, the vegetables are tender, and the liquid has evaporated. Serve warm or at room temperature.

HOW TO BOIL AND MASH POTATOES AND ROOTS

I think of root vegetables as the work horses of the kitchen, reliable, constantly available, and built by nature to last. I'm never quite at ease unless I have a little stock of carrots, turnips, and potatoes in the kitchen rack. They may get a bit dry and wrinkled, but I can always count on them. Choose root vegetables that are firm with bushy green tops and no moldy patches; avoid potatoes that have developed sprouts. Roots keep a couple of weeks or more in a cool place, best in the dark or loosely wrapped. Potatoes hate cold and will develop black patches if you store them in the refrigerator. Every root variety has its quirks. Potatoes, for example, divide into two groups, waxy or floury. Waxy varieties stay firm when cooked and are good for boiling, steaming, and potato salad; floury varieties are right for baking, mashing, sautéing, and French fries.

Steaming root vegetables on a rack above boiling water leaves them moist and tender, and is an alternative to boiling. The vegetable may be peeled or left with its skin—cooking with the skin adds flavor but may increase pesticide exposure. So that they cook at the same speed, roots should be even-sized and you may need to cut them in pieces. The cooking time for roots varies from vegetable to vegetable. As a rough guide, small potatoes, or larger ones cut in 2-inch chunks, take 15 to 20 minutes. Turnips, rutabaga, Jerusalem artichokes (sunchokes), and pieces of celery root (celeriac) of the same size cook a bit quicker. Carrots are robust, they take double the cooking time of most other roots and retain their shape long after they are tender, one reason for their value in slowly cooked stews.

Plain boiled roots, particularly potatoes, are dreary. Just a simple topping of butter, cracked pepper, and chopped parsley can make a world of difference. Better still, you can mash roots to a coarse or smooth purée along with a variety of flavorings. The plain mashed potatoes I was raised with—crushed with a masher and smoothed with milk and butter—have multiplied into mashed potatoes with roast garlic, with olives and olive oil, with basil pesto, even with smoked cheese and chives or rosemary and grated orange zest. Boiling a root vegetable can also be a preliminary to slicing and frying it like home fries, or dressing it with vinaigrette while still warm to serve as a salad. Consider celery root drizzled with balsamic and walnut oil, sweet potatoes with orange and mint, or parsnips with grapefruit juice and brown sugar.

1 For boiling, roots (here potatoes) may be peeled or left with their skins. Cut them in 2 to 3 even pieces, put them in cold salted water, and bring them to a boil, covering the pan with a lid. Simmer them gently—rapid boiling can break up the surface. Poke the roots with the point of a knife to test if they are tender through to the center. Underdone roots have an unpleasantly chewy center and form lumps if you try to mash them; if overdone they will be soggy with water. Drain roots at once and let them dry—I like to put them back in the pan and dry them further over low heat for a few minutes. Peel them or use them with the peel, depending on the recipe.

special cases

* Many root vegetables, including potatoes, celery root, turnips, and Jerusalem artichokes need to be covered with cold water once they are peeled, otherwise they will discolor. Most keep well in water for up to 24 hours.

* Boiling does not loosen the skin of carrots, sweet potatoes, celery root, parsnips, and turnips, so for mashing and puréeing they should be peeled before boiling.

* Beets bleed when peeled, so leave the root and a bit of stem when trimming them, and always cook them in their skins.

* For a truly smooth, fluffy purée, fibrous root vegetables such as celery root must be worked through a sieve.

Sweet Potatoes with Orange and Mint

An unusual accompaniment to lamb or pork chops or Virginia's Southern Fried Chicken (page 149). Any type of sweet potato is good.

Serves 4

Peel 2 to 3 sweet potatoes (about 1¹/₂ pounds), cut them in 1-inch dice, and put them in a large pan of cold salted water. Cover, bring them to a boil, and simmer until just tender, 8 to 12 minutes. Meanwhile, cream 4 tablespoons butter with 2 tablespoons chopped fresh mint, the grated rind of 1 orange and 1 tablespoon orange juice, ¹/₂ teaspoon each of ground coriander and white pepper, and a little salt. When the potatoes are done, drain them, pile them in a serving dish, and dot with the butter. Toss gently until the butter coats the potatoes. Taste and adjust seasoning.

Smashed Celery Root Purée

If left on their own, root vegetables such as celery root make disappointingly damp purées as they contain little starch. Therefore potato is usually added for the best of both worlds. You can substitute turnips, parsnips, or rutabagas. Rutabagas may cook more quickly, while parsnips may take more time.

Serves 4

> **1 medium celery root (about 2 pounds)**
> **2 medium potatoes (about 1¹/₂ pounds)**
> **¹/₂ lemon**
> **³/₄ cup milk, more if needed**
> **4 tablespoons butter**
> **salt and white pepper to taste**

Peel and cut the celery root and potatoes in large chunks. Put them in two separate pans of cold salted water and add half a squeezed lemon to the celery root so it does not discolor. Cover, bring to a boil, and simmer the vegetables until tender, 20 to 25 minutes for the celery root, 15 to 20 minutes for the potatoes.

Drain the vegetables, discarding the lemon, and put them together in one of the pans. Dry them over the heat, 1 to 2 minutes. In another pan, bring the milk just to a boil. Crush the vegetables by mashing them in the pan with a potato masher. Add the butter, milk, salt, and pepper and beat the purée over medium heat with a wooden spoon until light and fluffy, 2 to 3 minutes. Taste and adjust seasoning. The purée should just fall easily from the spoon, so add a little more milk if it is stiff.

GETTING AHEAD: Purées of root vegetables keep well up to 30 minutes if you leave them in the pan: Smooth the top of the purée, pour a little hot milk over it to prevent it from drying out, and keep it covered in a warm place or in a water bath. Before serving, beat the purée until smooth to mix in the milk.

how to mash potatoes

Potatoes contain more starch than other root vegetables and must be handled gently. If worked too vigorously, for example in a food processor, they become gluey, almost stringy in consistency. I know that some cooks swear by mashing potatoes in the electric mixer using the paddle, but I've never found it as satisfactory as a hand masher. For mashing, be sure the potatoes are thoroughly cooked and also dried of excess water. Then you can go ahead and mash potatoes to one of three different consistencies: crushed, mashed, or puréed. Crushed potatoes should have chunky bits and can be left unpeeled. They are quick to make, but can be heavy if not served at once. Traditional mashed potatoes, which are peeled after boiling, have a finer, smoother texture but still hold the mark of a spoon, while puréed potatoes, the fluffiest and most delicate, are worked through a ricer. All these preparations are best done with floury baking potatoes.

2 Continue crushing vigorously with the masher until smooth, holding the masher upright and working around the pan so all the pieces of potato are squashed.

3 Beat over low heat with a wooden spoon until light and fluffy, adding more hot milk and butter to make a smooth mash that holds a shape or falls easily from the spoon, whichever consistency you prefer.

Plain Crushed (or Smashed) Potatoes

Easy to do at the last minute for up to 4 people. Larger quantities require a strong arm.

Serves 4

Cut about 2 pounds potatoes into 3 to 4 chunks and put them in a large pan of cold water. Cover, bring to a boil, and simmer until very tender, 15 to 20 minutes. Drain them and peel if you wish. Return them to the pan and quickly crush them with a potato masher or large table fork, leaving chunks of potato for texture. Gently stir in 3 to 4 tablespoons butter or olive oil and season the potatoes to taste. Serve at once.

1 For mashed potatoes: Boil, drain, and dry the potatoes in a large pan. Bring milk or cream to a boil in a small pan. Peel the potatoes if not already done. Return them to the large pan and start crushing with a potato masher. Add butter and hot milk or cream.

Slow-Roasted Garlic and Parsley Mashed Potatoes

Whole heads of garlic, slow-roasted in the oven, are a wonderful flavoring for potatoes. Be sure to make plenty, as roast garlic keeps well and any leftover oil is invaluable for frying.

Serves 4

To roast the garlic: Preheat the oven to 375°F. Trim 2 to 3 heads of garlic so the tops of the cloves are exposed. Pack them in a small heavy pan and pour over enough oil to half cover them. Cover tightly and roast the garlic in the oven until very tender, 1 to 1½ hours. Drain and reserve the oil. Let the heads of garlic cool, 5 to 10 minutes, then break the cloves apart and squeeze out the pulp. Make Plain Crushed Potatoes using the garlic-flavored oil, and stir garlic pulp to your taste into the potatoes with 2 tablespoons chopped fresh parsley. Taste and adjust seasoning.

Plain Mashed Potatoes

These may have the odd lump or two but the taste is great. After mashing, add the butter or olive oil and cream or milk and beat until smooth. Don't beat for more than a minute or two or the potatoes will be heavy.

Serves 4

Follow the recipe for Plain Crushed Potatoes. When the potatoes are cool enough to handle, peel them. Crush them in the pan as described, then continue mashing them until smooth. Using a wooden spoon, work in 3 to 4 tablespoons butter or olive oil and 1 cup hot cream or milk, and beat over low heat until the potatoes are fluffy and hold a firm shape; if too stiff, add more cream or milk. Taste and adjust seasoning.

Crushed Potatoes with Black Olives and Olive Oil

A pungent mix, good with steak, lamb chops, and roast lamb.

Serves 4

In the recipe for Plain Crushed Potatoes, substitute ½ cup fruity olive oil for the butter, and add 1 cup oil-cured black olives, pitted and shredded.

Classic Puréed Potatoes

For a special occasion, the smooth, fluffy consistency of classic puréed potatoes is worth the extra effort of sieving rather than mashing them. The variety of potato you choose makes a big difference here—favorites are the French *ratte*, russet, or Yukon Gold.

Serves 3 to 4

> **3 to 4 medium potatoes (1½ pounds total)**
> **1 cup milk, more if needed**
> **3 tablespoons butter**
> **salt and white pepper to taste**
> **pinch of grated nutmeg, more to taste**

Cut the potatoes in 2 to 3 even pieces and cover with cold salted water. Add the lid, bring to a boil, and simmer until tender when pierced with a knife or skewer, 15 to 20 minutes. The potatoes should be quite soft. Scald the milk.

Drain the potatoes and peel them when cool enough to handle. Work them through a ricer or a bowl strainer back into the pan. Add the butter, milk, salt, pepper, and nutmeg, and beat the potatoes with a wooden spoon over low heat until they are light and fluffy—the heat expands the grains of starch in the potatoes. Taste and adjust seasoning, including nutmeg. Add more milk if necessary to make a soft purée that just falls from the spoon.

GETTING AHEAD: To keep the potatoes warm for up to 30 minutes, leave them in the pan, smooth the top, and pour a little hot milk over them to prevent them from drying out. Cover and keep in a warm place or in a water bath. Beat the potatoes until smooth before serving.

HOW TO BOIL GREEN VEGETABLES

Cooks make a big distinction between roots and greens, and rightly so. Roots are babied along, simmering gently in a covered pan (think of them growing underground and loving the dark), but greens get shock treatment. They are plunged into large amounts of rapidly boiling water and cooked in the light of day, without the lid. The quicker a green vegetable is cooked, the more nutrients and flavor are retained, and the brighter its color. Tender greens such as spinach and herbs are boiled only until the leaves barely wilt, 1 to 2 minutes or even less. Robust greens—cabbage, kale, or mustard greens are typical—take longer to cook. The same principle—lots of salted water and high heat—suits other green vegetables such as asparagus, broccoli, and green beans. Once cooked, all green vegetables must be "refreshed" by rinsing or plunging them in cold water. Refreshing sets the color and I'm always gratified by the brilliant flush of green that is captured.

A green vegetable that is perfectly cooked is tender but not soft, retaining a touch of crispness. The margin of error between overdone, just right, and underdone is narrow. An overcooked green vegetable is ruined, losing all its character, but I insist that undercooking is just as bad. By all means serve greens such as spinach raw, but a boiled green vegetable should be fully cooked with no lingering grassy tinge. Green beans and asparagus are commonly undercooked, particularly in fancy restaurants that should know better.

Storage time varies greatly—for instance tender leafy salad wilts within a day or two, while green cabbage stays good for a week or more. You can't get away with poor produce and this is especially true of green vegetables. Good greens are easy to spot, with their bushy leaves and firm stems; color should be vivid with no trace of yellow. Keeping them that way can be tricky. Greens like to be moist but not wet, so pierce a hole or two in plastic bags and stash them in the salad drawer of the refrigerator.

Fresh, crisp garden produce rewards the simplest of finishes such as tossing greens in melted butter or olive oil, or bathing them in a walnut and lemon dressing—lemon complements the peppery bite of many greens, as does garlic, nutmeg, and herbs such as parsley. Asian cooks are particularly adept with greens, steaming them and then adding ginger and soy, or perhaps a seasoning of scallion and sesame.

1 Lower the vegetable (here broccoli) into a large pan of boiling salted water, pushing it under the surface so it is immersed. Bring the water back to a boil and cook at a fast simmer.

2 To test cooking, lift out a piece of the vegetable and poke it with a knife. It should resist, but not fight back. The best test is to taste a piece—it should be tender but still firm. At once drain the vegetable, refresh it (rinse it with cold water), and drain it thoroughly.

Green Beans with Walnuts and Walnut Vinaigrette

This recipe is a popular appetizer salad, particularly when made with baby haricots verts. Serve it warm or at room temperature. The beans and dressing can be prepared ahead but should be mixed not more than 15 minutes before serving so the beans do not discolor.

Serves 4

Bring a large pan of salted water to a boil, add 1 1/2 pounds trimmed green beans, and boil until they are tender but still firm, 5 to 10 minutes depending on size and age. Drain them, refresh in cold water, and drain them thoroughly.

For the vinaigrette: Whisk 2 tablespoons red wine vinegar with 1/2 teaspoon Dijon mustard, salt, and pepper. Gradually add 6 tablespoons walnut oil, whisking vigorously so the dressing emulsifies and thickens slightly. Taste it for seasoning. Shortly before serving, mix beans with dressing and 1/2 cup coarsely chopped walnuts.

Great Sautéed Spinach

In northern Burgundy where we live for much of the year, spinach is the first of the long-awaited spring greens. Spinach can be sautéed half a dozen ways, and our family reckons this is the best.

Serves 4 to 6

Wash 2 pounds spinach, discarding stems. Bring a large pan of salted water to a boil, add the spinach, bring back to a boil and blanch it until just wilted, about 1 minute. Drain it and leave until cool enough to handle, and then squeeze out excess moisture with your fists. Chop the spinach on a board. Melt 2 tablespoons butter in a large frying pan and fry a finely chopped onion until tender, 5 to 7 minutes. Stir in the spinach with salt, pepper, and 1 teaspoon grated nutmeg, and cook until any moisture has evaporated, 2 to 3 minutes. Stir in 1 cup crème fraîche or heavy cream and heat until very hot and all the cream is absorbed, 2 to 3 minutes. Taste and adjust seasoning, including nutmeg.

Broccoli and Cauliflower Bouquet

Cauliflower, like broccoli, counts as a green vegetable. In this attractive recipe, the two vegetables are molded in a bowl and turned out to resemble a green and white cauliflower with a topping of hard-boiled egg and fried breadcrumbs for color and crunch. To simplify, use just one vegetable.

Serves 4 to 6

> **1/2 medium head of cauliflower (about 1 pound)**
> **medium bunch of broccoli (about 1 1/2 pounds)**
> **salt and pepper to taste**
>
> **FOR THE TOPPING**
> **3 slices white bread**
> **3 tablespoons butter, more for the bowl**
> **1 hard-boiled egg, chopped**
>
> **1-quart heatproof bowl**

Trim florets from the cauliflower and broccoli, discarding stems. Bring 2 large pans of salted water to a boil, add the vegetables, and boil until tender but still firm, 5 to 7 minutes for broccoli, 1 to 2 minutes more for cauliflower. Drain them, refresh in cold water, and drain thoroughly. Butter the bowl and pack the vegetable florets in it, arranging stems inward and alternating the colors. Fill the center of the bowl with leftover bits—it should be full. Press down on the vegetables lightly and leave in a warm place at least 5 minutes. Discard crusts from bread and cut it in chunks. Purée it to crumbs in a food processor.

To finish: Turn out the mold onto a platter. Melt the butter in a frying pan and sauté the crumbs, stirring, until golden brown. At once pour them with the butter over the mold. Top with the chopped egg and serve.

GETTING AHEAD: The vegetables can be cooked and molded up to 2 hours ahead. To reheat them, warm them, covered, in a low oven, 10 to 15 minutes. Unmold them and add the topping just before serving.

how to steam green vegetables

In terms of taste, there's very little differ-ence between boiling and steaming green vegetables so you can freely substitute one for the other. Some cooks prefer to steam them because they hold their shape well. In steam, the vegetables take longer to heat than when boiling, but then cook more rapidly in the higher temperature; in the end boiling and steaming take about the same time. Steamed vegetables are not usually refreshed with cold water after cooking. You'll find steamer attachments, some adjustable, for regular saucepans. Asian cooks often use bamboo steamers stacked one on another over a wok.

1

Set the vegetables (here snow peas) in a steamer over a pan of boiling water. Cover and

Asian Steamed Bok Choy or Chard

Leafy greens with thick stems such as bok choy and chard are often divided into leaves and stems so both can be cooked just right. I find these greens, with their Asian dressing, go well with fish.

Serves 4 to 6

Separate stems from the green leaves of 2 pounds bok choy or chard. Rinse them, drain, and cut the stems in ¹/₂-inch slices. Put about 2 inches water in the base of a steamer and bring to a boil. Put the sliced vegetable stems in the top of the steamer, set it over the boiling water, cover, and steam until nearly tender, 6 to 8 minutes. Lay vegetable leaves on the stems and continue steam-ing until wilted but still firm, 3 to 5 minutes more. In a small bowl, mix 3 tablespoons each of soy sauce and rice wine vinegar with a 1-inch piece of ginger, peeled and chopped. Taste and adjust seasoning. Transfer the vegetables to a deep platter, spoon over the dressing, and serve.

how to blanch green vegetables

Brief boiling of green vegetables is called blanching. It removes traces of bitterness, sets vivid color, and softens texture so that greens are easy to chop and either cook further or possibly mix into another preparation such as mayonnaise, stuffing, or a soufflé. Some greens may be blanched before braising or sautéing them. To blanch tender greens such as spinach or bok choy it is sufficient to bring them just to a boil. Tougher ones take 2 to 3 min-utes. After blanching, rinse the vegetable at once in cold water to stop the cooking.

Red Cabbage Salad with Roquefort

A little red cabbage stretches a long way, so I'm always happy to find an unusual way to use it. This cheerful salad is a great winter standby.

Serves 4

½ head of red cabbage (about 1 pound)
½ cup red wine vinegar
½ cup crumbled Roquefort cheese
1 large tart green apple

FOR THE DRESSING
3 tablespoons red wine vinegar
1 tablespoon Dijon mustard
salt and freshly ground black pepper to taste
¾ cup walnut oil

Bring a large pan of salted water to a boil. Discard any wilted leaves from the cabbage and shred it, discarding the core and thick stems. Put the cabbage into a large bowl. Bring the vinegar to a boil, standing back as the vapor will sting your eyes. (Vinegar prevents the cabbage from turning gray.) Pour it over the cabbage and mix well. Add the cabbage to the boiling water, return to a boil, and cook 1 to 2 minutes to soften it slightly. Drain, refresh with cold water, and drain thoroughly.

Make the dressing: Whisk the vinegar with mustard, salt, and pepper until mixed. Gradually add the walnut oil in a slow steady stream, whisking constantly so the dressing emulsifies. Taste and adjust seasoning.

Wipe the apple, quarter, and core it. Cut it in dice and stir into the dressing. Pat the cabbage dry with paper towels. Mix it into the apples and dressing, taste, and adjust seasoning. Pile the salad on individual plates and crumble the Roquefort cheese on top.

GETTING AHEAD: Make the salad and toss it with dressing up to 6 hours ahead—you'll find the flavor will mellow. Plate it and sprinkle with the Roquefort at serving time.

how to refresh boiled or blanched green vegetables

When green vegetables have been boiled or blanched, they should be "refreshed" that is to say drained and rinsed under cold water so cooking stops at once. This sets their color, texture, and flavor. To chill a big batch of vegetables evenly, it's best to plunge them into cold water—you should have a big bowl with ice cubes standing at the ready.

1 Drain the vegetable thoroughly (here broccoli). Tip it into a sinkful or bowl of ice water to cool it and set the color. After 1 to 2 minutes, when the vegetables are cold, drain them again so they do not get waterlogged. After refreshing, the vegetables may be reheated or cooked further, for example in a gratin.

HOW TO SAUTE VEGETABLES

If I'm asked how to cook a vegetable, I generally say sauté. In my opinion, almost all vegetables do well when sautéed over brisk heat in a little fat. There are really no rules: if you like your cabbage tossed with bacon fat and crispy diced bacon, go ahead. Some people prefer their spinach sautéed in olive oil, garlic, and onion, others like myself go for butter and freshly grated nutmeg. Butter is rich and refined, appropriate for peas, green beans, asparagus, and carrots, and by far the best choice if you want a crusty brown surface to the vegetable. Olive oil brings a touch of Mediterranean sun to tomatoes, bell peppers, and eggplant, while lighter peanut and other vegetable oils blend more discreetly with the flavors of zucchini, leeks, or bok choy. Lard belongs to hearty regional dishes featuring cabbage, onion, and kidney beans.

A seasoning of salt, pepper, onion, garlic, herbs, and aromatic spices such as coriander add Western atmosphere. Turning East, you find ginger, soy sauce, star anise, sesame, and the rest of the palette of Asian spices. When cooked, a sautéed vegetable should be golden and slightly crisp on the outside, yet moist within. Notice I say "within." Unless moist vegetables such as squash are fried over quite high heat, they will soften and stew in their own juices. I like to cook them fast, a few at a time, so they dry and brown quickly.

When you are sautéing a mixture of vegetables, don't throw them in all together. In ratatouille, for example, the onions are sautéed first, followed by the eggplant, and finally the squash, bell peppers, and tomatoes. Vegetables that take longer to cook, such as potatoes and root vegetables should go in first. Quite often roots are partially cooked (parboiled) before sautéing, and greens such as spinach and cabbage may be blanched (see How to Blanch Green Vegetables, page 244) to remove bitterness. Never forget that sautéing is a handy way to reheat leftover boiled or steamed vegetables. Cooked potatoes that have been cut up and fried as hash browns are often better than the originals. As a family, we all love green beans and when Emma was small she would have them reheated in butter for supper. "Emma's burnt beans," as she called them, have become a home tradition.

1 Sautéing is a different technique from deep-frying, where the food is immersed in a layer of hot fat. For sautéing you need just a few tablespoons of fat and a large frying pan, big enough for all the pieces to lie flat on the surface. To test whether the fat is hot enough, add a piece of a vegetable to the pan. If it sizzles the fat is ready. Add the remaining vegetables and cook briskly, stirring often, so they brown within 2 to 3 minutes. (Here are the ingredients for ratatouille). If the vegetables are not tender after browning, turn down the heat, cover the pan, and continue cooking.

Scrumptious Sautéed Potatoes (Home Fries)

Almost any potatoes, raw or cooked, with or without their skins, will be delicious sautéed in a fat with plenty of flavor—I think of butter, olive oil, bacon fat, or goose fat. The very best sautéed potatoes, however, are made from peeled potatoes that are already steamed or boiled—in other words, leftovers. They will take at least 20 minutes to brown and always remember that the longer you cook them, the browner and crisper they will be.

Serves 4

Cut 2 pounds potatoes, with or without peel, in $^1/_2$-inch chunks. The potatoes may be raw or cooked. Heat 5 tablespoons butter or other fat in a large frying pan. Spread the potatoes in the pan and sauté over medium heat until they start to brown, about 5 minutes. Stir and continue cooking, stirring often so the potatoes brown on all sides, though unevenly. This will take 10 to 15 minutes, or longer for raw potatoes. When you think they are brown enough, keep cooking at least 5 minutes longer. Just before serving, sprinkle with salt and 1 tablespoon chopped fresh parsley.

Home Fries with Onions

The same good things often exist in many countries, and here's an example: home fries with onions, one better than plain fried potatoes. Serve them with meats, particularly steak, pork chops, ham, and liver.

Serves 4

Follow the recipe for Scrumptious Sautéed Potatoes. In a separate frying pan (or the pan that you used to fry the potatoes), heat 3 tablespoons butter or other fat and add 3 medium onions, sliced. Sprinkle the onion slices with salt and pepper and sauté them over low to medium heat, stirring from time to time, until they are very brown, 15 to 20 minutes. When the potatoes are cooked, stir in the onions and taste for seasoning.

Sautéed Radicchio with Pancetta

Radicchio, and any other member of the endive family, is good sautéed. Simply slice the heads or divide them in leaves, depending on the type. This recipe is just right with roast chicken or veal.

Serves 4

Coarsely shred 3 small heads of radicchio (about 1 pound), discarding thick stems and any wilted leaves. Dice 4 ounces sliced pancetta and, in a large frying pan, fry it in 2 tablespoons olive oil until lightly browned. Stir in the radicchio with 1 tablespoon capers, rinsed and drained, pepper, and a little salt. Cover the pan, turn down the heat, and cook gently, 2 to 3 minutes, until the radicchio is wilted, stirring occasionally. Remove the cover, increase the heat, and stir-fry until the radicchio begins to brown, 1 to 2 minutes. Taste and adjust seasoning.

Sautéed Fennel with Bacon and Raisins

The sweet and salty mix of raisins, bacon, and Parmesan cheese is ideal with fennel (celery, too, so there's another idea). Serve it as an appetizer or side dish with roast pork, chicken, and duck.

Serves 4

Thinly slice 2 fennel bulbs (about 1 pound), cutting through the stem and root so the slices hold together. In a large frying pan, fry 4 slices diced bacon until brown. Remove bacon with a slotted spoon, add $^1/_2$ cup slivered almonds, and fry, stirring until brown, 2 to 3 minutes. Add almonds to the bacon. Stir the fennel into the frying pan with $^1/_4$ cup raisins and pepper (the bacon fat is salty so you won't need salt). Sauté until the fennel starts to brown, 2 to 3 minutes. Press a piece of aluminum foil on top, cover, and cook over low heat until the fennel is tender and browned, stirring once or twice, 15 to 20 minutes. Stir in $^1/_4$ cup grated Parmesan cheese, 2 tablespoons chopped fresh parsley, and pepper; taste and adjust seasoning.

Rapid Ratatouille

I like the vegetables in my ratatouille to have texture, so instead of baking them slowly in a stew, I sauté them. To save time, I leave skins on all the vegetables except the onion and garlic, and I don't bother to salt the eggplant. Be sure to cut the vegetables uniformly so they cook evenly. The coriander seasoning, popular in Provence where ratatouille originates, is my trademark, too.

Serves 4

> 1 medium eggplant (about ¾ pound)
> 2 small zucchini (about ¾ pound)
> 1 pound plum tomatoes
> 3 tablespoons olive oil, more if needed
> 1 onion, thinly sliced
> 1 red bell and 1 green bell pepper, cored, seeded, and cut in strips
> 3 garlic cloves, chopped
> 1 tablespoon ground coriander
> small bunch of thyme
> 2 bay leaves
> salt and pepper to taste
> medium bunch of basil

Cut the eggplant, zucchini, and tomatoes in ¹/₂-inch chunks, discarding stems. Heat a large frying pan and drizzle with a tablespoon of the olive oil. Add the onion and cook over brisk heat, stirring often, until soft, 2 to 3 minutes. Stir in the eggplant with the rest of the oil and cook, stirring often, 2 minutes longer. Stir in the peppers, zucchini, tomatoes, garlic, coriander, thyme, and bay leaves. Add salt and pepper and stir thoroughly, with a little more oil if the vegetables seem dry.

Lower the heat to moderate, cover, and leave the ratatouille to simmer, stirring occasionally, until the vegetables are soft but still hold their shape, 12 to 15 minutes. Meanwhile, shred the leaves from the basil in a chiffonade (page 24). When the ratatouille is done, discard the thyme and bay leaves and stir in the basil. Taste and adjust seasoning. Ratatouille is good hot or at room temperature, and it reheats well.

GETTING AHEAD: When first cooked, the flavor of ratatouille is fresh and bold. Over a day or two in the refrigerator it mellows, becoming rich and complex. Take your pick and plan cooking accordingly. You can reheat it once or twice as needed, so leftovers are no problem.

how to roast vegetables

Oven-roasted vegetables are delicious and remarkably easy. The steady heat of an oven is easier to control than the fire of a grill, so you can take time to do other things. It's true that roasting is not as quick as grilling, but if you already have a bird or roast meat in the oven, the vegetables can go in the pan, too, and basting with the pan juices from the meat improves them. The Trio of Roasted Root Vegetables (page 166) is good to serve with the Thanksgiving turkey (page 162) or Roast Pork with Cabbage, Potatoes, and Plums (page 178), but these pairings are just a start.

Roasted vegetables will shrink as they cook, so start off with a generous quantity. The skins can be left on or peeled, as you prefer. Potatoes and other whole unpeeled root vegetables need pricking with a fork to allow steam to escape as they cook. A little butter or oil, fresh herbs such as rosemary, sage, and thyme, and a seasoning of salt and pepper is all they will need. Once in the oven, stir them occasionally until they are tender and browned.

Roasted Cauliflower

I've always had a liking for cauliflower and this is my favorite way to prepare it. Sometimes I add unpeeled garlic cloves to the pan—they transfer flavor to the cauliflower and the soft pulp inside tastes great, too.

Serves 4 to 6

Preheat the oven to 400°F. Trim a head of cauliflower (about 3 pounds) and cut it in even-sized florets. Toss the florets in a roasting pan with 3 tablespoons olive oil and 3 tablespoons vegetable oil. Add 3 to 4 sprigs of thyme or a handful of sage leaves, salt, and pepper. Roast the cauliflower in the oven, stirring occasionally, until tender and browned, 1 1/4 to 1 1/2 hours. Taste and adjust seasoning.

how to grill vegetables

Emma's influence and the California climate have me hooked on grilled vegetables. Her local farmers' markets offer an abundance of produce including asparagus, fennel, and vegetables from the vine such as tomatoes, eggplant, peppers, and summer and winter squash. Many need only to be halved or sliced without peeling (the peel adds flavor during grilling and helps hold the vegetable in shape).

Vegetables do well on the grill if marinated beforehand—try Soy and Balsamic Vinaigrette (page 73) or Asian Marinade (page 124). When you are short of time, a simple brushing of olive oil and a sprinkling of salt and pepper does the trick, too—the oil adds flavor and also prevents sticking. Set the vegetables cut side down on the hot grill (brush the rack with oil first), and turn them when they are browned. Frequent basting with the marinade or olive oil keeps the vegetables moist. Cooking time will vary depending on the heat of the grill and the ripeness of the vegetables—what you're aiming for is an agreeably brown surface and tender center that is not too soft. Grilled vegetables can cook fast, so watch closely. A fierce flame or rack that is too close to the heat can spell ruin.

By all means, make an aluminum foil package filled with thinly sliced vegetables sprinkled with marinade and set it on the grill—strictly speaking this is steaming, not grilling, but the results are delicious, too. Skewering smaller pieces of vegetable, such as cherry tomatoes, halved mushrooms, and bell pepper chunks to make kebabs is a colorful alternative. Just be sure the vegetables are cut in pieces of about the same size so they cook evenly.

Grilled Spicy Salad of Belgian Endive

This Italian favorite is also good with radicchio and any of the other slightly bitter relatives of the endive family. Grilled endive is delicious on its own, or as an accompaniment to grilled chicken and fish.

Serves 3 to 4

Light the grill. Trim 1 pound endive, discarding any wilted outer leaves and leaving enough stem to hold the leaves together. Cut small heads in half and large heads in quarters. In a bowl, mix 1/2 cup olive oil, 1/2 teaspoon each of salt, ground coriander, and ground cumin, and 1/4 teaspoon each of ground black pepper and ground red chile pepper. Brush the endive generously all over with the spiced oil. Brush the grill rack with oil and set the endive on it about 3 inches from the heat. Grill the endive, brushing occasionally with more spiced oil, until it is slightly charred, 3 to 5 minutes. Turn and brown the remaining sides until tender but still firm when poked with a knife, 5 to 7 minutes longer.

HOW TO PREPARE AND WASH SALAD GREENS

There's really only one secret to a good salad—great greens. They are pretty easy to recognize as good fresh greens look crisp and curly, with plenty of color. Dried out stems and shriveled outer leaves are a bad sign. The more delicate the greens, the quicker they will wilt, even in the refrigerator. I'd count on a maximum of four days for robust heads, two days for loose-leaf greens, and only a day for watercress, which yellows very rapidly. With the exception of Belgian endive (which can simply be wiped with a damp cloth), all salad greens are trimmed and washed in the same way. First you trim the stem then discard the wilted outside until you reach the fresh inner leaves.

You'll soon learn just what to keep and how much to discard. Tender lettuces are usually totally edible except for a few outer leaves, but robust greens such as chicory (frisée) and escarole have a tough exterior, so its best to keep going to the paler center for the good stuff, tearing the close-packed fronds carefully apart. The solid red heads of radicchio must also be eased apart gently so the leaves do not tear. Iceberg lettuce is even denser; to ease its leaves apart, you can run it under the tap after scooping out the core. Simply pick over spinach, arugula, and the loose-leaf greens called mesclun and nip off any tough stems.

Add a memorable dressing to fresh salad greens and you're done—the section on vinaigrette has lots of ideas (page 72). In this chapter, I'm suggesting salads that go a bit beyond just greens and dressing. Zesty parsley salad has only five ingredients, but with sesame and lime, it becomes almost a relish. I've a duo of warm salads—I'm equally fond of hot dressings that wilt chewy greens like arugula and curly endive while mellowing their peppery, strident tastes. As for Caesar salad, it is so rarely done well that I thought you'd like to know how it ought to be. Vary the greens in any of these recipes and you'll be happy with the results.

1 Trim the stem and discard any wilted leaves from the greens. Separate the inner leaves and soak them in cold water, swirling them once or twice. Nowadays most salad greens are relatively clean, but they will always benefit from a reviving rinse in a sinkful of cold water. Robust garden greens should be soaked for at least 15 minutes, swirling them from time to time to loosen any grit and (heaven forbid) lurking bugs.

2 Lift the leaves out one by one and rinse them in cold running water to remove any remaining grit. Tear large leaves with your hands into 2 to 3 pieces. Dry the leaves using a salad spinner, or by patting them dry with paper towels or a dish towel.

salad sidenotes

* The more delicate the greens, the lighter and milder the dressing should be. Rich, creamy dressings or hot and spicy flavors rarely suit green salads.

* After washing, most greens will hold up for a day or two if you wrap them carefully so they remain moist. Roll unused greens loosely in paper towels or a dish towel and enclose them in a plastic bag. Store them in the refrigerator. If you have room in your refrigerator, you'll find greens also hold perfectly in a salad spinner after excess water has been spun off.

* By all means prepare dressing and greens ahead, but they should be tossed together only just before serving. Tender leaves wilt after 15 minutes, and robust greens do not hold up much longer. You can always mix more as demand dictates.

* Always taste salad greens after the leaves have been dressed and adjust seasoning as necessary.

Summer Salad of Parsley with Sesame

Delicious with charcuterie, cold ham, and shellfish, particularly shrimp.

Serves 4

Heat 2 tablespoons sesame seeds in a small dry frying pan over moderate heat, stirring until brown and fragrant, 2 to 3 minutes. Let them cool. Wash and dry 2 large bunches of flat-leaf parsley. Pull leaves from the stems. To make the dressing: In a salad bowl, whisk the grated zest and juice of 2 limes with $1/4$ cup mustard seed oil or walnut oil, $1^1/_2$ teaspoons dark sesame oil, salt, and pepper. Add the parsley, toss, and taste for seasoning. Sprinkle the salad with the sesame seeds and serve.

Peppery and Sweet Arugula

This salad, peppery from the greens and sweet with balsamic vinegar, expands to be an appetizer if you top it with curls shaved from a hunk of Parmesan cheese. It's good as accompaniment to lentils or rice. I rarely bother to peel the tomatoes, but you may prefer to do so.

Serves 4

Wash and dry 3 large bunches of arugula (about $1/2$ pound) and discard any thick stems. Put it in a large bowl. Halve 2 medium tomatoes crosswise, squeeze out the seeds, and dice the flesh. In a small frying pan, heat 3 tablespoons balsamic vinegar until bubbling. Add a small chopped sweet onion and cook until the onion softens and has absorbed almost all the vinegar, about 2 minutes. Add the tomato with salt and pepper and cook for 1 minute. Pour the tomato-onion mixture over the arugula and toss vigorously. Heat $1/4$ cup olive oil in the frying pan until almost smoking, pour it over the salad, and toss again. Taste and adjust seasoning—the salad should be quite peppery.

Warm Salad with Bacon and Egg

In the fall, we have a lot of chewy greens such as escarole and curly chicory from the garden, with spinach as an alternative. Hot bacon fat wilts them efficiently, and with a hard-boiled egg or two, there's lunch on the table.

Serves 4

> **medium head of curly chicory or escarole (about ¾ pound)**
> **1 tablespoon vegetable oil**
> **4-ounce piece of smoked lean bacon, diced**
> **⅓ cup red wine vinegar**
> **freshly ground black pepper to taste**
> **2 hard-boiled eggs, chopped**

Discard tough outer leaves from the greens, then wash and dry the leaves, tearing them into pieces. Put them in a salad bowl.

Heat the oil in a frying pan and fry the bacon until browned. Discard all but about 4 tablespoons fat from the pan and pour the rest, with the bacon, over the greens. At once toss vigorously, so heat from the fat wilts the leaves. Add the vinegar to the hot pan (stand back as the vapor may sting your eyes) and bring just to a boil, stirring to dissolve the pan juices. Pour the hot vinegar over the greens and toss again. Add pepper, taste, and adjust seasoning. Pile the salad on 4 plates, sprinkle with chopped hard-boiled egg, and serve at once while still warm.

GETTING AHEAD: You can wash the greens in advance, but the essence of this warm salad is to make it quickly at the last minute.

The Real Caesar Salad

Many versions of Caesar salad do the rounds, but this is the unbeatable original from Tijuana, creation of restaurateur Caesar Cardini. It involves an almost-raw egg, which can be omitted if you wish. The second step is traditionally done at the table.

Serves 4

> **medium head of romaine lettuce (about 1 pound)**
> **1 egg**
> **4 anchovy fillets in oil, finely chopped**
> **½ teaspoon Worcestershire sauce**
> **¼ cup olive oil**
> **juice of ½ lemon, more to taste**
> **salt and freshly ground black pepper to taste**
> **¼ cup grated Parmesan cheese**
>
> FOR THE CROUTONS
> **1 garlic clove**
> **3 tablespoons olive oil**
> **4 thick slices dry baguette, cut in uneven dice**

Trim and wash the romaine. Dry the leaves thoroughly and tear them into pieces. Make the croutons: Cut the garlic clove in half and very finely chop one half. Heat the other half with the olive oil in a frying pan. When very hot, add the diced bread and fry, stirring constantly, until brown, 1 to 2 minutes. Drain the croutons on paper towels, discarding the garlic. Boil the egg for 1 minute.

To finish the salad, at the table if you wish: Put the anchovy fillets and chopped garlic into a salad bowl and crush them together with a fork. Mix in the Worcestershire sauce followed by the olive oil. Add the lettuce pieces and toss thoroughly. Break the warm egg into the salad and toss again. Sprinkle with lemon juice, pepper, and very little salt and toss again. Finally, add the Parmesan cheese and croutons, toss, and taste the salad, adjusting the seasoning, including lemon juice, as you prefer. Serve at once.

GETTING AHEAD: The fun of Caesar salad is in the last-minute tossing, so there's no getting ahead here beyond preparing the individual ingredients.

HOW TO CORE, SEED, AND CHOP BELL PEPPERS

Bell peppers are a practical vegetable: just wipe them with a damp cloth. When raw, they are crisp and juicy. Once heated, they soon wilt and are best rapidly stir-fried or sautéed so they retain a bit of texture. If roasted, bell peppers soften and mellow to an aromatic, almost melting consistency.

Red peppers, glowing ripe and sweet, seem to be everyone's favorite, certainly mine. Green peppers are picked unripe and taste that way, juicy but slightly sharp, while orange and yellow peppers are somewhere in between. Purple peppers are fine raw but they discolor to tired gray if cooked. A medley of colors is the charm of mixed salads and recipes like Pepper Relish, while some dishes such as Gazpacho or Tuscan Roasted Red Pepper Salad with Anchovy call for a single variety.

When buying peppers, look for big shiny specimens with firm skins. Loosely wrapped in the refrigerator, they keep well for a week or more and are handy to have around to decorate a dish or fill out a salad. One caution, sweet bell peppers belong to the same family of capsicums as hot chiles, and a few varieties resemble bell peppers in size. In a Mexican market I once bought poblanos instead of green peppers for stuffing, with searing consequences.

Pepper Relish
Serve with grilled steak, hamburgers, or pot roast.

Makes 5 cups relish

Core, halve, seed, and chop 2 red, 2 yellow, and 2 green bell peppers. Mix them in a preserving pan or heavy saucepan with 3 chopped medium onions, 3/4 cup cider vinegar, 1/4 cup dark brown sugar, and 1 tablespoon soy sauce. Bring to a boil and simmer, stirring often, until the peppers are tender but still firm and the relish is thick enough to hold the trail of the spoon, 30 to 35 minutes. Let the relish cool slightly, pour it into jars that have been sterilized by running them through the dishwasher on the hottest cycle, and seal with a circle of wax paper and a lid. Store up to 2 weeks in the refrigerator.

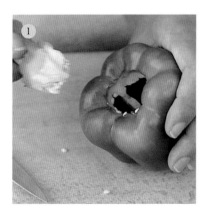

1 Cut around the core of the pepper with a small knife, twist, and pull it out.

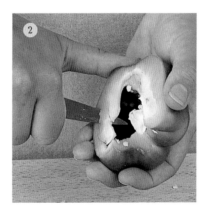

2 Halve the pepper and scrape out the seeds with your fingers or the knife. Cut away the white ribs.

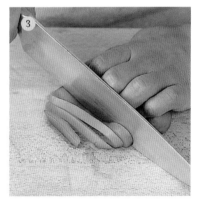

3 To slice the pepper, set one half cut side down on the board and push down with the heel of your hand to flatten it. With a large knife, slice lengthwise into even strips. If you want to chop the pepper, line up strips and cut them crosswise into dice.

Great Gazpacho

Salad in a soup bowl, chilled gazpacho is the ultimate refresher on a hot day. With slices of fresh crusty bread for dunking, it can become a light meal.

Serves 4

2 slices white bread
1 cup water
1 red bell pepper, cored, seeded, and
  cut in chunks
1 green bell pepper, cored, seeded, and
  cut in chunks
1 medium cucumber, peeled, seeded, and
  cut in chunks
1 pound very ripe tomatoes, peeled, seeded,
  and cut in chunks
½ onion, cut in chunks
1 garlic clove, cut in pieces
¼ cup olive oil
3 tablespoons red wine vinegar, more if needed
salt and pepper to taste
ice cubes

Discard the crusts from the bread and put it in a small bowl, pour the water over the bread, and leave it to soak for 5 minutes. Finely chop 3 to 4 pieces of the red pepper and set them aside for decoration. Squeeze the bread to remove excess water. In a food processor, purée one-half of the peppers, cucumber, tomatoes, onion, and garlic with one-half of the bread and olive oil until smooth. Pour the purée into a bowl and repeat with the other half of the ingredients. Stir in the vinegar, salt, and pepper and taste, adding more seasonings if needed. Cover and chill the gazpacho for at least 2 hours.

Just before serving, thin the gazpacho with a little cold water if necessary—it should have body but not be thick enough to hold a shape. Taste again for seasoning and spoon the soup into chilled bowls. Add an ice cube or two to each bowl and top with the reserved red pepper.

GETTING AHEAD: How far ahead to make gazpacho is an interesting question. When fresh, not more than an hour old, its flavor is bright and grassy. If you keep it, the flavor mellows until at the end of 24 hours it has become dark and complex, so make your choice. In any case, it must be thoroughly chilled in the refrigerator before serving.

Piquant Pepper Scramble (*Pipérade*)

The name for this Basque recipe comes from *piper*, meaning hot red pepper. A delicious purée of bell peppers and tomato spiced with chile pepper, it is thickened and enriched with eggs. In winter I find canned tomatoes do just fine.

Serves 6

3 tablespoons vegetable oil
2 onions, chopped
2 red bell peppers, cored, seeded, and chopped
1 green bell pepper, cored, seeded, and chopped
2 garlic cloves, chopped
large pinch of dried hot red pepper flakes
2 pounds tomatoes, peeled, seeded, and
  chopped
salt to taste
6 slices whole-wheat bread
8 eggs, beaten to mix

Heat the oil in a large deep frying pan, add the onions, and sauté them until soft and lightly browned, 5 to 8 minutes. Stir in the bell peppers, garlic, and hot red pepper flakes and cook over low heat, stirring often, 5 minutes. Stir in the tomatoes with some salt and continue cooking until the vegetables have reduced by half and melt together, 30 to 40 minutes. Taste and adjust seasoning.

To finish: Toast the bread and discard the crusts. Reheat the vegetable purée if necessary until hand-hot. Stir in the beaten eggs and cook over low heat, stirring constantly, until the mixture has thickened but remains soft and moist, 3 to 5 minutes. Check the seasoning again, spoon the *pipérade* onto the toast, and serve at once.

GETTING AHEAD: The vegetable purée can be cooked ahead and refrigerated up to 2 days. Reheat it with the eggs at the last minute.

how to roast and core bell peppers

When bell peppers are roasted until their skin blackens, the skin peels off easily and the core and seeds can be stripped away. The flesh develops a characteristically smoky sweet flavor that is incomparable in salads, soups, and dips. Red peppers, with their ripe sweetness, are favorites for roasting but yellow and green ones can be peeled this way, too. If you are roasting just one or two peppers, use a two-pronged fork held over an open gas flame, or toast them with a small blowtorch. (This handy kitchen tool is available at most hardware stores.) Larger quantities of peppers are best roasted under the broiler.

1 Preheat the broiler. Set the whole peppers on a broiler rack and broil about 3 inches from the heat until the skin is blistered and black, 10 to 12 minutes. Turn them from time to time so they are charred all over.

2 Drop the peppers while still hot into a plastic bag, or wrap them in plastic wrap and leave them to cool, so that steam helps loosen the skin. When cool, peel off the skins, discard the cores, and scrape out the seeds. (Rinsing removes delicious toasted flavor.) Cut the peppers in strips or chop them, according to the recipe.

Tuscan Roasted Red Pepper Salad with Anchovy

You'll need lots of crusty bread to serve with this vibrant salad, a mix of sweet peppers, sharp scallion, and salty anchovy. If you can find them, use anchovies preserved in salt for their more intense taste.

Serves 4 to 6

Roast 2 red bell peppers, then core, seed, and cut them in wide strips. Lay them on a serving dish and sprinkle with 1 to 2 tablespoons olive oil and black pepper. Soak 24 anchovy fillets in 2 to 3 tablespoons milk for 10 minutes to remove salt, then drain and dry them on paper towels. Lay them on the peppers. Scatter the green and white parts of 3 scallions, sliced, on top, and drizzle with 2 tablespoons more olive oil. Top with $^1/_4$ cup pitted oil-cured black olives and 3 to 4 tablespoons coarsely chopped fresh flat-leaf parsley. Cover with plastic wrap and leave for an hour at room temperature for flavors to mellow. Just before serving, squeeze the juice of $^1/_2$ lemon over the salad.

HOW TO ROAST AND GRILL EGGPLANT

Rarely in the U.S.A. does an eggplant resemble its name, though occasionally in a farmers' market you'll find white or pale green oval varieties that might have been mothered by a hen. From the cooking viewpoint, color makes no difference—purple, green or white, plain or striped, all eggplants behave and taste much the same. Some varieties have thicker skins, particularly the oversized purple ones. Small ones are handy for stuffing and easy to slice for vegetable stews. The best eggplants are heavy for their size, and shiny and tight in their skins, as if they want to burst. A warm climate plant, they do not like cold and are best stored in a cool corner of the kitchen, not in a refrigerator.

It seems to me that for vegetarians, eggplants must be the closest thing to meat. They have a rich, satisfying texture and pleasant taste that melds as well with Indian spices as with Mediterranean olive oil, garlic, anchovy, sesame, and olives. Versatile, eggplants are at home in purées and marinated salads, yet equally happy in vegetable stews such as ratatouille, along with their botanical cousins tomato and bell pepper. In Greek moussaka they marry with lamb, and in eggplant parmigiana with Parmesan cheese.

Personally I never peel eggplants as I like the color and slight chewiness of the skin. However I do usually salt them after halving or slicing them, both to draw out bitter juices and to get rid of excess moisture. Roasting, grilling, sautéing, or deep-frying eggplants all lead in very different directions. When an eggplant is roasted or grilled, either whole in its skin, or halved and cooked cut side down, the flesh acquires a characteristic smoky, slightly bitter taste that you'll love or loathe. The effect is less pronounced if eggplants are sliced and then grilled or roasted on a baking sheet, particularly if generously brushed with oil. The smokiness disappears altogether if eggplants are sautéed until meltingly soft and rich (invariably olive or vegetable oil is used, not butter). And if cut in sticks and deep-fried, eggplant will crisp invitingly.

2 To grill slices of eggplant: Preheat a stovetop or outdoor grill. Cut the eggplant in $3/8$- to $1/2$-inch slices, brush them with oil, and sprinkle with salt and pepper. Lay them on the hot grill and cook, 3 to 5 minutes, until browned. Turn and brown the other side, grilling until the eggplant is tender, 2 to 3 minutes longer.

1 To roast eggplant whole: Preheat the oven to 400°F. Trim stem and prick the eggplant all over with a fork; bake it in an oiled baking dish, allowing 30 to 40 minutes for a 1-pound eggplant. To roast eggplant halves: Trim the eggplant, halve it lengthwise, and slash in a lattice, cutting around the edge just inside the rim. Set the halves cut side down on an oiled baking sheet and roast for 25 to 30 minutes, until very tender. Scoop the pulp out with a spoon.

Todd's Italian Eggplant

Emma's husband Todd became addicted to this recipe when on junior year abroad in Rome. Recreating just the right balance of garlic and hot pepper took a bit of experimentation, but now it's perfect. Don't throw away any leftover oil as it makes a wonderful spicy topping for fettuccine.

Serves 4

2 pounds small eggplants
salt and pepper to taste
1 cup olive oil, more for brushing
large pinch of dried hot red pepper flakes
1 garlic clove, finely chopped

Trim and cut the eggplants lengthwise in ¼-inch-thick slices. Lay them on a tray, sprinkle with salt, turn, and sprinkle again. Leave for 15 to 30 minutes to draw out juices. Rinse and drain them. Light the grill. Brush the eggplant slices with olive oil, sprinkle with salt and pepper, and lay them on the hot grill. Grill them until browned, 3 to 5 minutes, turn, and continue grilling until tender and browned on the other side, 2 to 3 minutes more. Spread a layer of eggplant in a dish and sprinkle with part of the hot red pepper flakes and garlic. Repeat with more eggplant, pepper, and garlic until all are used. Pour the olive oil over the eggplant, adding more if needed to coat it thoroughly. Cover and leave to marinate at room temperature at least a day.

GETTING AHEAD: The longer this spicy eggplant sits the better it is. Allow up to 4 days, covered, in the refrigerator.

Eggplant Rolls of Pesto and Mozzarella

Grilled eggplant, brushed with pesto and wrapped around sticks of fresh mozzarella, makes an excellent hors d'oeuvre. For a simple appetizer serve three rolls on a bed of arugula. You'll find a recipe for basil pesto on page 94, or you can buy it ready prepared. The rolls are easy to vary—for example, try brushing them with balsamic vinegar instead of pesto, substituting half of an anchovy fillet for the mozzarella.

Makes about 30 eggplant rolls

4 to 5 small eggplants (about 2 pounds)
salt and pepper to taste
½ cup olive oil
1 pound fresh mozzarella
¼ cup basil pesto

toothpicks

Trim and cut the eggplants lengthwise in ¼-inch slices. Sprinkle salt generously over both sides and leave for 30 minutes. Rinse the slices thoroughly in cold water, drain well, and pat dry.

Light the grill or preheat the broiler. Brush the eggplant slices with olive oil, sprinkle with pepper, and lay them on the hot grill. Grill them until browned, 3 to 5 minutes, turn, and continue grilling until tender and browned on the other side, 2 to 3 minutes longer. Set the slices aside to cool.

Cut the mozzarella into sticks about 2 inches long and ⅜ inch thick. Spread a very thin layer of pesto on each slice of eggplant. Put a stick of mozzarella on one end, roll the eggplant around it, and secure with a toothpick. Serve at room temperature.

GETTING AHEAD: These rolls keep well for 3 to 4 hours at room temperature or in the refrigerator, no problem. Be sure they are tightly covered.

Eggplant Sandwiches in a Tomato Broth

Here's another easy yet inventive way to cook eggplant. The slices are sandwiched with a savory herbal stuffing dotted with raisins, baked in the oven, then served in a tomato broth.

Serves 4

2 medium globe eggplants (about 1½ pounds total)

salt and pepper to taste

½ cup mayonnaise, more if needed

1 cup dried white breadcrumbs

FOR THE TOMATO BROTH

2 pounds tomatoes, cored

½ cup dry white wine

2 tablespoons shredded fresh basil

FOR THE FILLING

2 tablespoons olive oil, more for the baking sheet

2 onions, chopped

2 garlic cloves, chopped

¼ cup golden raisins

1 tablespoon capers, rinsed and chopped

½ cup grated Asiago or Parmesan cheese

2 tablespoons chopped fresh mint

2 tablespoons chopped fresh basil

Make the broth: Quarter the tomatoes and purée them in a food processor. Simmer them 10 to 12 minutes in a saucepan. Sieve them into a bowl, pressing to extract all the purée, and return them to the pan. You should have at least $1^1/2$ cups purée. Add the white wine and basil to the strained tomato purée and simmer until well flavored, 5 to 8 minutes. Taste and adjust the seasoning.

Trim the eggplants and cut each one lengthwise into 4 slices, discarding the skin at top and bottom. Sprinkle the slices on both sides with salt and pepper. Spread one side of each slice with mayonnaise, dip in breadcrumbs, and lay 4 slices, crumb side down, on an oiled baking sheet. Set the remaining 4 slices aside.

For the filling: Heat the oil in a frying pan and fry the onions with salt and pepper until starting to brown, 5 to 7 minutes. Stir in the garlic and cook for 1 minute, until fragrant. Take the pan from the heat and stir in the raisins, capers, cheese, mint, and basil. Taste, adjust seasoning, and spread the filling on the eggplant slices on the baking sheet. Top with reserved slices, crumbed side up.

To finish: Preheat the oven to 400°F. Bake the sandwiches in the oven until browned and eggplant is tender, 35 to 45 minutes. If necessary, reheat the broth. Spoon it into 4 shallow bowls, set an eggplant sandwich in the center, and serve. The sandwiches should be moistened but not drowned by the broth.

GETTING AHEAD: The broth can be made up to 2 days ahead and reheated. The sandwiches, too, can be assembled up to 8 hours ahead and baked at serving time.

Grilled Eggplant Caviar
(Baba Ghanouj)

This Middle Eastern dip, made with eggplant purée and sesame paste, is even better with a touch of five-spice powder instead of the more usual cumin. Serve it with pita bread and black olives.

Serves 4 to 6

2 large eggplants (about 2 pounds total)
2 tablespoons olive oil
1 teaspoon five-spice powder, more to taste
1 teaspoon salt, more to taste
¼ cup sesame paste (tahini)
1 teaspoon dark sesame oil
¼ cup lemon juice, more to taste
2 garlic cloves, peeled
cilantro or flat-leaf parsley sprigs, for decoration

Light the grill or preheat the broiler. Trim eggplant stems and cut the eggplants lengthwise in half. Slash the cut flesh in a lattice, almost down to the skins. Brush with oil and sprinkle with five-spice powder and salt, pressing it well into the slashes.

Set the eggplants cut side down on an oiled rack and grill them, 2 to 3 inches from the heat. Turn them when browned, after 5 to 7 minutes, and continue grilling on the skin side until the flesh is soft and collapsed and the skin is charred (this adds wonderful smoky flavor).

Let the eggplant halves cool, then peel them, squeezing out any excess moisture with your fists. Purée the flesh in a food processor with the sesame paste, sesame oil, lemon juice, and garlic. Taste and adjust seasoning: the purée should be very smooth, piquant with spices and raw garlic, and mellow with sesame. Pile it in a bowl and decorate with cilantro or parsley sprigs. Serve at room temperature.

GETTING AHEAD: The longer you keep it, the better eggplant caviar will be; up to 3 days in the refrigerator is fine.

how to salt vegetables

A few vegetables, notably eggplants, cucumbers, and squash, have firm structures that enclose quantities of water, making them tricky to cook without diluting flavor. This is why they are often sprinkled with salt to break down cell walls and draw out moisture (also called by the French term *dégorger*). Salting also helps draw out any bitter juices. Start by cutting the vegetable in slices or chunks. Eggplants for stuffing are halved lengthwise, then slashed in a lattice to make them more absorbent. Sprinkle the vegetable generously with fine salt (coarse salt dissolves less easily and draws out juices unevenly), tossing so it is evenly coated, and leave it, 15 to 30 minutes, as directed. Moisture will bead on the surface and the texture of the vegetable will soften. Wash off the salt with cold running water and drain the vegetable thoroughly.

Salted Cucumber Salad with Mint

Versions of this salad turn up in many countries. In England it comes with cold salmon, in the Middle East it forms part of a mezze table, and in India it is called raita, a cooling accompaniment to curry.

Serves 4 to 6

Peel 2 English cucumbers or 3 medium regular cucumbers (about 2 pounds total). Cut them in half lengthwise and scoop out seeds with a teaspoon. Very thinly slice the cucumbers crosswise. Put them in a bowl, sprinkle generously with salt, and toss so the slices are coated. Leave, 15 to 30 minutes, until the slices are wilted and translucent. Rinse thoroughly in cold water and drain them. Mix with 1 cup plain yogurt, 3 tablespoons chopped fresh mint, 1 tablespoon white wine vinegar, and freshly ground black pepper. Taste and adjust seasoning. Chill and serve within an hour (the yogurt thins on standing).

HOW TO CUT CORN KERNELS FROM THE COB

One summer we rented a beach house on Delaware's eastern shore. Sam, a local farmer, picked the corn for supper at 6:00 P.M., not a minute before, and it was in the pot within the half hour. Compared with the tough, spindly ears of corn I had encountered in Europe, freshly picked corn was a revelation. (And, of course, freshly cooked corn kernels are a world away from those in a can.) We had it every day, sometimes twice a day after Sam showed me how to cut the kernels from the cob for salad. There are two ways to do it—cut off the kernels or slit them to extract the inner pulp. The corn may be raw or cooked, it makes no difference. An ear of corn will yield about a half cup corn kernels, rather less pulp.

Whole raw kernels of corn are good when you want a bit of texture, in creamed corn for example. Cooked kernels are a standby in many salads, adding color and sweetness. I think of corn kernels combined with bell peppers and tomato or tomatillo in chicken salad, tacos, and spicy relishes. Milky raw or cooked pulp, with the chewy skin left behind, is right for creamed corn, corn chowder, and other corn soups. For some corn dishes, such as pancakes, you can use any form of corn, raw or cooked, kernels or pulp. Taste and texture varies accordingly.

As you'll gather from Sam's insistence on gathering his corn as late in the day as possible, the fresher the ear the sweeter it will be, even though modern strains of corn are bred so the sugar converts less rapidly to starch. When corn is mature, the tassel at the tip will be dark and slightly dried. To doublecheck, pull away the husk to see whether the kernels are plump and full. If you must store corn, keep it cool. Pull off the husk only just before cooking, stripping away any silk still clinging to the kernels.

1 To remove whole corn kernels from the cob, remove husk and silk from the corn. Hold the ear upright on the chopping board. With a sharp knife, cut from the tip down to the board, removing as many kernels as possible, 3 to 4 rows at a time. A thin layer of pulp will be left.

2 To extract pulp from the kernels, leaving the skins behind, remove husk and silk from the corn. With a small knife, cut down each row of kernels to split them. Hold the ear vertically on the board and, starting halfway down, scrape the pulp from the cob with the back of a larger knife. Reverse the ear so the tip is on the board and extract the pulp from the other end. The flesh and milk will spurt out, so gather them together with the knife.

Boiled Corn on the Cob

Allow 1 to 3 ears of corn each, depending on appetites.

Bring a very large pot of salted water to a rolling boil. Strip the husk and silk from the corn. Boil rapidly, until the kernels are tender and can be popped fairly easily from the cob with a point of a small knife. Timing can vary from 3 to 8 minutes, depending on the size and age of the corn. Drain the corn and serve hot on the cob with a choice of salt, black pepper, melted butter, herbed olive oil, or lime wedges. Alternatively, cut off the cooked kernels to use for salad.

Grilled Corn on the Cob

Grilled corn kernels, cut from the cob, add memorable smoky flavor to summer salads. You can roast corn just as it is, in the husk. The husk dries during grilling, of course, so you'll have quite a strong grilled flavor—to lessen it, soak the corn in water for an hour before grilling.

Lay the ears in the husk directly on the grill or broiler rack, setting them about 2 inches from the heat and cook them, turning quite often so they cook evenly on all sides. Allow 8 to 15 minutes depending on the age of the corn and the intensity of heat. Let them cool, then strip off the husk—the silk will peel away with it. Serve with the accompaniments for Boiled Corn on the Cob.

Creamed Corn

The intense, sweet flavor of fresh corn is developed to the fullest in this recipe that tastes quite different from canned creamed corn. It's delicious with chicken or ham.

Serves 4 to 6

Extract the pulp from 6 to 8 ears of corn and put it in a pan with 2 tablespoons butter, salt, and pepper. Depending on the sweetness of the corn, stir in a teaspoon of sugar. Heat gently, stirring, 2 minutes. Add 1 cup heavy cream and simmer until the corn is tender and lightly thickened, 3 to 5 minutes. Taste and adjust seasoning, adding more sugar if you like.

Corn Dollars

These light fritters are quick to make and always disappear fast. I like to shape them the size of silver dollars for cocktails, but they can be bigger for a side dish. Serve corn dollars with roast chicken, or try them as a friend of mine enjoys them, cold with maple syrup. The sweeter the corn, the better they will be.

Makes about 12 cocktail dollars

> **5 ears of corn**
> **2 eggs, separated**
> **2 tablespoons flour**
> **1 tablespoon sugar**
> **salt and pepper to taste**
> **1½ tablespoons butter**
> **1½ tablespoons vegetable oil**

Cut the kernels from the corn and scrape the cobs to extract the pulp. You should have about $2\frac{1}{2}$ cups of corn. Mix the corn with the egg yolks, flour, sugar, salt, and pepper. Stiffly whisk the egg whites, adding a pinch of salt to help stiffen them. Fold them gently into the corn.

Heat the butter and oil in a large skillet or sauté pan. Drop tablespoonfuls of the batter into the hot pan and cook over moderate heat until browned, 2 to 3 minutes. Flip the dollars and brown the other side, 2 to 3 minutes longer. Serve at once.

GETTING AHEAD: Make the batter up to 2 hours ahead, and whisk and fold in the egg whites just before frying.

HOW TO PREPARE AND ROAST WINTER SQUASH

In any market, winter squash catch the eye with their exotic shapes and brilliant colors. When I first saw a full array of acorns, butternuts, turbans, hubbards, spaghettis, large and small pumpkins, and their cousins, I was entranced—the few winter squash that have emigrated to Europe are feeble in comparison. However, a winter squash can be a tough proposition so you'll need a large, robust knife with a sharp point. Giant pumpkins require a strong arm, too. Thinner-skinned types such as spaghetti and butternut can be peeled more easily, again using a large knife or possibly a vegetable peeler.

Unlike summer squash, which is edible either raw in salads or cooked, winter squash must be roasted, steamed, or simmered in stock or water. Once tender, the flesh can usually be puréed in a food processor or with an immersion blender leading to aromatic, creamy soups and purées. The bigger the squash, the more fibrous it is likely to be. Most winter squash can be substituted for each other, an exception being spaghetti squash with its characteristic stringy flesh.

Perhaps one reason for the popularity of winter squash is their affinity for warm seasonings, the spices, sugar, and caramel that taste so good when it's cold outside. Nuts and apples are around at the same time and early American settlers soon discovered other happy combinations such as baked winter squash with bacon and late-ripening plums. A cool dry basement or cupboard is the best storage place. Winter squash can survive for months in low temperatures without spoilage.

Steamed Spiced Pumpkin

Serve this as a side dish with roast chicken or turkey.

Serves 4

Peel 2 pounds pumpkin, discard seeds and fiber, and cut the flesh in $1^1/2$-inch chunks. Toss the pumpkin with 1 teaspoon salt and $^1/2$ teaspoon pepper to coat it. Put it in a steamer over a pan of boiling water, cover, and steam until tender, 15 to 20 minutes. Heat 2 tablespoons vegetable oil in a medium saucepan. Stir in 2 teaspoons five-spice powder and toast it over low heat until fragrant, stirring, about 1 minute. Add 2 to 3 chopped garlic cloves and continue frying until the garlic is fragrant also, 1 to 2 minutes. Add the pumpkin and toss to mix with the garlic and spice. Heat about 1 minute before serving.

1 To peel large winter squash (here pumpkin), cut it in wedges. Pull out the seeds and fiber with your fingers and discard them. Peel the wedges with a small knife, then cut them in chunks.

If the squash is smaller, for example butternut, trim the stem end and cut a slice from the base so the squash sits firmly. With a medium knife, cut off the peel, following the curve of the vegetable. Cut the squash in half, discard seeds and fiber, and cut the flesh in chunks as for pumpkin.

Colonial Roast Squash

The salt of bacon, sour of plums, and a touch of sugar are a classic trio in this roast pumpkin recipe that dates back to colonial times. Other winter squash such as butternut can be substituted for the pumpkin.

Serves 4

> **3 tablespoons butter**
> **1/2 pound thickly sliced bacon, diced**
> **1 pound purple plums**
> **3-pound piece of pumpkin**
> **1 tablespoon brown sugar**
> **1 teaspoon ground cinnamon**
> **1 teaspoon ground allspice**
> **1/2 teaspoon salt**
> **1/2 teaspoon ground black pepper**

Preheat the oven to 375°F. Melt a tablespoon of the butter in a frying pan and fry the bacon until lightly browned, 5 to 7 minutes. Add the remaining butter to the pan, turn the heat to low, and leave the butter to melt in the pan.

Meanwhile, halve the plums, discarding the pits, and put them in a large bowl. Discard seeds and fiber from the pumpkin, cut away the skin, and slice the flesh in 1-inch cubes. Add them to the plums.

Stir the brown sugar, cinnamon, allspice, salt, and pepper into the bacon and melted butter. Pour the mixture over the plums and pumpkin and mix well. Spread the mixture in a shallow baking dish to make a 1¹/₂-inch layer. Cover dish with aluminum foil and bake in the oven, 50 to 60 minutes, until the plums and pumpkin are tender. If necessary, remove foil toward the end of cooking so the pumpkin dries out and starts to brown. Serve very hot.

GETTING AHEAD: No problem. This dish keeps well in the refrigerator and can be baked at least 2 days ahead. Reheat the squash, covered in foil, in a 350°F oven until very hot.

Colonial Roast Squash

Caramelized Acorn Squash

Smaller squash such as acorns and baby pumpkins can act as their own attractive container for roasting with seasonings. This sweet, spiced version is particularly good with ham, pork, duck, and game. You may want to supply a small spoon for scooping out the flesh at table.

Serves 2

Preheat the oven to 400°F. Halve a medium acorn squash (about 1 pound) with a large knife, cutting through stem and flower end, and discard seeds and fiber. Cut a thin slice from each half so they sit flat and set in a small baking dish. Add ¹/₄ inch water. Melt 4 tablespoons butter and stir in ¹/₂ cup dark brown sugar, 1 teaspoon ground allspice, and ¹/₂ teaspoon each of grated nutmeg, ginger, and salt, with a pinch of ground cloves. Warm gently, 1 to 2 minutes. Spoon the mixture over the squash, cover with aluminum foil, and roast in the oven until tender when pierced with the point of a knife, ³/₄ to 1 hour. Remove foil about 15 minutes before the end of cooking so the squash browns.

how to prepare and grill summer squash

If pumpkin is the archetypal winter squash, zucchini plays the lead for the squash family in summertime. Soft-skinned and totally edible, summer squash are cook-friendly, needing no peeling and little preparation. Look for small firm squash as they hold their shape better. Yellow crookneck, pastel green patty-pan, and celadon scallop squash look especially inviting but in fact they all taste more or less the same, a bit bland. So I'd urge creative treatment with lively herbs such as thyme and sage, sprinklings of orange, lemon, and other citrus, scatterings of hot red pepper, and generous brushings with olive or nut oils. Summer squash keep up to a week in the refrigerator before they soften and wither, but like all vegetables, the fresher they are the better.

1 Trim the squash stem, leaving the skin for color and flavor. Young squash are completely edible, but if the squash is mature, you may want to halve it and scoop out the seeds with a teaspoon. Leave the squash (here zucchini) whole, or slice or dice it according to the recipe.

Squash, Raisin, and Pine Nut Gratin

You can use almost any winter squash for this gratin, which is excellent on its own or as a side for baked ham, pork, and turkey.

Serves 4 to 6

Preheat the oven to 350°F. Peel 3 pounds winter squash, discard seeds and fiber, and cut the flesh in 1-inch chunks. Toss with 4 tablespoons melted butter, 1/2 cup raisins, 1/2 cup pine nuts, and 1/2 cup grated Parmesan cheese. Sprinkle with a little salt and plenty of freshly ground black pepper. Spread in a buttered medium baking dish and cover with aluminum foil. Bake in the oven until the squash is tender when pierced with a knife, 3/4 to 1 hour. Remove foil for the last 30 minutes of cooking and sprinkle with 1/2 cup more Parmesan cheese so the gratin browns.

Striped Summer Squash on the Grill

I love grilled summer squash as its flabby texture is stiffened and its flavor concentrated. The grill marks look pretty, too (see eggplant, page 256). Serve the squash hot or as a salad at room temperature.

Serves 3 to 4

Heat 1/2 cup olive oil with 1 crushed garlic clove, 2 to 3 sprigs thyme, and a large pinch of dried hot red pepper flakes until very hot, then set aside to infuse. Light the grill or preheat the broiler. Trim 3/4 pound small zucchini and the same of yellow squash. Cut them lengthwise in 1/8-inch slices, preferably using a mandoline. Lay them on a tray or baking sheet, brush with the infused oil, turn and brush the other side. Sprinkle with salt and pepper. Lay squash on the hot grill and grill until browned, 2 to 3 minutes. Turn and brown the other side, brushing with more oil if you like, 2 to 3 minutes. The squash should be tender but not dry. Before serving, brush with lemon juice.

HOW TO TRIM, SLICE, AND CHOP MUSHROOMS

Cultivated mushrooms are such a useful ingredient. They are juicy enough to withstand the high heat of grilling, deep-frying, or stir-frying, yet firm enough to be simmered and stewed without losing their character. They complement a wide range of fish, meat, poultry, and vegetables. Little button mushrooms are an attractive side dish for grills and roasts, while larger portabellas are handy for stuffing and make a good appetizer. When you trim most of the stem from a button mushroom and slice it from head to toe, it forms an attractive tree shape, appealing in salads or sautéed as a garnish. Mushrooms have an affinity for lemon, nutmeg, garlic, Parmesan cheese, parsley, port wine, and cream—what a choice!

Good button mushrooms are firm and white, with the caps scarcely open. They keep quite well in the refrigerator if loosely wrapped, but if left uncovered they wither and turn brown, and if wrapped in plastic they mold rapidly. To prepare them, wipe the caps with damp paper towels and trim the stems. Bear in mind that mushrooms are 90 percent water and spoil if they absorb any more; rinse if you will, but do not soak. To peel portabellas, grasp the lip of skin at the edge of the mushroom and pull it toward the center of the cap. The skin on button mushrooms is so thin that I never bother to peel them.

Chopped mushrooms open a whole new dimension of taste. With a bit of butter, shallot, and garlic, they cook down to an extraordinarily concentrated purée called duxelles, named after a French nobleman. Firm and resilient as good mushrooms feel, if you chop them repeatedly they will gradually liquefy. For this reason I chop mushrooms by hand and rarely use the food processor; even with the pulse button, it is almost impossible to chop them finely without forming a muddy, wet purée. However, the processor does well if other ingredients are included with the mushrooms, as in the recipe for Ham-Stuffed Portabellas.

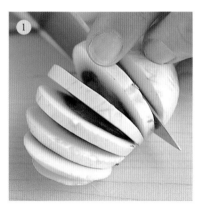

2 To chop mushrooms: Slice the mushrooms, pile slices on top of each other, and cut them into sticks. Chop the sticks, holding the point of the knife down with the flat of your hand and bouncing the blade up and down, to and fro across the board. When finished, the mushrooms should be very fine and crumbly with no coarse pieces.

1 To slice cultivated mushrooms: Wipe caps with a damp cloth and trim stems level with the caps. Set the mushroom stem down and slice vertically though the stem and cap, cutting thin or thick slices depending on the recipe. With your forefinger catch each slice you've just made so as to hold the slices together and keep them from sticking to the knife.

Duxelles Mushroom Purée

Good foods often have a long history—duxelles is named for a 17th-century French aristocrat. This concentrated mushroom purée is enormously useful for stuffing meats, flavoring sauces for fish and chicken, and making aromatic soups. Mixed with cream it forms a filling for tartlets, a teaspoonful on a cucumber slice makes a good cocktail hors d'oeuvre, and one of my favorite fish recipes calls for spreading duxelles on a thick fillet of halibut or cod and roasting it with a drizzle of olive oil. Duxelles keeps well in the refrigerator up to a week, so it is worth making a big batch.

Makes 1¹/₂ cups duxelles

Finely chop 1 pound button mushrooms. Melt 2 tablespoons butter in a deep frying pan and sauté 3 chopped shallots until soft, 2 to 3 minutes. Stir in 1 chopped garlic clove and cook until fragrant, 1 minute. Stir in the mushrooms with salt and pepper and cook over high heat, stirring occasionally, 5 to 7 minutes. At first, moisture will be draw out then the mushrooms will dry to a firm, concentrated purée. Stir in 2 tablespoons chopped fresh parsley, take from the heat, and taste and adjust the seasoning.

Old Emily's Mushroom Soup

Here's just one of the many uses for Duxelles Mushroom Purée, a recipe from a family friend that dates from my childhood when we gathered mushrooms in the paddock next door.

Serves 4

Make duxelles with 1 pound mushrooms and cook until most, but not all, moisture has evaporated. Stir in 2 tablespoons flour, then whisk in 1 quart chicken stock. Bring the soup to a boil, whisking until it thickens. Add ¹/₂ cup crème fraîche or heavy cream and simmer 2 minutes. If you like, stir in 2 tablespoons chopped fresh mint, tarragon, or parsley, taste and adjust seasoning.

Ham-Stuffed Portabellas

A quick first course or snack on a busy evening.

Serves 2

> **3 large portabella mushrooms**
> **2 slices cooked ham, cut in pieces**
> **1 scallion, including green part, cut in pieces**
> **1 garlic clove, sliced**
> **small handful of parsley sprigs**
> **2 tablespoons olive oil, more for the baking dish**
> **2 tablespoons Madeira, Marsala, or**
>   **sweet vermouth**
> **salt and pepper to taste**

Preheat the oven to 375°F. Peel 2 of the mushrooms, reserving the peel. Snap out their stems, then trim and cut the stems in chunks. Set the caps aside. Cut the third mushroom in pieces. Put the pieces, with the stems and peel, in a food processor and add the ham, scallion, garlic, and parsley. Purée until coarsely chopped. Tip the mixture into a bowl and stir in the oil, Madeira, pepper, and a little salt (the ham already adds salt). Taste and adjust the seasoning. Oil a small baking dish and put the mushroom caps in it. Pile the filling on top and cover with aluminum foil. Bake the mushrooms in the oven until tender, 25 to 30 minutes. Uncover during the last 10 minutes so the liquid evaporates. Serve warm.

GETTING AHEAD: Make the filling and stuff the mushrooms up to 6 hours ahead, storing them covered in the refrigerator. Bake them just before serving.

Salad of Mushrooms and Fennel

Be sure the mushrooms are fresh so they show white and firm beside the pale green fennel.

Serves 4

- **2 small fennel bulbs (about 1 pound)**
- **1/2 pound mushrooms**
- **3 ounces oil-cured black olives, pitted and halved**
- **3 to 4 tablespoons chopped fresh flat-leaf parsley**
- **2-ounce wedge of Parmesan cheese**

FOR THE VINAIGRETTE
- **juice of 1 lemon**
- **1 teaspoon Dijon mustard**
- **salt and pepper to taste**
- **1/2 cup olive oil**

Make the vinaigrette: Whisk the lemon juice with the mustard, salt, and pepper, then gradually whisk in the oil so the vinaigrette emulsifies and thickens slightly. Taste and adjust seasoning (remember the olives and Parmesan cheese will be salty).

Trim the stem and root of the fennel bulbs, reserving 4 tops for decoration, and halve them through the root. Slice them very thinly, cutting through stem and root, so the root holds each slice together. Toss with about half of the vinaigrette and marinate 1/2 to 1 hour.

Trim the stems of the mushrooms level with the caps and wipe the caps with a damp cloth. Set them stem side down on the cutting board and slice them as thinly as possible. Toss with the fennel mixture. Add the olives, parsley, and the rest of the vinaigrette and mix gently. Taste and adjust seasoning.

Pile the salad on 4 plates and decorate with the fennel tops. Hold the wedge of Parmesan cheese over each plate and, with a vegetable peeler, shave a few thin curls on top.

GETTING AHEAD: The fennel can be sliced ahead and left to marinate up to an hour, but the mushrooms and parsley should be added just before serving.

Salad of Mushrooms and Fennel

Mediterranean Mushroom Salad (*Mushrooms à la Grecque*)

This multipurpose recipe can be made with a variety of vegetables such as quartered baby artichokes, thickly sliced fennel, or florets of cauliflower or broccoli. Simply vary the cooking time.

Serves 6 as appetizer

> **2 tablespoons coriander seeds**
> **2 teaspoons black peppercorns**
> **2 bay leaves**
> **2 sprigs thyme**
> **¼ cup olive oil**
> **15 to 18 baby onions or shallots**
> **1 pound button mushrooms, trimmed**
>   **and quartered**
> **1 tablespoon tomato paste**
> **2 tomatoes, peeled, seeded, and chopped**
> **1 cup medium-dry white wine**
> **1 cup water**
> **juice of 1 lemon**
> **1 tablespoon chopped fresh dill**
> **1 tablespoon chopped fresh parsley**
> **salt to taste**

Tie coriander seeds, peppercorns, bay leaves, and thyme in a piece of cheesecloth. (If you like the crunch of coriander seeds, they can be left loose.) Heat the oil in a sauté pan or shallow saucepan, add the onions, and sauté until brown, 5 to 7 minutes. Add the mushrooms and stir in the tomato paste, tomatoes, white wine, water, lemon juice, spice bag, and a little salt. Bring the mixture to a boil and simmer uncovered, stirring often, until the onions and mushrooms are tender, 20 to 30 minutes.

At the end of cooking, the liquid should just cover the vegetables, but if there is too much, boil to reduce it. Stir in dill and parsley and let the vegetables cool. Discard the spice bag, then taste and adjust seasoning of the marinade. Serve the mushrooms warm or at room temperature.

GETTING AHEAD: Make these marinated vegetables a day or two ahead and store them, covered, in the refrigerator as flavor will mellow.

how to prepare wild mushrooms

Aren't we lucky to have so many wild mushrooms available almost everywhere, all year? Strictly speaking, most of them have been cultivated and are exotic, not wild. Never mind. They provide a simple treat with a whiff of adventure. Most common, and least expensive, are mild oyster mushrooms and meaty shiitake. Golden chanterelles add distinctive color, while boletus (also called cèpes or porcini) will perfume a whole dish of pasta or risotto at a price. Most valued of all are craggy morels with their intense perfume and color that shades from cappuccino to black. All these exotic varieties can be swapped one for the other. When you cannot find them fresh, dried wild mushrooms can be a good buy, particularly boletus and morels. Dried ones need a long soak of an hour or more in cold water, or an emergency 10 minutes in hot water before using.

1 To prepare wild mushrooms: Wipe mushrooms with a damp cloth or brush off any earth. Trim the stems. If the caps seem gritty, they can be rinsed quickly in cold water at this stage, but this is rarely necessary. Small wild mushrooms are usually left whole, large ones may be cut in chunks.

Sautéed Wild Mushrooms

I'd always insisted that butter, garlic, and parsley could not be equaled as companions for wild mushrooms—until I tasted chanterelles sautéed in olive oil with an undetectable touch of anchovy. You can use any type of wild mushroom, but you get what you pay for: oysters or shiitake will be pleasingly mild, while boletus (cèpes or porcini) will almost leap off the plate.

Serves 3

Clean 1 pound wild mushrooms and cut in large chunks. Heat 3 tablespoons olive oil in a frying pan and cook 2 finely chopped anchovy fillets and 2 chopped garlic cloves until the anchovy dissolves and the garlic is fragrant, about 1 minute. Add the mushrooms, 1 tablespoon lemon juice, and some pepper and sauté, stirring often, until the mushrooms are tender and all moisture has evaporated. If the mushrooms are dry, you may need to cover them when they start to cook. Allow 5 to 12 minutes of cooking time depending on the type of mushroom. When ready, stir in 2 tablespoons chopped fresh parsley, taste and adjust seasoning.

Fennel for Fish

The anise flavor of fennel has an affinity for fish, and this delicious sauté takes no time at all.

Serves 3 to 4

Thinly slice 2 fennel bulbs (about 1 pound), cutting through stem and root so the slices hold together. Melt 3 tablespoons butter in a large frying pan, add the fennel, and sprinkle with 2 teaspoons fennel seeds, salt, and pepper. Cover tightly with aluminum foil, add a lid, and cook over low heat so the fennel softens and cooks in its own juices until it is tender, 10 to 15 minutes. Remove the foil and lid, raise the heat, and sauté the fennel until lightly browned, 3 to 5 minutes. Stir in 2 tablespoons chopped fresh flat-leaf parsley and 2 teaspoons chopped fresh thyme, then taste and adjust seasoning.

how to choose and cook fennel

I love the taste of anise so of course I'm a fennel aficionado. The Italian habit of nibbling a slice or two of crisp raw fennel with an apéritif has strong appeal. So do all those marinated salads and gratins that include fennel, among other Mediterranean ingredients like tomatoes, zucchini, orange, Parmesan and goat cheese. Fennel can vary widely in quality, so look out for small pale green bulbs with a moist cut stem and no brown discoloration. Large bulbs can be quite fibrous.

Trim stems and root of the fennel bulb and halve it from the stems through the root. Set a half cut side down on the chopped board (as for an onion). Either slice crosswise, thickly or thinly according to the recipe, so the leaves of fennel fall apart, or slice from stem to root so each slice is held together by a piece of root. Fennel bulbs can also be chopped like an onion (page 32).

HOW TO PREPARE AND COOK WHOLE ARTICHOKES

I had an eccentric aunt who grew artichokes. They must have been the most prickly, least user-friendly artichokes ever, but as a child I loved pulling them apart, leaf by leaf, to nibble the meaty ends with their curiously bitter-sweet taste. Then came the challenge of removing the hairy central choke without leaving spikes behind—artichokes belong to the thistle family, and the choke is its infant purple flower. I still find these built-in artichoke defenses fun, and I can assure you they are easy to overcome. The best part comes last— a tender green disk for dipping in sauce. Like my aunt, I serve artichokes with melted butter flavored with fresh tarragon; other possibilities include lemon butter, citrus or herb vinaigrette, warm hollandaise, *aïoli*, and the roasted red pepper sauce I suggest here.

When choosing artichokes, look for firm, bright-colored globes with no brown patches on the leaves. (Note that I'm talking here about portion-sized globe artichokes, not the tender little heads that are sold with long edible stems.) You can keep raw artichokes, loosely wrapped in the salad drawer of the refrigerator, for 2 to 3 days. Cooked artichokes become rubbery in the refrigerator, so I leave them at room temperature a maximum of 12 hours. At table, you'll need extra-large plates, or bowls for discarded leaves.

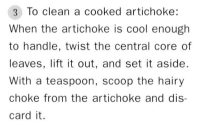

1 To trim an artichoke: Set the artichoke sideways on a board, grasp the head in one hand and the stem in another, and snap it. This pulls tough fibers from the artichoke heart.

2 Trim the base with a serrated knife so the artichoke sits flat. Cut off the pointed top of the artichoke parallel to the base. Since the cut surfaces of artichokes discolor quickly, rub them at once with a cut lemon wedge and drop them in a bowl of cold water.

3 To clean a cooked artichoke: When the artichoke is cool enough to handle, twist the central core of leaves, lift it out, and set it aside. With a teaspoon, scoop the hairy choke from the artichoke and discard it.

4 Turn the cone of leaves upside down and drop it into the center of the artichoke to form a shallow cup. Fill the cup with a sauce for serving.

Plain Boiled Artichokes

Bring a large pan of salted water to a boil and add a squeezed lemon half. Large artichokes require a pan of stockpot dimensions. Add the artichokes and press a folded dishtowel on top with a spoon, topping the towel with a pan lid or heatproof plate in order to keep the artichokes submerged. Simmer them for 30 to 45 minutes—cooking time varies a lot with age and size. To test, tug a leaf from near the center of the artichoke. If it yields easily, it is probably ready; nibble the leaf to make doubly sure. If not done, continue simmering 5 or 10 minutes longer. A well-cooked artichoke should be easy to eat but not so soft as to fall apart. A second test for tenderness is to pierce the base of the artichoke with the point of a knife. When done, drain artichokes in a colander, then leave them upside down on a rack to drain completely.

Artichokes Stuffed with Shrimp Salad

The same shrimp filling is delicious in hollowed out tomatoes.

Serves 2

Trim, boil, and clean the artichokes as described in Plain Boiled Artichokes. While they are cooking, mix 1/2 cup mayonnaise with 1/2 teaspoon Dijon mustard, 3 to 4 tablespoons chopped fresh tarragon, chervil, or chives, and salt and pepper. Fold in 1 cup cooked, peeled, chopped shrimp, taste and adjust the seasoning. When the artichokes are cool, fill them with the shrimp stuffing and top each one with a whole shrimp and a sprig of herb.

Artichokes with Roasted Red Pepper Coulis

Serve this eye-catching recipe warm or at room temperature so the smoky flavor of roasted red peppers is at its best.

Serves 4

4 large artichokes
1 lemon, halved
salt and pepper to taste

FOR THE COULIS
2 red bell peppers
small bunch of basil
2 tablespoons olive oil
1 pound tomatoes, seeded and chopped
1 garlic clove, chopped
2 scallions, including green parts, chopped

Trim, boil, and clean the artichokes as described in Plain Boiled Artichokes. While the artichokes are cooking, make the coulis: Roast and core the bell peppers (page 255). Cut them into chunks. Pull the basil leaves from the stems, reserving 4 sprigs for garnish. Coarsely shred the leaves. Heat the olive oil in a frying pan. Add the peppers, tomatoes, garlic, scallions, and basil with salt and pepper. Cover and simmer, stirring occasionally, until thickened, 15 to 20 minutes. Work the coulis in a food processor until puréed but still slightly chunky. Taste, adjust the seasoning, and set the coulis aside.

To finish: Set the artichokes on plates and spoon coulis into each cone. Garnish with a basil leaf and pass the remaining coulis separately. Serve the artichokes at room temperature.

CHAPTER TEN pastry fundamentals

To earn the title cook, you need to be able to put together pastry for a pie. Most of us have our favorites and Emma and I are no exception. She goes for the food processor, fast and clinical; I like to get my hands in the dough, the traditional way. That allows me to feel with my fingers if the fat is getting too warm and soft, and judge whether the crumbs are dry and need more water to bind them into a light, tender dough. It's all very tactile.

In this chapter I start with two versions of simple pastry dough: the plain pie pastry that is common in the U.S., and European-style pâte brisée. Both use the same ingredients but they are made differently: pie pastry is light and crumbly, while pâte brisée is pliable and easier to roll to a thin sheet. A third variation, biscuit dough, is made like pie pastry but with baking powder added so the dough rises in the oven to form homey toppings for pot pies filled with plenty of sauce. Finally, there is phyllo, which comes ready-prepared in frozen packages—today even Greek grandmothers hesitate to make phyllo at home.

Whatever the type of dough, we all agree that good pastry must be light and delicate. Much depends on the tender touch of the cook, but ingredients make a difference, too, most importantly the flour. Unbleached all-purpose flour, the type most commonly used, has variable levels of gluten, which is the protein that gives dough its elasticity. For pastry, gluten should be developed as little as possible, in contrast to pasta and bread doughs that need to be springy and resilient. Southern flour and many European flours have a comparatively low gluten content and make good pastry.

Butter gives outstanding flavor to pastry, while shortening lightens it. Lard yields a splendidly earthy dough that is characteristic of some regional recipes like the Yorkshire pork pies of my childhood. Some people ask if I use margarine and the answer is no. Margarine does not have the flavor of butter; furthermore, the firm type needed to make pastry does not seem to have any dietary advantages either. Olive oil enters the picture with flaky phyllo that is brushed with oil or melted butter to enrich and separate the layers. Nut oils such as walnut and hazelnut are alternatives. Egg yolks help make plain pastry doughs crumbly and rich, and water (or sometimes milk) binds them together. And don't forget that any pastry is bland without a dose of salt, and a bit of sugar added for sweet dough.

HOW TO MAKE PIE PASTRY

Pie pastry is the easiest and most versatile of all pastry doughs. Speed and a light touch are the key, so gluten in the flour is developed as little as possible. It helps to have a cool kitchen, cold butter and shortening, plus cold water—and cold hands, too, if you can manage it! (I was born with hot hands, designed by nature for making bread.) Finished pie pastry dough should be soft without being sticky and slightly rough. Quite a range of fat can be used: all butter for a rich dough; shortening for a crumbly dough with less flavor that's called "short dough"; or a mixture of the two if you want to hedge your bets. I was brought up with dough made with lard, tasty and surprisingly light.

Now we can move on to the fun—the fillings. Pie pastry's crumbly consistency and the taste of the chosen fat lend character to the finished dish. An all-butter crust, for instance, suits delicate fillings of seafood and vegetables such as asparagus, corn with bell peppers, or pumpkin with caramelized onions. A part butter, part shortening crust will be more crumbly and still have the flavor of butter. A pure shortening crust is right for hearty American pies such as beef pot pie. Mexicans make their tamale pies with lard. In Britain, a top crust of pie pastry covers steak and kidney pie, with a double crust used for fillings such as mushroom or spinach and anchovy in a cream sauce. Hungry anyone? I hope so!

1 Sift the flour and salt into a bowl. Add the fat and cut it into small pieces with a table knife held in each hand.

2 Rub with your fingertips until the mixture forms fine crumbs, lifting and crumbling to help aerate it. Lightness of touch as you rub is important at this stage.

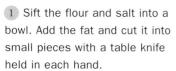

3 Add the water, and egg yolk if using, and mix quickly with a fork to form crumbs. You should start with the smallest quantity of liquid suggested, and then add more if the crumbs of dough seem dry as mixing proceeds.

4 When the flour mixture has formed even crumbs, test with your fingers to see if they are dry, and if so, work in 1 to 2 tablespoons more water. On the other hand, if crumbs seem wet and sticky, stop mixing at once. Sprinkle with 2 to 3 tablespoons of flour, toss the crumbs so they are coated, then continue mixing. The amount of liquid you need will depend on the heat and humidity of your kitchen, the dryness of the flour, and the moisture in the fat.

pie pastry pointers

* Pie pastry dough should cling together easily without being sticky. With too little water, the dough will crumble when rolled out and bake to be hard and dry; if too wet, the dough will be tough.

* Pie pastry dough can be wrapped and chilled up to 3 days in the refrigerator, or frozen. The dough will stiffen, so let it come to room temperature before rolling.

Plain Pie Pastry

This is the pie pastry recipe we always use at home, with half butter for good flavor and half shortening to cut the gluten and make a light crumbly dough.

Makes a 9½-inch pie shell

> **2 cups flour**
> **1 teaspoon salt**
> **5 tablespoons cold butter**
> **⅓ cup cold shortening or lard**
> **1 egg yolk (optional)**
> **¼ cup cold water, more if needed**

Sift the flour and salt into a bowl. Add the butter and shortening and use two knives or one of those pastry cutters designed to cut the fat in small pieces. With your fingertips, rub the mixture until fine crumbs form. Mix the egg yolk, if using, with the water and sprinkle over the crumbs. Stir quickly with a fork, tossing and turning to form crumbs again. If they are dry, sprinkle with 1 to 2 tablespoons more water and stir to form moist crumbs. Press the dough together with your fingers. It should be soft but not sticky. Knead it lightly a few times until you have a rough ball. Wrap it in plastic wrap and chill until firm, 15 to 30 minutes.

GETTING AHEAD: Pie pastry dough keeps well in the refrigerator up to 2 days, or it can be frozen. If chilling, wrap it loosely in plastic wrap—if too tightly wrapped, the dough tends to sweat and be sticky when you start to roll it.

All Butter Pie Pastry

For luxury pies, for example with a filling of seafood or chicken.

Makes a 9½-inch pie shell

In the recipe for Plain Pie Pastry, substitute 5 tablespoons more butter for the shortening or lard. Omit egg yolk and use 5 tablespoons water, more if needed.

All Shortening Pie Pastry

For American sweet and savory pies.

Makes a 9½-inch pie shell

In the recipe for Plain Pie Pastry, substitute ⅓ cup more shortening for the butter. Omit egg yolk and use 5 tablespoons water, more if needed.

Lard Pie Pastry

For traditional savory pies such as British steak and kidney pie.

Makes a 9½-inch pie shell

In the recipe for Plain Pie Pastry, use ⅔ cup lard instead of the butter and shortening. Omit the egg yolk and use 5 tablespoons water, more if needed.

how to make pie pastry dough in a food processor

Emma likes to make her pie pastry dough in a processor, and it certainly is speedy. To be sure the dough is light, use the pulse button in quick bursts. When the crumbs start to cling together, you've added enough water. Pâte brisée can also be mixed in a processor, but then the dough must be kneaded (*fraiser*) by hand. Put the flour in a processor with the salt. Work the pulse button 2 seconds to mix. Add the cold butter and shortening, cut into small pieces. Process, using the pulse button, until the mixture has formed fine crumbs, 10 to 15 seconds. Sprinkle crumbs with egg yolk, if using, and the water. Pulse again just until the crumbs start sticking together, about 30 seconds. Press them together with your fingers: if they seem dry, sprinkle with a tablespoon more water, pulse, and test again. When the crumbs cling lightly together, tip them onto a work surface and press them lightly into a ball. Wrap and chill the dough until firm, 15 to 30 minutes.

HOW TO MAKE PATE BRISEE

Pâte brisée uses the same ingredients as pie pastry but to different effect. (The French word *brisée* means broken and does not have an English equivalent.) Unlike pie pastry, which is handled as lightly as possible, pâte brisée is kneaded briefly to develop gluten in the flour just a little—the technical term for this, *fraiser*, is equally untranslatable. Kneading makes the dough pliable and easy to roll quite thinly to a variety of shapes.

Pâte brisée can be used as a top crust but it is more commonly associated with bottom and double crust pies, often with a rich savory filling. Quiches of all kinds, from the original Quiche Lorraine to contemporary versions laden with vegetables, do best with pâte brisée as the dough remains firm with moist fillings, especially when prebaked empty, or "blind" (page 286). Some of my favorites include an herbal Provençal mix of eggplant, zucchini, and tomato with garlic, and a perfumed, creamy mushroom tart with a lattice topping. Rolled very thin, pâte brisée is also easy to line into small molds for tartlets (page 288).

Unlike pie pastry, which is mixed in a bowl, pâte brisée is made on a flat work surface—unless you are Emma with her processor (I'll come to that later). The flour is tipped onto the surface (cool smooth marble if you have it), and swept into a wide circle with the back of your hand. Ground nuts are sometimes mixed in with the flour. Into the central well go the other ingredients. These will include fat (almost always butter), egg yolks for body and richness, a bit of salt, and some cold water. Other candidates include sugar and flavorings such as vanilla for sweet dough. Then the ingredients are combined to make a soft, slightly rough dough as you see in the pictures. So far, so good, but how does this differ from pie pastry? The answer is that pâte brisée has to be kneaded on the work surface so as to distribute the fat and assure a characteristically pliable consistency. It is this putty-like texture that makes it so easy to roll, and so resistant to moist fillings.

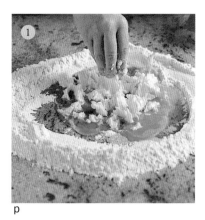

p

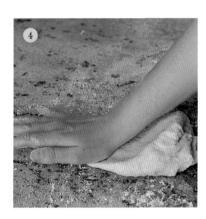

1 Have a pastry scraper or metal spatula ready. Sift the flour onto a work surface and sweep a large well in the center with the back of your hand. Pound the butter until pliable and add it to the well with the egg yolk, salt, sugar if using, and water. With the fingertips of one hand, pinch the central ingredients, dabbing and stirring for a minute or two until mixed.

2 With a pastry scraper, pull the flour into the central ingredients. Mix and cut the ingredients together using the pastry scraper until the water is absorbed. With practice, you'll find it easy to combine flour with the water so it does not run all over the counter.

3 With the tips of your fingers, work the flour with the other ingredients to form coarse crumbs, lifting them and letting them fall to aerate them. They should be tacky but if they seem dry, sprinkle them with 1 to 2 tablespoons more cold water and continue working a bit more. If sticky, add a little flour. Press the crumbs together in a ball. Here comes the split with pie pastry.

4 The dough must be kneaded *(fraiser)*: Lightly flour the work surface. Blend the dough by pushing it away from you with the heel of your hand then gathering it up. Rotate it through 90 degrees and repeat the action until it is very smooth, pliable as putty, and peels away from the work surface in one piece, 1 to 2 minutes. Shape it into a ball, wrap loosely in plastic wrap, and chill it until firm, 15 to 30 minutes.

how to make pâte brisée in a food processor

Put the flour in a processor with the salt, adding sugar for sweet pastry. Work 2 seconds to mix. Add cold butter, cut in small pieces. Process, using the pulse button, until the mixture has formed coarse crumbs, 10 to 15 seconds. Sprinkle the crumbs with egg yolk and cold water. Pulse again, just until the crumbs start sticking together, about 1 minute. Feel the crumbs with your fingers, and if they are dry and do not hold together, work in 1 to 2 tablespoons more water until they are slightly sticky. Tip them out onto the work surface and press them lightly into a ball. Blend the dough with the heel of your hand before chilling.

Plain Pâte Brisée

You'll find pâte brisée easy after a bit of practice, but on your first try the dough may seem elastic because you've overworked the gluten in the flour. If so, let it chill at least an hour for the gluten to relax.

Makes a 9 1/2-inch tart shell

> **1 3/4 cup flour**
> **1/2 cup (1 stick) butter**
> **1 egg yolk**
> **1/2 teaspoon salt**
> **3 tablespoons water, more if needed**

Sift the flour onto a work surface and make a well in the center. Pound the butter to soften it slightly and put it in the well with the yolk, salt, and water. Work the ingredients in the well together with the fingertips of one hand, dabbing and pinching so the butter softens and is partly mixed with the egg yolk and water. Using a pastry scraper, draw the flour in from the sides, mixing and cutting the ingredients together with the blade of the scraper.

When the butter has been mixed and cut into small chunks among the flour, start using both hands. With your fingertips, work the flour into the other ingredients until coarse crumbs form. If they are dry, sprinkle them with 1 or 2 tablespoons more water. When the crumbs are sticky, press them into a ball.

Work the dough on a lightly floured surface, pushing it away with the heel of your hand and gathering it up with your fingers until it is smooth, pliable, and peels away in one piece. Press it into a ball and wrap loosely in plastic wrap. Chill dough until firm, 15 to 30 minutes.

GETTING AHEAD: Pâte brisée dough keeps well in the refrigerator up to 2 days, or it can be frozen. Wrap it loosely in plastic wrap for the refrigerator—if too tightly wrapped, the dough tends to sweat and be sticky when you start to roll it.

White Wine Pastry Dough

Wine cuts the effects of gluten so the dough is easy to mix and roll, as well as having extra flavor. Use it for quiches, particularly of meat and seafood.

Makes a 9 1/2-inch tart shell

Substitute dry white wine for the water in the recipe for Plain Pâte Brisée.

Sour Cream Pastry Dough

A sturdy dough that is easy to work, excellent for meat pies and traditional for Russian *piroshki* turnovers.

Makes a 9 1/2-inch tart shell

In the recipe for Plain Pâte Brisée, substitute 3 tablespoons sour cream for the water.

Sweet Pâte Brisée (*Pâte Sucrée*)

A rich pliable dough that makes delicious cookie-like shells for open fruit tarts and tartlets.

Makes a 9 1/2-inch tart shell

In the recipe for Plain Pâte Brisée, add 1/2 cup sugar to the flour well with the butter. Omit the water and put 4 egg yolks instead of 1 in the well, with 1/2 teaspoon vanilla. Mix and knead the dough as described. Chill it thoroughly before rolling.

Sweet Almond Pastry Dough

A crumbly, tender pastry, delicious for cookies as well as sweet tart shells.

Makes a 9 1/2-inch tart shell

In the recipe for Plain Pâte Brisée, substitute 2/3 cup ground blanched almonds for half the flour. Mix the flour and almonds and make a well. Add 1/2 cup (1 stick) softened butter, 2 egg yolks, 1 tablespoon water, and 1/2 teaspoon vanilla or the grated zest of 1 lemon. Mix and knead the dough as described.

Brilliant Biscuits

What Southern brunch is complete without homemade biscuits? The dough is made just like pie pastry, with the addition of baking powder so the crust puffs in the oven. Often I use milk instead of water so the dough is more tender, and I like to include chopped herbs or flavorings such as toasted sesame or caraway seeds. Biscuit dough is also a favorite topping for savory pot pies. A single round is fine on individual pies, with several rounds arranged overlapping on larger ones.

1 Biscuit dough must be handled very lightly so, rather than rolling, it is usually patted out with your fist on a generously floured board to about a ¹/₂-inch thickness, then stamped into rounds.

Plain Biscuits

You can't go wrong with these classic plain biscuits. Spread them with butter and honey or jam, or layer them with thinly sliced ham and cheese.

Makes about 14 biscuits

> **2 cups flour**
> **1 tablespoon baking powder**
> **1 teaspoon salt**
> **4 tablespoons cold butter**
> **³/₄ cup milk, more if needed**
> **milk or melted butter for brushing the tops**
> **(optional)**

Preheat the oven to 425°F. Sift the flour into a large bowl with the baking powder and salt. Make a well in the center and add the butter. Cut it in small pieces using two table knives or a pastry blender. Rub the mixture with your fingertips until it forms fine crumbs, lifting

and crumbling to aerate it. Again make a well in the center. Add the milk and cut it in quickly with a knife to form coarse crumbs. If the mixture seems dry, add more milk. Mix the dough with your fingers just until it comes together.

Turn the dough onto a floured surface and knead lightly for a few seconds until smooth. With your fingers, pat it out to ¹/₂-inch thickness. Cut out rounds with a 2-inch cookie cutter and set them on a baking sheet. Press the scraps together and cut out more biscuits. If you like crusty biscuits, set them 1 inch apart. If you prefer soft sides, place them close together but not quite touching. Brush the tops with milk if you like, for browner tops. Bake until the biscuits are golden brown, 12 to 15 minutes. Serve hot.

GETTING AHEAD: Sure, you can bake biscuits ahead, but they never taste quite the same as when they are warm from the oven.

Herbed Biscuit Topping

A mixture of herbs or just plain parsley can be used in this dough, which is a variation of Plain Biscuit dough. I like to use it to cover chicken pot pie—you'll find a recipe on page 155. The biscuits are good on their own, too.

Makes enough topping for a large 10-inch pie or 6 individual pies

Preheat the oven to 425°F. In the recipe for Plain Biscuits, after cutting in the butter, stir 3 tablespoons chopped mixed fresh herbs or parsley into the pastry crumbs. Finish making and baking dough as directed.

HOW TO ROLL, SHAPE, AND BAKE PIES AND TARTS

Dough in hand, we can now get down to the business of rolling, shaping, and baking. A cold surface such as marble or granite is ideal for rolling pastry, or failing that, a countertop that is smooth (not made of wood). A rolling pin is a matter of personal preference—I like a heavy plain wooden cylinder, but others find it easier to manipulate a rolling pin that rotates on handles. In an emergency I use a slim wine bottle, an item commonly at hand in our home (it should be full as you need the weight, so drinking the wine must be deferred). Pans for pies and tarts vary from traditional metal or heatproof glass dishes to French-style tart pans with a removable base. Quiche dishes made of pottery, and with fluted sides, are often deeper and hold more filling.

Basically, there are three types of pie: top crust, bottom crust (often referred to as a shell), and double crust, with two layers of dough sealed around the edge in a decorative pattern. Top crusts are a simple matter of filling the pie pan, then brushing the rim with water or egg glaze so the dough adheres. The dough is rolled about an inch larger than the pie pan to allow for shrinkage.

Bottom crust pies (called tarts if the sides are vertical) act as containers—if the base of the pan is removable the pie can be unmolded. The difficulty with bottom crust pies is ensuring that the crust is fully cooked, especially if the filling is moist. Double crust pies suffer the same inconvenience. It helps to preheat a baking sheet so the pie shell starts cooking as soon as it goes in the oven. The best solution, however, is to bake the shell "blind" (page 286). This means that you partly bake an empty shell before adding the filling and cooking further. For fillings such as fresh fruit that need no cooking, the empty shell may be baked completely.

You can eliminate the work of pastry shells by baking pastry dough in flat sheets, like cookies. Firm fillings of goat cheese, vegetables such as asparagus, sautéed mushrooms with garlic and parsley, or tomatoes chopped in a coarse coulis and flavored with basil can be built into two- or three-layer towers. Serve them individually, or make one large pastry round and cut it in wedges for serving.

recommendations for rolling

* The diameter of pie and tart pans is measured at the widest point of the rim.
* When lining a pie or tart pan, pâte brisée is rolled a bit thinner than pie pastry and cooks to be tender and delicate though not as crumbly and light.
* If your dough seems elastic and shrinks when you try to roll it, it has been overworked. Best remedy is to slide it onto a floured baking sheet, cover it, and let it rest in the refrigerator at least 15 minutes for the gluten to relax. Then continue rolling.
* Pie pastry dough trimmings can be useful but when rerolled, the dough will never be as light as the original.
* Pie shells, whether baked or raw, freeze well; baked shells are best warmed briefly before you serve them, and raw dough should be thawed before baking. Store baked pie shells in an airtight container for a day and warm them through before using; shells of raw dough can be kept covered in plastic wrap in the refrigerator, also up to a day.

1 Butter or grease the pan (here a tart pan with removable base). Sprinkle the rolling pin and board lightly with flour (use just a little so you do not change the proportions of the dough). Start with the ball of dough in the shape you want at the finish: round for a round pan, square if you are aiming for a square or a rectangle. Pound the dough lightly with the rolling pin to flatten it somewhat, then start rolling from the nearest edge, working always away from you. Work quickly and firmly, keeping the dough moving on the work surface. Rotate the dough 90 degrees from time to time so the sheet expands to an even round, square or rectangle. To make rotating easy, when the sheet gets larger wrap it loosely around the rolling pin, turn it, lightly flour the work surface, and unwrap the dough onto the counter to be rolled again.

2 Once you've started rolling your dough, here's a quick guide to size: Mark the diameter of your pie pan with a finger on the rolling pin and compare this length with the dough. When the dough round is 2 inches larger than the diameter of the pan, it is the right size. Wrap the dough loosely around the rolling pin, and lift it gently into the pie pan. Unroll it over the pan, taking care not to stretch it or it will shrink during baking.

3 Lift the edges and press the dough well into the corners of the pan, leaving a generous overlap at the rim. If using a metal tart pan, roll the rolling pin over the pan to cut off the dough; if using a ceramic pie or quiche pan, trim the edge with a knife or scissors.

4 With your fingers, press the dough evenly up the sides of the pan and neaten the rim. It can be left plain or scalloped (see Pastry Finishes, page 285), as you prefer. Prick the base of the pie shell with a fork so it cooks more evenly and does not develop air pockets during baking. Preheat the oven. While it is heating, chill the tart shell until it is very firm (for quick results, I put it in the freezer).

Provençal Vegetable Tart

Aromatic Provençal vegetables baked in a pastry shell are the ideal summer lunch.

Serves 6 to 8

1 recipe Plain Pâte Brisée dough (page 278)
3 tablespoons olive oil
1 small onion, finely chopped
2 garlic cloves, chopped
6 medium tomatoes, peeled, seeded, and chopped
1 small eggplant, trimmed and diced
1 medium zucchini, trimmed and diced
salt and pepper to taste
bouquet garni of 2 bay leaves, 3 sprigs thyme, and 3 to 4 parsley stems
4 to 5 tablespoons browned breadcrumbs
½ cup grated Gruyère cheese
melted butter for brushing the tart pan

9½-inch tart pan with removable base

Make the Plain Pâte Brisée dough and chill it for 15 to 30 minutes.

For the filling: Heat the olive oil in a large frying pan, add the onion, and sauté until brown, 5 to 7 minutes. Stir in the garlic, tomatoes, eggplant, zucchini, salt, and pepper and add the bouquet garni, pushing it down among the vegetables. Cover and cook over medium heat, stirring often, until the vegetables soften, 8 to 12 minutes. Take off the lid, increase the heat, and continue cooking until the tomatoes break apart and the vegetables are tender, 15 to 18 minutes longer. Discard bouquet garni, taste and adjust seasoning, and let the filling cool.

Preheat the oven to 400°F and set a baking sheet on a low rack in the oven to heat. Brush the tart pan with melted butter. Roll out the pastry dough, line the tart pan, and chill for 15 minutes. Sprinkle breadcrumbs on the base of the pie shell and spread the vegetable filling on top. Sprinkle with grated cheese.

To finish: Bake the tart on the heated baking sheet until the pastry is browned and starts shrinking from the sides of the pan, 25 to 35 minutes. Let the tart cool for 5 minutes before unmolding, and serve it warm or at room temperature.

GETTING AHEAD: Provençal Vegetable Tart is best the day of baking, but you can make the tart shell and filling a day ahead and bake it up to 2 hours before serving.

how to make a lattice

Lightly flour the work surface and roll out two-thirds of the dough into a round 2 inches larger than the tart pan. Transfer the dough into the pan and press it into the bottom and sides. Trim the edge and press the dough up the sides, neatening the edge. Prick the base all over with a fork and chill until firm, at least 15 minutes. Arrange your filling in the base.

Roll out the remaining dough and trim it to an 11-inch square. Cut it in 3/4-inch strips. You should have 14 strips. Lay 7 strips over the filling, about 3/4 inch apart. Let the ends hang over the edge of the pan. Fold back alternate strips halfway. Lay an eighth strip across the middle of the unfolded strips. Unfold the folded strips over the crosswise strip, again leaving the ends to hang over the edge. Fold back alternate strips in between. Lay the ninth strip about 3/4 inch from the eighth. Continue until half of the surface is latticed. Turn the pan and repeat the process on the other half of the tart. Brush the ends of the strips with cold water and, using your fingers, seal the strips to the pastry shell, pinching off excess dough. Brush the lattice with the egg glaze and chill the tart for 15 minutes.

Maryland Ham Pie

On Maryland's Eastern Shore, the Easter ham is often sliced, layered, and baked with spicy greens. Here country ham and greens are packed in a pie, ideal for a party. I often cover the tart with a lattice of pastry strips, but a simple round of pastry as a lid would do fine, too. Serve the pie hot or at room temperature.

Serves 6 to 8

> **Plain Pâte Brisée dough (page 278), made with ³⁄₄ cup (1¹⁄₂ sticks) butter, 2¹⁄₂ cups flour, 2 egg yolks, 1 teaspoon salt, ¹⁄₃ cup water, more if needed**
>
> **5 or 6 leaves of kale or green cabbage**
>
> **green leaves of a bunch of celery**
>
> **green tops of 4 to 6 scallions**
>
> **¹⁄₂ teaspoon dried hot red pepper flakes**
>
> **¹⁄₂ teaspoon mustard seed**
>
> **¹⁄₂ teaspoon celery seed**
>
> **a few drops of Tabasco**
>
> **salt and pepper to taste**
>
> **melted butter for brushing the pan**
>
> **¹⁄₂ pound cooked sliced country ham, cut in julienne strips**
>
> **¹⁄₂ cup heavy cream**
>
> **2 egg yolks**
>
> **1 egg whisked with ¹⁄₂ teaspoon salt for pastry glaze**

9¹⁄₂-inch tart pan with removable base

Make and chill the Plain Pâte Brisée dough. For the filling: Wash and drain the kale, celery leaves, and scallion tops and shred them. Bring a pan of salted water to a boil and boil the greens until wilted, 2 to 3 minutes. Drain and run them under cold water, then squeeze them with your fists to remove excess water. Mix them in a bowl with the hot red pepper flakes, mustard and celery seeds, Tabasco, and salt and pepper. Set the greens aside.

Brush the tart pan with melted butter. Set aside about one-third of the pastry dough. Roll out the remaining two-thirds and line the pan. Chill the shell until firm, at least 15 minutes.

Spread half the ham in the pie shell and top with the greens. Mix the cream and egg yolks and spoon over the greens. Top with remaining ham. Roll out the remaining dough, trim it to an 11-inch square, and cut it in strips to make a lattice topping (see opposite page). Brush the lattice with the egg glaze and chill the pie for 15 minutes. Preheat the oven to 375°F and set a baking sheet on a low rack to heat.

Bake the pie on the heated baking sheet until the pastry is browned and crisp, 35 to 45 minutes. Let the pie cool on a wire rack. To unmold it, set it on an upturned bowl so that the pan rim slips down over the bowl. Using a metal spatula, slide the pie from the base onto a flat serving plate.

GETTING AHEAD: This pie is equally good hot or at room temperature, so make it up to 8 hours ahead and warm it briefly before serving.

Maryland Ham Pie

Marvelous Mushroom Tart

This tart, using simply button mushrooms, tastes marvelously rich, equally good hot or at room temperature.

Serves 6 to 8

> **Plain Pâte Brisée dough (page 278), made with**
> **¾ cup (1½ sticks) butter, 2½ cups flour,**
> **2 egg yolks, 1 teaspoon salt, ⅓ cup water,**
> **more if needed**
> **3 tablespoons butter, more for brushing the pan**
> **2 shallots, finely chopped**
> **1 garlic clove, finely chopped**
> **1 pound button mushrooms, chopped**
> **2 tablespoons flour**
> **1¾ cups heavy cream**
> **3 tablespoons chopped fresh parsley**
> **salt and pepper to taste**
> **1 egg whisked with ½ teaspoon salt for**
> **pastry glaze**
>
> **9½-inch tart pan with removable base**

Make the Plain Pâte Brisée dough, and chill it 15 to 30 minutes.

For the filling: Melt the butter in a skillet and fry the shallots and garlic until fragrant and soft, 1 to 2 minutes. Add the mushrooms and cook over high heat, stirring often, until all the moisture has evaporated, 5 to 7 minutes. Stir in the flour then the cream and cook the filling, stirring until it thickens enough to just pour. Stir in the parsley, taste, and adjust the seasoning. Set the filling aside to cool.

Brush the tart pan with melted butter. Roll out the dough and line the pan as in Maryland Ham Pie. Chill until firm, at least 15 minutes.

Spread the mushroom filling in the base of the chilled tart shell. Top the pie with a lattice (page 282), chill until firm, and bake as directed in Maryland Ham Pie.

GETTING AHEAD: This tart refrigerates well, so make it up to a day ahead and warm it in a low oven just before serving. It can be frozen for up to 3 months.

Cornish Pasties

A pasty is a pastry case containing meat, vegetables, and sometimes a spoonful or two of applesauce squashed into one end as dessert.

Makes 3 pasties

> **1 recipe Plain Pie Pastry dough (page 275)**
> **1 pound beef chuck**
> **3 medium potatoes**
> **3 medium carrots**
> **2 onions, chopped**
> **salt and pepper to taste**
> **grated nutmeg to taste**
> **small bunch of thyme**
> **½ cup beef stock or water**
> **3 to 6 chunks of apple (optional)**
> **1 egg whisked with ½ teaspoon salt for**
> **pastry glaze**

Preheat the oven to 350°F. Trim the beef and cut it in ½-inch cubes. Peel and cut the potatoes and carrots in chunks like the beef. Mix them with the onions, salt, pepper, and a generous grating of nutmeg. Mix vegetables and thyme with the beef in a small casserole and add the stock or water. Cover and cook in the oven, stirring occasionally, until beef and vegetables are very tender, 1¼ to 1½ hours. They should be fairly dry, so remove the lid if necessary toward the end of cooking. Discard thyme sprigs, taste and adjust seasoning, including nutmeg, and let the filling cool.

Make the Plain Pie Pastry dough and chill it 15 to 30 minutes. Divide it in thirds and roll each portion to an 8-inch round. Spoon the filling along the center of each round. If you like, add a bonus of some apple at one end. Brush edges of dough with glaze and pull the sides up over the filling to meet in the middle to make a boat shape. Seal this central seam with your fingers across the top of the pie, then flute it and poke a small hole for steam to escape. Brush the pasties with glaze and chill until firm, about 15 minutes.

Preheat the oven to 400°F. Bake the pasties in the oven until browned and crisp, 30 to 35 minutes. Serve hot or at room temperature.

Pastry Finishes

Your pastry dough has been made, rolled, and shaped, but it is still not quite ready to go in the oven. Now come the finishing touches that can transform plain pastry into a triumph. Most important is a glaze, usually of egg, brushed on the surface so it gleams with a golden shine. I cannot resist showing you how to make pastry decorations, the scalloped borders and leaves that make a plain pie crust festive. I'm including just a few.

egg glazes for pastry

Glaze made from egg yolk or a whole egg, brushed on before baking, adds brilliance to pastry, and is also useful for glueing decorations or holding layers of dough in place. Apply glaze with a pastry brush in a smooth layer and, for extra color, leave it for 10 to 15 minutes to dry, then add a second coat.

To make egg glaze, whisk a whole egg and a half teaspoon of salt in a small bowl with a fork until the egg is broken up. (An egg yolk and a tablespoon of water can be substituted for the whole egg). Let the glaze stand at least 5 minutes until it is smooth (salt breaks down albumin in the egg white). Glaze made from 1 egg goes a long way, so you rarely need to make more.

pastry finishes for a pie

Decorations not only add a personal finish, they often serve a practical purpose. A scalloped edge, for instance, is a useful seal for a double-crust pie. Leaves will cover blemishes in a dough crust and also disguise the vent that must be cut in a top crust to let steam escape.

1 With a small knife or scissors, trim the top crust even with the bottom crust. Press the edges together to seal them. Put your forefinger and thumb on the edge of dough and, with the forefinger of the other hand, push the dough outward to make a scallop. Brush the dough with egg glaze. To shape leaves, cut pointed ovals with a small knife, brush them with egg glaze, and mark veins with the back of the knife. Arrange leaves on the pie crust and brush them with glaze also. Chill the pie thoroughly to set the dough before baking.

HOW TO BLIND BAKE PIES AND TARTS

Oddly enough, here it's Emma who is the traditionalist, not me. As a lover of quiche, she goes to the trouble of first baking a pastry shell "blind," without a filling, so the pastry is thoroughly cooked on the bottom before adding the moist custard filling of eggs and cream or milk. I grant that partially or completely baking a pie shell before filling it helps guarantee crisp, brown pastry. It is no more than an extra step in the process.

You start by lining the pan with dough and chilling it as usual. Chilling beforehand is important, otherwise the dough will shrink and collapse when it goes in the oven. Then the cold, firm shell of dough is lined with foil or parchment paper—I find foil easier to shape—and filled with a layer of dried beans or rice to hold the base flat so air pockets do not develop.

Empty pastry shells are baked in quite a hot oven; again the aim is to set the dough's shape before it can melt and collapse. After 15 minutes or so, when the edges of the dough are lightly browned, it is safe to remove the foil and beans. The pastry shell will still be damp on the bottom, so it must be dried for a few minutes at a lower temperature. If it is to be further cooked with a filling inside (as with quiche), take the partially baked shell from the oven. If you want it fully cooked, continue baking.

For these open pies, the filling itself is often the main eye-catcher, with no further decoration needed. The gleaming surface of a custard-filled quiche is temptation enough, surrounded by its golden, neatly scalloped border of pastry. A browned topping of Gruyère or Cheddar cheese is equally seductive—remember to rotate a pie once or twice in the oven so the surface browns evenly. Vegetable combinations have their own colorful appeal. However, plain fillings cry out for a lattice topping, or a decoration of leaves (see Pastry Finishes, page 285). The extra bit of time pays off!

1 Line the pie pan with dough, prick it all over with a fork, and chill until very firm, 15 to 30 minutes. Preheat the oven to 425°F and set a baking sheet on a low rack to heat. Trim a round of aluminum foil or parchment paper about 2 inches larger than the diameter of the pan and crumple it to make it more pliable. Press it into the pie shell, pushing it down into the corners. Fill it three-quarters full with dry beans or rice to hold the base flat. (You can use the beans or rice again and again.)

2 Bake the pie shell in the oven until the dough is brown around the edges and firm enough to hold its shape, about 15 minutes. Take the pie pan, still on the baking sheet, from the oven and lift out the foil and beans. To partially bake the pie shell: Lower the oven heat to 375°F and continue cooking until the bottom pastry is dry, 5 to 10 minutes. At this stage, remove the pie shell and let it cool if it is to be cooked further after filling has been added. To fully bake the pie shell: After removing the beans, lower the oven heat to 375°F and continue baking until the pastry is golden brown and has begun to shrink from the sides of the pan, 8 to 12 minutes longer.

the shell game

* Don't forget a brushing of egg glaze (see Egg Glazes for Pastry, page 285) for your border decoration to shine.

* A liquid filling such as the custard in quiche can easily slop over the edges when you move it to the oven. Spread the filling in the shell, put the tart pan on the oven shelf, and only then add the custard.

* To help prevent moist fillings from soaking a prebaked pie shell, sprinkle the base of the shell with dry breadcrumbs.

* Pans with a removable base are designed for unmolding: Let the pastry cool for 5 minutes. Turn a small bowl upside down and set the base of the tart pan on top so the sides slip down. Using a metal spatula, slide the tart shell onto a rack to cool completely. Or that's what the books say. I often leave a pie shell in the pan until I've filled it, so the weight of the filling does not collapse the sides. Don't try to unmold a baked pie shell if you are using a pie pan with sloping sides.

Quiche with Country Pâté

French-style country pâté makes a simple, deliciously meaty filling for quiche.

Serves 6 to 8

Partially blind bake a 9 1/2-inch tart shell. Dice 6 ounces country pâté and spread it over the base of the shell. Make a custard by whisking 3 eggs with 1 1/2 cups heavy cream or crème fraîche. Whisk in 3 tablespoons chopped mixed fresh herbs (parsley, chives, tarragon, or basil) with salt and pepper. Pour the custard over the pâté and bake in a preheated 375°F oven until the filling is set and lightly browned, 35 to 40 minutes.

Killer Quiche Lorraine

All the pundits say that authentic Quiche Lorraine should not contain cheese, but I find the addition of just a few thin slices of Gruyère transforms quiche into a killer.

Serves 6 to 8

> 1 recipe Plain Pâte Brisée dough (page 278)
> 1 tablespoon butter, more for brushing the tart pan
> 7 ounces lean bacon, diced
> 2 ounces thinly sliced Gruyère cheese
> 3 eggs
> 1 1/2 cups heavy cream or crème fraîche
> salt and pepper to taste
> freshly grated nutmeg to taste
>
> 9 1/2-inch pie pan or tart pan with removable base

Make and chill the Plain Pâte Brisée dough. Brush the tart pan with melted butter, line it with the pastry (page 281), and chill until firm, about 30 minutes. Preheat the oven to 425°F and put a baking sheet on a low rack to heat.

Line the pie shell with aluminum foil and fill with dry beans or rice. Put the pan on the heated baking sheet and bake the shell until the edges of the pastry are lightly browned and firm, about 15 minutes. Remove the foil and beans, lower the oven heat to 375°F, and continue cooking, 5 to 10 minutes longer, until the pastry is no longer damp. Remove the shell and leave it to cool. Leave the baking sheet in the oven.

Melt the butter and sauté the bacon in it until brown and crisp. Drain and sprinkle the bacon over the base of the tart shell. Top it with the sliced cheese. Whisk the eggs and cream together in a bowl and season with salt, pepper, and a generous grating of nutmeg. Put the tart shell on the hot baking sheet and pour the egg and cream mixture over the bacon and cheese. Bake until the filling is set and lightly browned, 30 to 35 minutes. Serve warm or at room temperature.

GETTING AHEAD: Quiche Lorraine can be baked and kept up to 12 hours in the refrigerator. Warm it in a low oven just before serving.

Pancetta and Fennel Tart

A tempting Italian version of Quiche Lorraine. For a lighter tart, I use half cream, half milk.

Serves 6 to 8

Partially blind bake a 9$^{1}/_{2}$-inch tart shell. Dice 7 ounces pancetta and fry it in 1 tablespoon butter until lightly browned, stirring often, 5 to 7 minutes. Trim, halve, and thinly slice a medium bulb of fennel and stir it into the pancetta with $^{1}/_{2}$ teaspoon fennel seed, a bit of salt, and pepper. Cover and cook over low heat, stirring often, so the fennel softens and cooks in its own juices, until it is very tender and lightly browned, 15 to 20 minutes. Spread filling in the tart shell. Mix 2 eggs with 1 cup heavy cream or crème fraîche, salt if needed (the pancetta is already salty), and pepper, and pour into the tart shell. Bake in a preheated 375°F oven until the filling is set and lightly browned, 30 to 35 minutes.

Catchall Cheese Quiche

The more varied the bits of cheese for this recipe, the better. Ideally, you'll round up a slice or two of goat cheese, a half cup of crumbled blue, and something sharp for grating such as Cheddar, Gruyère, or Parmesan. The same filling does well in tartlets, too.

Serves 6 to 8

Partially blind bake a 9$^{1}/_{2}$-inch tart shell. Melt 2 tablespoons butter and sauté 2 thinly sliced onions with salt and pepper until lightly browned, 5 to 8 minutes. Spread them in the tart shell and top with $^{1}/_{2}$ pound sliced, diced, or grated mixed cheeses, spreading them evenly over the onions. Whisk 3 eggs with 1$^{1}/_{2}$ cups milk, salt, pepper, and a generous grating of nutmeg until mixed, then pour into the tart shell. Bake in a preheated 375°F oven until the filling is set and lightly browned, 30 to 35 minutes.

HOW TO SHAPE AND BLIND BAKE TARTLETS

To line a tartlet mold, you can use either pie pastry or pâte brisée. So the dough does not collapse during baking, it must be lined with foil or with another mold to hold the sides of the shell in place. Tartlet shells are fragile, so let them cool to tepid before unmolding them. When filling shells after they are baked, it helps to replace them in the molds for stability, removing them after filling them.

Leek Tartlets with Sage and Hazelnuts

At home in Burgundy, our garden abounds in leeks, hazelnuts, and bushes of sage, hence these tempting tartlets are the perfect lunch or light supper. When I'm short on time, I buy ready baked tartlet shells, the best I can find.

Serves 6

> **1 recipe Plain Pâte Brisée dough (page 278)**
> **$^{1}/_{3}$ cup peeled hazelnuts**
> **2 leeks (about $^{1}/_{2}$ pound)**
> **salt and pepper to taste**
> **melted butter for the pans**
> **$^{1}/_{4}$ cup mascarpone**
> **1$^{1}/_{2}$ cups heavy cream**
> **2 tablespoons chopped fresh sage**
> **generous grating of fresh nutmeg, more to taste**
> **$^{1}/_{4}$ cup grated Parmesan cheese**
>
> **six 4$^{1}/_{2}$-inch tartlet pans**

Make and chill the Pâte Brisée dough. To toast the hazelnuts, preheat the oven to 350°F. Put them on a tray and bake in the oven until browned, 12 to 15 minutes. Let cool. Put the nuts in a plastic bag and coarsely crush with the base of a heavy pan. Increase the oven heat to 425°F.

Cook the leeks: Trim leeks, leaving some of the green tops. Split them lengthwise and cut crosswise into $^{3}/8$-inch slices. Rinse them thoroughly in a bowl of cold water and transfer to a colander, lifting leeks out with your hands so grit is left behind. Bring a large pan of salted water to a boil, add leeks, and simmer until tender, 5 to 7 minutes. Drain, rinse with cold water, and drain again thoroughly. Season them with salt and pepper.

Make the tartlet shells: Brush the tartlet pans with melted butter. Roll out the Pâte Brisée dough, cut 6-inch rounds, and line the pans. Chill thoroughly, then line them with aluminum foil and beans and bake them blind until the pastry is firm and the edges are lightly browned, 8 to 10 minutes. Remove the foil and beans and let the shells cool in the pans. Lower the oven heat to 350°F again.

To fill the tartlets: Stir the mascarpone, cream, sage, nutmeg, salt, and pepper together

in a small saucepan and bring this sauce just to a boil. Remove from the heat and stir in the Parmesan cheese. Taste and adjust seasoning, including nutmeg. Spread leeks in the tartlet shells with all but 2 tablespoons of the hazelnuts. Spoon the cream sauce on top, covering the filling completely. Sprinkle top with the reserved hazelnuts.

To finish: Bake the tartlets until the filling is very hot and bubbling and the dough is browned, 15 to 20 minutes. Serve hot, or just warm.

GETTING AHEAD: The tartlet shells can be baked blind, filled, and kept up to 4 hours in the refrigerator. Finish cooking them just before serving.

1 To line tartlet molds with dough: Butter or grease the molds. Roll the dough quite thinly, 1/8 inch or less. With a plain or fluted cutter, stamp out rounds about 3/4 inch larger than the diameter of the molds and transfer them to the molds. Press dough into the base of the molds with your fingers. Push the dough up above the rim of the mold to make a deep shell. Prick the dough with a fork and chill until very firm, 15 to 30 minutes. Preheat the oven to 425°F.

2 To line and blind bake tartlet shells: The simplest method is to line the pastry shells with a tartlet mold of slightly smaller diameter. Alternatively, crumple a round of aluminum foil and press it into the base of the chilled tartlet shell, smoothing the foil up the sides, and add dry beans or rice to the foil. Set the molds on a baking sheet.

3 To partially bake the tartlet shells: Bake them in the oven until the edges of the tartlets are light gold and the dough is firm, 8 to 10 minutes. To fully bake the tartlet shells: Remove liner mold or the foil and beans and continue baking until the dough is browned, 8 to 12 minutes longer.

HOW TO SHAPE AND BAKE PHYLLO DOUGH

Phyllo is fun, or so I always thought until I landed on live television with a bad batch of dough, with leaves that refused to peel apart. Ever since, I've taken care to have a backup package of phyllo on hand in case of an emergency. Don't even think of making phyllo at home—everyone collects it from the frozen section of the nearest market, and I do the same. Store it in the freezer, and before use, let it thaw slowly for at least 6 hours (or longer in the refrigerator).

Phyllo is used by stacking the dough in layers, brushing each one with oil or melted butter to keep it moist and flaky. You'll find every brand of phyllo differs in size and thickness. Recipes will give dimensions for the finished pie or package, and it's not a problem to cut and shape your dough

accordingly. Here, for example, we're making a big phyllo pie filled with spinach and ricotta, a favorite for small pastries, too. The dough is draped into the tart pan and the excess folded back to make a decorative edge. For small pastries, you'll find ideas below. Look out for many more in displays at ethnic bakeries.

Fillings for layered pastries must be pungent—consider salty ingredients such as feta cheese, goat cheese, olives, ham, and anchovies. A touch of green herbs, particularly parsley and chives, is helpful. In the oven, a moderate, steady heat is important so the pastry leaves bake through. It's tempting to shape pretty, fluffy decorations from just a few layers of phyllo, but take care as they scorch easily, baking faster than the rest.

1 To make a phyllo pie: Unroll the package of dough onto a dampened dish towel. Brush a quiche or tart pan with olive oil or melted butter. Uncover the dough sheets, brush the top one with oil or butter, and transfer it to the pan, letting the edges overlap. Brush another layer of dough with oil or butter and lay it at a slight angle to the first—you'll be using 12 sheets and they should follow the hours on a clock.

2 Brush and add 2 more sheets, then cover the remaining dough with the damp towel.

3 Spread half the filling (here spinach with ricotta cheese) over the 4 sheets of dough. Continue adding sheets of dough to make another layer of 4, then top with the remaining spinach and more dough to make 12 sheets.

4 Brush the top of the pie with oil or butter. Loosely roll the overlapping dough back on top of the pie to form a decorative edge. Sprinkle with a little more oil or butter.

Phyllo Pie with Spinach and Ricotta

If you substitute feta for the ricotta, you'll have the classic Greek spanakopita.

Serves 8

12 sheets phyllo dough (about ½ pound), more for decorating the pie (optional)
4 tablespoons butter, more if needed
⅓ cup olive oil, more if needed

FOR THE FILLING
2 packages (10 ounces each) frozen chopped spinach
3 tablespoons olive oil
2 onions, finely chopped
freshly grated nutmeg to taste
salt and pepper to taste
½ pound ricotta cheese
12 anchovy fillets, finely chopped

11-inch quiche pan or tart pan with removable base

Make the filling: Defrost the spinach and coarsely chop it. Heat the olive oil in a large sauté pan. Add the onions and sauté, stirring until soft but not brown, 3 to 4 minutes. Stir in the chopped spinach, nutmeg, salt, and pepper. Cook, stirring, until very hot and any liquid has evaporated, about 2 minutes. Remove from the heat and stir in the ricotta cheese and anchovies. Taste, adjust the seasoning, including nutmeg, and leave the filling to cool.

Preheat the oven to 350°F. Melt the butter with the olive oil. Brush the tart pan with melted butter and oil. Lay a damp dish towel on the work surface and unroll the phyllo on it. Brush the top sheet with butter and oil and transfer it to the pan. Brush the next sheet with butter and oil and lay it on the first sheet at a slight angle. Continue brushing and layering 2 more sheets, then cover the rest of the phyllo with a damp towel. Spread half the filling over the phyllo in the tart pan. Continue adding layers of phyllo and the rest of the filling, finishing with layers of phyllo.

Brush the top of the pie with butter and oil and roll and neaten the edges. If you like, cut another sheet of phyllo into 2-inch strips and crumple them lightly into loose round flowers. Arrange them on top of the pie, brush with butter and oil, and bake until the pie is lightly puffed, crisp, and evenly browned, 50 to 60 minutes. (If it starts to brown too much before the end of cooking, cover it loosely with aluminum foil.) Serve the pie warm or at room temperature.

GETTING AHEAD: Spinach phyllo pie can be made up to 8 hours ahead and refrigerated; warm it in a low oven before serving.

phyllo facts

* Because sheets of phyllo are so thin, they dry out easily. When you are not working with them they must be kept covered with a slightly dampened dish towel, or the plastic sheet that is included in most packages.
* Before baking, a completed pie or pastry needs a brush of melted butter or oil to moisten the top layer (sweet pastries are often glazed with honey or sugar syrup).
* Too many layers or a filling that is very moist will make the pastry heavy.
* Phyllo need not be chilled before baking.
* Baked phyllo pastries keep well, and need only to be warmed briefly before serving. Freezing is the best way to store pastries that are shaped and ready to bake; wrap them carefully and they will keep well for a month or two. Thaw them before baking.
* Leftover phyllo dough can be refrozen, but it will dehydrate if not tightly sealed.
* Don't count on leftover dough being usable; always have a fresh package ready in case the layers won't peel apart

how to shape phyllo packages

Phyllo packages are terrific fingerfood—they're easy to pick up yet keep the contents a surprise. A single layer of dough makes two cocktail-sized packages and can be folded several ways into triangles, rolls, or purses. Start by brushing the dough with melted butter or oil, according to the recipe, and add a teaspoonful of filling (don't overdo it or the packages will leak). The filling should be intense; Mediterranean flavors such as tapenade (page 119) and the feta cheese mixture below are traditional. Use only a small amount of filling and wrap it quite loosely so it does not burst in the heat of the oven.

1   To shape triangles: Brush a sheet of phyllo dough with olive oil and cut it lengthwise in half. Fold each rectangle in half lengthwise. Put a small teaspoonful of filling at one end. Lift a corner of dough and fold it diagonally over the filling to cover it and make a triangle. Fold the triangle over to the first side. Keep folding, as you would fold a flag, until all the dough is used.

To shape rolls: Cut a buttered or oiled sheet of dough in half lengthwise. Fold each rectangle in half lengthwise. Spread a line of filling along one short edge, leaving a 3/4-inch border. Fold the border inward at both ends, then roll the dough to enclose the filling.

To shape purses: Cut a buttered or oiled sheet of dough in 6 more-or-less even squares. Layer 2 squares, setting each at an angle to the other. Add a small spoonful of filling. Gather up the dough to form a purse and twist, fluffing the corners of dough. Repeat with the remaining squares of dough.

Phyllo Cheese Triangles

Dry aged feta is best in these little pastries, in Greek called *tiropetes*, that can be made small for cocktails, or larger as an appetizer.

Makes about thirty-six 2-inch pastries

Crumble 1 cup dry feta cheese and beat until smooth with 1 egg yolk, 1/2 teaspoon ground black pepper, and a generous grating of fresh nutmeg. Preheat the oven to 400°F and oil a baking sheet. Cut 18 sheets of phyllo (3/4 pound) lengthwise. Brush 2 strips lightly with olive oil and fold them in half lengthwise. Put a teaspoonful of filling at one end of each strip and fold in triangles as illustrated. Set the triangles on the baking sheet and continue making more. If you work fast, you will not have to cover the dough. Bake in the preheated oven until the triangles are puffed and brown, 12 to 15 minutes.

Caponata Phyllo Purses

Caponata is Sicilian, an eggplant and celery salad that is so highly seasoned as to be almost a pickle, a perfect filling for phyllo purses. Small purses make good hors d'oeuvre, while three on a bed of peppery greens are a great appetizer.

Makes about 24 purses

> **12 sheets phyllo dough (about ½ pound)**
> **⅓ cup olive oil for brushing the phyllo,**
>   **more if needed**

> **FOR THE CAPONATA**
> **¼ cup red wine vinegar**
> **¼ cup pitted green olives**
> **1½ tablespoons capers, drained**
> **1½ teaspoons sugar**
> **4 tablespoons olive oil**
> **1 medium eggplant (about 1 pound),**
>   **diced including peel**
> **salt and pepper to taste**
> **4 to 5 stalks of celery, sliced**
> **4 ounces canned tomatoes, drained and chopped**
> **1½ teaspoons tomato paste**

Make the caponata: Combine the vinegar, olives, capers, and sugar in a pan, simmer 2 minutes, and set aside. Heat 3 tablespoons of the olive oil in a sauté pan or wok, add the eggplant with salt and pepper, and fry, stirring, until tender and lightly browned, 10 to 12 minutes. Remove the eggplant and set it aside. Heat the remaining oil in the pan and fry the celery until tender, 4 to 5 minutes. Stir in the eggplant, vinegar mixture, tomatoes, and tomato paste. Simmer the caponata, stirring often, until dense and very thick, 15 to 20 minutes. Taste, adjust seasoning, and leave to cool.

Preheat the oven to 400°F and brush a baking sheet with oil. To shape the purses: Lay a damp dish towel on the work surface and unroll the phyllo on it. Cut the sheets in half lengthwise and then crosswise to make 5- to 6-inch squares. (You may have some leftover trimmings.) Brush a square with oil and transfer it to the work surface. Brush a second square and lay it on the first, at a 45-degree angle. Cover the remaining phyllo with another damp towel. Spoon a heaping tablespoon of caponata in the center of a square and bunch the phyllo up and around the filling, pinching it to make a purse with a frill of pastry at the top. Set it on the baking sheet. Repeat with more phyllo and the remaining filling. Brush the pastry frills with olive oil.

Set the baking sheet on a low rack in the oven and bake the purses until browned, 12 to 15 minutes.

GETTING AHEAD   Fill and shape the purses ahead of time. They hold up to 4 hours, covered, in the refrigerator, or they can be frozen for up to 1 month.

Curried Turkey Purses

This quick curry makes a tasty filling for phyllo packages or Curry Crêpes (page 110).

Makes 16 to 20 purses

In a medium saucepan, heat 2 tablespoons oil and fry a chopped onion until golden brown, 5 to 7 minutes. Stir in a chopped garlic clove and cook until fragrant, 1 to 2 minutes. Stir in 1½ tablespoons curry powder and cook also until fragrant, about 1 minute. Add ½ pound turkey, cut in ½-inch cubes, and stir to coat. Add 2 tomatoes, peeled, seeded and chopped and ½ cup water with salt and pepper. Simmer, covered, 20 to 25 minutes, until the turkey is tender. Uncover and cook over high heat to thicken the sauce if necessary. Taste and adjust the seasoning, including curry powder. Leave to cool. Shape and bake the phyllo purses as in the recipe for Caponata Phyllo Purses.

MAIN BOOKS CONSULTED

The following books have been a particular help in researching *The Good Cook*. We all have our favorite works of reference and these are some of mine; most, but not quite all, are recent works, often released by one publisher in New York and another in London.

Boni, Ada, *Italian Regional Cooking*, Thomas Nelson, 1969.

Child, Julia and Jacques Pépin, *Julia and Jacques: Cooking at Home*, Knopf, 1999.

Cook's Illustrated: *The Best Recipe*, Boston Common Press, 1999.

Davidson, Alan, *The Oxford Companion to Food*, Oxford, 1999.

Del Conte, Anna, *Gastronomy of Italy*, Prentice Hall, 1987.

Grigson, Jane, *Jane Grigson's Vegetable Book*, Michael Joseph, 1978.

Kafka, Barbara, *Roasting: A Simple Art*, William Morrow, 1995.

Morash, Marian, *The Victory Garden Cookbook*, Knopf, 1982.

Norman, Jill, *The New Penguin Cookery Book*, Penguin, 2001.

Raichlen, Steven, *The Barbecue Bible*, Workman, 1998.

Rombauer, Irma et al, *The Joy of Cooking*, revised edition, Scribner, 1997.

Schneider, Elizabeth, *Vegetables from Amaranth to Zucchini*, Morrow, 2001.

Tropp, Barbara, *China Moon Cookbook*, Workman, 1992.

Yan, Martin, *Martin Yan's Feast*, Bay Books, 1998.

METRIC CONVERSION CHARTS

WEIGHT EQUIVALENTS

The metric weights given in this chart are not exact equivalents, but have been rounded up or down slightly to make measuring easier.

Avoirdupois	Metric
1/4 oz	7 g
1/2 oz	15 g
1 oz	30 g
2 oz	60 g
3 oz	90 g
4 oz	115 g
5 oz	150 g
6 oz	175 g
7 oz	200 g
8 oz (1/2 lb)	225 g
9 oz	250 g
10 oz	300 g
11 oz	325 g
12 oz	350 g
13 oz	375 g
14 oz	400 g
15 oz	425 g
16 oz (1 lb)	450 g
1 1/2 lb	750 g
2 lb	900 g
2 1/4 lb	1 kg
3 lb	1.4 kg
4 lb	1.8 kg

VOLUME EQUIVALENTS

These are not exact equivalents for American cups and spoons, but have been rounded up or down slightly to make measuring easier.

American	Metric	Imperial
1/4 t	1.2 ml	
1/2 t	2.5 ml	
1 t	5.0 ml	
1/2 T (1 1/2 t)	7.5 ml	
1 T (3 t)	15 ml	
1/4 cup (4 T)	60 ml	2 fl oz
1/3 cup (5 T)	75 ml	2 1/2 fl oz
1/2 cup (8 T)	125 ml	4 fl oz
2/3 cup (10 T)	150 ml	5 fl oz
3/4 cup (12 T)	175 ml	6 fl oz
1 cup (16 T)	250 ml	8 fl oz
1 1/4 cups	300 ml	10 fl oz (1/2 pt)
1 1/2 cups	350 ml	12 fl oz
2 cups (1 pint)	500 ml	16 fl oz
2 1/2 cups	625 ml	20 fl oz (1 pint)
1 quart	1 liter	32 fl oz

OVEN TEMPERATURE EQUIVALENTS

Oven Mark	F	C	Gas
Very cool	250-275	130-140	1/2-1
Cool	300	150	2
Warm	325	170	3
Moderate	350	180	4
Moderately hot	375	190	5
	400	200	6
Hot	425	220	7
	450	230	8
Very hot	475	250	9

INDEX

Note: Pages in *italics* refer to recipe photographs.